DILEMMAS OF DEMOCRACY

READINGS IN AMERICAN GOVERNMENT

DILEMMAS OF DEMOCRACY

READINGS IN AMERICAN GOVERNMENT

edited by PETER COLLIER

HARCOURT BRACE JOVANOVICH, INC.
New York   Chicago   San Francisco   Atlanta

PREFACE

Battered by the long trauma stretching from the first escalations of the war in Vietnam to the final revelations of Watergate, contemporary America has often seemed bent on proving the truth of John Adams' observation in a letter written some two hundred years ago: "There was never a democracy yet that didn't commit suicide."

American institutions have faced tremendous pressures over the last decade. Gaps—credibility, generational, and intellectual—have opened up between parents and children and between voters and elected leaders. Disturbing questions have been raised about the disposition of power in this society and the way decisions are made. There has been a break with the smooth continuity of the past, and future shock is a common ailment. Shaken by kaleidoscopic images of riot and assassination, by body counts in Southeast Asia and corruption in high places, citizens have become openly skeptical about the integrity of their government and its political processes. They are convinced that they are not told the truth by their leaders. They are stunned by their country's sudden decline as the preeminent global superpower. When polled, they indicate a surprising lack of faith in the presidency, Congress, political parties, the efficacy of voting, and the regenerative powers of the "system" itself. For good reason political analysts point out that beneath the apparent calm of the mid-seventies is the potential for social upheaval and reorganization unparalleled since the New Deal.

This anthology attempts to deal with some of these issues. It cannot present the whole truth about American government. But it does seek to do justice to the complexity of that truth through a series of essays that, whatever their differences, are all concerned with the gap between the rhetoric and realities of government in America. This approach is admittedly not new, but the unpredictability—the ambiguities—of the American experience, often noted since the time of de Tocqueville, have kept its possibilities from being exhausted.

Part One, "Consent of the Governed," surveys aspects of the electoral process and the distance that has been created between Americans and the institutions and leaders that govern them. Part Two, "Public Policies, Private Interests," focuses on some of the crucial areas where government impinges on the daily life of the individual and examines how decisions are made and to whose ultimate benefit. And Part Three, "Democratic Vistas," considers some of the philosophic issues in the social upheaval of the past few years and in the widening distance between democratic theory and practice.

I have purposely avoided filling this book with articles from the professional journals. It seems clear that the insights of individuals like Representative Donald Riegle and former presidential aide Richard Goodwin, both of whom have seen the governmental process firsthand, have a place in a book about government. The same is true for official government studies like the Rockefeller Commission Report on the CIA and the House Judiciary Committee's selection of taped conversations from the Nixon White House. I also feel that the work of journalists like Jessica Mitford and Studs Terkel nicely complements that of scholars like Richard Hofstadter and Robert Coles. The only homogeneity between the essays in this collection derives from the fact that they are all provocative arguments about issues of common importance to American citizens.

PREFACE

Dilemmas of Democracy does not pretend to be an exhaustive documentation of the workings of American government. Rather, by presenting a few carefully selected essays on the electoral process, problems of governance, and strategies for change, it seeks to engage the reader imaginatively in a broad range of considerations. It is best regarded as a sourcebook of ideas: a number of diagnoses of the nature of the ills besetting the body politic, as well as some prescriptions for reforms that might have a curative effect.

PETER COLLIER

CONTENTS

CONTENTS

impact on the political process. One of their most serious political acts may be the way alarming numbers of citizens are cutting ties with the major political parties and choosing not to vote.

The mass media have contributed significantly to the growth of image politics. Television, particularly in the making (and remaking) of candidates such as Richard Nixon, has often proven more adept at communicating the illusion than the realities.

In the hands of political management firms, opinion polls have become an important part of the arsenal of campaigning. The future could bring a new generation of politicians without ideas of their own, dummies to the ventriloquist-pollster who puts words in their mouths based on his analysis of what the public wants to hear.

The anomie of the big-city voter contrasts sharply with the idyllic image of the villager making his opinions known through the town meeting. Even here, however, influence and decision-making power are inevitably consolidated in the hands of the few.

From parents and teachers children inherit a strong regard for the authority of elected leaders and a somewhat sentimental view of American institutions. From their own observations they often encounter realities that are quite

different from the egalitarianism they are told is the central
feature of national political life.

PUBLIC POLICIES, PRIVATE INTERESTS

Captives of the very interests and industries they were
designed to protect against, the regulatory agencies are a
window through which distortions of the governmental
process can be seen.

Exceeding its original mandate regarding the gathering of
foreign intelligence, the Central Intelligence Agency has
become hated and feared abroad. By transferring its
operations to America and targetting individual citizens,
this "invisible government" has caused serious questions
to be raised about the nature of political freedom in this
country.

Although it has functioned admirably in its efforts to check
the corruption and secrecy of government during the last
few years, the press remains big business with its own
prerogatives to protect. A major conflict could arise as the
public demands more and better access to the organs of
opinion.

The term "middle class" has often been used as a
smokescreen by politicians and social critics who have

CONTENTS

attempted to convince Americans that they inhabit a society based on full equality and an absence of class distinctions.

DEMOCRATIC VISTAS

CONTENTS

CONSENT
OF
THE
GOVERNED

RICHARD HOFSTADTER

The Founding Fathers

Disturbed by economic dislocation, boundary disputes between the states, and the specter of radicalism conjured up by Daniel Shays' recent uprising in western Massachusetts, delegates arrived at the Constitutional Convention in Philadelphia in 1787 with a mandate to revise the Articles of Confederation. Their deliberations accomplished far more than that, of course, eventually resulting in a remarkable piece of work that would henceforth stand, in the Constitution framers' own phrase, as the "supreme Law of the Land." Generations of American schoolchildren would learn to regard the Founding Fathers' handiwork as a hallowed symbol, the ark of the American covenant. In fact, studying this document through a patriotic haze would often tend to obscure the fact that it was also a masterwork of compromise and statecraft, every part marked by the distinctive philosophy of individuals who in their own time were seen not as saints but as eminently practical men. As political scientist Richard Hofstadter suggests in the following selection, the Constitution reflects not only the Founding Fathers' hopes but their fears and prejudices as well, especially regarding the role of the common men they mistrusted as potential torch carriers in the mob. The decisions made at Philadelphia in sorting out and ranking the competing claims of liberty, democracy, property, and other complex abstractions would echo subtly during the development of the American enterprise over the next two hundred years.

> *Wherever the real power in a government lies, there is the danger of oppression. In our Government the real power lies in the majority of the community.* JAMES MADISON

"The Founding Fathers" (Originally "The Founding Fathers: An Age of Realism"). From THE AMERICAN POLITICAL TRADITION AND THE MEN WHO MADE IT, by Richard Hofstadter. Copyright 1948, © 1973 by Alfred A. Knopf, Inc. Reprinted by permission of Alfred A. Knopf, Inc.

*Power naturally grows . . . because human pas-
sions are insatiable. But that power alone can
grow which already is too great; that which is
unchecked; that which has no equal power to control it.* JOHN ADAMS

Long ago Horace White observed that the Constitution of the United States "is based upon the philosophy of Hobbes and the religion of Calvin. It assumes that the natural state of mankind is a state of war, and that the carnal mind is at enmity with God." Of course the Constitution was founded more upon experience than any such abstract theory; but it was also an event in the intellectual history of Western civilization. The men who drew up the Constitution in Philadelphia during the summer of 1787 had a vivid Calvinistic sense of human evil and damnation and believed with Hobbes that men are selfish and contentious. They were men of affairs, merchants, lawyers, planter-businessmen, speculators, investors. Having seen human nature on display in the market place, the courtroom, the legislative chamber, and in every secret path and alleyway where wealth and power are court-ed, they felt they knew it in all its frailty. To them a human being was an atom of self-interest. They did not believe in man, but they did believe in the power of a good political constitution to control him.

This may be an abstract notion to ascribe to practical men, but it follows the language that the Fathers themselves used. Gen-eral Knox, for example, wrote in disgust to Washington after the Shays Rebellion that Americans were, after all, "men—actual men possessing all the turbulent passions belonging to that animal." Throughout the secret discussions at the Constitutional Conven-tion it was clear that this distrust of man was first and foremost a distrust of the common man and democratic rule. As the Revolu-tion took away the restraining hand of the British government, old colonial grievances of farmers, debtors, and squatters against merchants, investors, and large landholders had flared up anew; the lower orders took advantage of new democratic constitutions in several states, and the possessing classes were frightened. The members of the Constitutional Convention were concerned to create a government that could not only regulate commerce and pay its debts but also prevent currency inflation and stay laws, and check such uprisings as the Shays Rebellion.

Cribbing and confining the popular spirit that had been at large since 1776 were essential to the purposes of the new Constitution.

Edmund Randolph, saying to the Convention that the evils from which the country suffered originated in "the turbulence and follies of democracy," and that the great danger lay in "the democratic parts of our constitutions"; Elbridge Gerry, speaking of democracy as "the worst of all political evils"; Roger Sherman, hoping that "the people . . . have as little to do as may be about the government"; William Livingston, saying that "the people have ever been and ever will be unfit to retain the exercise of power in their own hands"; George Washington, the presiding officer, urging the delegates not to produce a document of which they themselves could not approve simply in order to "please the people"; Hamilton, charging that the "turbulent and changing" masses "seldom judge or determine right" and advising a permanent governmental body to "check the imprudence of democracy"; the wealthy young planter Charles Pinckney, proposing that no one be president who was not worth at least one hundred thousand dollars—all these were quite representative of the spirit in which the problems of government were treated.

Democratic ideas are most likely to take root among discontented and oppressed classes, rising middle classes, or perhaps some sections of an old, alienated, and partially disinherited aristocracy, but do not appeal to a privileged class that is still amplifying its privileges. With a half-dozen exceptions at the most, the men of the Philadelphia Convention were sons of men who had considerable position and wealth, and as a group they had advanced well beyond their fathers. Only one of them, William Few of Georgia, could be said in any sense to represent the yeoman farmer class which constituted the overwhelming majority of the free population. In the late eighteenth century "the better kind of people" found themselves set off from the mass by a hundred visible, tangible, and audible distinctions of dress, speech, manners, and education. There was a continuous lineage of upper-class contempt, from pre-Revolutionary Tories like Peggy Hutchinson, the Governor's daughter, who wrote one day: "The dirty mob was all about me as I drove into town," to a Federalist like Hamilton, who candidly disdained the people. Mass unrest was often received in the spirit of young Gouverneur Morris: "The mob begin to think and reason. Poor reptiles! . . . They bask in the sun, and ere noon they will bite, depend upon it. The gentry begin to fear this." Nowhere in America or Europe—not even among the great liberated thinkers of the Enlightenment—did democratic ideas appear respectable to the cultivated classes. Whether the

5

Fathers looked to the cynically illuminated intellectuals of contemporary Europe or to their own Christian heritage of the idea of original sin, they found quick confirmation of the notion that man is an unregenerate rebel who has to be controlled.

And yet there was another side to the picture. The Fathers were intellectual heirs of seventeenth-century English republicanism with its opposition to arbitrary rule and faith in popular sovereignty. If they feared the advance of democracy, they also had misgivings about turning to the extreme right. Having recently experienced a bitter revolutionary struggle with an external power beyond their control, they were in no mood to follow Hobbes to his conclusion that any kind of government must be accepted in order to avert the anarchy and terror of a state of nature. They were uneasily aware that both military dictatorship and a return to monarchy were being seriously discussed in some quarters—the former chiefly among unpaid and discontented army officers, the latter in rich and fashionable Northern circles. John Jay, familiar with sentiment among New York's mercantile aristocracy, wrote to Washington, June 27, 1786, that he feared that

> "the better kind of people (by which I mean the people who are orderly and industrious, who are content with their situations, and not uneasy in their circumstances) will be led, by the insecurity of property, the loss of confidence in their rulers, and the want of public faith and rectitude, to consider the charms of liberty as imaginary and delusive."

Such men, he thought, might be prepared for "almost any change that may promise them quiet and security." Washington, who had already repudiated a suggestion that he become a military dictator, agreed, remarking that "we are apt to run from one extreme to the other."

Unwilling to turn their backs upon republicanism, the Fathers also wished to avoid violating the prejudices of the people. "Notwithstanding the oppression and injustice experienced among us from democracy," said George Mason, "the genius of the people is in favor of it, and the genius of the people must be consulted." Mason admitted "that we had been too democratic," but feared that "we should incautiously run into the opposite extreme." James Madison, who has quite rightfully been called the philosopher of the Constitution, told the delegates: "It seems indispensable that the mass of citizens should not be without a voice in making the laws which they are to obey, and in choosing the magistrates who are to administer them." James Wilson, the outstanding jurist of the age, later appointed to the Supreme Court by Washington, said again and again that the ultimate power of government must of necessity reside in the people. This the Fathers commonly accepted, for if government did not proceed from the people, from what other source could it legitimately come? To adopt any other premise not only would be inconsistent with everything they had said against British rule in the past but would open the gates to an extreme concentration of power in the future. Hamilton saw the sharp distinction in the Convention when he said that "the members most tenacious of republicanism were as loud as any in declaiming the vices of democracy." There was no better expression of the dilemma of a man who has no faith in the people but insists that government be based upon them than that of Jeremy Belknap, a New England clergyman, who wrote to a friend: "Let it stand as a principle that government originates from the people; but let the people be taught . . . that they are not able to govern themselves."

II

If the masses were turbulent and unregenerate, and yet if government must be founded upon their suffrage and consent, what could a Constitution-maker do? One thing that the Fathers did not propose to do, because they thought it impossible, was to change the nature of man to conform with a more ideal system. They were inordinately confident that they knew what man always had been and what he always would be. The eighteenth-century mind had great faith in universals. Its method, as Carl Becker has said, was "to go up and down the field of history looking for man in general, the universal man, stripped of the accidents of time and place." Madison declared that the causes of political differences and of the formation of factions were "sown in the nature of man" and could never be eradicated. "It is universally acknowledged," David Hume had written, "that there is a great uniformity among the actions of men, in all nations and ages, and that human nature remains still the same, in its principles and operations. The same motives always produce the same actions. The same events always follow from the same causes."

Since man was an unchangeable creature of self-interest, it would not do to leave anything to his capacity for restraint. It was too much to expect that vice could be checked by virtue; the Fathers relied instead upon checking vice with vice. Madison once objected during the Convention that Gouverneur Morris was "forever inculcating the utter political depravity of men and the necessity of opposing one vice and interest to another vice and interest." And yet Madison himself in the *Federalist* number 51 later set forth an excellent statement of the same thesis:[1]

> Ambition must be made to counteract ambition . . . It may be a reflection on human nature that such devices should be necessary to control the abuses of government. But what is government itself, but the greatest of all reflections on human nature? If men were angels, no government would be necessary. . . . In framing a government which is to be administered by men over men, the great difficulty lies in this: you must first enable the government to control the governed; and in the next place oblige it to control itself.

Political economists of the laissez-faire school were saying that private vices could be public benefits, that an economically beneficent result would be providentially or "naturally" achieved if self-interest were left free from state interference and allowed to pursue its ends. But the Fathers were not so optimistic about politics. If, in a state that lacked constitutional balance, one class or one interest gained control, they believed, it would surely plunder all other interests. The Fathers, of course, were especially fearful that the poor would plunder the rich, but most of them would probably have admitted that the rich, unrestrained, would also plunder the poor. Even Gouverneur Morris, who stood as close to the extreme aristocratic position as candor and intelligence would allow, told the Convention: "Wealth tends to corrupt the mind and to nourish its love of power, and to stimulate it to oppression. History proves this to be the spirit of the opulent."

What the Fathers wanted was known as "balanced government," an idea at least as old as Aristotle and Polybius. This an-

---

[1] Cf. the words of Hamilton to the New York ratifying convention: "Men will pursue their interests. It is as easy to change human nature as to oppose the strong current of selfish passions. A wise legislator will gently divert the channel, and direct it, if possible, to the public good."

cient conception had won new sanction in the eighteenth century, which was dominated intellectually by the scientific work of Newton, and in which mechanical metaphors sprang as naturally to men's minds as did biological metaphors in the Darwinian atmosphere of the late nineteenth century. Men had found a rational order in the universe and they hoped that it could be transferred to politics, or, as John Adams put it, that governments could be "erected on the simple principles of nature." Madison spoke in the most precise Newtonian language when he said that such a "natural" government must be so constructed "that its several constituent parts may, by their mutual relations, be the means of keeping each other in their proper places." A properly designed state, the Fathers believed, would check interest with interest, class with class, faction with faction, and one branch of government with another in a harmonious system of mutual frustration.

In practical form, therefore, the quest of the Fathers reduced primarily to a search for constitutional devices that would force various interests to check and control one another. Among those who favored the federal Constitution three such devices were distinguished.

The first of these was the advantage of a federated government in maintaining order against popular uprisings or majority rule. In a single state a faction might arise and take complete control by force; but if the states were bound in a federation, the central government could step in and prevent it. Hamilton quoted Montesquieu: "Should a popular insurrection happen in one of the confederate states, the others are able to quell it." Further, as Madison argued in the *Federalist* number 10, a majority would be the most dangerous of all factions that might arise, for the majority would be the most capable of gaining complete ascendancy. If the political society were very extensive, however, and embraced a large number and variety of local interests, the citizens who shared a common majority interest "must be rendered by their number and local situation, unable to concert and carry into effect their schemes of oppression." The chief propertied interests would then be safer from "a rage for paper money, for an abolition of debts, for an equal division of property, or for any other improper or wicked project."

The second advantage of good constitutional government resided in the mechanism of representation itself. In a small direct democracy the unstable passions of the people would dominate lawmaking; but a representative government, as Madison said, would "refine and enlarge the public views by passing them through the medium of a chosen body of citizens." Representatives chosen by the people were wiser and more deliberate than the people themselves in mass assemblage. Hamilton frankly anticipated a kind of syndical paternalism in which the wealthy and dominant members of every trade or industry would represent the others in politics. Merchants, for example, were "the natural representatives" of their employees and of the mechanics and artisans they dealt with. Hamilton expected that Congress, "with too few exceptions to have any influence on the spirit of the government, will be composed of landholders, merchants and men of the learned professions."

The third advantage of the government the Fathers were designing was pointed out most elaborately by John Adams in the first volume of his *Defence of the Constitutions of Government of the United States of America*, which reached Philadelphia while the Convention was in session and was cited with approval by several delegates.[2] Adams believed that the aristocracy and the democracy must be made to neutralize each other. Each element should be given its own house of the legislature, and over both houses there should be set a capable, strong, and impartial executive armed with the veto power. This split assembly would contain within itself an organic check and would be capable of self-control under the governance of the executive. The whole system was to be capped by an independent judiciary. The inevitable tendency of the rich and the poor to plunder each other would be kept in hand.

III

It is ironical that the Constitution, which Americans venerate so deeply, is based upon a political theory that at one crucial point stands in direct antithesis to the main stream of American democratic faith. Modern American folklore assumes that democracy and liberty are all but identical, and when democratic writers take

[2]"Mr. Adams' book," wrote Benjamin Rush, often in the company of the delegates, "has diffused such excellent principles among us that there is little doubt of our adopting a vigorous and compounded Federal Legislature. Our illustrious Minister in this gift to his country has done us more service than if he had obtained alliances for us with all the nations of Europe."

the trouble to make the distinction, they usually assume that democracy is necessary to liberty. But the Founding Fathers thought that the liberty with which they were most concerned was menaced by democracy. In their minds liberty was linked not to democracy but to property.

What did the Fathers mean by liberty? What did Jay mean when he spoke of "the charms of liberty"? Or Madison when he declared that to destroy liberty in order to destroy factions would be a remedy worse than the disease? Certainly the men who met at Philadelphia were not interested in extending liberty to those classes in America, the Negro slaves and the indentured servants, who were most in need of it, for slavery was recognized in the organic structure of the Constitution and indentured servitude was no concern of the Convention. Nor was the regard of the delegates for civil liberties any too tender. It was the opponents of the Constitution who were most active in demanding such vital liberties as freedom of religion, freedom of speech and press, jury trial, due process, and protection from "unreasonable searches and seizures." These guarantees had to be incorporated in the first ten amendments because the Convention neglected to put them in the original document. Turning to economic issues, it was not freedom of trade in the modern sense that the Fathers were striving for. Although they did not believe in impeding trade unnecessarily, they felt that failure to regulate it was one of the central weaknesses of the Articles of Confederation, and they stood closer to the mercantilists than to Adam Smith. Again, liberty to them did not mean free access to the nation's unappropriated wealth. At least fourteen of them were land speculators. They did not believe in the right of the squatter to occupy unused land, but rather in the right of the absentee owner or speculator to preempt it.

The liberties that the constitutionalists hoped to gain were chiefly negative. They wanted freedom from fiscal uncertainty and irregularities in the currency, from trade wars among the states, from economic discrimination by more powerful foreign governments, from attacks on the creditor class or on property, from popular insurrection. They aimed to create a government that would act as an honest broker among a variety of propertied interests, giving them all protection from their common enemies and preventing any one of them from becoming too powerful. The Convention was a fraternity of types of absentee ownership. All property should be permitted to have its proportionate voice in government. Individual property interests might have to be sacrificed at times, but only for the community of propertied interests. Freedom for property would result in liberty for men—perhaps not for all men, but at least for all worthy men.[3] Because men have different faculties and abilities, the Fathers believed, they acquire different amounts of property. To protect property is only to protect men in the exercise of their natural faculties. Among the many liberties, therefore, freedom to hold and dispose property is paramount. Democracy, unchecked rule by the masses, is sure to bring arbitrary redistribution of property, destroying the very essence of liberty.

The Fathers' conception of democracy, shaped by their practical experience with the aggressive dirt farmers in the American states and the urban mobs of the Revolutionary period, was supplemented by their reading in history and political science. Fear of what Madison called "the superior force of an interested and overbearing majority" was the dominant emotion aroused by their study of historical examples. The chief examples of republics were among the city-states of antiquity, medieval Europe, and early modern times. Now, the history of these republics—a history, as Hamilton said, "of perpetual vibration between the extremes of tyranny and anarchy"—was alarming. Further, most of the men who had overthrown the liberties of republics had "begun their career by paying an obsequious court to the people; commencing demagogues and ending tyrants."

All the constitutional devices that the Fathers praised in their writings were attempts to guarantee the future of the United States against the "turbulent" political cycles of previous republics. By "democracy," they meant a system of government which directly expressed the will of the majority of the people, usually through such an assemblage of the people as was possible in the small area of the city-state.

[3]The Fathers probably would have accepted the argument of the Declaration of Independence that "all men are created equal," but only as a legal, not as a political or psychological proposition. Jefferson himself believed in the existence of "natural aristocrats," but he thought they were likely to appear in any class of society. However, for those who interpreted the natural-rights philosophy more conservatively than he, the idea that all men are equal did not mean that uneducated dirt farmers or grimy-handed ship calkers were in any sense the equals of the Schuylers, Washingtons, or Pinckneys. It meant only that British colonials had as much natural right to self-government as Britons at home, that the average American was the legal peer of the average Briton. Among the signers of the Constitution, it is worth noting, there were only six men who had also signed the Declaration of Independence.

A cardinal tenet in the faith of the men who made the Constitution was the belief that democracy can never be more than a transitional stage in government, that it always evolves into either a tyranny (the rule of the rich demagogue who has patronized the mob) or an aristocracy (the original leaders of the democratic elements). "Remember," wrote the dogmatic John Adams in one of his letters to John Taylor of Caroline, "democracy never lasts long. It soon wastes, exhausts, and murders itself. There never was a democracy yet that did not commit suicide."[4] Again:

> If you give more than a share in the sovereignty to the democrats, that is, if you give them the command or preponderance in the . . . legislature, they will vote all property out of the hands of you aristocrats, and if they let you escape with your lives, it will be more humanity, consideration, and generosity than any triumphant democracy ever displayed since the creation. And what will follow? The aristocracy among the democrats will take your places, and treat their fellows as severely and sternly as you have treated them.

Government, thought the Fathers, is based on property. Men who have no property lack the necessary stake in an orderly society to make stable or reliable citizens. Dread of the propertyless masses of the towns was all but universal. George Washington, Gouverneur Morris, John Dickinson, and James Madison spoke of their anxieties about the urban working class that might arise some time in the future—"men without property and principle," as Dickinson described them—and even the democratic Jefferson shared this prejudice. Madison, stating the problem, came close to anticipating the modern threats to conservative republicanism from both communism and fascism:

> In future times, a great majority of the people will not only be without landed but any other sort of property. These will either combine, under the influence of their common situation—in which case the rights of property and the public liberty will not be secure in their hands—or, what is more probable, they will become the

---

[4]Taylor labored to confute Adams, but in 1814, after many discouraging years in American politics, he conceded a great part of Adams's case: "All parties, however loyal to principles at first, degenerate into aristocracies of interest at last; and unless a nation is capable of discerning the point where integrity ends and fraud begins, popular parites are among the surest modes of introducing an aristocracy."

tools of opulence and ambition, in which case there will be equal danger on another side.

What encouraged the Fathers about their own era, however, was the broad dispersion of landed property. The small landowning farmers had been troublesome in recent years, but there was a general conviction that under a properly made Constitution a *modus vivendi* could be worked out with them. The possession of moderate plots of property presumably gave them a sufficient stake in society to be safe and responsible citizens under the restraints of balanced government. Influence in government would be proportionate to property: merchants and great landholders would be dominant, but small property-owners would have an independent and far from negligible voice. It was "politic as well as just," said Madison, "that the interests and rights of every class should be duly represented and understood in the public councils," and John Adams declared that there could be "no free government without a democratical branch in the constitution."

The farming element already satisfied the property requirements for suffrage in most of the states, and the Fathers generally had no quarrel with their enfranchisement. But when they spoke of the necessity of founding government upon the consent of "the people," it was only these small property-holders that they had in mind. For example, the famous Virginia Bill of Rights, written by George Mason, explicitly defined those eligible for suffrage as all men "having sufficient evidence of permanent common interest with and attachment to the community"—which meant, in brief, sufficient property.

However, the original intention of the Fathers to admit the yeoman into an important but sharply limited partnership in affairs of state could not be perfectly realized. At the time the Constitution was made, Southern planters and Northern merchants were setting their differences aside in order to meet common dangers—from radicals within and more powerful nations without. After the Constitution was adopted, conflict between the ruling classes broke out anew, especially after powerful planters were offended by the favoritism of Hamilton's policies to Northern commercial interests. The planters turned to the farmers to form an agrarian alliance, and for more than half a century this powerful coalition embraced the bulk of the articulate interests of the country. As time went on, therefore, the main stream of American

political conviction deviated more and more from the antidemo-
cratic position of the Constitution-makers. Yet, curiously, their
general satisfaction with the Constitution together with their growing nationalism made Americans deeply reverent of the founding
generation, with the result that as it grew stronger, this deviation
was increasingly overlooked.

There is common agreement among modern critics that the debates over the Constitution were carried on at an intellectual level
that is rare in politics, and that the Constitution itself is one of
the world's masterpieces of practical statecraft. On other grounds
there has been controversy. At the very beginning contemporary
opponents of the Constitution foresaw an apocalyptic destruction
of local government and popular institutions, while conservative
Europeans of the old regime thought the young American Republic
was a dangerous leftist experiment. Modern critical scholar-
ship, which reached a high point in Charles A. Beard's *An Economic Interpretation of the Constitution of the United States*, started a new turn in the debate. The antagonism, long latent, between
the philosophy of the Constitution and the philosophy of American democracy again came into the open. Professor Beard's work
appeared in 1913 at the peak of the Progressive era, when the
muckraking fever was still high; some readers tended to conclude
from his findings that the Fathers were selfish reactionaries who
do not deserve their high place in American esteem. Still more
recently, other writers, inverting this logic, have used Beard's facts
to praise the Fathers for their opposition to "democracy" and as
an argument for returning again to the idea of a "republic."
 In fact, the Father's image of themselves as moderate republicans standing between political extremes was quite accurate. They
were impelled by class motives more than pietistic writers like
to admit, but they were also controlled, as Professor Beard himself
has recently emphasized, by a statesmanlike sense of moderation
and a scrupulously republican philosophy. Any attempt, however,
to tear their ideas out of the eighteenth-century context is sure
to make them seem starkly reactionary. Consider, for example,
the favorite maxim of John Jay: "The people who own the country
ought to govern it." To the Fathers this was simply a swift axio-
matic statement of the stake-in-society theory of political rights, a
moderate conservative position under eighteenth-century conditions of property distribution in America. Under modern property
relations this maxim demands a drastic restriction of the base of

15

political power. A large portion of the modern middle class—and it is the strength of this class upon which balanced government depends—is propertyless; and the urban proletariat, which the Fathers so greatly feared, is almost one half the population. Further, the separation of ownership from control that has come with the corporation deprives Jay's maxim of twentieth-century meaning even for many propertied people. The six hundred thousand stockholders of the American Telephone & Telegraph Company not only do not acquire political power by virtue of their stock-ownership, but they do not even acquire economic power: they cannot control their own company.

From a humanistic standpoint there is a serious dilemma in the philosophy of the Fathers, which derives from their conception of man. They thought man was a creature of rapacious self-interest, and yet they wanted him to be free—free, in essence, to contend, to engage in an umpired strife, to use property to get property. They accepted the mercantile image of life as an eternal battleground, and assumed the Hobbesian war of each against all; they did not propose to put an end to this war, but merely to stabilize it and make it less murderous. They had no hope and they offered none for any ultimate organic change in the way men conduct themselves. The result was that while they thought self-interest the most dangerous and unbrookable quality of man, they necessarily underwrote it in trying to control it. They succeeded in both respects: under the competitive capitalism of the nineteenth century America continued to be an arena for various grasping and contending interests, and the federal government continued to provide a stable and acceptable medium within which they could contend; further, it usually showed the wholesome bias on behalf of property which the Fathers expected. But no man who is as well abreast of modern science as the Fathers were of eighteenth-century science believes any longer in unchanging human nature. Modern humanistic thinkers who seek for a means by which society may transcend eternal conflict and rigid adherence to property rights as its integrating principles can expect no answer in the philosophy of balanced government as it was set down by the Constitution-makers of 1787.

F. G. HUTCHINS

Presidential Autocracy in America

Some delegates, notably young Alexander Hamilton, arrived at the Constitutional Convention ready to argue that the new government should be headed by a king, elected to office for life tenure. But most of the delegates feared monarchy quite as much as they did the mob and sought a governmental system based on balance—each faction or interest blocking the potential dominance of its competitor, one branch of government checking another in what Richard Hofstadter calls "a harmonious system of mutual frustration."

George Washington refused to be addressed as "Your Excellency"; Andrew Jackson celebrated his inaugural with the common man. For well over a hundred years the office of the Chief Executive was relatively unassuming in its relations with the other branches of government. By the beginning of the twentieth century, in fact, foreign observers frequently commented on the weakness of the presidency. Yet, by the 1930s, as the size and function of the federal government increased under the New Deal and America began to reach out for an enlarged role in international affairs, the balance of power began to tilt toward an executive with its own special privileges. The power of the presidency increased, Harvard government professor F. G. Hutchins argues in the following selection, by absorbing judicial and legislative functions; the inevitable result was the consolidation of these incursions in a presidential "autocracy."

The tyranny of the legislature is really the danger most to feared, and will continue to be so for many years to come. The tyranny of the executive power will come in its turn, but at a more distant period.

THOMAS JEFFERSON,
letter to James Madison, March 15, 1789

"Presidential Autocracy in America," by F. G. Hutchins. From *The Presidency Reappraised*, edited by Rexford G. Tugwell and Thomas E. Cronin (Santa Barbara, Calif.: The Center for the Study of Democratic Institutions, 1974), pp. 35–55. Reprinted by permission of the Center for the Study of Democratic Institutions.

17

The American Presidency has today become the "tyranny" that Jefferson foresaw. The executive branch, the Cinderella of the Constitution of 1789, which fell into such disrepute and inconsequence in the nineteenth century that Lord Bryce felt compelled to explain "Why Great Men are not Elected President," has in the twentieth century come into an inheritance greater than that ever enjoyed by her two sister branches of government.

The triumph of the Presidency was accomplished without constitutional alteration, because the federal government, from the beginning, was a system of separation of power, but fusion of function. Each of the separate branches of government—the Congress, the Presidency, the Court—was assigned legislative, executive, and judicial functions. The "strengthening of the Presidency" has resulted not simply from the growth in the importance of executive authority in an increasingly complex, developed society, but, more importantly, from the fused growth of the legislative, executive, and judicial authority of the Presidency. This has not appeared to involve usurpation of functions from the other two branches, because the constitutional framework did give the Presidency a foothold in all three areas from which to develop.

The image of the President as an elective monarch had been present in the minds of the Founding Fathers from the beginning. Monarchy—enlightened or otherwise—was the normal pattern of governance in the eighteenth century, and the availability of a suitable candidate in the person of George Washington made the notion of elective monarchism—articulated most forcefully by Alexander Hamilton—the pattern of the constitutional Presidency. This idea, latent in the Constitution, never died completely. For the time being, however, the expansion of Presidential power was eclipsed in 1801, when Jefferson, a Presidential minimalist, succeeded Adams. Jefferson was effective as President, but his *purpose* as President was to further the independence of individuals rather than to establish and consolidate an autocratic form of government.

Lincoln expanded the powers of the Presidency in practice; but this expansion did not survive, because Lincoln did not develop a rationalization for the retention of these expanded powers. Lincoln expanded his powers because the nation was threatened by an emergency; he increased the *executive* powers of the Presidency because decisions needed to be centralized in wartime. Lincoln was willing to do almost anything to save the Union. But the Union Lincoln wanted to save was a land of free yeomen, and in this land there was no room for an institutionalized monarchy. Lincoln viewed his actions as extraordinary. He took extreme measures under the press of circumstances without trying to build these actions into permanent Presidential prerogatives, and without conducting himself as licensed, in his representative capacity, to articulate newly discovered general principles. The Emancipation Proclamation was viewed as exceptional by Lincoln himself, and its moralistic phraseology was urged upon him by others.

The methodical consolidation of Presidential supremacy required more than monarchical instincts or the *de facto* expansion of powers under the press of emergency. The institutionalization of Presidential supremacy required a theory, and this was not developed until the twentieth century, when the Progressives concluded that the President could wield best all three of the traditional functions of government.

The legislative, executive, and judicial powers of the President have not only been expanded but also used to justify one another. Enthusiasts stress the representative character of the Presidency; the role of Presidential leadership in foreign and domestic affairs; and the judgmental power of the President, who, because of his special representativeness and responsibilities as well as his special advantages of position and access to advice, is able to arbitrate issues in a uniquely judicious way. The Presidency, in short, is three branches in one. The definition that the Presidency gives to each of these functions is not, however, identical with the definition of these functions traditionally upheld by the other branches. The President's apologists have defined the prime functions associated with the other branches in ways that make it appear that the President is better suited to pursue them than the originally constituted branch.

The most grandiose conception of the President's representativeness was that first articulated by Woodrow Wilson, that the President represents all the people. If the Presidency could be made to seem more truly representative of the "people" than was the Congress, where arguably only "interests" were represented, then the Presidency could, in the name of the people, exercise ultimate power with righteous vigor. If the President really, effectively represents everybody, then the Congress, in opposing the President, may seem to represent nothing more than selfishness. Legislators have themselves helped strengthen this impression by their willingness to accept a role as little more than lobbyists for their constituents, exerting influence in the bureaucratic labyrinth on behalf of their constituents, thereby appearing, in fact, to represent nothing that cannot be rightfully subordinated to a larger national interest. If the President is the only true representative institution, or even only a representative institution that is somewhat preferable to the Congress, then there is logically no reason why the President should feel bound by the Congress; the moral pressure, indeed, moves in the opposite direction.

In 1885, Woodrow Wilson, in his book *Congressional Government*, argued that America needed majestic leadership, and that the Congress was not supplying it. At this time, with the power of the American President at its nadir, and with the brilliant parliamentary duels of Gladstone and Disraeli fresh in Wilson's mind, the remedy for the sorry state of Congress that recommended itself to Wilson was a form of Cabinet government for America on the British model. It was only later, after Theodore Roosevelt had demonstrated in practice the Presidency's potential as a platform for strong leadership, that Wilson finally found the proper solution for America. In 1908, he paired his denunciation of Congress with a eulogy for the President:

> The nation as a whole has chosen him, and is conscious that it has no other political spokesman. His is the only national voice in affairs. Let him once win the admiration and confidence of the country, and no other single force can withstand him, no combination of forces will easily overpower him. His position takes the imagination of the country. He is the representative of no constituency, but of the whole people. When he speaks in his true character, he speaks for no special interest. If he rightly interprets the national thought and boldly insists upon it, he is irresistible; and the country never feels the zest for action so much as when its President is of such insight and calibre.[1]

The Wilsonian conception of the Presidency has triumphed far beyond Wilson's wildest imaginings. The President, representing all the people, can act in his executive capacity in response to his representative capacity. He need not think of himself as the executive of the Congress; he is the executive of the people. He does not need a law upon which to base his actions. Actions can

---

[1]Woodrow Wilson, *Constitutional Government in the United States,* quoted in James MacGregor Burns, *Presidential Government* (Boston: Houghton Mifflin, 1965), p. 96.

be justified by reference to the President's "constitutional powers," which means, in effect, his direct representativeness. In 1973, President Nixon, for example, defended his bombing of Cambodia as an exercise of his "inherent authority" as commander in chief and pointed to his re-election margin of 1972 to refute the apparent constitutional requirement of congressional authorization for military initiatives. Originally, the President's constitutional powers meant little more than the power to enforce the laws approved by Congress. Being commander in chief did not seem initially a license to use force if the President, exercising his personal judgment, deemed it necessary. Now, the President's constitutional power is defined to mean the power to make and enforce decisions in response to a direct popular mandate. The Congress is frequently urged to pass laws that amount to little more than the authorization of administrative discretion in new areas. Many other laws passed by the Congress contain saving clauses stating that they can be set aside by the President in response to some "emergency." The President in fact is considered derelict by the public if he does not himself initiate the bulk of legislation placed before Congress. The President may use Congress's laws with discretion and further has innumerable direct discretionary powers.

Most recent Presidents have seemed to take literally the Wilsonian aspiration to "represent all of the people all of the time." John Kennedy, however, while still a senator, defended the election of the President by the electoral college against the proposal that the college be abolished in order to ensure a more representative Presidency, on the grounds that the President represented the industrial North to a greater extent than other parts of the country, under the present arrangement, and that this was desirable because other parts of the country were better represented in other parts of the government. Since the Congress was a stronghold of Southern strength, the slight advantage the North had in the contest for the Presidency was important to preserve, in Kennedy's eyes. This argument implied a conception of representation that included the entire government, in which the Presidency was seen as a competing representative institution, representing a part of the whole, while the Congress represented another part.

While few Presidents have advanced such an explicit argument as Kennedy made, all Presidents feel representative of a primary constituency as well as of the people as a whole. One's primary constituency may be only characterized vaguely as "the forgotten man" or "the silent majority," or its existence may be denied altogether. The significant consideration, however, is that the direct, fractional representativeness of the President is not thought to make it impossible for him to be, when necessary, also the representative of all. The President may feel that the better half of the nation that supports him is also more representative of the nation's future, and that, in responding to it, he is thereby responding to the interests of all, properly and prospectively defined.

The representativeness of the Presidency is inherent and desirable. What and whom the President actually represents is important and affects the decisions he makes. It is consequently possible to argue about the impact of the President's constituency on his decisions. The President's ability, in individual cases, to decide whether or not to act as a representative of his constituency, and to alter the definition of the group he will consider himself representative of, suggests the other half of the story: The President is a representative not only of the people but also of the inherent power of the Presidency in his dealings with the people.

The complexity of the meaning of the Presidency, answerable and yet not answerable to the people, is similar to the complexity inherent in the medieval concept of dual sovereignty, according to which sovereignty resided both in the King and in the people. The King was both God's representative on earth and the representative of all the people. The "confusion" of legal texts on the issue of sovereignty, as perceived by later, more logical generations, was no more than the confusion of reality, a complex balance in which neither the King nor the people claimed exclusive rights. It was only the eventual breakdown of this confused but viable system that necessitated the location of sovereignty in either King or Commons, in the seventeenth century. The medieval King ruled by virtue of his divine position, but only in the way in which a divinely sanctioned monarch was supposed to rule. Beyond the bounds of conventionally sanctioned behavior, the King might seem to be acting nakedly, without the divinity that hedged him— but also hedged him in. The people could not rule without the King, but a bad King could be replaced, though, of course, only to be followed by another King.[2]

The people might have a role in protesting the conduct of the King, or the state of the kingdom, but once the act of confirming

---

[2]See Donald Hanson, *From Kingdom to Commonwealth* (Cambridge, Mass.: Harvard University Press, 1970).

a new King had been completed, the people were expected to settle down and watch the new King address himself to the country's problems. The people could hope that the new King would remedy their problems and be different from his predecessor, but all they could do was wait and see. And the active process of selecting a new King determined nothing about the set of personal advisers he might choose—quite possibly the same ones who had surrounded his hated predecessor. The new King might have witnessed the old King's fate but have concluded that the hatred directed against him was now expended and that it would be safe for him to act in precisely the same way—certainly safe for a period.

The practice in America is not too different. The President is chosen by the people, more or less, and can be removed by the normal process of election, by the extraordinary process of impeachment and conviction for high crimes and misdemeanors, or by the illegal action of assassination. Once chosen, however, he is the President. There is only one President at a time. Certain things can be done only by Presidents. Thus, as in the Middle Ages, the exercise of popular sovereignty is circumscribed.

The American people are involved in the exhausting process of substituting one President for another. But the range of substitutes available is limited, and the degree of popular control that can be exercised on the President in the day-to-day performance of his duties is also limited. The new President may choose as his deputies the same people, or the same kind of people, used by his predecessor. The Constitution provides that the Senate, representing the people, should have a role in the screening of Presidential advisers, but even the formality of Senate confirmation is now frequently evaded by the utilization of special Presidential assistants not subject to Senate approval for duties once performed by Cabinet officers.

Some feel that the President, though freed from most congressional and popular restraints, is nonetheless still effectively controlled by the groups who helped put him in office. This is true only with qualification. Presidential candidates are selected by powerful coalitions in American society who hope to sustain their power by association with a person who may become the legitimate President of all Americans. Every four years competing coalitions offer alternative candidates, and the acquisition of the largest number of votes is accepted as proof of constitutional legitimacy. The President is then able, if he acts with circumspection, to dispense with the services of the coalition behind him.

23

Once in the office the office is his, and he belongs to the office, not to his backers. Only the sustained opposition of the nation as a whole—not the withdrawal of the support of his backers—can bring him down. He is now motivated by his own sense of who he is—a person placed in a historic office who will be judged in retrospect in terms of his ability to radiate the full majesty of that office. The President tries to act as the legitimate spokesman of an entire people. As a spokesman, he speaks not only to the people but also to history. By history, he means the court of future public opinion that will assign him his rank. Speaking to the court of history, the President is speaking to his own moral conscience, to his own conviction that certain values will be shared by future generations. In speaking for the people, the President also hopes to retain his legitimacy in the eyes of the present generation of voters, from whom he must secure re-election.

Being above politics is the best, the only politics for a legitimate President. If being above politics means that the President must dissociate himself from some of those who put him in office, he will do so.

Once installed, a President is hedged by the divinity of his office. Although selected by a coalition and elected by the people, once sworn in he is also the representative of the Constitution, from which stems the Presidential line. The President must safeguard the source of his legitimacy by identifying himself with his precursors in this office, an office which only its holders, so they say, can understand. By convention there are areas in which the President's sole responsibility is respected; in recent decades, foreign policy has been championed as one such. By convention there are other areas—primarily domestic—in which the President is conceived as relatively helpless. In these areas, continual defeats for the President will not damage his dignity, because here the dual sovereignty of the people is recognized. The people, through Congress, have a right to settle directly for themselves certain matters affecting their fate, just as the President has a right to the unfettered exercise of his power in certain other matters, not so directly affecting people in his country. When the President ventures beyond the hedge of his office, he is naked. Defeats within the hedge will not damage his image; victories beyond it may be ruinous.

The Presidency's insulation from popular pressure in specified areas has not discouraged Presidents from trying to expand their room for maneuver by pushing the hedge of their divinity outward. Presidents, like others, create wishing worlds. Presidents may find themselves, for example, tantalized by the thought that the deference they inspire in a self-selected circle of sycophants abroad might be replicated at home.

A supposedly representative leader is naturally interested in appearing to be responding to "demands" in taking a given action, even if this means orchestrating the demands to order. If a demand comes from a source beyond the immediate familiarity of those the President is addressing, they will not know how to refute the assertion that a demand has been received from this other source. A President may make a claim to be responding to invisible parts of the electorate or to the higher imperatives of the office he holds, just as he may pretend to be responding to foreign obligations—and to have no choice but to do so. A President elected in the purest democratic manner with no evident way of pretending to be the representative of any group other than the electorate will be tempted to build up foreign alliances to create obligations to which he may respond if he wishes to act in opposition to a popular mandate. Such obligations, the electorate will be told, are obligations of the Presidential office, and hence of the nation as a whole; failure to fulfill them would disgrace the nation. In reality, they may have been created by Presidential pump-priming and may be used to disguise arbitrary actions the President wishes to take for his own purposes.

Presidents who grasp the potential of their office have seldom had difficulty being re-elected, even if opposed on specific issues by a majority of the people. The President can easily hold out against transitory opposition. A President may not even claim to represent more than a plurality; even if he claims to represent the people as a whole, he will not think of himself simply as their representative, with no choice but to bend to every public pressure. The President thinks of his representativeness as an attribute compatible with, but subordinate to, his other attributes, as leader and rational decision-maker. The President, as a representative institution, wants to be representative enough to be re-elected; but as an executive institution, he wishes to do grand things worthy of his office.

Montesquieu contended that the governing principle of a constitutional monarchy is honor, whereas that of a republic is virtue. The leader of a republic, Montesquieu suggested, is satisfied with the existence in it of many individually virtuous men. A monarchy, whether elective or hereditary, is concerned with grandeur, with putting all its subjects to tasks of appropriate magnitude, with justifying the awe in which it is held abroad by acting in accordance with the dignity of its power.[3] In advocating a step-up in military activity in Vietnam, Presidential adviser McGeorge Bundy, for example, argued that America's power imposed an obligation. In a memorandum to President Johnson written on February 7, 1965, Bundy noted "that in all sectors of Vietnamese opinion there is a strong belief that the United States could do much more if it would, and that they are suspicious of our failure to use more of our obviously enormous power."[4]

The concentration of power in the President's hands, which has permitted him to indulge in international exploits in a manner befitting a powerful monarch, was first urged, ironically, by liberals attempting to replace conflict for conflict's sake with regulation for regulation's sake. Governing institutions, standing above others, it was felt, would not need to engage in petty competition with those below them and would be able to govern in the interest of all. The Presidency was to be the one place where all competing interests would be viewed from a superior "vantage point," to use Lyndon Johnson's phrase. Since no one had his perspective, no one could be entirely sure that the President's judgment was flawed; everyone consequently ought to be expected to give the President the benefit of the doubt. But the President's liberal eulogists did not succeed in placing above the chaos of competition a single individual who was liberated from the ambitions that drove men placed lower. Rather, they succeeded in elevating a single man driven by the same passions as others into a position in which the only way he could gratify his passions was in a vastly more dangerous arena. The man who was supposed to act in the public interest, because it was at his personal disposal, became a man who could subordinate the public interest to his personal drive for glory. It was, in fact, tempting to the man exalted above others to endeavor to fulfill his particular drive for recognition by utilizing all his citizens in a competition with powerful enemies. James MacGregor Burns has noted that "for a man with Theodore Roosevelt's need for personal fulfillment it was a sort of tragedy that he had no war—

---

[3]Baron de Montesquieu, *The Spirit of the Laws*, trans. Thomas Nugent (New York: Hafner, 1962).

[4]*The Pentagon Papers* (New York: Bantam Books, 1971).

not even a Whiskey Rebellion."[5] President Kennedy referred to the week of the Cuban missile crisis as a week in which he "really earned his pay." This was pre-eminently the week in which Kennedy felt that his conception of his proper activity as President of all Americans was fulfilled; the power of all Americans was pitted against a worthy antagonist in a way that permitted him to test his leadership ability. Kennedy saw the Presidency as a position of great power; he defined his personal challenge as the holder of that office as the grasping of opportunities to exemplify "grace under pressure." In planning the strategy of the Vietnam conflict, Lyndon Johnson felt that a large group "with 100 people sitting around was not the place . . . to build a military effectiveness. . . . I want to put it off as long as I can, having to make these crucial decisions. I enjoy this agony."[6]

Ruling, as President, as a neutral arbiter of lower conflicts among his subject has not afforded equal gratification. Only Eisenhower, of recent Presidents, has come close to the conception of a neutral Presidency, and this was clearly a reflection of his life-stage, as a man of proven skill in grand combat now in semi-retirement.

Montesquieu was right: If you make a man a King he will begin to think in terms of glory. How could proponents of the enhancement of Presidential power not have anticipated that a great leader armed with great discretion would seek glory rather than goodness? They failed to anticipate this result because they had also written into the drama a role for themselves. The President, subordinating representativeness to the imperatives of executive leadership of a great power, in turn was to subordinate executive leadership to the directives of a "rational" decision-making process. A judicious President, exercising discretion wisely, would be guided at every juncture by the expert advisers at his side.

The original purpose of the Constitution was to give necessary power to officials hamstrung by legal strictures. As Herman Melville put it, "If there are any three things opposed to the genius of the American Constitution, they are these: irresponsibility in a judge, unlimited discretionary authority in an executive, and the union of an irresponsible judge and an unlimited executive in one person."[7] The rule of laws, not men, meant that, though men would rule, they

---

[5]Burns, *op. cit.*, p. 66.
[6]*The Pentagon Papers*, p. 496.
[7]Herman Melville, *White-Jacket* (New York: Russell and Russell, 1963), p. 178.

could not rule as idiosyncratically as they would wish. Implicit in the contemporary vision of Presidential government, in contrast, is a vast role for discretion. Centralized action is obviously more efficient; if it can be claimed that it is also more just, then the old fears of the Founding Fathers can be dismissed as out of date.

A judicious President, it is argued, can act with speed, flexibility, and on the basis of expert advice. Is not the President the best-informed person, the best-situated person to make a decision? Actually, the availability of expert advice has served to isolate the President. Whether advised by an elite of independently accomplished men, or by specialists on his own payroll, the President is trapped by those trying to help him. The President may be the worst-informed person in the country if he is systematically shielded from the normal experience and outlook of citizens. Akbar the Great of India and Henry V of England used to disguise themselves as ordinary men and wander freely amongst their subjects to learn what was really going on. Surrounded by sycophants and specialists, these monarchs went to their lowly subjects in search of unbiased views on the needs of the kingdom. A President who honors his advisers with the highest possible praise—his trust that their presentation of this country's need makes him well informed—is the most pathetic of captives, a bear on a string.

The myth of the judicious President is not only factually inaccurate, it is deeply destructive of the character of the occupant of the office. The President, we are told, is a different sort of person from the generality of Americans. As he has a special nature, so he has special duties. He alone, for example, can determine when his political opponents are endangering "national security" and giving "comfort to America's enemies." His special duties necessitate his possession of special privileges—picture-phones, jet airplanes, summer and winter palaces, and a prescriptive right to impound the consciences of the highest and lowest members of his realm. The Watergate affair demonstrated graphically that a surprising number of Americans of high patriotism felt unable to refuse a request from "the White House" that they break the law of the land.

A structure wrought to ensure rational decision-making has instead hopelessly entangled private whims with national needs. A President, freed to do as he wishes, is expected to be right; in fact, he is permitted no defense against his own fallibility. He is routinely tempted by the logic of false determinism; having made a decision, he is likely to say, and come to believe, that he had "no choice" but to make the decision he did. George Reedy has argued that, with the possible exception of Franklin Roosevelt, recent Presidents have been ordinarily unable to profit from their mistakes. In Reedy's view, a person who enters the Presidency with normal, or even above-normal, intelligence and political sensitivity will soon start making political blunders which would make a ward-heeler blush.[8] Together, the forces around and within the President are likely to destroy even the elementary political sensitivity of men who show enormous subtlety in their march to the throne.

No person can rule without help; no sane person can come to believe he is infallible without frequent testimony to that effect from others. The President is unlikely to experience a rude awakening at the hands of his staff. In fact, the greater effort he makes to surround himself with apparently distinguished, independent, accomplished professionals with standing in their own fields, the greater may be the resulting delusion that their praise is accurate. Independent American intellectuals have offered their services to the President to ensure the rationality of his decisions; ironically, their willingness to serve negates the goal they seek. Their availability feeds the vanity of the President and offers no obstacle to his ability to toy with them for his own purposes, while they remain subject to the delusion that the President values them for their wisdom. A King and his courtiers feed one another's vanity. Pride in servility for the adviser, pleasure in adulation for the King: both are satisfied by a mutually corrupting relationship.

Many observers have been puzzled by the reluctance of the President's "independent" advisers to resign when the President disregards their advice. Yet, if they sense their impotence within the inner circle, they also realize that they would be even more powerless outside of it, capable only of making appeals to "public opinion." A class of notables may put pressure on the person they advise if, as a class, they possess independent bases of power and regulate admission to their class—and if the class is not very large. If a group of would-be advisers lacks cohesion, the task of selecting favorites who will identify with the King rather than the class from which they are drawn will be child's play. A regulating class, such as the Barons at Runnymede or, on rare occasions, the British Prime Minister's Cabinet colleagues, even in the best of circumstances, purchases its power of regulation at a high price. It

---

[8]George Reedy, *The Twilight of the Presidency* (New York: New American Library, 1970). This book provides an excellent insider's account of the "court" atmosphere of the contemporary White House.

can only perform a restraining function, pinning the King down. It cannot actively advise the King on the positive manner in which he should conduct his affairs in those areas which remain his prerogative. Its preference for defiance is a self-denying ordinance, tying its hands from accepting a position as a trusted ally of the King. An adviser can only influence an autocrat in a positive manner by presenting himself as a person who presumably advises the autocrat to do what is in his own interest—who claims to be putting the interest of his master above the retention of his class affiliation. He may use his class identity to present himself to the autocrat as an analyst of his class, an interpreter of the way in which it can be best exploited by the autocrat, but he cannot act as a spokesman for his class. In a sense, the most salient question is the simplest: Who rewards his services?[9]

A President needs different sorts of advisers from different backgrounds. A President's advisers are drawn from many sources —business, the professions, politics, the bureaucracy. In their new role, however, they become the President's agents in his dealings with these estates, and they most probably will remain in this role, even if they formally return to the estates from which they came. A high government official who returns to his bank or airplane factory or university may well remain informally a member of the President's staff, even though he is now only engaged in a rearguard action of defending his past actions.

The King's men are not likely to provide him with the corrective advice that might shake his confidence. Even the designation of a devil's advocate within the inner circle may only reinforce the impression that all possible objections have been anticipated and can be coped with. Beyond the circle of Presidential appointees, however, there remain the great bureaucratic establishments, which have, on occasion, been portrayed as an immovable "fourth branch of government," fiercely resistant to Presidential prodding. In fact, this tenured establishment can only rarely provide a corrective to the President. Bureaucrats have even less independence than private advisers. The bureaucrat is an employee who must look up to the President and his agents as the embodiment of the public interest he has sworn to serve. In this sense, even a merit bureaucracy becomes, to a degree, a personal household staff. The

---

[9]For a heroic but ultimately unpersuasive effort to formulate a procedure which will encourage "rational" Presidential decision-making by a rearrangement of the President's advisory establishment, see Alexander George, "The Case for Multiple Advocacy in Making Foreign Policy," *American Political Science Review*, September, 1972.

bureaucrats' job is not to analyze reality, but to make their presentation of reality one that will appeal to their superiors. The simple fact that a bureaucrat is right is no guarantee of his credibility in the eyes of his superiors. The bureaucracy is not a class capable of limiting the President's freedom of action; it is a group of servants dependent on his attention.

A sizable bureaucracy is naturally difficult to control, but by making careful appointments and promotions, the President can usually drive opposition underground, whatever the organizational structure of the bureaucracy may be. In dealing with obstructive agency heads, he can threaten the creation of competing policy-making units within the White House. The State Department in recent years, for example, far from "influencing" the President, has had to acquiesce in the concentration of foreign-policy–making in the White House. This lesson has not been lost on other bureaucratic establishments. It has seemed far safer to be accommodating than to oppose and then be circumvented. Even those apparently indispensable and autonomous specialized agencies, the CIA and the FBI, have found it difficult to withstand pressure to perform unwelcome tasks set by the White House when threatened with the possible establishment of competing units within the White House. J. Edgar Hoover—a uniquely powerful bureaucratic fixture —did prevent the creation of a White House "crime" unit desired by President Nixon, but lesser men have ordinarily been unwilling to risk their agencies' prospects by defying clear White House preferences. Far from encouraging open deliberation of policy alternatives, the President's elevation has only intensified Presidential arrogance and bureaucratic servility.[10]

What, finally, can be said of the effect of the myth of the judicious President on the morale of the public at large? The President's superhuman prerogatives ultimately rest on the assumption that it is in the interest of all of us to have a person who is pure and high-minded, and who consequently must be presented publicly as such even if there are good grounds for believing differently. The feeling persists that something dreadful would happen to all of us, and to the entire structure of government from which we benefit so substantially, if anybody acted publicly on the basis of his private knowledge of the personal character of the President.

---

[10]Concerning Hoover's opposition to Nixon, see Nixon's statement, *New York Times*, May 23, 1973. The Watergate hearings turned up elaborate evidence of White House pressure on the CIA and the post-Hoover FBI and of the reluctance of their senior officials to oppose or report to the public illegal requests made by White House aides.

If all avert their eyes, the President will not be in danger of damaging his image by walking around naked. The myth of the Presidency is the creation of people who know better but who are appalled by the prospect of having to consider the alternatives. We cling to the hope that a person, even though an ordinary man to all appearances, when supplied with a magical apparatus, can bring about a complete change in the entire polity. The irony is, we know that the President's magic is manufactured and maintained by our own efforts and that a man riding on a wish is not really a magician; he is a confidence artist. We supply him with the confidence that makes him look like an artist. You can't fool all the people all the time; but can all the people fool themselves all the time?

The myth of the magical President is of relatively recent origin. The contemporary phenomenon of Presidential autocracy was created by the strengthening of one of the three constituted branches of government, a strengthening resulting not from necessity but from choice, the considered preference of idealists for a kind of decision-making that somehow seemed more just because it was made on high by one man. Today many people recognize that the system has not worked as hoped but are uncertain why that is, and how it might be remedied. The most natural response is to assume that there is nothing wrong with the basic approach but only with its implementation. The easiest argument is that all that is lacking for the system to function as planned is the right individual. If all our troubles can be said to stem from the tragic unsuitability of the individuals catapulted into office by a series of historical accidents, why is it not reasonable to hope that all will be set aright through one more swing of the pendulum?

As in the Middle Ages, so in America today, much political discourse ranges between two poles, from romantic optimism to grim pessimism, from hope for the succession to the throne of a truly good King, to tyrannicide. This discourse, as in the Middle Ages, is limited by the assumption that the extent of political change possible is to replace one monarch by another—by natural or surgical means. Such a preoccupation with the possibility that the replacement of one man with another will produce a total transformation in the policy and posture of government is as intense as it would be in any divine-right monarchy; the basis for such a preoccupation is so fragile as to be pathological. Like any entrenched pathology, it is an effort to adjust to the presence in the organism of a searing disease and may consequently be stabilizing in the short run. Since the effort to adjust cannot halt the progress of the disease, however, the effort at adjustment only makes things worse in the long run. Intense hope in the magical transformation that a change of regime will produce turns to appalling disillusionment when the change occurs and nothing happens. The engine of hope is once again revved up. Attention focuses once again on the next succession and the high-minded, pure people whose elevation will make all the difference. And yet, as the cycles of hope and disillusionment expand their duration and intensity, they begin to overlap, and people become increasingly aware of the similarity between the new vain hope and the last blasted hope.

The answer lies not in pursuing the present course to the end but in changing course. Instead of attempting to remove the human need to demonstrate adequacy by wielding power, one should attempt to neutralize the danger of wielding power by restricting the scope of possible conflicts. Placing men above ambition simply releases them from normal restraints and forces them to invent new and more reckless forms of moral testing. To attempt to institutionalize virtue is to guarantee disaster.

The President should be respected for what he is—a man representative of the forces that put him in office—not what it is hoped he may become once in office, through the magic of disinterestedness or the brilliance of his advisers. If the President ceases to pretend that he does not represent some more than others, he will be a more candid, more effective person. He will be less deferential to his predecessors in office, who represented other coalitions, and by his candid partisanship, he will make it easier for ordinary citizens to recognize him for the significant, partial person that he is. A series of Presidents with alternating constituencies would make it possible for each President to pursue an active policy of representing primarily the interest of some, with the implicit understanding that others would have their turn. This could be said to be the situation currently in existence in Great Britain. In Britain, the representative and executive functions are formally consolidated in one man, the Prime Minister. The Prime Minister, in fact, does represent little more than one-half of the electorate, and the country is governed by two halves, each taking turns at the exercise of substantial, directly representative executive power.

A second alternative would be to establish a purer division of legislative and executive power, in which the Congress decided policies and the President merely implemented them. Firm lines of division between functions embodied in separate institutions do not offer much promise on the basis of past performance. The classic example of a clear-cut division between executive and legislative bodies is in the meeting of the French Estates-General, which led to the outbreak of the French Revolution. The monarchy and the Estates-General were so completely out of touch that inevitably each was driven to try to govern without resort to the other. First the monarchy tried to get along without the Estates; then the Estates tried to get along without the monarchy. The American system has never been characterized by the separation of legislative and executive powers ascribed to it, and there seems little reason to hope for improvement by making that separation a practical reality. The balance of *power* between legislative and executive branches should be redressed more favorably to the Congress, but a viable system would retain fused functions in each of the branches of government. The Congress thus should increase its legislative and executive roles, while those of the Presidency should be diminished.

One should be cautious, in strengthening the Congress, that one is, in fact, strengthening it in the name of an alternative vision of governmental functioning. There is an ominous tendency, for example, to speak of the strengthening of Congress by providing congressmen with longer terms and more staff and amenities. It is possible that the Congress might, in consequence, be strengthened in relation to the President, and that both these branches would then be even more isolated from the citizenry. The Congress should not be strengthened to make it more like the present Presidency; the current appeal of Congress is in the fact that it shares many of the hardships experienced by ordinary citizens. Television viewers of the Senate's Watergate hearings saw a disorderly, contradictory human spectacle—in contrast to the cut-and-dried imperial pronouncements from the closed Presidential suite to which the American public had become so accustomed. The Senate's hearings were accessibly, persuasively inefficient.

The main direction of congressional reform should be to bring Congress even closer to the ordinary citizen, by eliminating the rigidities in the internal structure of the Congress that make it most representative of the public opinion of twenty or thirty years ago. A strict seniority system for selecting committee chairmen is ludicrous in a body such as the House of Representatives that the Constitution directed should be freshly elected once every two years.

One may safely assume that the main structural outlines of the American political system will remain: that an individual will continue to be selected by powerful coalitions and accepted by the general public as a legitimate ruler because of their minimal role in his final ratification. One may safely assume that the uniqueness of the office will continue to hold a fascination for its occupant, and that he will never be simply a creature of those who put him in a position where he can dispense with their services. There is no great reason to hope for significant change from the assembling of a new coalition of interests for the purpose of putting a new man into this unique office. The only hope of significant change in the nature of Presidential conduct lies in the alteration of the expectations a President is supposed to live up to, an alteration in the constraints on his actions in office rather than in the obligations he may assemble on his way to the office. Such constraints would have to be reflected in popular expectations of what a good President would be like. Such expectations would have to be clear and deep enough to impress every President with the belief that they will still be around when history puts him in his place.

What constitutes greatness in a President? Is a great President one who permits the gigantic bureaucracy he heads to occupy itself in vindicating his special privileges and powers? Is a great President one who patterns his personal life and public conduct after Louis XIV? Is a great President one who, like monarchs of the past, engages in warfare to preserve personal vanity, to avoid, for instance, being the first President to lose a war? (Countries can usually survive the loss of a war; Presidents cannot.) Can one not conceive of a country that insisted that its President did not have a special nature, did not have a special wisdom stemming from his vantage point and number of advisers? Such a country's President would not be permitted to pretend to infallibility; if he spoke with pious smugness or implied that his policy was inevitable, he would be laughed at.

Citizens are too sensible to want to concern themselves all the time with everybody else's business, but the President in Washington should be made aware that citizens want public men directing the polity politically, with the force of argument, not administratively, with the assistance of advertising. Citizens should demand responsible leaders and not settle for covert controllers.

From The Watergate Tapes

As Watergate so clearly demonstrated, the final consequence of unchecked presidential power is government by stealth and imperiousness. Opponents become "enemies" who must not only be defeated but broken as well. "Executive privilege" is elevated to the level of high principle and defended as necessary to national security. The essence of the office becomes the accumulation of power even more than its exercise. When finally cornered by critics, the "imperial" presidency retreats behind the secrecy of a stone wall. In this magisterial isolation, as the following selection from the Watergate tapes suggests, the ordinary rules of political conduct and morality no longer obtain.

Meeting:
The President, Dean, Oval Office
March 21, 1973. (10:12-11:55 A.M.)

P Well, sit down, sit down.

D Good morning.

P Well what is the Dean summary of the day about?

D The reason that I thought we ought to talk this morning is because in our conversations, I have the impression that you don't know everything I know and it makes it very difficult for you to make judgments that only you can make on some of these things and I thought that—

P In other words, I have to know why you feel that we shouldn't unravel something?

D Let me give you my overall first.

P In other words, your judgment as to where it stands, and where we will go.

"The Watergate Tapes." From *Submission of Recorded Presidential Conversations to the Committee on the Judiciary of the House of Representatives by Richard Nixon* (Washington, D.C., Government Printing Office, 1974).

D I think that there is no doubt about the seriousness of the problem we've got. We have a cancer within, close to the Presidency, that is growing. It is growing daily. It's compounded, growing geometrically now, because it compounds itself. That will be clear if I, you know, explain some of the details of why it is. Basically, it is because (1) we are being blackmailed; (2) People are going to start perjuring themselves very quickly that have not had to perjure themselves to protect other people in the line. And there is no assurance—

P That that won't bust?

D That that won't bust. So let me give you the sort of basic facts, talking first about the Watergate; and then about Segretti; and then about some of the peripheral items that have come up. First of all on the Watergate: how did it all start, where did it start? O.K.! It started with an instruction to me from Bob Haldeman to see if we couldn't set up a perfectly legitimate campaign intelligence operation over at the Re-Election Committee. Not being in this business, I turned to somebody who had been in this business, Jack Caulfield. I don't remember whether you remember Jack or not. He was your original bodyguard before they had the candidate protection, an old city policeman.

P Yes, I know him.

D Jack worked for John and then was transferred to my office. I said "Jack come up with a plan that, you know—a normal infiltration, buying information from secretaries and all that sort of thing." He did, he put together a plan. It was kicked around. I went to Ehrlichman with it. I went to Mitchell with it, and the consensus was that Caulfield was not the man to do this. In retrospect, that might have been a bad call because he is an incredibly cautious person and wouldn't have put the situation where it is today. After rejecting that, they said we still need something so I was told to look around for someone who could go over to 1701 and do this. That is when I came up with Gordon Liddy. They needed a lawyer. Gordon had an intelligence background from his FBI service. I was aware of the fact that he had done some extremely sensitive things for the White House while he had been at the White House and he had apparently done them well. Going out into Ellsberg's doctor's office—

P Oh, yeah.

D And things like this. He worked with leaks. He tracked these things down. So the report that I got from Krogh was that he was a hell of a good man and not only that a good lawyer and could set up a proper operation. So we talked to Liddy. He was interested in doing it. I took Liddy over to meet Mitchell. Mitchell thought highly of him because Mitchell was partly involved in his coming to the White House to work for Krogh. Liddy had been at Treasury before that. Then Liddy was told to put together his plan, you know, how he would run an intelligence operation. This was after he was hired over there at the Committee. Magruder called me in January and said "I would like to have you come over and see Liddy's plan."

P January of '72?

D January of '72.

D "You come over to Mitchell's office and sit in a meeting where Liddy is going to lay his plan out." I said "I don't really know if I am the man, but if you want me there I will be happy to." So I came over and Liddy laid out a million dollar plan that was the most incredible thing I haver laid my eyes on: all in codes, and involved black bag operations, kidnapping, providing prostitutes to weaken the opposition, bugging, mugging teams. It was just an incredible thing.

P Tell me this: Did Mitchell go along—?

D No, no, not at all, Mitchell just sat there puffing and laughing. I could tell from—after Liddy left the office I said "That is the most incredible thing I have ever seen." He said "I agree." And so Liddy was told to go back to the drawingboard and come up with something realistic. So there was a second meeting. They asked me to come over to that. I came into the tail end of the meeting. I wasn't there for the first part. I don't know how long the meeting lasted. At this point, they were discussing again bugging, kidnapping and the like. At this point I said right in front of everybody, very clearly, I said, "These are not the sort of things (1) that are ever to be discussed in the office of the Attorney General of the United States—that was where he still was—and I am personally incensed." And I am trying to get Mitchell off the hook. He is a nice person and doesn't like to have to say no when he is talking with people he is going to have to work with.

P That's right.

D So I let it be known. I said "You all pack that stuff up and get it the hell out of here. You just can't talk this way in this office and you should re-examine your whole thinking."

P Who all was present?

D It was Magruder, Mitchell, Liddy and myself. I came back right after the meeting and told Bob, "Bob, we have a growing disaster on our hands if they are thinking this way," and I said, "The White House has got to stay out of this and I, frankly, am not going to be involved in it." He said, "I agree John." I thought at that point that the thing was turned off. That is the last I heard of it and I thought it was turned off because it was an absurd proposal.

P Yeah.

D Liddy—I did have dealings with him afterwards and we never talked about it. Now that would be hard to believe for some people, but we never did. That is the fact of the matter.

P Well, you were talking with him about other things.

D We had so many other things.

P He had some legal problems too. But you were his advisor, and I understand you had conversations about the campaign laws, etc. Haldeman told me that you were handling all of that for us. Go ahead.

D Now. So Liddy went back after that and was over at 1701, the Committee, and this is where I come into having put the pieces together after the fact as to what I can put together about what happened. Liddy sat over there and tried to come up with another plan that he could sell. (1) They were talking to him, telling him that he was putting too much money in it. I don't think they were discounting the illegal points. Jeb is not a lawyer. He did not know whether this is the way the game way played and what it was all about. They came up, apparently, with another plan, but they couldn't get it approved by anybody over there. So Liddy and Hunt apparently came to see Chuck Colson, and Chuck Colson picked up the telephone and called Magruder and said, "You all either fish or cut bait. This is absurd to have these guys over there and not using them. If you are not going to use them, I may use them." Things of this nature.

P When was this?

D This was apparently in February of '72.

P   Did Colson know what they were talking about?

D   I can only assume, because of his close relationship with Hunt, that he had a damn good idea what they were talking about, a damn good idea. He would probably deny it today and probably get away with denying it. But I still—unless Hunt blows on him—

P   But then Hunt isn't enough. It takes two doesn't it?

D   Probably. Probably. But Liddy was there also and if Liddy were to blow—

P   Then you have a problem—I was saying as to the criminal liability in the White House.

D   I will go back over that, and take out any of the soft spots.

P   Colson, you think was the person who pushed?

D   I think he helped to get the thing off the dime. Now something else occurred though—

P   Did Colson—had he talked to anybody here?

D   No. I think this was—

P   Did he talk with Haldeman?

D   No, I don't think so. But here is the next thing that comes in the chain. I think Bob was assuming, that they had something that was proper over there, some intelligence gathering operation that Liddy was operating. And through Strachan, who was his tickler, he started pushing them to get some information and they—Magruder—took that as a signal to probably go to Mitchell and to say, "They are pushing us like crazy for this from the White House." And so Mitchell probably puffed on his pipe and said, "Go ahead," and never really reflected on what it was all about. So they had some plan that obviously had, I gather, different targets they were going to go after. They were going to infiltrate, and bug, and do all this sort of thing to a lot of these targets. This is knowledge I have after the fact. Apparently after they had initially broken in and bugged the DNC they were getting information. The information was coming over here to Strachan and some of it was given to Haldeman, there is no doubt about it.

P   Did he know where it was coming from?

D   I don't really know if he would.

P   Not necessarily?

D   Not necessarily. Strachan knew it. There is no doubt about it, and whether Strachan—I have never come to press these people on these points because it hurts them to give up that next inch, so I had to piece things together. Strachan was aware of receiving information, reporting to Bob. At one point Bob even gave instructions to change their capabilities from Muskie to McGovern, and passed this back through Strachan to Magruder and apparently to Liddy. And Liddy was starting to make arrangements to go in and bug the McGovern operation.

P   They had never bugged Muskie, though, did they?

D   No, they hadn't, but they had infiltrated it by a secretary.

P   By a secretary?

D   By a secretary and a chauffeur. There is nothing illegal about that. So the information was coming over here and then I finally, after—. The next point in time that I became aware of anything was on June 17th when I got word that there had been this break in at the DNC and somebody from our Committee had been caught in the DNC. And I said, "Oh, (expletive deleted)." You know, eventually putting the pieces together—

P   You knew what it was.

D   I knew who it was. So I called on Monday morning and said, "First, Gordon, I want to know whether anybody in the White House was involved in this." And he said, "No, they weren't." I said, "Well I want to know how in (adjective deleted) name this happened." He said, "Well, I was pushed without mercy by Magruder to get in there and to get more information. That the information was not satisfactory. That Magruder said 'The White House is not happy with what we are getting.'"

P   The White House?

D   The White House. Yeah!

P   Who do you think was pushing him?

D   Well, I think it was probably Strachan thinking that Bob wanted things, because I have seen that happen on other occasions where things have said to have been of very prime importance when they really weren't.

P   Why at that point in time I wonder? I am just trying to think. We had just finished the Moscow trip. The Democrats had just nominated McGovern. I mean, (expletive deleted), what in the hell were these people doing? I can see their doing it earlier. I can see the pressures, but I don't see why all the pressure was on then.

D   I don't know, other than the fact that they might have been looking for information about the conventions.

P   That's right.

D Because, I understand that after the fact that there was a plan to bug Larry O'Brien's suite down in Florida. So Liddy told me that this is what had happened and this is why it had happened.

P Where did he learn that there were plans to bug Larry O'Brien's suite?

D From Magruder, long after the fact.

P Magruder is (unintelligible)

D Yeah. Magruder is totally knowledgeable on the whole thing.

P Yeah.

D Alright now, we have gone through the trial. I don't know if Mitchell has perjured himself in the Grand Jury or not.

P Who?

D Mitchell. I don't know how much knowledge he actually had. I know that Magruder has perjured himself in the Grand Jury. I know that Porter has perjured himself in the Grand Jury.

P Who is Porter? (unintelligible)

D He is one of Magruder's deputies. They set up this scenario which they ran by me. They said, "How about this?" I said, "I don't know. If this is what you are going to hang on, fine."

P What did they say in the Grand Jury?

D They said, as they said before the trial in the Grand Jury, that Liddy had come over as Counsel and we knew he had these capacities to do legitimate intelligence. We had no idea what he was doing. He was given an authorization of $250,000 to collect information, because our surrogates were out on the road. They had no protection, and we had information that there were going to be demonstrations against them, and that we had to have a plan as to what liabilities they were going to be confronted with and Liddy was charged with doing this. We had no knowledge that he was going to bug the DNC.

P The point is, that is not true?

D That's right.

P Magruder did know it was going to take place?

D Magruder gave the instructions to be back in the DNC.

P He did?

D Yes.

P You know that?

D Yes.

P I see. O.K.

D I honestly believe that no one over here knew that. I know that as God is my maker, I had no knowledge that they were going to do this.

P Bob didn't either, or wouldn't have known that either. You are not the issue involved. Had Bob known, he would be.

D Bob—I don't believe specifically knew that they were going in there.

P I don't think so.

D I don't think he did. I think he knew that there was a capacity to do this but he was not given the specific direction.

P Did Strachan know?

D I think Strachan did know.

P (unintelligible) Going back into the DNC—Hunt, etc.—this is not understandable!

D So—those people are in trouble as a result of the Grand Jury and the trial. Mitchell, of course, was never called during the trial. Now—

P Mitchell has given a sworn statement, hasn't he?

D Yes, Sir.

P To the Jury?

D To the Grand Jury.—

P You mean the Goldberg arrangement?

D We had an arrangement whereby he went down with several of them, because of the heat of this thing and the implications on the election, we made an arrangement where they could quietly go into the Department of Justice and have one of the assistant U.S. Attorneys take their testimony and then read it before the Grand Jury.

P I thought Mitchell went.

D That's right, Mitchell was actually called before the Grand Jury. The Grand Jury would not settle for less, because the jurors wanted him.

P And he went?

D And he went.

P Good!

D I don't know what he said. I have never seen a transcript of the Grand Jury. Now what has happened post June 17? I was under pretty clear instructions not to investigate this, but this could have been disastrous on the electorate if all hell had broken loose. I worked on a theory of containment—

P Sure.

D   To try to hold it right where it was.

P   Right.

D   There is no doubt that I was totally aware of what the Bureau was doing at all times. I was totally aware of what the Grand Jury was doing. I knew what witnesses were going to be called. I knew what they were asked, and I had to.

P   Why did Peterson play the game so straight with us?

D   Because Peterson is a soldier. He kept me informed. He told me when we had problems, where we had problems and the like. He believes in you and he believes in this Administration. This Administration has made him. I don't think he has done anything improper, but he did make sure that the investigation was narrowed down to the very, very fine criminal thing which was a break for us. There is no doubt about it.

P   Do you honestly feel that he did an adequate job?

D   They ran that investigation out to the fullest extent they could follow a lead and that was it.

P   But the way point is, where I suppose he could be criticized for not doing an adequate job. Why didn't he call Haldeman? Why didn't he get a statement from Colson? Oh, they did get Colson!

D   That's right. But as based on their FBI interviews, there was no reason to follow up. There were no leads there. Colson said, "I have no knowledge of this" to the FBI. Strachan said, "I have no knowledge." They didn't ask Strachan any questions about Watergate. They asked him about Segretti. They said, "what is your connection with Liddy?" Strachan just said, "Well, I met him over there." They never really pressed him. Strachan appeared, as a result of some coaching, to be the dumbest paper pusher in the bowels of the White House.

P   I understand.

D   Alright. Now post June 17th: These guys immediately—It is very interesting. (Dean sort of chuckled) Liddy, for example, on the Friday before—I guess it was on the 15th, no, the 16th of June—had been in Henry Peterson's office with another member of my staff on campaign compliance problems. After the incident, he ran Kleindienst down at Burning Tree Country Club and told him "You've got to get my men out of jail." Kleindienst said, "You get the hell out of here, kid. Whatever you have to say, just say to somebody else. Don't bother me." But this has never come up. Liddy said if they all got counsel instantly and said we will ride this thing out. Alright, then they started making demands. "We have to have attorneys fees. We don't have any money ourselves, and you are asking us to take this through the election." Alright, so arrangements were made through Mitchell, initiating it. And I was present in discussions where these guys had to be taken care of. Their attorneys fees had to be done. Kalmbach was brought in. Kalmbach raised some cash.

P They put that under the cover of a Cuban Committee, I suppose?

D Well, they had a Cuban Committee and they had—some of it was given to Hunt's lawyer, who in turn passed it out. You know, when Hunt's wife was flying to Chicago with $10,000 she was actually, I understand after the fact now, was going to pass that money to one of the Cubans—to meet him in Chicago and pass it to somebody there.

P (unintelligible) but I would certainly keep that cover for whatever it is worth.

D That's the most troublesome post-thing because (1) Bob is involved in that; (2) John is involved in that; (3) I am involved in that; (4) Mitchell is involved in that. And that is an obstruction of justice.

P In other words the bad it does. You were taking care of witnesses. How did Bob get in it?

D Well, they ran out of money over there. Bob had $350,000 in a safe over here that was really set aside for polling purposes. And there was no other source of money, so they came over and said "You all have got to give us some money." I had to go Bob and say, "Bob, they need some money over there." He said "What for." So I had to tell him what it was for because he wasn't just about to send money over there willy-nilly. And John was involved in those discussions. And then we decided there was no price too high to pay to let this thing blow up in front of the election.

P I think we should be able to handle that issue pretty well. May be some lawsuits.

D I think we can too. Here is what is happening right now. What sort of brings matters to the (unintelligible). One, this is going to be a continual blackmail operation by Hunt and Liddy and the Cubans. No doubt about it. And McCord, who is another one involved. McCord has asked for nothing. McCord did ask to meet with somebody, with Jack Caulfield who is his old friend who had gotten him hired over there. And when Caulfield had him hired, he was a perfectly legitimate security man. And he wanted to talk about commutation, and things like that. And as you know Colson has talked indirectly to Hunt about commutation. All of these things are bad, in that they are problems, they are promises, they are commitments. They are the very sort of thing that the Senate is going to be looking most for. I don't think they can find them, frankly.

P Pretty hard.

D Pretty hard. Damn hard. It's all cash.

P Pretty hard I mean as far as the witnesses are concerned.

D Alright, now, the blackmail is continuing. Hunt called one of lawyers from the Re-Election Committee on last Friday to leave it with him over the weekend. The guy came in to see me to give a message directly to me. From Hunt to me.

P Is Hunt out on bail?

D Pardon?

P Is Hunt on bail?

D Hunt is on bail. Correct. Hunt now is demanding another $72,000 for his own personal expenses; another $50,000 to pay attorneys fees; $120,000. Some (1) he wanted it as of the close of business yesterday. He said, "I am going to be sentenced on Friday, and I've got to get my financial affairs in order." I told this fellow O'Brien, "If you want money, you came to the wrong man, fellow. I am not involved in the money. I don't know a thing about it. I can't help you. You better scramble about elsewhere." O'Brien is a ball player. He carried tremendous water for us.

P He isn't Hunt's lawyer?

D No he is our lawyer at the Re-Election Committee.

P I see.

D So he is safe. There is no problem there. So it raises the whole question. Hunt has now made a direct threat against Ehrlichman. As a result of this, this is his blackmail. He says, "I will bring John Ehrlichman down to his knees and put him in jail. I have done enough seamy things for he and Krogh, they'll never survive it."

P Was he talking about Ellsberg?

D Ellsberg, and apparently some other things. I don't know the full extent of it.

From THE WATERGATE TAPES

P I don't know about anything else.

D I don't know either, and I hate to learn some of these things. So that is that situation. Now, where are the soft points? How many people know about this? Well, let me go one step further in this whole thing. The Cubans that were used in the Watergate were also the same Cubans that Hunt and Liddy used for this California Ellsberg thing, for the breakin out there. So they are aware of that. How high their knowledge is, is something else. Hunt and Liddy, of course, are totally aware of it, of the fact that it is right out of the White House.

P I don't know what the hell we did that for!

D I don't know either.

P What in the (expletive deleted) caused this? (unintelligible)

D Mr. President, there have been a couple of things around here that I have gotten wind of. At one time there was a desire to do a second story on the Brookings Institute where they had the Pentagon papers. Now I flew to California because I was told that John had instructed it and he said "I really hadn't. It is a mis-impression, but for (expletive deleted), turn it off." So I did. I came back and turned it off. The risk is minimal and the pain is fantastic. It is something with a (unintelligible) risk and no gain. It is just not worth it. But—who knows about all this now? You've got the Cubans' lawyer, a man by the name of Rothblatt, who is a no good, publicity seeking (characterization deleted), to be very frank with you. He has had to be pruned down and tuned off. He was canned by his own people because they didn't trust him. He didn't want them to plead guilty. He wants to represent them before the Senate. So F. Lee Bailey, who was a partner of one of the men representing McCord, got in and cooled Rothblatt down. So that means that F. Lee Bailey has knowledge. Hunt's lawyer, a man by the name of Bittmann, who is an excellent criminal lawyer from the Democratic era of Bobby Kennedy, he's got knowledge.

P He's got some knowledge?

D Well, all the direct knowledge that Hunt and Liddy have, as well as all the hearsay they have. You have these two lawyers over at the Re-Election Committee who did an investigation to find out the facts. Slowly, they got the whole picture. They are solid.

P But they know?

D But they know. You've got, then an awful lot of the principals involved who know. Some people's wives know. Mrs. Hunt was the savviest woman in the world. She had the whole picture together.

P Did she?

D Yes. Apparently, she was the pillar of strength in that family before the death.

P Great sadness. As a matter of fact, there was a discussion with somebody about Hunt's problem on account of his wife and I said, of course commutation could be considered on the basis of his wife's death, and that is the only conversation I ever had in that light.

D Right.

D So that is it. That is the extent of the knowledge. So where are the soft spots on this? Well, first of all, there is the problem of the continued blackmail which will not only go on now, but it will go while these people are in prison, and it will compound the obstruction of justice situation. It will cost money. It is dangerous. People around here are not pros at this sort of thing. This is the sort of thing Mafia people can do: washing money, getting clean money, and things like that. We just don't know about those things, because we are not criminals and not used to dealing in that business.

P That's right.

D It is a tough thing to know how to do.

P Maybe it takes a gang to do that.

D That's right. There is a real problem as to whether we could even do it. Plus there is a real problem in raising money. Mitchell has been working on raising some money. He is one of the ones with the most to lose. But there is no denying the fact that the White House, in Ehrlichman, Haldeman and Dean are involved in some of the early money decisions.

P How much money do you need?

D I would say these people are going to cost a million dollars over the next two years.

P We could get that. On the money, if you need the money you could get that. You could get a million dollars. You could get it in cash. I know where it could be gotten. It is not easy, but it could be done. But the question is who in the hell would handle it? Any ideas on that?

D That's right. Well, I think that is something that Mitchell ought to be charged with.

P I would think so too.

D And get some pros to help him.

P Let me say there shouldn't be a lot of people running around getting money—

D Well, he's got one person doing it who I am not sure is—

P Who is that?

D He has Fred LaRue doing it. Now Fred started out going out trying to solicit money from all kinds of people.

P No!

D I had learned about it, and I said, "(expletive deleted) It is just awful! Don't do it!" People are going to ask what the money is for. He has apparently talked to Tom Pappas.

P I know.

D And Pappas has agreed to come up with a sizeable amount, I gather.

P What do you think? You don't need a million right away, but you need a million? Is that right?

D That is right.

P You need it in cash don't you? I am just thinking out loud here for a moment. Would you put that through the Cuban Committee:

D No.

P It is going to be checks, cash money, etc. How if that ever comes out, are you going to handle it? Is the Cuban Committee an obstruction of justice, if they want to help?

D Well they have priests in it.

P Would that give a little bit of a cover?

D That would give some for the Cubans and possibly Hunt. Then you've got Liddy. McCord is not accepting any money. So is not a bought man right now.

P O.K. Go ahead.

D Let me continue a little bit right here now. When I say this is a growing cancer, I say it for reasons like this. Bud Krogh, in his testimony before the Grand Jury, was forced to perjure himself. He is haunted by it. Bud said, "I have not had a pleasant day on my job." He said, "I told my wife all about this. The curtain may ring down one of these days, and I may have to face the music, which I am perfectly willing to do."

P What did he perjure himself on, John?

D Did he know the Cubans. He did.

P He said he didn't?

D That is right. They didn't press him hard.

P He might be able to—I am just trying to think. Perjury is an awful hard rap to prove. If he could just say that I—Well, go ahead.

D Well, so that is one perjury. Mitchell and Magruder are potential perjurers. There is always the possibility of any of these individuals blowing. Hunt. Liddy. Liddy is in jail right now, serving his time and having a good time right now. I think Liddy in his own bizarre way the strongest of all of them. So there is that possibility.

P Your major guy to keep under control is Hunt?

D That is right.

P I think. Does he know a lot?

D He knows so much. He could sink Chuck Colson. Apparently he is quite distressed with Colson. He thinks Colson has abandoned him. Colson was to meet with him when he was out there after, you know, he had left the White House. He met with him through his lawyer. Hunt raised the question he wanted money. Colson's lawyer told him Colson wasn't doing anything with money. Hunt took offense with that immediately, and felt Colson had abandoned him.

P Just looking at the immediate problem, don't you think you have to handle Hunt's financial situation damn soon?

D I think that is—I talked with Mitchell about that last night and—

P It seems to me we have to keep the cap on the bottle that much, or we don't have any options.

D That's right.

P Either that or it all blows right now?

D That's the question.

50

MARK J. GREEN, JAMES M. FALLOWS,
and DAVID R. ZWICK

Congress:
The Broken Branch

The way the Johnson and Nixon administrations conducted the war
in Indochina, even more than the startling revelations of the White
House taping system, showed the dangers of an unchecked presidency. By the early seventies, Arthur Schlesinger, Jr., former Roosevelt brain truster Rexford Tugwell, and others who had once vigorously defended the accumulation of power by the Chief Executive now
began to question the imbalance between the branches of government and to look to a strengthened Congress as a counterbalance
to the presidency. Especially after the Nixon resignation there was
talk of a reassertion of congressional prerogatives. Yet, as the following selection points out, the legislative branch has been complicit
in the long usurpation of its powers by the White House. The authors
(members of the Ralph Nader Congress Project) argue that Congress
has become "incapable of creation, with authority but little power,"
and that it will take a massive effort to reverse this tendency.

D uring its springtime sessions in 1972, the Senate at times had
difficulty gathering a quorum, because so many of its members
were out campaigning for the presidency. It now seems logical
that a member of Congress should want to rise to be president,
but it was not always this way. More than a hundred years ago,
in the decades leading to the Civil War, those who remained in
Congress—men like Daniel Webster, Henry Clay, John C. Cal-
houn—had more to do with directing the nation's policies than
did presidents like Millard Fillmore or Franklin Pierce. John

"Congress: The Broken Branch" (Originally "The Broken Branch: Congress vs. the
Executive"). From *Who Runs Congress?* by Mark J. Green, James M. Fallows, and
David R. Zwick. A Ralph Nader Congress Project. Copyright © 1972 by Ralph Nader
Reprinted by permission of Grossman Publishers, a division of The Viking Press, Inc.

Quincy Adams ran for a seat in the House after retiring from the presidency in 1829; one can hardly imagine Lyndon Johnson or Richard Nixon doing the same today.

This change in the president's relation to Congress—the transformation of the presidency into the summit of prestige and power—happened so long ago that it is no longer newsworthy. What the newspapers do cover when they compare Capitol Hill with the White House are the legislative skirmishes which mark each congressional session. Regularly come reports of showdowns over bills the president wants and Congress obstructs or items that Congress has passed and the president threatens to veto. More recently, the popular image of the president and Congress has come from Congress's attempts to limit the president's apparent right to conduct a war for as long as he wants, in the way he chooses.

The danger of these incidents is their suggestion that a true struggle is on between two strong sides, and that whichever side is stronger on an issue will win. This impression becomes even firmer whenever Congress seems to dominate the president—as the House Rules Committee did when it stifled many of President Kennedy's proposals, or as the Senate did in rejecting two of President Nixon's Supreme Court nominees.

A battle does go on, but the field has been moved miles within one side's lines. No matter how hard the Congress may struggle on one issue, it is overwhelmed by the vastly greater forces of the presidency. Whether Congress wins or loses, the president ends up on top. The clearest example of this change is in proposing new laws—the most basic of Congress's jobs. In the years before 1900, the heavy majority of laws passed each year originated within Congress; senators or representatives drafted them, pushed them, saw them passed. During this century, however, the source has shifted. The greatest change came at the beginning of the New Deal, when the president was so firmly in control of lawmaking that the speaker of the House could address freshman representatives like a pack of Marine recruits and say, "We *will* put over Mr. Roosevelt's program." Since then, according to political scientist James Robinson, Congress has "yielded to virtually exclusive initiation by the executive." Putting it more plainly, a Republican congressman told a witness from President Kennedy's administration, "We're not supposed to draw up these bills—that's your job, and then you bring them to us."

In the last two decades, roughly 80 percent of the major laws passed have started in the executive branch. So, even when the president is stymied in one area—as President Nixon has been, when Congress refused to pass his six "key proposals"—most of the laws that *do* pass will be his.[1]

This change is important to all of us, not just the academics or congressmen. For all its flaws, Congress is still the most responsive and open branch of the government. As the executive has grown more powerful, it has also become more isolated. Power has flown to an isolated staff of White House advisers, accountable only to themselves and liable to strong temptations from private interests. These members of the president's staff, along with more traditional parts of the executive bureaucracy, have matched their grip on legislative initiative with control of Congress's other jobs: getting laws passed, apportioning money for them, and reviewing the way they are carried out. These incursions are less newsworthy than antiwar resolutions or nomination fights, but they say far more about what's gone wrong with our government.

. . .

To a surprising degree, Congress knows little more than what the president tells it. When it gets ready to pass a new law for missiles or highways, it turns to the Defense Department and the Federal Highway Administration. While a stray outside witness—from a public interest group, or a wandering refugee from academia—turns up at congressional hearings, the bulk of what congressmen find out about new laws comes from the president's departments. Congress itself is largely to blame, since committees can choose their own witness list.

Explanations for this range from sloth to inability; a major practical barrier is a shortage of staff. Another important reason is that Congress has not figured out that "Information Is Power." Executive departments started to get the message shortly after World War II, and jumped into action. Led by the ever-vigilant Defense Department, they set up the congressional liaison system—which is another phrase for congressional lobbying by the executive. Starting with one lone assistant secretary of defense

---

[1] Of course, there are exceptions. In consumer and environmental legislation, recent Congresses have been far more creative than presidents. The Joint Committee on Atomic Energy has been the main force behind nuclear energy development, and Senator McGovern's Select Committee on Nutrition and Human Needs forced a reluctant administration to expand food stamp programs.

for congressional liaison, the network has grown to include at least 531 agents from twelve departments.[2] They have charmed their way into not only the congressional heart but its buildings as well; the alleged space shortage on Capitol Hill does not keep the Army from spreading its offices over a huge suite in the Rayburn Office Building.

The point of stashing these agents within the halls of Congress is to make sure Congress knows the right facts about each department. In theory, the liaison agents are not supposed to "influence" the congressman, especially by appealing to the public to put pressure on Congress. A 1913 law, the Executive Anti-Lobbying Act, says "no funds may be used . . . to influence in any manner a member of Congress to favor or oppose, by vote or otherwise, any legislation or appropriation by Congress." The only exception is that executive agents may "communicate with Members of Congress on request, through proper channels"—a clause that has been opened up to let the whole liaison troop roll through. No one has ever been prosecuted under the law, although it is routinely violated—as with the administration's efforts for the SST. Ready to answer any congressional request with an illustrated brochure about, say, New Steps in Defense or Advances in Securities Regulation, ready even to anticipate requests and shove possibly interesting documents into open hands, the liaison offices steadily mold congressmen's minds. Assuming that politicians, like mountains, can be worn away by light but steady pressure, they see constant evidence of their success when Congress rubber-stamps executive bills.

Many congressmen are unhappy about the hazards of relying on the executive, but their moans are often muffled as they sink deeper and deeper into the executive lap. Congressman John Rooney, for example, uses FBI agents to help his committee evaluate the performances of the Justice Department, of which the FBI is a part. The House Ways and Means Committee relies on experts loaned from the Treasury to help draw up committee reports. When it convenes in closed session to vote on tax bills, the doors stay shut to all outsiders except dozens of Treasury

---

[2]In 1970, the Center for Political Research reported the following liaison staffs: Defense, 312 (with 177 for the Air Force); Army, 95; Navy, 67; Treasury, 28; Post Office, 33; Securities and Exchange Commission, 35; Office of Economic Opportunity, 10; Veterans Administration, 43; Transportation, 28; State, 26. The CIA has a liaison office, but refuses to say how many people work in it.

Department officials who come to advise. When the House Public Works Committee wants to evaluate new transportation plans, it turns to the Transportation Department. What's wrong with this cooperation? Not just danger that the departments will deceive— as a former liaison for the Equal Employment Opportunity Commission said, "We don't lie to them. We just tell them what will be the most persuasive, and don't volunteer all the facts." The real issue is that Congress might as well not even bother studying or approving the executive's plans when all it has to go on is the executive's information.

The final problem is that Congress often can't even get the information it specifically asks for. More and more, the real policy decisions are made, not by the secretary of state, or the Department of Health, Education, and Welfare, but by the president's personal staff—the Henry Kissingers and John Ehrlichmans and Peter Flanigans. These men don't have to talk unless they want to. The Senate Foreign Relations Committee can always get commonplace figures like the secretary of state to testify, for what it is worth; one week before the Cambodian invasion of 1970, Secretary of State William Rogers calmly said that nothing big was about to happen. Henry Kissinger, on the other hand, is recognized as the most important foreign policy adviser in the government—but he has never publicly appeared before Congress. Senator William Fulbright considered it a great coup when Kissinger deigned to eat lunch with him, in lieu of showing up before the Foreign Relations Committee. The domestic policy advisers—John Ehrlichman and Peter Flanigan—similarly turn down invitations to testify. In fact, the only senior White House aide to testify before Congress during the Nixon administration has been Flanigan—who gave in to public pressure and testified about the ITT affair, but only after giving a specific list of questions he would and would not answer.[3]

As the presidential staff grows strong from sustenance gained at the expense of its satellite departments, Congress might well contemplate two further threats to its power. One is the president's blunt intrusion into the mechanics of legislating. Like the

---

[3]This simultaneous oozing of power from Congress to the executive, and from the executive department's to the president's own staff, has led to strange alliances. As part of his committee's assault of the president, for example, Fulbright has sponsored bills that would strengthen the State Department; it, unlike Kissinger, is subject to congressional scrutiny.

55

"liaison officers," the presidential staff is not supposed to lobby Congress. But, as columnist Jack Anderson has reported, "Lobbyists for the Nixon administration swarm over Capitol Hill in flagrant disregard of the law. Before an important Senate vote, they often operate right out of Vice President Agnew's office, a few steps from the Senate floor." Another example of this backstage lobbying came in August, 1972, when the Senate was voting on the president's arms-limitation agreement with the Russians. As reported in the *Congressional Record:*

> *Sen. Church:* Some could be misled as a result of what is going on right now out in the Vice President's office. I was taken in there a few minutes ago and shown two models. One model is of the [Russian] SS-9. It stands ... fully 2 feet off the table. It is a very menacing looking weapon. One is especially struck by the size of the scale model of the SS-9 when it is compared with the model, also to scale, of the [U.S.] Minuteman missile which sits next to it. . . .
>
> *Sen. Fulbright:* May I ask the senator, since I have not been invited into the Vice President's room, whether the Vice President is now a substation of the National Security Council? Is it used for the purpose of influencing the votes of the senators? . . . I thought it was a ceremonial hall for the Vice President. However, it is now an exhibit hall for the National Security Council. Is that what it is now?
>
> *Sen. Church:* Apparently so.
>
> *Sen. Fulbright:* Mr. President, this is rather peculiar in view of the fact that officials of the National Security Council, including Mr. Kissinger, refuse to come to the Hill for committee hearings. Now instead of coming to the Hill to testify, they have the exhibits here and ask senators into the Vice President's room so they can see these models.

Unlikely as it sounds, the other danger of increased presidential power is the *even greater* amount of pandering to private intersts it encourages. After even a brief look at Congress's many cozy ties to private lobbies, it is hard to imagine that any other part of the government could be as thoroughly influenced. Recent presidents, however, have not just responded to the secret desires of private industries, but have actually spurred them on. The Clean Water Bill of 1971 illustrates the story.

Trying to please both sides, President Nixon had talked himself into a corner on this bill. Early in 1971, he had nagged Congress for not passing his environmental bills, concluding with a rhetorical outburst:

> The fundamental fact is that of choice. We can choose to debase the physical environment in which we live, and with it the human society that depends on that environment, or we can choose to come to terms with nature, to make amends for the past, and build the basis for a balanced and responsible future.

Congress responded more eagerly than Nixon had expected, and by November the Senate had passed a strict water-quality bill that meant high pollution-control outlay for many industries. The law's sponsors, notably Edmund Muskie, had packed in a series of tough clauses, including one which let the federal government veto state water standards if they seemed too lenient.

In public, the president's staff opposed the bill because it infringed on "states' rights." But four days before that, in an extraordinary display of concern for the struggling corporations of America, the president's staff had held a pep rally to encourage private interests to fight the bill. "The notion that somehow industry 'got to' the administration and pushed them into [opposing the bill] is really the reverse of what happened," said Douglas Trussel, vice president of the National Association of Manufacturers. "The administration took the initiative, and many executives were ignorant of what was going on." At the November 4 meeting—when seven trade representatives came to the White House to see presidential aides John Whitaker and Richard Fairbanks—Fairbanks made what one trade agent called "an incredible speech": "His pitch was, 'We fought a lonely battle over here on this bill. Where the hell were you guys when we needed you? We could have gotten some of the worst provisions changed if you'd gotten into this in a big way.'"

This view of the president as promotion man is hardly cheering to those who dream of a separation of Business and State. But it cannot come as a surprise, since Congress is so weak—when so many administration officials are on brief sabbatical from corporate work. President Nixon's former congressional liaison, Bryce Harlow, had to leave his job as congressional liaison for Procter and Gamble to come to the White House. When he left the administration, he returned to P&G where he teamed up with Mike Manatos—former special assistant for Lyndon Johnson. John

Connally, man-of-all-work for Nixon, has been a private-interest lobbyist; Peter Flanigan, before coming to the White House in 1969, was an investment banker and president of the Barracuda Tanker Corporation of Liberia. Lyndon Johnson's former aides, Clark Clifford and Myer Feldman, now work as lawyer-lobbyists in Washington law firms. All in all, they make the presidential lobby into what Lambert Miller, senior vice president of the National Association of Manufacturers, called in 1971 "the most pervasive, influential, and costly of any such in the whole country."

Power of the Purse

Money can't buy happiness, but it should buy power. If Congress gets ignored, or lied to, or lobbied, or manipulated in passing legislation—why should it care? It still holds the purse strings. Let the president send up missile plans or domestic programs: since Congress determines where the money goes, it should be able to reorder the priorities to suit its taste. War getting costly? Trim down the funds. People starving in the city? Send in a little more aid. President bowling congressmen over? Just use the Power of the Purse to put him in his place.

In practice, Congress has not been able to find salvation through appropriation. Even more miserably than in passing laws, Congress has failed to manage the budget. It retains the right to control the budget, but not the ability to do so. In the few cases where it does not dutifully rubber-stamp the president's programs (usually with a few modifications to salve its conscience), it finds that the president can do what he wants anyway—and often keeps Congress totally unaware of what he is doing.

As in information-gathering techniques, Congress has simply been passed by time in the budgeting system. Forty years ago, economists figured out that if countries wanted to avoid the boom-and-bust cycles which had led to the Great Depression, then *someone* had to keep track of how much money was coming into the government (through taxes) compared with amount flowing out. The president was set to take on this job, since the Budget and Accounting Act of 1921 had given him the power to draw up a "national budget" for the whole federal government. Congress might have tried to share the power—and, for a few brave years in the forties, it did prepare a "legislative budget"—but it gave up. In this simple abdication we have the full story of why the president appropriates money now, not Congress. He who makes the budget sends the money on its way. Those who "approve" the budget are spectators.

The trouble Congress has dealing with the budget is a much exaggerated version of its troubles passing laws: it arrives too late and knows too little. By the time the congressional appropriations committees sit down to examine budget requests, the president's staff has already invested more than a year of research and scheming in them. Through rounds of haggling and calculation, the Office of Management and Budget (OMB) and the various executive departments have worked out compromise estimates for the next year's programs. When they send the figures to Congress, they're not in the mood to make many more changes. However much HEW may have protested (in the secret counsel of the executive) when OMB decided to end a special education program or shift funds elsewhere, few bureaucrats want to bring the complaint into the open before Congress.

Congress, too, is in a hurry. It gets the budget estimates at the start of each calendar year—and must pass new budgets before the next fiscal year starts in June. Even if the Appropriations committees had staffs as large as the OMB, that would leave then only half as much time as the budgeters had. With Congress's diminished resources, five months is barely time to insert the pork barrel items each legislator loves. The Senate, which waits for the House to act, has even less time.

The Appropriations committees still make an attempt to review the budget. When they do, they find the familiar roster of information problems facing them. Whom do they interview to find out more about the programs and estimates? Why the same officials who drew up the program—whose testimony must be approved by the OMB. Congressmen often do a creditable job of asking about successes and failures, but the instances of surprising revelations are few. At times, the agencies may even dissemble in front of their congressional superiors. Usually this takes the form of telling less than one knows. Each agency, for example, prepares a program memo—an evaluation of its different projects—to send to the OMB at budget time. Congressmen do not get to see the memoranda. More overt cases of deception usually involve the Pentagon—whose customs of waste, conflict of interest, secrecy, and classification may confuse the line between truth and fiction. In the mid-sixties, congressional committees were reduced to speechlessness by Defense Secretary Robert McNamara's virtuoso budget presentations. Now, they have become more suspicious. Recently, for example, Defense experts rolled out a chart showing the relative strengths of Soviet and American fleets. A suspicious congressional investigator later discovered that the figures had been doctored to exaggerate the Pentagon claim that the Navy needed more ships. While the American fleet total had been reduced to take account of ships idle in port, the Russian total was not.

Even this distorted testimony is better than nothing at all, which is sometimes the alternative. When Wisconsin's Senator William Proxmire began to press Budget Director Robert Mayo, asking questions about items in the Defense request, Mayo loftily replied that "the president's flexibility is better served by not getting into a debate on what is and what is not in the Defense budget."

If relatively true information, and more time for study, are two reasons why the OMB can make a budget and Congress cannot, the third is that Congress works in a fashion so fragmented that no overall planning is possible. There are parts of the legislative process where that doesn't matter: those who authorize agricultural subsidies don't need to know a thing about new airplane projects. But when dividing a set amount of money among many competing needs, there must be one giant funnel through which all the decisions pass. OMB and the White House provide that; Congress is a funnel turned upside down. Budget power is split between the House and the Senate; between the dozen fiefdoms which each Appropriations subcommittee creates; between taxing committees and spending committees; between committees that pass new programs and committees that allot the money. As long as there is someone else to take an overview, then Congress's anarchy is not disastrous; it simply means that the president will make the budget and Congress can make only minor, tinkering repairs. A country can run this way (as ours has for the past twenty years)—but it faces the prospect of one-man or one-agency rule from the White House (as ours has for the past twenty years). The solution is not to hobble the executive, bringing it down to Congress's level, but rather to make Congress move into the modern budgetary world. As the *Journal of Commerce* put it: "What Congress needs—'as we and many others have said before'—is a prestigious joint committee on the budget. It needs a committee to perform for the legislature the function performed by the [OMB] for the executive department."

Despite these obstacles—information, staffing, fragmentation—when Congress applies its pressure to one small point in the budget, it can, like a spike heel, make a dent. In August, 1972, Congress brazenly took $1.7 billion from the Defense budget and added the same amount to the appropriations for the Departments of Labor and HEW. The change, said Senate Majority Leader Mansfield, "demonstrated Congress's sense of priorities—a will to spend more for health, schools, and manpower programs, and less for providing arms for allies." President Nixon then vetoed the HEW bill, and Congress conceded.

More often, Congress's changes reflect a motive less subtle than "sense of priorities": the ancient rite of carving up the pork. Such gothic figures as South Carolina's Mendel Rivers or Mississippi's John Stennis provide easy illustrations of how closely committee chairmanship may be tied to government benefits. This is not to suggest that only foxy Southern politicians reach into the greasy barrels up to the elbows. In fact, New England patricians and Iowa farmboys succumb to the same temptation. Senator Warren Magnuson, the farthest cry from a Southerner in the Senate, has used his chairmanship of the Commerce Committee and his high rank on Appropriations to funnel outlandish amounts of public works money to Washington state. As numerous reference works show (the best of them are the *Almanac of American Politics*, by Michael Barone and others, and the Nader Congress Project profiles), the simplest way to tell whether a district is rich or poor in government projects is to see how long its representative has been in Congress.

The success of pork-barreling proves, in its perverse way, that Congress has not entirely faded out of the appropriations picture. Throughout the executive bureaucracy, administrators cater to the whims of powerful legislators. Often, in the desire to please a powerful and fussy chairman, the executive will bow to his demands, no matter how bizarre they may be. For example, when Assistant Secretary of the Navy Graeme Campbell Bannerman came to the House Armed Services Committee to ask that the outmoded midshipmen's dairy at Annapolis be closed, committee chairman Mendel Rivers made it clear that he would defend the middies' right to home-made ice-cream:

> *Congressman Rivers:* I just want to tell you if you have any notion of closing it I would advise you to get it out of your head

because if you have any notion of closing it, it will be written into that law and I would rather hear you say you have abandoned that idea. . . .

Secretary Bannerman: The plan to close it has not been abandoned. . . . Mr. Chairman, if I had my "druthers" at this moment, I would close it.

Rivers: I'm glad to hear it. You don't have your "druthers."

Bannerman: That is entirely possible.

Rivers: That is a fact of life. . . . Those boys over there . . . want to get that milk, and you can't get it. I lived through Parris Island. . . . They were cutting out the ice cream at Parris Island.

Now they don't get any ice cream, period, unless they happen to get a little old thing at lunch. Before . . . they had all these machines making ice cream. . . . Everybody was happy. . . .

Bannerman: I think the original . . . creation of the dairy . . . was undoubtedly a very wise thing. This happened about sixty years ago. I guess at that time there was no assured source of healthful milk.

I think for this reason the dairy was created. . . .

There isn't any question now, however, in anybody's mind, that you can't get good healthy milk commercially. We are all drinking it.

Rivers: You can't get it in abundance.

Bannerman: We are doing it, Mr. Chairman, all over the country.

Rivers: I don't think we can get the milk in abundance. We own it; we operate it; why get rid of it?

Such small-scale congressional tyranny is about as reassuring a sign of Congress's power as are its piqued delays and obstructions of selected admininstration bills. If Congress's contribution to the budget is silly or venal, should even these powers be taken away? A better solution would be to restore some significant budgetary power to Congress. To do this will require a legislative budget, a congressional OMB, or some similar drastic change.

The Executive Shell Game

Even if Congress passes a law on its own initiative and funds it according to its own ideas, the executive can still get its way. In the civics textbooks, there is not a hint that the president can run programs that Congress has outlawed, or delay forever laws the Congress thinks have gone into effect. But a set of innocuous-sounding practices—"impoundment," "reprogramming," "transfers"—gives the president surprising and almost unbounded control over the government's financial affairs.

The catfish farmers of Tupelo, Mississippi, know what impoundment can mean. In 1965, Congress had voted $32,500 to build an experimental carfish hatchery in Tupelo. The Interior Department, however, had scheduled the national catfish project for extinction. Congressmen knew that, but they decided Tupelo's farm was worth preserving. If the president was sufficiently annoyed, they reasoned, he could veto the bill. Johnson signed the bill, but the money never got to Tupelo. It lay "impounded" in the federal treasury.

How could this happen? The legal answer is a clause in the 1950 Budget Act. "In apportioning any appropriation," it says, "reserves may be established to provide for contingencies or to effect savings whenever savings are made possible by or through changes in requirements, greater efficiency of operations, or other developments." In other words, the president need not spend all the money Congress gives him, if the reasons are good. This sounds acceptable in theory. In practice, the president has repeatedly withheld funds, often for blatantly political reasons. In these cases, the Congress might as well never have bothered to propose bills, pass them, and appropriate money. By impounding funds, the president can ignore the Congress:

- In 1971, Congress appropriated $8 million extra for the Veterans Administration hospital system—intending that the VA use it to hire 8,600 more workers, including 800 more doctors. Meanwhile, the OMB refused to release $71 million of VA funds, which prevented the hiring of 11,000 people.
- The administration asked for $2 billion for the food stamp program in 1972; Congress added $200 million more. Instead of vetoing the bill, the president just told the OMB to set the "allowable spending" level at $2 billion.
- As thirty-six senators complained in a letter to Nixon, mass transit funds totaling $900 million have been frozen by the OMB.
- The Farmers Home Administration lends money to rural families to improve their farms; but it lends $75 million less than Congress intended, because of an OMB freeze.
- According to Congressman Paul Rogers, chairman of the Public Health subcommittee, the administration has spent only half the money Congress voted for anticancer research.

- While the Environmental Protection Administration complains that tight funds hamper it, the administration requests
less money than authorized by the Clean Air Act of 1970,
and spends less than is appropriated.
- In water pollution control, the administration spent only $262
million of the $800 million appropriated in 1970, and $475
million of a $1-billion appropriation for 1971. Together with
freezes in urban renewal, highway construction, and dozens
of other programs, the impoundments totaled $12 billion in
1971, when Congress finally got the first complete list of
them.

The impounded funds may be used as political bargaining
pieces. In the fall of 1970, California Democrat B. F. Sisk found
that some $10 million was being withheld from the Wetlands
Water Project in his district. Since his district had an extremely
high unemployment rate, Sisk complained. There was no action
until October 31, only a few days before the election in which
Republican Senator George Murphy would try to hold his seat
against John Tunney. Murphy appeared on a telethon that day
with Ronald Reagan and Richard Nixon. Reagan announced that,
due to Murphy's dogged efforts, the water project money had
been released. A week later, Murphy had lost. Since then, Sisk
has not been able to get the promised funds from the OMB. But,
late in 1972, the funds suddenly began to flow more quickly than
the project could absorb them. Election time had come again.

Unlike the executive branch's lead in the appropriations process, this is not simply one branch getting a superior grasp on
a power the other could share if it tried. The impoundments represent an arrogation of power which Congress is unable to fight,
unless it amends the Budget act. Presidents have always had some
discretion over the timing of federal spending, but as political
scientist Louis Fisher points out,

> An entirely different situation has developed under the Nixon ad-
> ministration, where funds have been withheld from domestic pro-
> grams because the president considers those programs incompat-
> ible with his own set of budget priorities. . . . To impound funds
> in this prospective sense—holding onto money in anticipation that
> Congress will enact an administration bill—is a new departure. . . .
> Impoundment is not being used to avoid deficiencies, or to effect
> savings, or even to fight inflation, but rather to shift the scale of

priorities from one administration to the next, prior to congressional action.

By spending money only where he pleases, the president writes his own laws.

Its resentment smoldering, Congress began to challenge the use of impoundment. In 1971, North Carolina Senator Sam Ervin, quick to notice branches of constitutional balance, held special hearings on impoundment. "What concerns me," Ervin said, "is the use of impounding practice to void or nullify congressional intent." At the hearings, Ervin accomplished what many believed impossible: he managed to get a list of all impounded funds from the OMB. The list, the most recent version of which appears on pages S 3847–3849 of the *Congressional Record* for March 31, 1972, is the best available guide to the comparative priorities of Congress and the president.

The OMB submitted another list in 1972, this one showing an apparent total of "only" $1.7 billion impounded, not the $12 billion which OMB had admitted the year before. Ervin quickly detected the crude accounting trick the OMB had tried. The $1.7 billion was only the impoundments for which the executive branch could find no other excuse; they were purely political decisions which, in Ervin's words, "fly in the face of the constitutional duty of the Congress to set the priorities of our government." Another $10.5 billion more had been withheld for "routine" or "administrative" reasons. Together, they total $12.2 billion—an increase from 1971.

Until 1971, and Senator Ervin's hearings, congressmen fought impoundment on an item-by-item level. Since impoundment's greatest advantage is its secrecy—there are troublesome news stories when the president vetoes a clean-water bill, but no one knows if he freezes the funds—Congressmen have tried to focus attention on the cases they have discovered. Shortly before the 1970 elections, for example, criticism from Democrats led to the release of impounded education funds. More recently, Ervin has proposed a bill which would require the president to tell Congress whenever he impounded money. If Congress did not ratify the impoundment within sixty days, the president would have to spend the money. The obvious intention of the bill is to restore the constitutional balances—to eliminate the possibility of a secret veto on an item he doesn't like. Because of opposition from Holifield and others, the bill will probably not pass in this session.

Impoundment is only half the picture. If the president could *spend* money with the same abandon with which he withholds it, his bypass of Congress would be complete. He's not there yet; but, like impoundment, "reprogramming" and "transfers" have vastly expanded the president's ability to run the country the way he wants.

Defense Secretary Melvin Laird learned about these tactics in 1971, when he was worried that Congress would cut off $52 million he wanted to send as military aid to Cambodia. In August, 1971, the Joint Chiefs of Staff told Laird not to fret; he could get the money (1) by transferring the $52 million from economic aid programs to military aid, (2) by applying $52 million from some other program with both military and civilian uses, which could then be sent to Cambodia, (3) by jacking up the Army's request by $52 million, and then "loaning" the money to Cambodia, or (4) by declaring some of the Army's equipment obsolete, and then selling it at bargain rates to Cambodia.

In an article in the *Washington Monthly*, journalist Timothy Ingram pointed out the full range of devices the executive branch can use to write its own appropriations. His list includes:

- Transfer authority: The secretary of defense is allowed to shift up to $600 million from the program Congress authorized to some other use. He may also send funds from civilian to military programs if "security" demands it. A provision of the Foreign Assistance Act says that 10 percent of the money earmarked to any one country may be rechanneled to another. President Nixon took advantage of all these loopholes when financing the Cambodian invasion of 1970. By the time he asked Congress for $255 million to pay for the project, he had already spent $100 million of it.
- "Obsolete" excess stocks: At a time when Congress kept reducing money for aid to Taiwan, the Defense Department kept a flow of military goods running from its piles of extra weapons.
- Secret funds: Louis Fisher estimates that $15–20 billion of appropriations, mainly for defense, is never even explained to Congress. While some congressmen denounce this—but cannot, of course, find many details to support their argument—the late Senator Allen Ellender took a milder view. "What can you do?" he asked. "I believe in having one strong commander in chief. Once war matériel is ordered, no

member of Congress—no one—is supposed to follow through to see how it's used. It's to be used by the commander in chief as he sees best."

- The pipeline: Some appropriations have to be used up during the fiscal year or returned to the Treasury. Others have "full-funding" clauses, which means that the money stays in the department's hands if not spent. Ingram estimates that the Pentagon has $50 billion waiting in the pipeline—enough to run the war with no congressional appropriations, and enough so that for the last several fiscal years the Pentagon has spent more than Congress voted it.
- Cost overruns: A Defense Department statute allows the Pentagon to pay for cost overruns whenever the "national defense" is at stake. Liberally defined, this has excused many billions of dollars in overpayments. The Pentagon can go even further to accommodate erring contractors, by changing the terms of the deal along the way. When, in 1968, the Pentagon discovered that its C5-A was going to cost roughly $2 billion more than estimated—$5.3 billion instead of $3.4—its accountants obligingly changed the contract from a fixed-price one to "cost-plus," an open ticket for whatever the company wanted to spend.

Congress can now and then rebuke the executive for the worst of these abuses. But, as Timothy Ingram says,

> It can threaten fund cutoffs, mandate the use of funds as directed, and exercise its oversight function. But as the executive detours proliferate, Congress discovers that its problems go beyond relative weakness. Increasingly, Congress is less the underdog and more the old fighter who is no longer even invited into the ring.

Congress's "Oversight"

Congress is, or ought to be, the watchdog of the public purse. Even if it no longer initiates legislation, even if it abdicated much of the budget-making process, even if the president can play a shell game with the funds Congress has appropriated, Congress should vigorously and constantly yap at the executive's heels to make sure that funds are not squandered, that incompetent administrators don't fritter taxpayer dollars away on worthless or marginal projects, that the executive is obeying the laws and enforcing the laws. Congress is the only representative of the people—whose money, after all, is being spent—that has the power to see that the executive is doing its work.

With felicity rare for congressional jargon, this area is called "legislative *oversight*." The double meaning is a perfect guide to the topic. For just as Congress tries to oversee its laws once they are passed, much of its weakness here is due to oversights. The reason for oversight—or "review"—is that laws don't always live up to their ambitions. Everyday experience provides examples of legislation that has not accomplished its purpose—such as the "War on Poverty." A series of lesser-known illustrations shows how pervasive the problem is:

- In 1967, after a series of nauseating articles about meat packinghouses, Congress passed the Wholesome Meat Act. By 1969, all state slaughterhouses were supposed to meet federal standards or be taken over by the U.S. (except for a special one-year grace period in some cases). The deadline came and went, and federal inspectors moved into only one state. The others were approved—not, in most cases, because they had improved their standards, but because the federal standards had dipped to meet them.
- The Civil Rights act of 1964 said that no federal funds could be spent to support projects practicing racial discrimination. Five years later, the Agriculture Department was running an extension service which, in many states, was overtly segregated.

   In addition, Congress is responsible for the "quasi-legislative" agencies. These regulatory bodies, such as the Interstate Commerce Commission and the Federal Trade Commission, officially function with powers delegated by Congress. Because Congress cannot deal with each railroad rate claim or advertiser's complaint, it passes the powers to regulatory agencies. Congress is still responsible to see that the powers it has delegated to the agencies are used well.
- Finally, there are the problems which affect any bureaucracy—waste, inefficiency, corruption. Someone has to guard against possible abuses, and in theory Congress is the one.

The procedures for congressional oversight range from special hearings, or investigations of an agency, to informal queries, or questions at appropriations time. The important fact about all of them is that they have proved increasingly inadequate. As Jerry Cohen and Morton Mintz say in *America, Inc.,*

> In theory the deficiencies of the independent regulatory agencies and of units of the executive branch with regulatory powers would be alleviated and on occasion maybe even corrected if Congress reliably and seriously exercised its responsibility to oversee their performance. The unhappy truth is that reliable, serious, and sustained oversight is the exception rather than the rule on Capitol Hill. Not even in remote degrees have the oversight mechanisms of Congress kept pace with the enormous growth of the executive.

The reasons behind the failures of oversight are displayed clearly in one of the few *successful* instances of oversight. The House Government Operations Committee is, in the main, a useless appendage. Under the gerontocracy of, first, Representative William Dawson of Illinois, and recently Chet Holifield, its investigations into government performance have led to more trivial reports than substantive ones. But its Subcommittee on Intergovernmental Operations is another story. The subcommittee's chairman, L. H. Fountain of North Carolina, shows few of the traits of an agitator. In the mid-sixties, however, he became obsessed with the Food and Drug Administration and the ways in which it was not fulfilling its responsibilities. For the last six years, Fountain's subcommittee has grilled a succession of FDA commissioners on an impressive range of topics. The agency has had to defend its policies on the sale of birth control pills, on control of pesticides, on recalls of poisonous foods, on removal of cyclamates from the market, and, most recently, on its approval of the cattle-fattening but cancer-causing hormone DES. Aided by two committee staffers, one of whom once worked for the FDA, Fountain's committee has come closer than any other to exercising good oversight.

That is fine as far as it goes—but consider what has been left out in the process. One of the committee's Republican members, Guy Vander Jagt of Michigan, complained in a letter to Fountain that the committee's single-minded inquisition into the FDA was forcing it to ignore many other areas. The committee was simultaneously responsible for at least a dozen other agencies, many of them as big and important as the FDA. Even with best intent, Congress cannot supervise the ever-expanding, ever-more-complex activities of the federal government. After a while, the frustration may make congressmen give up: as Vander Jagt said, "You wait two hours so you can get a shot at the secretary of defense, and then it lasts only five minutes. The only thing you know is that you're getting bullshit from him, and there's nothing you can do about it."

Many congressmen show a decided distaste for oversight, because it seems pointless and because it does not interest the electorate. Bills sponsored and projects obtained can be used in the constant quest for reelection, but oversight usually wins little public attention. There are exceptions—as Fountain shows at the best end of the scale, and Joseph McCarthy at the worst—but not frequently enough to give legislators an incentive to spend their time in oversight hearings. It is significant that during the last few years, the more effective oversight has come in "glamour" areas: consumer protection (Fountain and others), Defense spending (led by Senator William Proxmire), foreign policy and the war (Senator Fulbright's Foreign Relations Committee has taken a notable step by hiring its own investigators to make on-the-spot studies in Laos, Greece, and elsewhere). At times, Appropriations committees also conduct effective oversight. Jamie Whitten's House Agricultural Appropriations subcommittee, while promoting some of its chairman's pet plans, also reviews agriculture programs in detail. Other areas, equally important but less newsworthy, are for the most part neglected.

Congressmen may at times even go out of their way to avoid oversight. Thus, Wright Patman of Texas, usually an effective overseer, accused Nixon of unfair price and profit guidelines. If the administration didn't shape up, Patman warned, he might hold oversight hearings. But he also made clear this was only as a last resort: "It should be emphasized that we prefer to avoid oversight hearings," he said. And when, in 1967, a few rash congressmen suggested that revelations about the CIA's role in funding the John Hay Whitney Trust Fund might merit an investigation, Everett Dirksen quashed the idea, saying, "I can't imagine the British Parliament investigating the British intelligence system."

The New Czars

If Congress has abandoned its oversight responsibilities, two outcomes are possible. The agencies and departments might roll along, unsupervised, or someone else might pick up the reins Congress has dropped. The second has happened, with the presidential staff in the driver's seat.

To see how the White House has succeeded, we need only review why Congress failed. To do a good job of oversight, Congress would need, first, a much larger staff of investigators. It would need some system for regular reviews of the agencies, instead of relying on haphazard coverage. It would need to know when policies or performance changed. Most of all, it would need to know that what the administrators told it was true.

Rolled together and placed on the White House staff, these reasons describe the Office of Management and Budget. As part of the reorganization which changed its name from the Bureau of the Budget, the OMB was given greater responsibility for reviewing the impact and worth of programs, as well as their budgets. This, of course, is another way of phrasing "oversight." The OMB has gone at its task with a vigor the Congress might well imitate.

Because of its privileged position within the executive, the OMB can exercise both before- and after-the-fact review. Before any programs get under way, OMB analysts have screened budget requests and program proposals. While the projects are running, the OMB parcels out the money, or withholds it. And when agencies propose new rules or decisions, the OMB can often screen them before Congress has its chance.

This has led to a situation in which an appointed agency, entirely shielded from public scrutiny, has more impact on administrative policy than any elected congressman, or group of them. A few illustrations show the danger. While the president should have the right to coordinate the policies of the Labor Department or HEW, he has no place setting the policy or priorities of the independent agencies, which are not part of the executive branch. But in February, 1972, the chairman of the Federal Power Commission, John P. Nassikas, came to Congress to complain that the president was doing just that. Nassikas told a Senate subcommittee that his agency was disappearing into the White House. Because he must send his budget requests through the OMB—not directly to Congress—his agency is subject to the same policy coordination as the executive departments. This OMB screening, Nassikas said, "results in some control of the policies, programs, and priorities of the independent regulatory agencies."

More than "some control" was evident in the OMB's treatment of the Federal Communications Commission. As its most ambitious project ever, the FCC undertook a mammoth audit of American Telephone and Telegraph. In 1972, however, the FCC dropped the study, saying it was short of funds. Senator John Pastore pointed out that the OMB had withheld $1.8 million from the FCC—enough to pay for the project. Only after another wing of the executive—one section of the Pentagon, one of AT&T's largest customers—complained that AT&T was being let off the hook, and offered to supply spare auditors if needed, did the FCC resume the study. (Shortly afterwards, Defense Secretary Laird withdrew the offer.) Drawing on this example and Nassikas's testimony, Senator Lee Metcalf has proposed a bill which would let the independent agencies send their budgets directly to Congress, avoiding the OMB filter.

The OMB can interfere even more directly in the agencies' policy process. A famous memorandum, issued on October 5, 1971, requires *all* federal departments and agencies to send the OMB copies of new regulations "which could be expected to . . . impose significant costs on, or negative benefits to, non-Federal sectors" (that is, private industry) before they are publicly announced in the *Federal Register*. Congress has no such chance for a preview screening of regulations; the public certainly does not. And OMB has even altered the regulations. In 1971, the Environmental Protection Agency drew up a new set of guidelines for state air pollution control boards. They were tough—so tough that OMB diluted them before they were published. Peter Bernstein of Newhouse News Service described the process:

> OMB intervened at the request of Commerce Secretary Maurice Stans, Federal Power Commissioner John Nassikas, and several other federal officials who share big industry's viewpoint. Government sources say [EPA Administrator William] Ruckelshaus defended the original draft at subsequent meetings, but finally lost out when two key White House aides intervened on the side of big industry. They were presidential assistants John D. Ehrlichman and Peter M. Flanigan.

A year later, in 1972, the OMB struck again. The EPA prepared a report on a plan to clean the Great Lakes. It was ready for Nixon's February 8 message on the environment, but along the way it disappeared into OMB's maw. Congressman Abner Mikva of Illinois then found out about the plan; with twelve other congressmen, he appealed to OMB to reconsider its decision. The plan would have cost $141 million in its first year—less than just the research costs for the space shuttle.

While exercising this tight supervision over executive departments and "independent" agencies, OMB can also interfere with whatever attempts Congress may make to assert its own supervisory power. The most important technique for doing so is OMB's screening of testimony administration witnesses plan to give Congress. Combined with the witnesses' usual ellipsis, this means that congressmen are often frustrated when they try to oversee the executive. On July 26, 1972, a Pentagon witness demonstrated an extreme degree of his noncooperation. Appearing before a Senate subcommittee investigating "environmental war" (rainmaking) in Vietnam, Benjamin Foreman, assistant general counsel at the Defense Department, refused to answer Claiborne Pell's questions:

> *Pell:* Are you under instructions not to discuss weather modification in Southeast Asia?
> *Foreman:* Yes, sir:

The expanded OMB is just one part of the extreme suction of executive power toward the White House, which began years ago but has accelerated under Nixon. Perturbed by the growth of what he called "palace guard government," Congressman Morris Udall commissioned a study in 1972 to see just how many people were working directly for the president. After considerable difficulty, Udall found that the presidential staff had grown 25 percent in Nixon's first three years, from 1,766 members to 2,206. The annual growth rate had quadrupled from its level under Johnson. The OMB had grown by 60 percent, the National Security Council by 50 percent, and nine new satellite agencies had joined them under the presidential aegis, including the Domestic Council, the Office of Telecommunications Policy, special assistants to the president, the Council on Environmental Quality, the Office of Intergovernmental Relations, and several more. The total payroll for the executive office of the president had risen from Johnson's $32 million to $41 million in fiscal year 1973.

Udall's study rose from a sense of congressional unease about presidential government; another manifestation of unease came from Congressman J. J. Pickle, in June, 1972. Offering an amendment to cut appropriations for the OMB by $4 million, Pickle said:

> The Office of Management and Budget is the unseen government of today. It is an invisible force that has more to do sometimes with your own district than you do. . . . This is not a severe cut . . . just to try to get the office to tighten its belt a little and let them know Congress should be running the government and not the Office of Management and Budget.

Aside from its denunciations, what more does Congress have to throw against the OMB? Not too much. For supervision of the executive, congressmen must mainly rely on committee staff members.

In all, the congressional committees have 1,600 staff members, and half of them are secretaries or clerks. For the range of jobs to be covered—from appropriating money to passing laws to overseeing the executive—this is too few. Congress's other potential ally is the General Accounting Office, the legislature's staff of investigators. The GAO is a relatively bright spot in Congress's general prospect, and any reassertion of congressional power will probably begin there. But its manifold problems and weaknesses once more emphasize how Congress has lost control.

The GAO is an arm of Congress; its job is to help congressmen study the government. Before 1950, it spent most of its time doing purely accounting work. After the Korean War, however, Comptroller General Joseph Campbell led GAO into more adventuresome areas. Campbell began a series of studies of war industries and produced, during the fifties, reports on profiteering and wasteful construction. Campbell, who had been treasurer of Columbia University before coming to the GAO in 1954, favored a candid style rare in government reports. His audits were studded with phrases like "excessive cost" and "congressional intent as to cost limitations circumvented," shockers in a society accustomed to squishy government prose.

Campbell soon ran afoul of the Defense Department and the defense contractors; by 1965, they had conveyed their unhappiness to Chet Holifield. In his response to the Pentagon complaints, Holifield illustrates one of the most potent executive tactics for controlling the legislature: by setting up one congressman with favors and patronage, the executive can count on him to beat down other critics. Holifield's Committee on Government Operations held hearings on the GAO in 1956, which Holifield began by mentioning "the great concern that has been shown in industry circles, and, recently, in the Department of Defense over the difficult and sometimes awkward situations created by the GAO audit reports." By the end of the hearings, the GAO had been tamed. It agreed to a list of conditions, including an agreement to stop using company names in the reports and an effort to be more "constructive."

With that behind it, and with cautious bureaucrat Elmer Staats now as comptroller general, the GAO walks a fine line between toadyism and giving offense, but it still is the most important investigative tool Congress has. It showed its split personality well in a recent study of, once again, defense contractors. While the audit itself was factual and critical—revealing that seventy-seven weapons systems would cost $28.7 billion more than estimated—and that the average profit rate was a fantastic 56 percent—the GAO sent the report to the industry before publishing it, and then incorporated many industry alibis into the text and toned down its own charges.

Despite its occasional disappointments, the GAO offers congressmen their main defense against the analysts of the White House and the OMB. Whenever congressmen ask, the GAO will make studies of specific problems. And in 1970, it was authorized to make cost-benefit studies of programs. Unfortunately, few members of Congress take advantage of the service. An average of 300 requests per year come from Congress—nearly all of them from a few enthusiasts. Between July, 1969, and April, 1972, for example, of the 160 Senate requests, 37 came from Proxmire; of the 200 House requests, 11 came from H. R. Gross of Iowa, 6 each from two other congressmen, and the rest in ones and twos from others.

If, as we have argued, information is the key to the executive's power, Congress will have to do more than ask for an occasional GAO study. What is needed is a major overhaul of Congress's information sources, so that it can deal on a more equal basis with the executive. As former White House special assistant Joseph Califano wrote recently in the *Washington Post:*

> The Congress is presently the separate but unequal branch of the
> federal government.... The basic reason for the decline in congressional effectiveness and status, however, lies not with the executive

branch or some federal bureaucrats. . . . Responsibility for its separate but unequal status rests largely with the Congress
itself. . . .

The Congress is dependent upon the executive branch for most
of its information, with an occasional and too often superficial
assist from outside experts. . . .

Congress has ignored the revolution in analytical technology.
. . . The Congress has only three or four computers, and those
computers operate in large measure on payrolls and housekeeping
matters. . . . Contrast the executive branch, which now has some
4,000 computers working almost entirely on substantive policy
issues. . . .

The stark fact is that neither the Congress nor any of its committees has the consistent capability—without almost total reliance
on the informational and analytical resources of the executive
branch—of developing coherent, large-scale federal programs.

Incapable of creation, with authority but little power, Congress
has become a broken branch. If it becomes upset with the executive branch, it expresses itself in the only way it can—by obstruction or delay. The country needs more.

As a secret government replaces the one elected by the voters—
as Congress placidly hands its remaining powers over, one by
one, to the president and his advisers—the president's thirst for
power seems actually to increase. Along with assuming Congress's
normal powers of lawmaking, appropriating, and overseeing, the
president in the last few years has increasingly extended the
powers inherent in his office:

- He has made law by "regulation," as with the "Accelerated
  Depreciation Range." As part of President Nixon's economic
  measures in 1971, this gave corporations tax breaks worth
  some $3.9 billion. When Congress began to complain about
  the enactment of this tax charge through "alterations in Treasury regulations," Nixon agreed to submit it to Congress. On
  short notice, it was rammed through by Congressman Wilbur
  Mills, whom presidential aides had courted by flying to his
  Arkansas home.
- In foreign affairs, the president has obviously had just as
  free a hand. Whenever Congress prepares to curb the presidential war—by repealing the 1965 Gulf of Tonkin resolution,
  by voting a series of end-the-war amendments in the seven-

ties—it finds either that (as Nicholas Katzenbach told a hearing in 1967) the president didn't need the Tonkin resolution in the first place, or that (as Nixon said after an antiwar resolution was passed in 1971) the president can simply ignore antiwar clauses.

- With a slightly more plausible pretense of legality, the president has used Executive Orders to write laws Congress won't give him. In 1971, after Congress had turned down President Nixon's request to revive the literally useless Subversive Activities Control Board (which had so little to do that its members would not come to the office for long stretches), Nixon evaded Congress by issuing an executive order to keep the board in operation.

- The foreign-policy equivalent of executive orders are executive agreements. Although these secret deals, signed by the president and a foreign country, bind the nation with the force of treaties, Congress knows nothing about them. According to Senator Clifford Case, some four thousand of the agreements are now in effect. In an attempt to limit them Case has proposed a bill which would make the president report the agreements to Congress and have them approved.

If this is not tyranny, autarchy, abuse of power, then the Constitution writers had nothing to fear. Congress has its problems, but the only way to restore balance to the government is for it to stand up for the rights it retains—and to fight for the return of those that have been taken from it.

DONALD RIEGLE, JR., with TREVOR AMBRISTER

A Congressman's Diary

If Congress is seemingly incapable of defending itself against incursions into its authority by the executive, at least part of the reason can be found in the bureaucracy, ritual, and self-interest that have encrusted its channels and encumbered its deliberations. Ralph Nader echoed the feelings of many students of the contemporary legislative process when he charged that Congress has "shackled itself with inadequate political campaign laws, archaic rules, the seniority system, secrecy, understaffing, and grossly deficient ways to obtain crucial information." In the following excerpts from *O Congress,* a personal diary of life in the United States House of Representatives, Donald Riegle, Jr., a maverick Republican congressman from Flint, Michigan, considers some of these problems. His conclusion: "You're playing against a stacked deck virtually all the time."

Wednesday, *June 9.* . . .   The man whose power within the Congress probably counts for more than all the other members put together is Wilbur Mills of Arkansas. He's the man who writes the tax bills that come out of the Ways and Means Committee; he writes them the way he wants or they just don't come out. His power is enormous. After lunch I spotted him and asked if I could see him privately in the next day or two. Although I didn't say so, I wanted to urge him to support the Nedzi-Whalen amendment to cut off funds for the war. He was extremely gracious. "You don't need an appointment," he said, "and if you don't know that yet, well, it's time you found out. You just look me up on the floor tomorrow and we'll step off the floor and talk for as long as you need."

Later this afternoon I ran into Bill Steiger and we had a chance to chat. Both of us were twenty-eight when we first came to the

"A Congressman's Diary" (Originally "June," "July," "September," "December," "February"). From *O Congress,* copyright © 1972 by Donald W. Riegle, Jr., and Trevor Armbrister. Reprinted by permission of Doubleday & Co., Inc.

Congress in January 1967, but our respective styles and adjustments have differed enormously since then. A diabetic, Bill is probably the thinnest man in the House. He's deadly serious, a tough, able "inside man" who's very much at home with the internal legislative process: the day-to-day piecemeal adjustments, the perfecting amendments, the above-average participation in the succession of floor statements on pending bills, the base-touching and necessary courtesies to senior members, the laughing at their unfunny jokes. He's a dependable team player and he's learned how to dissent occasionally without burning his bridges.

His is the chip-away method—the occasional reform of consequence, the steady, methodical attempt to make small but regular incremental impacts on the flow of legislation. It's a necessary function and it serves a useful, if limited, purpose.

In my opinion, though, that approach will not enable America to beat the train to the crossroads. A continuation of business as usual in the Congress won't help us stave off approaching disasters. We're trapped by a traditional momentum that makes it impossible for us to shift into an emergency state of mind and operation and come to grips with urgent problems.

After being here for a while, I learned what the limitations are in terms of making things happen. The legislative process is slow and has a million roadblocks in it. The seniority system plays a big part and there's almost no way a newer member can affect the shape of legislation. There's damn little you can get your hands on, make happen or influence.

Even your vote doesn't count for much. Since I've been here only one major bill has been decided by a single vote. If you try to evaluate your incremental impact, you have to decide that, unless you're Speaker, chairman of an important committee or part of the House leadership—and all these assignments are a function of seniority—you just can't have much impact on normal congressional operations.

There are three approaches you can take. The first is to play the game and be one of the boys. Essentially, that's what Steiger is doing. Avoid major controversy, get yourself re-elected time after time and accumulate power slowly. The second is to leave the House when you see the barriers to getting things done. If you're John Lindsay, you run for mayor of New York. If you're Mel Laird, you become Secretary of Defense. If you're Don Rumsfeld, you leave to head OEO. In these positions it's possible to have an incremental impact.

The third approach is to stay in the House and become an outside man. Develop ad hoc initiatives, mechanisms that lie outside the established, traditional paths. By dramatizing the public debate on some critical issues, you force the legislative and executive branches and the press to deal with realities more quickly and more honestly than they'd otherwise prefer.

Congress is really a body of followers, not leaders, and it's often necessary to build a significant public mandate to get Congress to move. Congress usually won't face up to a problem until it has to, before it's forced to. By using these outside methods to bring pressure on your colleagues, you tend to burn your bridges behind you. You can become an "outsider" within the club.

But if the country is in jeopardy and you're not prepared to try to force a change, then your political future doesn't mean anything on moral or practical grounds. It doesn't stand for anything. If you choose the role of outsider, you just can't worry about what happens to you as a consequence. That philosophy is a violation of the traditional rules around here. That's why some people think I've lost my mind.

. . .

Friday, July 30. . . . This was the day of the vote on whether the government should guarantee a loan to rescue Lockheed Aircraft from its financial troubles. There were some early parliamentary skirmishes and procedural maneuvers, but it wasn't until late afternoon that the House got down to business. The final vote was very close. The chamber was hushed so everyone could hear each response. Several members kept running tallies on the backs of envelopes.

After the first roll-call vote, the nays were ahead by two. As the clerk began calling the remaining names again, activity picked up on the floor. Jerry Ford was moving about, looking for potential switches, trying to glean additional votes. Majority Leader Hale Boggs, a Democrat from Louisiana, was doing the same thing on the other side of the aisle. Then I noticed something very interesting.

Bill Steiger hadn't answered on the first roll-call vote. Yet he had been standing on the floor and obviously had heard his name called. Bill is a party man; he's careful to play the game by the established rules. He knew the Lockheed loan wouldn't be popular in his district. Hence he wanted to vote against it. But at the same time he's close to the Republican leadership. They wanted him to vote aye. So he intended to vote for the loan only if it developed that one or two votes were needed to pass it. He'd go with the party and thereby earn the leadership's gratitude. Either way, he'd score numerous brownie points.

The clerk was completing the second calling of the roll. "Steiger of Wisconsin." Again Bill didn't answer. The vote was a virtual dead heat. Plainly, the issue was going to be decided in the well of the House—the open space between the members' seats and the raised Speaker's platform. Once the roll has been called twice, those who haven't yet voted or who wish to change their votes can stand in the well and be recognized for that purpose. Because the Democrats control the House, the Democratic side of the well is the first to be "cleared." Democrats are recognized before Republicans—and women are recognized before men.

When the Democrats had voted, the clerk turned toward the dozen or so Republicans who were waiting to be recognized. Steiger was standing in the far corner of the well so he could vote at the end of the line and be absolutely certain that his vote was needed. Because the leadership of both parties wanted this bill to pass, announcement of the final vote result by the Speaker, Carl Albert, was going to be delayed. That would give Hale Boggs, Jerry Ford and Les Arends more time to round up additional votes.

At this point, only four or five members remained in the well. The margin of ayes was big enough to let Steiger vote no, and with a look of obvious relief on his face, that's exactly what he did. The bill passed by three votes, 192 to 189.

. . .

Thursday, September 30. . . . The House remained in session until nine o'clock tonight to consider a slew of proposed amendments to the Economic Opportunity Act of 1964. We had token sessions Monday, Tuesday and Wednesday; then we had to go until nine o'clock tonight. That's typical of the regular inefficiency here. The membership just goes along, sheeplike, with a leadership that does a second-rate job. There were a number of recorded teller votes during the afternoon and they necessitated much running back and forth.

At one point, in the men's room off the floor, I noticed Frank Brasco, a Democrat from New York, standing on the scales carefully adjusting the weights. In his late thirties, he stands about five feet five and speaks through his nose with a Brooklyn accent.

Ferdie St. Germain, a Democrat from Rhode Island, was sitting in the raised shoeshine chair watching Brasco intently. "Be sure to take out the cigar, Frank," Ferdie said finally, "before you weigh yourself." Brasco smiled and laid his six-inch stogie in an adjacent ashtray.

Several weeks ago Ohio Republican Chalmers Wylie introduced legislation that would allow officially designated prayers in public schools—in effect, repealing the Supreme Court's 1962 decision. His bill went to the House Judiciary Committee. Chairman Emanuel Celler, a Democrat from New York, arbitrarily refused to hold hearings on it. When a bill is blocked in committee, its sponsor can try to persuade 218 members—a majority of the House—to sign a discharge petition that is kept at a desk in the well. If he succeeds in acquiring that many signatures, the bill automatically comes to the floor for a vote.

Since 1900, members have tried to bring bills to the floor 836 times via the discharge petition. Until today, they'd succeeded only twenty-four times. Now, with Wylie's prayer amendment, they've notched their twenty-fifth victory; the amendment will probably come to the floor next month. The reason their victories have been so few is that Congress runs on the committee system. And integral to that is the seniority system.

We select committee chairmen not on the basis of merit but rather on the basis of their seniority. The man who has served on the committee for the longest period becomes its chairman. At the present time in the House, we have seven committee chairmen in their seventies and four in their eighties. Eight of the remaining ten are in their sixties. One chairman, John McMillan from South Carolina, has actually gotten younger. Now in his seventies, he recently changed his biographical data in the Congressional Record to indicate that he's only sixty-nine years old. Some of these men can't hear very well, can't see very well, have difficulty working a full day. Congress is the only major institution in America that selects its leaders this way.

A man can come to Congress when he's thirty-five, serve here twenty years and emerge, at age fifty-five, as the ablest man on his committee. But because he has to wait for all the members ahead of him to either retire or die, he may have to wait another twenty years—until he's seventy-five—before he becomes a chairman. The practical and psychological implications of this are obvious. Members realize they can't afford to lose an election. They can win nineteen, lose one and find themselves at the bottom of the seniority list. They have to win twenty in a row. That means they have to do things that minimize their chances for defeat. Nearly five years ago, Cederberg gave me some of his friendly advice. "Remember, Riegle," he said, "you'll never be defeated by the speech you didn't give." In other words, keep quiet and avoid risks; if you can get re-elected year after year and outlive your colleagues, you will climb to the top of the ladder eventually. The only catch is that you may be in your seventies when the big moment comes.

Why, then, do members go along with this? The answer is that chairmen of congressional committees have enormous, almost authoritarian power, if they choose to exercise it. My own chairman, George Mahon, for example, is chairman of the Appropriations Committee; he's also chairman of the Defense Appropriations Subcommittee. He and the other subcommittee chairmen have great influence over *multibillion*-dollar segments of the federal budget.

Analyzing the Administration's budget requests for Defense, Agriculture and HEW is an enormously time-consuming job, and while Mahon works as diligently as any man in the House, the workload is incredible. This year, for example, his Defense Appropriations Subcommittee produced nine volumes of hearings—a total of 8296 pages. Another 5924 pages were classified and taken out of the record. When a spending bill is reported out by its subcommittee, it goes to the full Appropriations Committee. As a rule, the full committee gives it only a cursory hearing. It listens to reports from the ranking majority and minority members, then reports out the bill to the floor. Once it is there, it is virtually impossible for any member to alter it.

Say, for example, that a member wants to offer an amendment to the Defense appropriations bill having to do with a certain type of aircraft. He can rise on the floor to propose his legislation; he will be recognized for five minutes. But few members ever avail themselves of this opportunity. They don't have the time or the expertise to take on the House "establishment." When the Appropriations Committee reports out a bill, it's reflecting the will of its chairman and, to a considerable extent, of the Speaker himself. Any member who hopes to offer a successful amendment has an almost herculean task.

When I first came to the Congress—and before I understood how things work around here—I offered several amendments on the floor. Most were to delete items from the Interior Department appropriation that I thought could be postponed. I was convinced, for example, that the Hirshhorn Sculpture Garden in Washington, D.C., was a luxury that could wait. The taxpayers shouldn't have had to pay for it when there were so many urgent needs for their money. However, the momentum was so strong on the side of the committee structure that none of my amendments was successful. You're playing against a stacked deck virtually all the time. In fact, Julia Hansen, the Interior Subcommittee chairman, is still miffed at me, five years later, for challenging "her bill."

The Appropriations Committee and its subcommittees can't function properly for at least two reasons. The first is a lack of staff. Chairman Mahon has only three staff aides. For years, the Republican minority on the committee had only two staff members—although that number has recently been increased to three. Each subcommittee has from one to three staff members (five for Defense) who work for its Democratic chairman, and while these people are non-partisan they have little time to assist the other members of the subcommittee. On Foreign Ops, for example, we have one staff member for nine subcommittee members. Even if I could have one ninth of his time available to me directly, I couldn't scratch the surface of the budget that our subcommittee is considering. Either I must do it myself or assign the job to someone on my office staff, usually Carl Blake. I could use at least five full-time assistants on my Appropriations Committee work alone.

The men in power, however, usually don't see themselves as needing more staff. And to many other, less senior, members, the lack of committee staff just isn't a pressing concern. It doesn't relate directly to their re-election hopes. They'd much rather take the people they have on their personal staffs and direct them toward servicing their districts, performing chores for constituents. That's far more important to them and their long-term chances of becoming committee chairmen than digging into the intricacies of the federal budget or pending legislation.

The second reason the committee doesn't function properly is that it isn't an accurate reflection of the House as a whole. As long as the Democrats have been in control, the existing power structure has been dominated by the Southerners. For decades, the one-party South automatically returned Democratic congressmen who accumulated great seniority. Of the seven highest-ranking Democrats on the Appropriations Committee today, six are from the South. The South is guaranteed the chairmanship of this committee for years to come—if the Democrats continue to control Congress. Southern congressmen tend to be more hawkish and fiscally conservative, less oriented toward domestic spending measures. Subcommittees tend to be special-interest-oriented. Members who have a strong interest in the military or have large numbers of defense installations in their districts usually seek assignment to the Defense Appropriations Subcommittee. That subcommittee usually smiles on Pentagon requests.

The same thing is true with respect to the Agriculture Subcommittee; most of its members come from farm states. Each subcommittee tries to enlarge its slice of the federal budget pie. But there is no mechanism for evaluating priorities, for questioning the wisdom, say, of taking $500 million away from Defense and plugging it into HEW. We don't know how to begin to weigh questions like that.

The Democratic leadership has another built-in bias that reflects itself in terms of committee assignments. Often, the more conservative Democrats will assign liberals to such "liberal" committees as Education and Labor. They know that, as long as they control the appointment of members to the Appropriations Committee, they can put on the brakes at that point. Both Democrats and Republicans have gone to great pains to screen out from the Appropriations Committee those who would spend more for domestic needs. I'm a fluke. If the Republican leadership had a second chance, they probably wouldn't appoint me to Appropriations. I'd more likely get Education and Labor.

This built-in bias also reflects itself in the unwillingness to form new committees. In the last twenty-five years this nation's problems have multiplied and grown increasingly complex. Yet the leadership has appointed only two new committees—on Science and Astronautics and on Ethics. David Pryor, a thoughtful, even-tempered Democrat from Arkansas, has tried to dramatize the problems of the elderly and feels that Congress should appoint a committee to consider these problems in detail. The chances that it will are almost non-existent. The favorite argument used by the leadership to thwart Pryor's request is lack of space to house a new committee. (So Pryor sought private donations, rented a trailer and parked it at a gas station a few blocks from the Capitol, where volunteers continue work on the problems of the elderly.)

But that's not the only reason for their reluctance to appoint a new committee. Existing committee chairmen don't want to dilute their own power. They had to spend all those years waiting to climb the ladder. They're loath to create competing ladders. This is especially true in Pryor's case. He's only been here for four terms and is still in his thirties. Few senior members, who've been waiting in line for years, would want to grant a charter to a new committee and give the prerogatives of a chairman to so young a member.

.   .   .

Tuesday, December 14. . . .   On the floor this afternoon, I spotted Bill Hungate, a thoughtful, prematurely graying Democrat from Missouri who has just announced his resignation as chairman of the House District Judiciary Subcommittee. For any chairman to resign voluntarily is almost unprecedented, so I stopped him to ask the circumstances. Despite his best efforts, he replied, lobbyists from collection agencies, small loan companies and other businesses were succeeding in their efforts to influence legislation before his subcommittee. Invited to testify publicly, these lobbyists have declined and chosen to keep pressing their efforts behind the scenes. Apparently, staff members of the House District Committee and its subcommittees have been going along with that.

As far as Hungate knows, Chairman John McMillan of the House District Committee doesn't seem to object to this practice and hasn't disciplined or warned the staffers. On occasion, McMillan has even called Hungate's Judiciary Subcommittee into session himself to consider measures affecting these local firms. Hungate never learned about this until after the fact. He told me he thought a major scandal might erupt over the way the legislation is being developed. He felt powerless to stop these end-run plays; he couldn't function effectively. Under the circumstances, he said, his only real alternative was to resign.

One of the prevailing myths about the House is that many congressmen and their staff members spend time accepting money, gifts or the favors of call girls from omnipresent lobbyists in return for their help with special-interest legislation. It *may* happen occasionally but certainly not to the extent that some people believe. Because I'm on the Appropriations Committee, whose duties are general, I don't see as many lobbyists as I would if I belonged to a specialized committee like Public Works or Post Office and Civil Service. No one has ever approached me to suggest a bribe of any sort. That could be because the people who might try such a thing feel I'm so powerless here that it wouldn't be worth the effort. I'd like to think it's because they know I'd throw them out of the office. I *have* heard rumors about kickback-type situations involving members of committees that handle big contracts, but I've seldom seen them substantiated. In fact, I know of only one or two instances of that happening during my time in office.

The one incident that I recall most vividly actually occurred before I came to Congress. In 1965, as a casewriter at the Harvard Business School, I was doing a study of how the Post Office Department and Congress agreed on increases in postal rates for different classes of mail. I flew to Washington to conduct my interviews. At the time, Post Office and Civil Service was probably the most corruption-prone committee in the House. There was a direct relationship between its decisions and the amount of money that a mail-order company, for example, would have to pay to send its packages. Lobbyists swarmed all over the members of that committee. The favorite ploy they used to reward sympathetic members was to hold phony testimonial dinners. A sponsoring organization might come in and buy a hundred tickets at fifty dollars each and maybe only two or three ticket holders would actually attend the event. Funds spent for the rest of the tickets would go to the "deserving" member. It was all a charade, a devious way to funnel money to a member who would be expected to show his appreciation for this largesse by favoring the sponsors' legislative proposals.

One afternoon the late Joe Pool, a Democrat from Texas and a member of the committee, invited me to attend a testimonial dinner that was being given for him that night at a Washington hotel. I had nothing better to do, so I went along. There was Pool in a rather small room with about two dozen people including the lobbyists who had underwritten the affair. Sales of the bogus tickets probably produced five or ten thousand dollars for Pool. Later, those same lobbyists appeared before the committee. They asked for help in keeping the rate structure low and the government subsidy high. I don't know how Pool reacted, but the whole situation was a disgrace.

Lobbyists here range from the inept and pitiful to the really powerful. Some national trade associations put out an awful lot of material which suggests to their members across the country that terrific things are being done. In reality, the Washington end

of the operation may have no influence at all. Other organizations—the road builders' group, for example, and most of the
larger unions—get in there and shoulder for position. They do
their homework. They know what they want and how to get it.
They reward compliant members with campaign contributions
and votes at election time. That's really the best currency in this
town.

. . .

Tuesday, February 22. After a busy two-day trip to Flint, I returned to Washington. At two o'clock this afternoon the Foreign
Operations Subcommittee met behind closed doors to discuss
last-minute developments before going on to the long-awaited
Senate-House conference on the foreign aid appropriation bill.
Otto Passman was talking excitedly, shuffling his papers and ex-
horting us to support all of his recommendations. Conscious of
his own fidgeting, he muttered, "I feel as nervous as a reformed
whore the first time in church."

Frowning and waving his arms, Otto warned that the Senate
conferees wanted to "roll us" in the conference. They wanted
to cut out military assistance programs and would seek an agreement that the House would have to reject. Otto lamented the
the fact that he had been forced to become "a defender of foreign
aid." But he was only against "these irresponsible reductions, ya
understand?" Sweeping his arms, blinking his eyes and looking
over the rims of his glasses, he urged us to concentrate on his
words. "As Governor Long used to say, 'Listen good.' Now Senator
Fulbright . . ."

"You mean Senator Half-Bright," John Rooney interrupted.

". . . Senator Fulbright," Otto went on, "has kept this bill bottled
up for nearly eight months. Obviously, those people want to em-
barrass the President while he's in China. I'm not gonna let them
do it." Otto ran through the list of items to be considered in the
conference: Alliance for Progress, international organizations,
population control programs, American schools abroad.

"What's the money for in this population control program?"
Doc Long asked in a nasal voice.

Otto ignored him, but Long persisted. "The population control
money—what's it being spent on?"

"Rubbers!" Otto thundered, and the subcommittee roared.

Later we walked as a group to the Senate-House conference—five Republicans and five Democrats—with Otto setting a

brisk pace. It was clear he took a dim view of Wisconsin Senator William Proxmire, the chairman of the Senate conferees, who was thought to oppose many of his favorite projects.

"This man Proxmire," Otto said, grabbing my arm, "he doesn't know sheep shit from cotton seed."

Bill Hathaway, a Democrat from Maine, overheard his remark. "Is this the Agriculture Committee?" he asked with a smile.

The conference itself lasted two and a half hours but turned out to be no contest. Proxmire seemed preoccupied. In a gesture of seeming good will and flexibility, Otto conceded several minor points to the Senate conferees. But when it came time to discuss the major items his graciousness turned to granite. He had his facts and figures in order and used his expertise to bulldoze the conference. Everything considered, Otto won the day. Had this been a football game, the score would have been something like 52 to 6. As one of the conferees remarked to me when we left the room, "Otto sure took Proxmire's pants down this afternoon."

Wednesday, February 23. The Republican cloakroom was crowded at noon today. Sober-faced H. R. Gross was standing at the food counter holding a cup of coffee; seven or eight other members were sitting in their leather chairs eating lunch or waiting to be served. Sam Steiger from Arizona was wearing his cowboy boots. With something of a beer gut hanging over his belt, he remarked that he had just talked to a lobbyist who was complaining that he had 162 fund-raising cocktail parties to attend between now and April 7. The new campaign financing disclosure bill takes effect on that date and contributions after that will have to be recorded publicly. Understandably, the lobbyists and large contributors are scrambling to disburse their 1972 gifts while they can still do so anonymously.

Les Arends from Illinois began telling us about his opponent in the Republican primary. "Twenty-three years without opposition [in the party] and now this," he said, shaking his head resignedly. He had just booked forty-two billboards at a cost of $4500. Don Clancy, a smoothly conservative Republican from Cincinnati, said he was in the same boat. He's being challenged by a twenty-six-year-old woman. Arends and Clancy aren't used to such challenges. While they pretend to kid about them, they're nervous.

Later this afternoon I stopped by the news ticker in the speaker's lobby and read that John Dowdy from Texas had just been fined $25,000 and sentenced to eighteen months in prison. He has said he will appeal and won't seek re-election to Congress this November. His wife, J.D., has announced that she will run in his place. Another story on the wire reported that Senator Proxmire had appeared on the floor with his head swathed in bandages. Several days ago, he showed up with a pair of unexplained black eyes and it was generally acknowledged that he had undergone surgery to have the bags removed from under his eyes. Now it appears that he's getting a hair transplant as well. In a statement today, he noted that the treatments would continue for several months and that his hair wouldn't grow out fully for another year and a half. "Even then," he said, "I will still be a semi-baldy, but a little more semi and a little less baldy. I expect humorous, critical, outraged or even ridiculing reactions, but I will acknowledge none of them. I consider the hair transplant to have no public significance." Now I know what was on Proxmire's mind when Otto Passman was working him over the other day.

Thursday, February 24. Early this afternoon, rushing to the floor for a quorum call, I found myself wedged into an elevator with about ten other members. Ed Derwinski towered above us. Spotting Leonor Sullivan in the rear of the car, he drowned out all other conversations by saying, "If you weren't here, Mrs. Sullivan . . ."

"I'm closing my ears," she said.

"Then I'd tell the joke about the Polish grandmother who began taking birth control pills . . . because she didn't want any more grandchildren." Noticing a member of Polish descent in the elevator, Derwinski grinned sheepishly. "Oh, I shouldn't have said that," he continued. "Our colleague here doesn't like these Polish jokes."

The Detroit *Free Press* this morning carried a column by Saul Friedman on the busing dilemma. It excoriated white liberals —especially Democrats—who have jumped on the anti-busing bandwagon. He criticized "the knee-jerk panic and the unstatesman-like stampede that swept through the House when the entire Michigan delegation save the two blacks voted for a barrage of anti-busing legislation, even including one measure to deprive Federal funds for busing from those districts complying with court orders."

Friedman went on to portray a black-white split on the issue. The truth of the matter is that on the occasion in question Charlie

Diggs, a black from Detroit, was absent from the chamber and didn't vote at all. The other black in the state delegation, John Conyers from Detroit, did vote against several amendments including the one Friedman specifically mentioned. But then so did I. It really hurts to be carelessly reported on. This struck me as the sort of journalism that deepens divisions on this explosive issue.

Friday, February 25. When I arrived at my district office in Flint today eight young black mothers were waiting to urge a continuation of federal financing for the Follow-Through Program, an effort to help inner-city youngsters break out of the depressing cycle of poor education, poor self-development, poor achievement and lifetime potential. They were concerned because they'd heard that funds for the program might be cut. We agreed to seek ways to keep the program alive.

Then I asked their views on school busing programs to achieve racial balance. If given the choice of equal resources for neighborhood schools in all black areas—or integrated schools with busing—they indicated by a vote of 7 to 1 they would prefer the upgraded neighborhood school. Only one mother said she would prefer to bus her children—arguing that, for blacks, racially unmixed education could not really be equal. Ola Mae Young, a former schoolmate of mine, was adamant the other way. "No busing for my kids," she said.

There was a reception at the Durant Hotel this evening before the start of the fund-raising program that featured Jerry Ford. Jerry urged my re-election and appealed for a party broad enough to accommodate different views. He went so far as to say that he himself couldn't be elected in this district, "but Don can and with overwhelming majorities." Considering that he's the Republican's top man in the House, it took some courage and largeness of spirit for him to openly endorse a maverick like me. Not only that, but Jerry announced that he would co-sponsor my community schools bill next week.

· · ·

Monday, February 28. At ten-thirty this morning I attended a meeting of our Foreign Operations Subcommittee. The Export-Import Bank—Eximbank, as it's called—is seeking financing authority in the amount of $7.3 billion to stimulate world trade—particularly the export of American products. Bank president Henry

Kearns, a rotund, florid-faced man, was a non-stop talker. On the surface he seemed to be agreeable enough; friendly, open and obliging. Yet under cross-examination he turned out to be just another slippery bureaucrat.

U.S. trade problems, he told me, stem primarily from poor American selling efforts abroad. More aggressive marketing would solve the problem, he said. I pursued the point, using an old cross-examination ploy. "Am I right, then, Mr. Kearns, in assuming that I can tell the workers and business firms in my area not to worry about the trade differentials because more aggressive marketing of our products is all that's required to solve the problem?"

To my surprise and disappointment, he said that I could do just that. I'm certain he's wrong. The reasons behind our trade problems are surely more complex and I think he's damaged his credibility with the members of this subcommittee. His statement was overdrawn and deceptive. Sometimes you can learn a lot about a witness in a very short time.

Tuesday, February 29.   Early this afternoon I was walking to a meeting of the Foreign Operations Subcommittee when I overtook Andy Jacobs from Indiana and Ken Hechler from West Virginia. We exchanged hellos and I remarked that it was encouraging for me to see "two of the good guys" walking together. They are so few in number that two constitutes a group. Pretending that we made too tempting a target, Jacobs chuckled and replied, "Yeah, don't bunch up."

In the subcommittee room I began reading the prepared statement of the witness testifying on behalf of the Inter-American Development Bank. It was a standard pitch. Glancing around the room, I noticed Doc Long sucking on his finger, seemingly lost in his own thoughts. Otto Passman was fondling an antique pocket watch. Bill Hathaway was poring over background information on the bank. Bob McEwen from New York was sitting on my right. We whispered briefly about the ITT case and the apparent involvement of Attorney General-designate Richard Kleindienst. Referring to back-room wheeling and dealing, McEwen deadpanned that his seventeen years in politics had taught him a valuable lesson: "Honesty is no substitute for experience."

After answering a quorum call I walked into the Republican cloakroom and bumped into Ed Derwinski. "Did you just get married?" he asked.

"Yes," I replied, "over a month ago."

"I guess that's why you haven't found time to get your hair cut," he said.

"Are you kidding? I married my barber."

Some of the members in the cloakroom were talking about the recent flock of retirement announcements by our senior colleagues. It's without precedent for nine ranking minority members to call it quits voluntarily over the span of several months.

. . .

Included in this group are the ranking Republicans on the Appropriations, Ways and Means and Judiciary Committees as well as the senior Republicans on Rules, Interstate and Foreign Commerce and Merchant Marine and Fisheries. This exodus surely reflects a collective belief that the party has no chance to capture control of the Congress in the foreseeable future. Otherwise, these men would be determined to hang on until they received the chance to serve as chairman of their respective committees. It reflects other factors as well: the pressures of redistricting, the higher pension benefits available for retiring members—it's possible now for some of them to draw as much as $34,000 per year; the frequency with which senior members are being stricken fatally while in office here; the longer sessions of Congress and the growing assertiveness of the newer members.

In recent years a congressman's job has changed dramatically and this has imposed a new set of pressures on the old soldiers of both parties. Fifteen years ago the House was largely an island unto itself. Few Americans knew or seemed to care very much about what happened here. That's not true any longer. Today the country is peering directly over our shoulder. It's Ralph Nader who is watching us, and Common Cause and the League of Women voters. It's newly politicized groups of blacks, women, young people and chicanos. It's such groups as SOS, NAG and Vietnam Veterans against the War. They've learned that Congress determines our national priorities; that we provide the men and money to fight undeclared wars; that we have the power to clean up the environment, restore the cities and help old people. They're letting us know their demands and lobbying aggressively to make sure we act. The pressures on members, already intense, are multiplying rapidly. As Cederberg said to me, "It's just not as much fun to be here any more."

RICHARD HARRIS

Trial by Jury

One constitutional scholar has called the Supreme Court "the least dangerous branch" of American government. Indeed, because of landmark decisions in criminal law, civil rights and liberties, and other areas where the president and Congress either would not or could not take action, it came to be regarded as a court of last resort in the truest sense on issues of inequality and injustice. Its crucial rulings of the 1950s and 1960s were supremely political ones, however, and the Court was plunged into deep political controversy. Billboards calling for the impeachment of the Chief Justice sprang up all over the country, and Richard Nixon took office promising to create a Court devoted to "strict constructionism."

The Burger Court did not immediately turn its back on the decisions of its predecessor, nor has it become an overtly political tool of the Chief Executive as was feared during the Haynsworth and Carswell confirmation hearings. (In fact, Nixon's appointees joined the holdovers from the Warren era in voting unanimously against the president on the issue of the White House tapes in 1974.) Like the Warren Court, which repeatedly refused to consider such controversial issues as the war in Vietnam, the present Supreme Court has failed to issue definitive decisions on busing and affirmative action. Yet its decisions in areas such as capital punishment and obscenity have begun to delineate its personality and the constituency it responds to. In the following essay, legal analyst Richard Harris considers the intricacies of one such important decision, on citizens' recourse to jury trials.

Trial by jury is one of liberty's oldest and most dependable safeguards. In the United States, the Constitution provides for jury trials in both civil and criminal cases, but, as with most of the

"Trial by Jury" (Originally "Annals of Law: Trial by Jury"), by Richard Harris. From *The New Yorker*, December 16, 1972, pp. 117–25. Reprinted by permission; © 1972 The New Yorker Magazine, Inc.

other rights enumerated in that document, there are few details to show how this one should be assured in practice. On the subject of juries in criminal cases, for example, Article III says only that "trial of all crimes, except in cases of impeachment, shall be by jury . . . in the state where the said crimes shall have been committed," and the Sixth Amendment adds that the jury shall be "impartial" and chosen locally. Thousands of cases have been heard since those few words were written to decide what they mean.

One thing they didn't mean until very recently was that every citizen was Constitutionally guaranteed a jury trial in any criminal prosecution. Although state constitutions have all along provided for jury trials in criminal cases under state jurisdiction, that has largely been a matter of imitation of the federal Constitution rather than obedience to it, and up to four years ago any state could have abolished its jury system, because until the Supreme Court ruled on this point, in 1968, the Constitution was understood to offer an explicit guarantee of jury trials only to defendants in federal courts. Since the states have always been more jealous guardians of their own powers, particularly their police powers, than of their citizens' individual rights, the Bill of Rights was long interpreted, first by tradition and then by law, to apply only to federal matters. But after ratification of the Fourteenth Amendment, in 1868, there was a growing movement to interpret its key clause, "nor shall any state deprive any person of life, liberty, or property without due process of law," to mean that due process demands "incorporation" of the Bill of Rights into state as well as federal laws and procedures. That movement was fiercely resisted—chiefly by the Supreme Court—and to some extent it still is. The idea of total incorporation has never been accepted by a majority of the Court, although slowly, and often grudgingly, the Court has conceded over the years that *some* provisions in the Bill of Rights are so "fundamental" that they apply equally to the states and to the nation. The first use of this doctrine by the Court came in 1925, when it declared that freedom of speech is a fundamental personal right, and has to be protected by state governments as well as by the national government. Once the legal wall in the federal system was breached by this ruling, the fundamental doctrine was gradually expanded by succeeding Courts, most of all by the Warren Court, to apply to state cases nearly all the criminal protections in the Bill of Rights, including the Sixth Amendment right to a jury trial. This last right was extended to the states in 1968, when the Supreme Court ruled, in Duncan v. Louisiana, that they must offer anyone who is accused of committing a serious crime a trial by jury.

A jury trial is a fundamental right, the Court stated in the Duncan decision, because it offers the only Constitutional way to protect defendants "against the corrupt or overzealous prosecutor and against the compliant, biased, or eccentric judge." In 1970, the Court—now the Burger Court—went on to address itself to the question, raised in Williams v. Florida, of whether it is also fundamental for a jury to consist of twelve members, as tradition and statute had long demanded. The issue was not of "Constitutional stature," a five-member majority of the Court replied, since "the essential feature of a jury obviously lies in the interposition between the accused and his accuser of the common-sense judgment of a group of laymen," whatever their number; the size of juries, then, must be left up to the states to determine for themselves. Finally, in 1971, the Court accepted two other cases that dealt with a basic issue in jury trials of criminal cases—namely, whether the rule that verdicts must be unanimous in criminal trials is fundamental to the jury system. The principle of unanimity in jury verdicts has been traced back as far as an English trial, recorded as Anonymous Case, in 1367. Although the unanimity rule is nowhere mentioned in the Constitution, it was generally accepted, apparently without question, under English common law and in the American Colonies and the United States as an essential part of any jury trial. The specific issue of unanimity for juries in criminal trials had never been decided by the Court before, but once states were compelled by federal law to provide trials for all serious offenses, it was inevitable that the rules governing those trials would have to be clarified. The Court heard arguments on the issue in March, 1971, and then heard rearguments in January, 1972, and on May 22, 1972, handed down its decision. Four members—Chief Justice Warren E. Burger, along with Justices Byron R. White, Harry Blackmun, and William H. Rehnquist—concluded that unanimous verdicts are not required in *any* criminal trial. Four other members—Justices William O. Douglas, William J. Brennan, Jr., Potter Stewart, and Thurgood Marshall—concluded that unanimous verdicts are required in *all* criminal trials. And the last member—Justice Lewis F. Powell, Jr.—concluded that unanimous verdicts are required in federal trials but not in state trials. Because of the peculiar nature of the four-to-four standoff, Powell's view prevailed, and is now the law in this country.

At the time of the Court's ruling, two states—Louisiana and Oregon—permitted less-than-unanimous juries to convict defendants in serious but non-capital cases. Louisiana allowed as many as three dissenting jurors out of twelve, and Oregon allowed as many as two out of twelve. Both state laws were reviewed by the Court at the same time, and its decisions on them were announced together. One case, Johnson v. Louisiana, was an appeal from a decision by the Louisiana Supreme Court upholding a conviction for armed robbery by a nine-to-three jury vote. In the other case, Apodaca et al. v. Oregon, the Supreme Court reviewed the convictions of three defendants who were found guilty, respectively, of assault with a deadly weapon by an eleven-to-one vote, grand larceny by an eleven-to-one vote, and burglary by a ten-to-two vote. One of the Chief Justice's prerogatives is to decide who is to write the Court's opinion when he is a member of the majority, and in both cases Chief Justice Burger chose Justice White, the sole member of the majority in these two decisions who had not been appointed by President Nixon.

In the Johnson case, the appellant argued that a verdict of guilty by only nine of the twelve jurors clearly showed reasonable doubt on the part of the jury as a whole. And since the reasonable-doubt rule is rooted in the basic Constitutional principle of due process, it was claimed, any verdict that was not based on a finding of guilt beyond a reasonable doubt abrogated due process and thus violated the Constitution itself. Justice White disagreed. Replying that the Supreme Court had never stated that jury unanimity was an essential part of due process, he continued, "Indeed, the Court has more than once expressly said that 'in criminal cases due process of law is not denied by a state law . . . which dispenses with the necessity of a jury of twelve, or unanimity in the verdict.'" The quotation was from Jordan v. Massachusetts, which was decided in 1912, and Justice White also cited Maxwell v. Dow, decided in 1900, to the same effect. He did not mention that these rulings were handed down before the incorporation doctrine began to be applied, in 1925, to extend the Bill of Rights to the states. Moreover, the two early rulings had allowed the states to dispense with juries altogether—an opinion that was flatly reversed in 1968 by Duncan v. Louisiana. But that decision had been made after Johnson was tried, and was not retroactive, so it didn't apply to the case at hand, as the appellant had conceded in his appeal. And, for that matter, if Duncan wasn't pertinent to this case, neither was the Sixth Amendment right to a jury trial that it had applied to the states.

While Justice White agreed that due process of law requires a finding of guilt beyond a reasonable doubt before a defendant can be convicted, he saw no reason to conclude, as the appellant had, that the reasonable doubt of three jurors constitutes reasonable doubt for an entire jury. In effect, he wrote, the Court was being asked to assume that if dissenters on a jury express sincere doubts about a defendant's guilt, the jurors who are convinced of that guilt will simply ignore them, without fully debating the questions they raise or allowing themselves to be converted, and will, instead, carelessly proceed to convict the accused. Rejecting this view, Justice White set out to develop what might be called the doctrine of the conscientious juror. It is far more likely, he wrote, that when a juror presents "reasoned argument in favor of acquittal," his fellow-jurors will either answer his arguments satisfactorily or enough of them will come around to his side to prevent conviction. In practice, the Justice continued, the majority members of a jury "will cease dicussion and outvote a minority only after reasoned discussion has ceased to have persuasive effect or to serve any other purpose—when a minority, that is, continues to insist upon acquittal without having persuasive reasons. . . ." At that point, he concluded, those in the majority should not be blamed for acting with improper haste; rather, the dissenter, in the words of an earlier Court opinion, "should consider whether his doubt was a reasonable one [when it made] no impression upon the minds of so many men, equally honest, equally intelligent with himself."

Justice Douglas delivered a long and angry dissent that combined the Johnson and Apodaca cases, and he disagreed with the majority on almost every point that was raised. But on none of them did he disagree as vehemently as on the subject of the way jurors actually behave in a jury room. Juries that do not have to reach a unanimous finding for a conviction, he wrote, are far less likely to "debate and deliberate as fully" as juries that do. As for the claim that there is no evidence to suggest that a majority will refuse to listen to a minority when its votes aren't needed for a conviction, he replied, "Yet human experience teaches that polite and academic conversation is no substitute for the earnest and robust argument necessary to reach unanimity." To support his view, Justice Douglas cited "The American Jury," by Harry Kalven, Jr., and Hans Zeisel, the leading work on the subject, which pointed out that in roughly one-tenth of all jury trials "the minority eventually succeeds in reversing an initial majority, and these may be cases of special importance." A likely explanation for this figure, Justice Douglas went on, was that in many courtrooms members of juries are not permitted to take notes, and since "they have imperfect memories, the forensic process of forcing jurors to defend their conflicting recollections and conclusions flushes out many nuances which otherwise would go overlooked." However, he added, in Louisiana and Oregon any "collective effort to piece together the puzzle of historical truth . . . is cut short as soon as the requisite majority is reached," and "indeed, if a necessary majority is immediately obtained, then no deliberation at all is required in these states." That may well have occurred in the Apodaca case, he suggested parenthetically, since the jury there was out for only forty-one minutes. In any event, he concluded on this point, the Court had now removed the "automatic check against hasty fact-finding by relieving jurors of the duty to hear out fully the dissenters" in a disputed case.

Justice Powell, the swing voter, chided Justice Douglas for his doubts about jurors' fidelity to the truth as they see it, and observed that "our historic dedication to jury trial" is based on "the conviction that each juror will faithfully perform his assigned duty." Passing over the fact that this historic dedication was also based, in part, on the assurance that a single juror could prevent unjust conviction by deciding that the only way to faithfully perform his assigned duty was to hold out for acquittal, Justice Powell went on to mention a couple of procedural safeguards that protect defendants against a "willfully irresponsible jury." One was that a defense lawyer has the right to use peremptory challenges and challenges for cause when prospective jurors appear unreliable. And the other was that every judge protects every defendant by reminding every jury, in his instructions to it, that the state carries the burden of proof and that each juror is obliged by oath to weigh the views of fellow-jurors. All this, he concluded, sufficiently "diminished the likelihood of miscarriage of justice."

In Apodaca et al. v. Oregon, Justice White cited the Court's refusal, in Williams v. Florida, to insist that a jury must have twelve members in support of his contention that the Oregon law maintained the essential bulwark between the state and those it accused of crimes; like the number of jurors considering a case, he argued, the old unanimity rule provided nothing of Constitutional stature and could be harmlessly dispensed with. Justice Powell agreed—in the matter of state trials, anyway—that a jury was a bulwark whether the verdict was reached by ten or by twelve out of twelve jurors. Justice Brennan, on the other hand, sharply disagreed, claiming that the premise underlying the majority's argument was unsound. Once there are enough jurors to reach a majority verdict for conviction, he wrote in his dissent, there is nothing, except perhaps common sense, at best, to restrain them from delivering it without paying much attention to the minority's views, however cogent these might be. Like Justice Douglas, Justice Brennan found the majority's opinion based on an excessive faith in human reason. "I think it simply ignores reality to imagine that most jurors in these circumstances would, or even could, fairly weigh the arguments opposing their position," he stated. In a separate dissent, Justice Stewart was even more emphatic on this point, and told the Court that it had "never before been so impervious to reality in this area." He reminded his fellow-justices on the majority side that the Court's long-standing concern about the "serious risks of jury misbehavior" had prompted a series of decisions over the years aimed at preventing juries from carelessly or willfully abusing defendants' rights. These decisions now stood in jeopardy, the Justice declared, and went on to ask a number of questions:

> Why, if juries do not sometimes act out of passion and prejudice, does the Constitution [as interpreted by earlier Court decisions] require the availability of a change of venue? Why, if juries do not sometimes act improperly, does the Constitution require protection from inflammatory press coverage and . . . influence by court officers? Why, if juries must be presumed to obey all instructions from the bench, does the Constitution require that certain information must not go to the jury no matter how strong a cautionary charge accompanies it? Why, indeed, should we insist that no man can be constitutionally convicted by a jury from which members of an identifiable group to which he belongs have been

systematically excluded? . . . The requirement that the verdict of the jury be unanimous, surely as important as these other constitutional requisites, preserves the jury's function in linking law with contemporary society. It provides the simple and effective method endorsed by centuries of experience and history to combat the injuries to the fair administration of justice that can be inflicted by community passion and prejudice.

The Sixth Amendment's relationship to the unanimity rule was raised in Apodaca when the petitioners contended that their convictions by less-than-unanimous juries violated the right to trial by jury under that amendment as it was applied to the states, through Duncan, by the due-process clause of the Fourteenth Amendment. This time, Justice White accepted the relevance of the Sixth Amendment, since the three cases at issue had been tried after the Duncan decision made the amendment's right to a jury trial binding on the states. But that right, he retorted to the petitioners' claim, was *all* that Duncan provided in state courts. In the Williams case, for instance, the Court stated that the size of juries was not a Constitutional issue and was up to the states; the same principle and the same reasoning, the Justice said for the majority, also applied to the question of unanimity. Relegating the common-law history of the question to a long footnote, he concentrated in the body of his opinion on the legislative history of the unanimity rule in the United States. That history, he reported, was "scanty," the "most salient fact" being Representative James Madison's attempt to persuade the House to accept his version of the Sixth Amendment—including "the requisite of unanimity for conviction"—when the Bill of Rights was under debate in the First Congress. The House accepted his version, but the Senate rejected it, and a conference committee produced a compromise amendment that didn't mention unanimity or, for that matter, any of the other specific safeguards that Madison had recommended. History has left no evidence to explain why the change was made, but Justice White observed that in the Williams case the Court had considered it plausible to conclude, and had concluded, "that the deletion was intended to have some substantive effect." Since the Court was now unable "to divine 'the intent of the Framers,' " he continued, the soundest recourse was to examine "the function served by the jury in contemporary society."

That function had been defined in Williams v. Florida as "the inter-position between the accused and his accuser of the common-sense judgment of a group of laymen," and, in the opinion of the Court's present majority, that barrier remained unaffected by unanimity or the lack of it. Nor, Justice White insisted once more, did the reasonable-doubt principle demand a unanimous verdict, as the petitioners claimed. In proof, he cited the precedent of Johnson v. Louisiana, which was then several minutes old.

Justice Powell disputed the claim made by Justices Burger, White, Blackmun, and Rehnquist that unanimity was not essential to any kind of criminal jury trial. "In an unbroken line of cases reaching back into the late 1800s, the justices of this Court have recognized, virtually without dissent, that unanimity is one of the indispensable features of *federal* jury trial," he wrote. Reference to the First Congress's revision of Madison's proposal struck him as an ambiguous kind of justification that was assuredly "not sufficient . . . to override the unambiguous history of the common-law right." Still, he agreed that the states were not bound by the unanimity rule, since, in his view, it was not the Sixth Amendment that imposed jury trials on the states, as the other members of the Court seemed to believe, but rather the Fourteenth Amendment. And that amendment, he claimed, did not impose *all* the features of federal trials on state courts—a position that put him firmly in disagreement with the four other members. One of the latter, Justice Douglas, insisted that the Sixth Amendment was wholly applicable to the states by way of the Fourteenth Amendment. And Justice Stewart agreed, on the ground that this was precisely what the Duncan decision had "squarely held." Unless the court meant to overrule Duncan, he added, the only question left was whether the Sixth Amendment right to a jury trial carries with it the requirement of a unanimous verdict. "The answer to that question," Justice Stewart concluded, "is clearly 'yes,' as my brother Powell has cogently demonstrated in that part of his concurring opinion that reviews almost a century of Sixth Amendment adjudication."

Justice Douglas found the Court's decision "so radical a departure" from two centuries of American history and six centuries of common-law tradition that he could scarcely believe it had been made. The Court majority, he charged, had embarked on a "vast restructuring of American law," which could legally be done only by Constitutional amendment, not by the Court sitting as "a Committee of revision." In sum, he characterized the decision as being not in the tradition of this nation's accusatorial system but "more in the tradition of the inquisition." Justice Douglas went on to point out that this decision created an obvious, and obnoxious, disparity. The Court had long and explicitly held, he explained, that the Seventh Amendment, which governs civil trials, unquestionably requires unanimous juries in civil cases tried in state courts. "After today's decision," he wrote, "a man's property may only be taken away by a unanimous jury vote, yet he can be stripped of his liberty by a lesser standard." Although the decision would apply theoretically to everyone, he added, it would "in cold reality touch mostly the lower castes in our society ... the blacks, the Chicanos, the one-mule farmers, the agricultural workers, the off-beat students, the victims of the ghetto."

The petitioners claimed in Apodaca that since 1880 the Fourteenth Amendment had been taken to mean, in part, that jury panels must reflect a cross-section of the community. If the court now allowed less-than-unanimous juries, they argued, it would thereby allow the exclusion of minority viewpoints as effectively as if members of minority groups were not permitted to serve on juries at all. In response, Justice White brought up the conscientious-juror theory, and said, "We simply find no proof for the notion that a majority [of jurors] will disregard its instructions and cast its votes for guilt or innocence based on prejudice rather than the evidence." Once again, Justice Stewart disagreed, and pointed out, in the Johnson case, that if one could rely on jurors to be so open-minded, the Court wouldn't have been obliged to rule again and again against "systematic discrimination in the selection of criminal-court juries." He added, "Under today's judgment, nine jurors can simply ignore the views of their fellow panel members of a different race or class." Justice Powell, for his part, vigorously supported the majority view on this issue, and stated that dissenters who held out in the face of a majority opinion were displaying their own "irrationality," against which some protection was essential.

Justice Marshall confronted this view—that dissent is unreasonable—head on. After observing that "if the jury has been selected properly and every juror is a competent and rational person, then the 'irrationality' that enters into the deliberation process is precisely the essence of the right to a jury trial," he went on to say that the fundamental feature of any jury is that it represents the community, and he argued that to "fence out a dissenting juror fences out a voice from the community, and undermines the principle on which our whole notion of the jury now rests." As a member of a racial minority, Marshall may have been especially sensitive to the problem of exclusion, but he warned that far more was at stake than the right of minorities. "The juror whose dissenting voice is unheard may be a spokesman, not for any minority viewpoint, but simply for himself—and that, in my view, is enough," he explained. "The doubts of a single juror are . . . evidence that the government has failed to carry its burden of proving guilt beyond a reasonable doubt."

Louisiana law allows five-man juries with unanimous verdicts to convict defendants who *may* be sentenced to hard labor, twelve-man juries with a majority of at least nine to convict defendants who *must* be sentenced to hard labor, and twelve-man juries with unanimous verdicts to convict defendants who *may* be sentenced to death. According to Johnson, the appellant, this scale deprived him of the equal protection of the law guaranteed by the Fourteenth Amendment, which, all hands for once agreed, *is* binding on the states. Justice White conceded that Johnson might well have been acquitted if he had killed the person he was charged with having robbed, since three jurors doubted that he had robbed the victim in the first place, but concluded for the majority that the state law didn't violate the equal-protection clause, because there was no "invidious . . . classification" and the law served "a rational purpose." As described by the Louisiana constitution, he went on, that purpose was to "facilitate, expedite, and reduce expense in the administration of justice." Accordingly, the different kinds of juries were fully Constitutional.

In the days of the Warren Court, Justice White often spoke for the minority there against decisions asserting "new" rights for individuals in criminal prosecutions; the state had rights, too, he repeatedly emphasized—chiefly the pressing need not to be further hampered, in time and expense, by the imposition of more and more procedural safeguards upon a system that was almost at a standstill as it was. That minority viewpoint—in effect, a kind of cost-efficiency approach to justice—was not the majority viewpoint, and Justice Douglas, a holdover from the liberal majority of the Warren days, held that the Court was dangerously increasing the power of the state over its citizens by the new decision. Pointing out that the Court had allowed fewer than twelve jurors in state trials because its studies had shown "no discernible difference between the results reached by the two different-sized juries," he went on to say that experience and other studies had shown that "the less-than-unanimous jury overwhelmingly favors the states." In effect, he explained, non-unanimous juries convict defendants about twice as often as unanimous juries do. "While the statutes on their face deceptively appear to be neutral, the use of the non-unanimous jury stacks the truth-determining process against the accused," Douglas wrote. "Thus, we take one step more away from the accusatorial system that has been our proud boast." Once other state legislatures learn that they can nearly double conviction rates by means of such laws, they will undoubtedly move to enact their own, and Douglas warned that the Supreme Court's historic example of preferring to "err on the side of letting the guilty go free rather than sending the innocent to jail" had been virtually destroyed by the new decision. Then, in conclusion, he charged that a "law-and-order judicial mood" had persuaded the Court's majority to lower the barricades against tyranny, and asked, "Is the next step the elimination of the presumption of innocence?"

MICHAEL PARENTI

The Harvesting of Votes

In the 1972 presidential election only 55 percent of potential voters bothered to cast ballots. In many municipal elections the figure has been even lower, with as little as 10 percent of the electorate turning out. Moreover, for nearly half of those who do vote (as Sidney Verba and Norma Nie point out in their study *Participation in America*), this single act ends their political activity. This "apathy" has had an impact on all political institutions, but especially on the Republican and Democratic parties. Once a primary force for mobilizing voters and inspiring participation, their credibility is now at a low ebb, and they are being deserted in record numbers, especially by young voters. In the following essay political scientist Michael Parenti considers some of the implications of these developments. He concludes that what often appears to be voter cynicism should not be seen as mere laziness but as a way of protesting against a process that seems beyond their influence; if people have become "apathetic" it is in large measure because the electoral system and party organizations resist the kind of creative involvement that democracy is supposed to nurture.

The Harvesting of Votes

The harvesting of votes is the specialized task of the political parties. The job has gone to men who have enjoyed a class and ethnic familiarity with the common voters and who have been sufficiently occupied by the pursuit of office and patronage to remain untroubled by questions of social justice. Alan Altshuler provides an apt description of the machine politicians:

> Though they distributed favors widely, they concentrated power tightly. Though their little favors went to little men, the big favors went to land speculators, public utility franchise holders, govern-

"The Harvesting of Votes" (Originally "The Sound and the Fury: Elections and Parties" and "The Politics of Discouragement: Nonvoters and Voters"). From *Democracy for the Few* by Michael Parenti. Reprinted by permission of St. Martin's Press, Inc.

ment contractors, illicit businessmen, and of course the leading members of the machines themselves. . . .

The bosses were entrepreneurs, not revolutionaries. They provided specific opportunities for individual representatives of deprived groups, but they never questioned the basic distribution of resources in society. Their methods of raising revenue tended toward regressivity. On the whole, the lower classes paid for their own favors. What they got was a *style* of government with which they could feel at home. What the more affluent classes got, though relatively few of them appreciated it, was a form of government which kept the newly enfranchised masses content without threatening the socio-economic status quo.[1]

Today, the party politician still performs little favors for little men but seldom addresses himself to the larger problems facing ordinary citizens. He might investigate a complaint by a mother that her welfare checks are not arriving, but he would not challenge the more demeaning features of the welfare system nor the conditions that fostered it. He might find a municipal job for a faithful precinct worker, but he will not advance proposals for an attack on unemployment. He might procure an apartment for a family, but he will not ask the landlord, who himself is sometimes a party contributor, to make housing improvements, nor would he think of challenging his right to charge exorbitant rents. The party regular will "look into" everything except certain of the more harrowing realities of lower-class life and the wider social forces that help create those realities.[2] Party regulars take "the existing socio-economic structure . . . as given," Dahl notes. They assume "that the physical and economic features of the city are determined by forces beyond their control."[3]

These same politicians, however, are quite ready to serve those "forces beyond their control." "When Mayor Daley took office," reports Banfield in his study of Chicago,

he immediately wrote to three or four of the city's most prominent businessmen asking them to list the things they thought most needed doing. . . . He may be impressed by the intrinsic merit of a proposal . . . but he will be even more impressed at the prospect

[1]Alan A. Altshuler, *Community Control: The Black Demand for Participation in Large American Cities* (New York: Pegasus, 1970), pp. 74–75.
[2]See Michael Parenti, "Power and Pluralism: A View from the Bottom," *Journal of Politics*, 32, August 1970, p. 514.
[3]Robert Dahl, *Who Governs?* (New Haven: Yale University Press, 1961), p. 94.

107

of being well-regarded by the highly respectable people whose proposal it is.[4]

The machine depends on the sufferance and direct aid of urban capitalist interests. In most cities this alliance is one of the important assets of the political organization.[5] Since their primary concern is to maintain their own positions of influence within society's established order, machine politicians, like most churchmen, union leaders and college administrators, generally take a conservative approach, showing little sympathy for new and potentially disruptive ideas and demands and little taste for the kind of dialogue and confrontation that one associates with the democratic process. "The man who raises new issues," observed Walter Lippman more than a half century ago, "has always been distasteful to politicians."[6]

Democrats and Republicans:
Fraternal Twins

"The rigidity of the two-party system is, I believe, disastrous," added Lippmann. "It ignores issues without settling them, dulls and wastes the energies of active groups, and chokes off the protests which should find a civilized expression in public life."[7] That scathing judgment has stood the test of time. Today the two parties are still more ready to blur than clarify political issues, adopting stances that seldom move beyond conventional formulas. Electoral contests, supposedly providing democratic heterodoxy, have generated a competition for orthodoxy. In politics, as in economics, competition is rarely a safeguard against monopoly and seldom a guarantee that the competitiors will offer the consumer a substantive choice.

This is not to say there are no differences between (and within) the major parties or that one party is not preferred by some people over the other. Generally the racial minorities, union workers, lower-income urban groups and more liberally oriented professionals support the Democratic party, while the White Protestant,

[4]Edward Banfield, *Political Influence* (New York: Free Press, 1961), p. 251.
[5]Gerald Pomper, "The First, New-Time Boss," *Transaction*, January 1972, p. 56.
[6]Walter Lippman, *A Preface to Politics* (Ann Arbor: University of Michigan Press, 1962), p. 195. Originally published in 1914.
[7]*Ibid.*, p. 197.

rural, upper-income groups, big and small businessmen and the more conservative elements of the electorate make their home in the Republican party. These differences are sometimes reflected in the voting records of Democratic and Republican legislators, albeit in a most imperfect way and within a narrow range of policy alternatives

When magnified by partisan rhetoric, the differences between the parties appear worrisome enough to induce many citizens to vote—if not *for* then *against* someone. While there is no great hope that the party of their choice will do much for them, there persists the fear that the other party, if allowed to take office, or remain in office, will make things even worse. This lesser-of-two-evils approach is perhaps the most important inducement to voter participation.[8] It is not quite accurate to characterize the Republicans and Democrats as Tweedledee and Tweedledum. Were they exactly alike in all manner of image and posture, they would have even more difficulty than they do in maintaining the appearances of choice. Therefore, it is preferable that the parties be fraternal rather than identical twins.

From the perspective of those who advocate "a fundamental change in our national priorities," the question is not, "Are there differences between the parties?" but "Do the differences make a difference?" For the similarities between the parties in organization, funding, electoral methods, ideological commitment, priorities and policy output loom so large as frequently to obscure the differences. The Democratic and Republican parties are both committed to the preservation of the private corporate economy; the use of subsidies, deficit spending and tax allowances for the bolstering of business profits; the funneling of public resources through private conduits, including whole new industries developed at public expense; the concoction of domestic programs which are supposedly to assist the less fortunate segments of the population but which provide little assistance to anyone but private contractors; the use of repression against opponents of the existing class structure; the defense of the multinational corporate empire and forceful intervention against social revolutionary elements abroad. In short, Republicans and Democrats are dedicated to strikingly similar definitions of the public interest, at great cost

---

[8]See Murray Levin, *The Alienated Voter* (New York: Holt, Rinehart and Winston, 1960), pp. 37–39; a similar sentiment was expressed by many lower-income voters in Newark and New Haven when explaining their somewhat reluctant preference for the Democratic party.

109

to the life chances of underprivileged people at home and abroad. Disagreements between the two parties focus principally on which of them is better qualified to achieve commonly shared goals within a fairly narrow range of means.

The similarities between the parties do not prevent them from competing vigorously and even vehemently for the prizes of office, expending countless hours and huge sums in the doing. The very absence of significant disagreement on fundamentals makes it all the more necessary to stress the peripheral, personalized and stylistic features that advantageously differentiate oneself from one's opponent. As with industrial producers, the merchants of the political system have preferred to limit their competition chiefly to techniques of packaging and brand image. With campaign buttons and posters, leaflets and bumper stickers, television commercials and radio spots, sound trucks and billboards, with every gimmick and ballyhoo devoid of meaningful political content, the candidate sells his image as he would a soap product to a public conditioned to such bombardments.[9] His family and his looks; his experience in office and devotion to public service; his sincerity, sagacity and fighting spirit; his military record, patriotism and ethnic background; his determination to limit taxes, stop inflation, improve wages and create new jobs by attracting industry into the area; his desire to help the workingman, the farmer, and the businessman, the young and the old, the rich and the poor and especially those in between; his eagerness to fight poverty but curb welfare spending, while ending government waste and corruption and making the streets and world itself safe by strengthening our laws, our courts and our defenses abroad, bringing us lasting peace and prosperity with honor and freedom and so forth—such are the inevitable appeals which like so many autumn leaves, or barn droppings, cover the land, only to be collected in piles and carted away each November.

The Two-Party Monopoly

The two major parties have long cooperated in various stratagems to maintain their monopoly over electoral politics and discourage

[9]On the methods of selling a candidate as one might sell a commodity, see Joe McGinnis, *The Selling of the President 1968* (New York: Simon and Schuster, 1970). For an earlier collection of case studies of mass media merchandising of political issues and candidates, see Stanley Kelley, Jr., *Professional Public Relations and Political Power* (Baltimore: Johns Hopkins Press, 1956).

the growth of radically oriented third parties. "Each views with suspicion the third party movements in America," writes one Washington observer. "Each in effect is committed to the preservation of the other as its chief competititor."[10] For all their election-time rancor, Republicans and Democrats understand something about each other: they know that neither will go "too far"; neither will move beyond a narrow range of goals and means; neither has much appetite for the risks of social change; each helps to make the world safe for the other.[11]

All fifty states have laws, written and enforced by Republican and Democratic officials, regulating party representation on the ballot. Frequently the provisions are exacting enough to keep smaller parties from participating. In order to win a place on the ballot, minor parties are required to gather a large number of signatures on nominating petitions, an expensive, time-consuming task. In some states they must pay exorbitant filing fees ($5,000 in Louisiana for an independent candidate) and observe exacting deadlines when collecting and filing nominating petitions. In Pennsylvania, in 1972, third-party candidates for statewide office had to obtain the signatures of 36,000 registered voters within a three-week period. Sometimes a 5-percent requirement for signatures of registered voters has been interpreted to mean 5 percent of voters from every district within the state—an impossible task for a third party whose base might be confined to a few urban areas. Persons who sign nominating petitions for unpopular third parties sometimes find their names publicized by town clerks in an effort to embarrass them into withdrawing their names, as happened in Vermont in regard to Communist party petitions in 1972. In some states voters who are registered with the major parties are not allowed to sign or circulate minor-party nominating petitions. Petitions are often thrown out on technicalities arising from ambiguities in election laws, compelling the minor party to pursue costly court battles which, whether won or lost, usually are decided *after* the election.

The system of representation itself limits the opportunities of third parties. The single-member district elections used throughout most of the United States tend to magnify the strength of the major parties and the weakness of the smaller ones, since

[10]Douglass Cater, *Power in Washington* (New York: Random House, 1964), p. 180.
[11]At least this was true until the Nixon administration began its campaign of political espionage and sabotage against the Democrats—some of which was exposed in the Watergate hearings.

the party that polls a plurality of the vote, be it 40, 50 or 60 percent, wins 100 percent of a district's representation with the election of its candidate, while smaller parties, regardless of their vote, receive zero representation. This is in contrast to a system of proportional representation that provides a party with legislative seats roughly in accordance with the percentage of votes it wins, assuring minor parties of some parliamentary presence. Duverger notes that under the winner-take-all system

> the party placed third or fourth is under-represented compared with the others: its percentage of seats is lower than its percentage of votes, and the disparity remains constantly greater than for its rivals. By its very definition proportional representation eliminates this disparity for all parties: the party that was at the greatest disadvantage before is the one to benefit most from the reform.[12]

The winner-take-all, single-member-district system not only deprives the minority parties of representation but eventually of voters too, since not many citizens wish to "waste" their ballots on a party that seems incapable of achieving legislative representation. Some political scientists argue that proportional representation is undesirable because it encourages the proliferation of "splinter parties" and leads to legislative stalemate and instability. In contrast, the present two-party system muffles rather than sharpens ideological differences and allows for the development of a consensus politics devoid of fragmentation and polarization. But one might question why the present forms of "stability" and "consensus" are to be treated as innate social virtues. Whose stability and whose consensus are we talking about? And one might wonder whether stalemate and fragmentation—with their consequent ill effects on the public interest—do not characterize the *present* political system in many important policy areas.

If, despite rigged rules and official harassments, radical groups continue to prove viable, then authorities are likely to resort to more violently coercive measures. Almost every radical group that

---

[12]Maurice Duverger, *Political Parties* (New York: Wiley and Sons, 1955), p. 248 and the discussion on pp. 245–255; also E. E. Schattschneider, *Party Government* (New York: Holt, Rinehart and Winston, 1960), pp. 74–84. Not long after World War II, Benjamin Davis, a Communist elected to the city council in New York, lost his seat when the city shifted from PR to single-member districts. The change was explicitly intended to get rid of Davis and limit the growth of other dissident parties. Proposals were introduced to abolish PR in local elections in Cambridge, Mass., in 1972 after victories by a few radically oriented candidates.

has ever managed to gain some grass-roots organizational strength, from the Populist movement in the last century to the Black Panther party of today, has become the object of official violence. The case of the American Socialist party is instructive. In 1919, after having increased its vote dramatically in various locales and having won control of some thirty-two municipal governments, the Socialists suffered the combined attacks of state, local and federal authorities. Their headquarters in numerous cities were sacked by police, their funds confiscated, their leaders jailed, their immigrant members deported, their newspapers denied mailing privileges and their elected candidates denied their seats in various state legislatures and in Congress. Within a few years, the party was finished as a viable political force. While confining themselves to legal and peaceful forms of political competition, the Socialists discovered that their opponents were burdened by no similar compunctions. The guiding principle of the establishment was (and still is): *when change threatens to rule, then the rules are changed.*

The weeding out of political deviants is carried on *within* as well as outside the major parties. It begins long before the election campaign and involves social forces that extend beyond the party system. First, the acceptable candidate must be born or educated into the middle or upper class, displaying the linguistic skills and social styles of a bourgeois personage. This requirement effectively limits the selection to business and professional people. Then he must express opinions of a kind that win the support of essentially conservative community leaders, party bosses and other established interests. Finally the aspiring candidate must have large sums of money of his own or access to those who do. As one Senator remarked: "The fundamental problem is that the ability to raise money starts the screening-out process. If you can't get the money, you don't get the nomination."[13] On election day, John Coleman reminds us, "the voters will have their choice between *two* such carefully chosen candidates. But the real election in which the candidates compete for the backing of business and of its representatives in the parties and the press, has already occurred."[14]

---

[13]Senator Mathias quoted in Richard Harris, "Annals of Politics: A Fundamental Hoax," *New Yorker*, August 7, 1971, p. 54.

[14]John Coleman, "Elections Under Capitalism, Part 2" *Workers' Power*, September 1–14, 1972, p. 11.

113

Money is not just one of many campaign resources; it is the life blood of electoral politics, helping to determine the availability of manpower, organization, tactical mobility and media visibility. Without money, the politician's days are numbered. Commenting on the plight of reformers in Congress, Representative Charles Vanik observed: "As things are now, the public-interest members here have no reward except personal satisfaction. In the long run most of them face defeat by the big-money people. Many of the best men who come here lose after one or two terms."[15]

The abortive attempt by Senator Fred Harris of Oklahoma to win the Democratic presidential nomination is instructive. Harris had been considered one of the more promising men in his party until, in the early stages of the 1972 primary campaign, he announced his intention to build a new coalition of working-class and underprivileged groups to wage a war against monopoly corporations. Within a short time Harris' campaign was without funds, and he withdrew from the race, being unable to pay his telephone bills and travel expenses. He noted that principal backers had become alienated by his anti-business stand. (One erstwhile donor had urged him to confine his attentions to such "safe" subjects as drug addiction and the Vietnam war.) The Senator concluded that this kind of financial control "explains why our Government is approaching such paralysis. For now it is very difficult to get American politicians, including many who are quite liberal, to advocate more than just *tinkering* with fundamental wrongs or simply adding a little more to existing New Deal-type programs."[16]

The man who became the Democratic presidential candidate in 1972, Senator George McGovern, found himself abandoned in the early stages of his campaign by wealthy liberal financiers who opposed his proposals for tax reform and income redistribution.[17] McGovern quickly retreated from these positions, placing an advertisement in the *Wall Street Journal* to assure its readers of his faith in the private-enterprise system. In subsequent speeches he informed businessmen that if he were elected, profits would "be bigger than they are now under the Nixon Administration."

[15]Quoted in Harris, "Annals of Politics," p. 59.
[16]Quoted in Erwin Knoll, "It's Only Money," *Progressive*, March 1972, pp. 25–26 (italics in the original).
[17]"McGovern's Views Alarm Big Donors on Wall Street," *New York Times*, July 3, 1972.

114

McGovern eventually did receive support from some wealthy donors, although hardly as much as Nixon.

The radical candidate faces far greater difficulties than do candidates like McGovern. Besides severe money problems, he or she must try to develop some kind of plausible image among a citizenry that has been conditioned for more than a century to hate and fear "anarchists," "socialists," "communists," "leftists," etc. He finds himself dependent for exposure on mass media that are owned by the conservative interests he is attacking. He sees that, along with the misrepresentations disseminated by a hostile press, the sheer paucity of information and haphazard reportage can make any meaningful campaign dialogue nearly impossible. The dissenter competes not only against well-financed opponents but against the media's many frivolous and stupefying distractions. Hoping to "educate the public to the issues," he discovers that the media allow little opportunity for the expositions needed to make his position comprehensible to those voters who might be willing to listen.

Dissenters who, in the face of all obstacles, decide to make the long march through the electoral process soon discover that it absorbs all their time, money and energy while leaving them no closer to the forces that make the important decisions of this society. Those few reformers who do win elections may subsequently find themselves redistricted out of existence, as happened during the 1970–1972 period in New York City to three of the more outspokenly liberal Democratic Congressmen and five of the more liberal Democratic state legislators. Once in office dissenters are often relegated to obscure legislative tasks and receive little cooperation from legislative leaders or bureaucratic agencies.

To achieve some effectiveness in an institution whose dominant· forces easily outflank him, the newly arrived representative frequently decides that "for now" he must make his peace with the powers that be, holding his fire until some future day when he can attack from higher ground. To get along he decides to go along; thus begins the insidious process that lets a person believe he is still opposing the ongoing arrangements when in fact he has become a functional part of them. There are less subtle instances of co-optation, as when reformers are bought off with promotions and favors by those who hold the key to their advancement. Once having won election, they may reverse their

115

stands on fundamental issues and make common cause with established powers, to the dismay of their supporters.

In sum, of the various functions a political party might serve—
(1) selecting candidates and waging election campaigns, (2) articulating and debating major issues, (3) formulating coherent and distinct programs, (4) implementing a national program when in office—our parties fulfill only the first with any devotion or success. The parties are loose conglomerations of local factions organized around one common purpose: to gain power. Issues come and go, but the party's *raison d'être* is the pursuit of office. For this reason, American parties have been characterized as "non-ideological." And indeed they are—in the sense that their profound ideological commitment to capitalism at home and abroad and to the ongoing class structure is seldom made an explicit issue. But even as they evade most important policy questions and refrain from commitment to distinct, coherent programs, the parties have a real conservative effect on the consciousness of the electorate and on the performance of representative government. They operate from a commonly shared ideological perspective which is best served by the avoidance of certain ideas and the suppression or co-optation of dissenters.

Democratic Competition: Does It Exist?

According to democratic theory, electoral competition keeps political leaders accountable to their constituents: politicians who wish to remain in office must respond to voter preferences in order to avoid being replaced by their rivals at the next election. This model presumes that the conditions of electoral competition actually exist. But as noted earlier, a host of political, legal and economic forces so limit the range of alternatives as to raise serious questions about the meaning of popular participation.

Furthermore, with so much of electoral politics reduced to an issueless publicity contest, the advantages go to the incumbent, he who has the financial support, legitimacy, exposure and other resources that come with public office, be he an ordinary Congressman or President of the United States.[18] Obviously, the man

[18]If the advantages of incumbency are great for the average member of Congress, they are all the greater for the President, especially in modern times when the presidency

who has won office already has built some kind of winning combination of money, organization and influence. But even if appointed as a replacement, he can use the resources of office to promote his own subsequent election, catering to the needs of important financial groups and performing favors that win him backing from special interests. He gets roads, irrigation projects, airports, bridges, harbors, post offices and various other government "pork barrel" projects for his home district, carries on a correspondence with thousands of voters, uses his official staff and mailing privileges for publicity purposes and enjoys an access to the local newspapers and radio and television stations that helps establish him as a "brand name." The most important and often most difficult task facing any candidate for public office is getting his name known to the voters, and here the incumbent has a usually decisive advantage over the challenger.

The trend in Congress over the last century has been for members to serve for longer and longer periods and to suffer fewer defeats by challengers. In the 1870s about 50 percent of the Representatives in each new Congress were newcomers; in 1970 the number had dropped to 12 percent.[19] From 1924 to 1956, 90 percent of the Congressmen who stood for reelection were victorious. In 1970, 94 percent of those seeking reelection to the House were returned by the voters. (Three percent were defeated in primaries, and 3 percent lost in the election.)[20]

Over the last two decades there has been a noticeable breakup of one-party regions: Republicans are now winning victories in Mississippi and Democrats get elected in Maine. Yet one-party dominance is still the rule in a good many locales throughout the rural Northeast, Midwest and South and in many cities. In 1970 one out of every ten Representatives was elected to Congress with *no opposition in either the primary or the general election.*

---

has become the object of mass attention and the repository of much popular sentiment. The only White House incumbents in the twentieth century who failed to be reelected were William Howard Taft in 1912, because the Republican party was split in two by Teddy Roosevelt's Bull Moose party, and Herbert Hoover, who was swept away by the Great Depression. Lyndon Johnson chose not to run in 1968, but it is not certain he would have lost in a reelection bid. His poll ratings in early 1968 were not much lower than Nixon's rating in early 1972, and the latter won a smashing victory the following November.

[19] Mark J. Green, James M. Fallows and David R. Zwick, *Who Runs Congress?* (New York: Bantam Books/Grossman, 1972), p. 229.

[20] See David Leuthold, *Electioneering in a Democracy* (New York: Wiley and Sons, 1968), p. 127. For the breakdown on the 1970 election I am indebted to Garrison Nelson.

In states like Vermont it is common for a majority of state and local officeholders to be elected to uncontested seats. One-party rule, considered the peculiar disease of "communist tyranny," is not an uncommon condition of American politics.

Death and voluntary retirement seem to be the important factors behind the turnover in representative assemblies. In this respect, legislative bodies bear a closer resemblance to the nonelective judiciary than we would imagine. One study of municipal governments found that upwards of half the city councilmen anticipated their own voluntary retirement after one term and about one fourth held nonelective appointments to fill unexpired terms. Many of the councilmen admitted that they paid little heed to constituent complaints. They entered and left office "not at the whim of the electorate, but according to self-defined schedules," a procession of like-minded men of similar social background.[21]

The prevalence of victorious incumbents is both a cause and an effect of low voter participation. As voters become increasingly discouraged about the possibility of affecting meaningful change through the ballot box, they are less likely to mobilize or respond to reformist electoral movements, thus increasing the unassailability of the incumbents. As the incumbents show themselves unbeatable, their would-be challengers become fewer in number and weaker in spirit. This is not an iron law of politics and the cycle has sometimes been dramatically reversed; but the reversals are usually the notable exceptions. The predominant situation is one of officeholders who are largely unresponsive to unorganized voters and voters who are often cynical and skeptical of office-holders.

Much has been written about the deficiencies of ordinary voters, their prejudices, lack of information and low civic involvement. More should be said about the deficiencies of the electoral representative system that serves them. It has long been presumed that since the present political system represents the best of all worlds, those who show an unwillingness to vote must be mani-

---

[21]Kenneth Prewitt, "Political Ambitions, Volunteerism, and Electoral Accountability," *American Political Science Review*, 64, March 1970, pp. 5–17; the quotation is from p. 10. Prewitt presents data on eighty-two municipal governments. The noncompetitive leadership selection he found at the local level exists to a lesser extent in the more visible and prestigious U.S. Congress, but as Prewitt points out, the more than 35,000 municipalities, towns and townships and the equal number of school boards have a cumulative impact that may be more important than the influence exercised by the Congress or any of its special committees.

festing some failing in themselves. Seldom is nonparticipation treated as a justifiable reaction to a politics that has become somewhat meaningless in its electoral content and disappointing in its policy results.

In the United States during the nineteenth century, the small-town democratic system "was quite adequate, both in partisan organization and dissemination of political information, to the task of mobilizing voters." according to Walter Dean Burnham.[22] But by the turn of the century most of the political means for making important decisions had been captured by powerful industrial elites. Business interests perfected the arts of pressure politics, wielding a heavy influence over state legislatures, party organizations, governors and congressmen. At the same time, the judiciary extended its property-serving controls over the national and state legislatures, imposing limitations on taxation powers and on regulatory efforts in the fields of commerce, industry and labor. "Confronted with a narrowed scope of effective democratic options an increasingly large proportion of the eligible adult population either left, failed to enter or—as was the case with the Southern Negro . . . was systematically excluded from the American voting universe."[23] Much of the blame for the diminishing popular participation, Burnham concludes, must rest with "the political system itself."

Nonvoting as a Rational Response

The percentage of nonvoters has climbed to impressive levels, running as high as 55 to 60 percent in congressional contests and 40 to 45 percent in recent presidential elections. In many local elections, voter participation is so low as to make it difficult to speak of "popular" representation in any real sense. Observing that in a municipality of 13,000 residents an average of 810 voters elected the city council, Prewitt comments:

> Such figures sharply question the validity of thinking that "mass electorates" hold elected officials accountable. For these councilmen, even if serving in relatively sizable cities, there are no "mass

[22]Walter Dean Burnham, "The Changing Shape of the American Political Universe," *American Political Science Review*, 59, March 1965, p. 22.
[23]*Ibid.*, p. 26.

electorates"; rather there are the councilman's business associates, his friends at church, his acquaintances in the Rotary Club, and so forth which provide him the electoral support he needs to gain office.[24]

The political significance of low participation becomes apparent when we consider that nonvoters are disproportionately concentrated among the rural poor, the urban slum dwellers, the welfare recipients, the underemployed, the young, the elderly, the low-income and nonunion workers and the racial minorities. The entire voting process is dominated by middle-class styles and conditions which tend to discourage lower-class participation.[25] Among the reasons poor Whites in one city gave for not voting were the humiliating treatment they had been subjected to by poll attendants in previous elections, the intimidating nature of voting machines, the belief that they were not entitled to vote because they had failed to pay their poll tax (a misapprehension encouraged by tax collectors and town clerks), the feeling that they lacked whatever measure of education, specialized information and ability gives one the right to participate in the electoral process, and the conviction that elections are a farce and all politicians are ultimately out to "line their own pockets."[26] Residency requirements and the registration of voters at obscure locations during the political off-season discriminate against the less informed and less established community elements, specifically the poor, the unemployed and transient laborers.[27]

Working long hours for low pay, deprived of the kind of services and material security that the well-to-do take for granted, made to feel personally incapable of acting effectively and living in fear of officialdom, those of lower-class background frequently are reluctant to vote or make political commitments of any kind. The entire social milieu of the poor militates against participation. As Kimball describes it:

[24]Kenneth Prewitt, "Political Ambitions, Volunteerism, and Electoral Accountability," p. 9.
[25]Penn Kimball, *The Disconnected* (New York: Columbia University Press, 1972); Guiseppe De Palma, *Apathy and Participation: Mass Politics in Western Societies* (New York: Free Press, 1970).
[26]Opinions reported by Democratic campaign workers in Burlington, Vt., in 1972. I am indebted to Cheryl Smalley for gathering the information.
[27]See Charles E. Merriam and Harold F. Gosnell, *Non-voting, Causes and Methods of Control* (Chicago: University of Chicago Press, 1924) pp. 78 ff.; and Kimball, *The Disconnected*, p. 15.

Tenements, rooming houses, and housing projects—the dormitories of the ghetto electorate—provide . . . a shifting, changing human environment instead of the social reinforcements that encourage political involvement in more stable neighborhoods. And the immediate struggle for subsistence drains the reservoirs of emotional energy available for the distant and complex realms of politics. . . . Elections come and go, and the life of poverty goes on pretty much as before, neither dramatically better nor dramatically worse. The posturing of candidates and the promises of parties are simply irrelevant to the daily grind of marginal existence.[28]

Nor is it unreasonable that lower-strata groups are skeptical that any one candidate can change things. Their suspicions might be summarized as follows: (1) the reform-minded candidate is still a politician and therefore is as deceptive as any other; (2) even if he is sincere, the reformer is eventually "bought off" by the powers that be; (3) even if he is not bought off, the reformer can do little against those who run things. The conviction that politics cannot deliver anything significant leaves many citizens unresponsive, even if not unsympathetic, toward those who promise meaningful changes through the ballot box.[29]

It has been argued that if nonvoters tend to be among the less informed, less educated and more apathetic, then it is just as well they do not exercise their franchise. Since they are not all that capable of making rational choices and are likely to be swayed by prejudice and demagogy, their activation would constitute a potential threat to our democratic system.[30] Behind this reasoning lurks the dubious presumption that the better-educated, upper-income people who vote are more rational, less compelled by narrowly defined self-interests, and less bound by racial, political and class prejudices that upper- and middle-class people (including social scientists) have of themselves. As Kimball reminds us:

The level of information of the most informed voters is not very high by objective standards. The influence of ethnic background, family upbringing, and party inheritance is enormous in comparison to the flow of political debate. The choices in a given situation

---

[28]Kimball, *The Disconnected*, p. 17.
[29]Michael Parenti, "Power and Pluralism: A View from the Bottom," p. 515; and Kimball, *The Disconnected*, pp. 61–62.
[30]A typical example of this kind of thinking is found in Seymour M. Lipset, *Political Man* (Garden City, N.Y.: Doubleday, 1960), pp. 215–219.

are rarely clearcut, and the decision to vote for particular candidates can be highly irrational, *even at the highest levels of education and experience.*[31]

Some writers argue that the low voter turnout in the United States is symptomatic of a "politics of happiness": people do not bother to participate because they are fairly content with the way things are going.[32] But the 40 to 50 million adult Americans outside the voting universe are not among the more contented but among the less affluent and more alienated, displaying an unusual concentration of socially deprived characteristics.[33] The "politics of happiness" may be nothing more than a cover for the politics of discouragement or what Lane describes as the "alienation syndrome": "I am the object not the subject of political life. . . . The government is not run in my interest; they do not care about me; in this sense it is not my government. . . ."[34] The nonparticipation of many people often represents a feeling of powerlessness, a conviction that it is useless to vote, petition or demonstrate, useless to invest precious time, energy and hope and risk insult, eviction, arrest, loss of job and police assault, useless to do anything because nothing changes and one is left only with an aggravated sense of affliction and impotence. For many ordinary citizens, nonparticipation is not the result of brutish contentment, apathy or lack of civic virtue but an understandable negative response to the political realties they experience.[35]

With that in mind, we might question those public-opinion surveys which report that underprivileged persons are more apathetic and less informed than better-educated, upper-income citizens.

[31]Kimball, *The Disconnected*, p. 63. Italics added. Occasionally there is an admission by the well-to-do that voting should be limited not to protect democracy but to protect themselves. A letter to the *New York Times* (December 6, 1971) offered these revealing words: "If . . . everybody voted, I'm afraid we'd be in for a gigantic upheaval of American society—and we comfortable readers of the Times would certainly stand to lose much at the hands of the poor, faceless, previously quiet throngs. Wouldn't it be best to let sleeping dogs lie?"

[32]Heinz Eulau, "The Politics of Happiness," *Antioch Review*, 16, 1956, pp. 259–264; Lipset, *Political Man*, pp. 179–219.

[33]Burnham, "The Changing Shape of the American Political Universe," p. 27; and Kimball, *The Disconnected*.

[34]Robert Lane, *Political Ideology* (New York: Free Press, 1962), p. 162.

[35]A similar conclusion can be drawn from Studs Terkel, *Division Street: America* (New York: Pantheon, 1967); Kimball, *The Disconnected*; Levin, *The Alienated Voter*; Harold V. Savitch, "Powerlessness in an Urban Ghetto: The Case of Political Biases and Differential Access in New York City," *Polity*, 5, Fall 1972, pp. 17–56; Parenti, "Power and Pluralism"; Lewis Lipsitz, "On Political Belief: The Grievances of the Poor," in Philip Green and Sanford Levinson (eds.), *Power and Community* (New York: Pantheon, 1969), pp. 142–172.

If by *apathy* we mean the absence of affect and awareness, then the poor, the elderly, the young, the racial minorities and the industrial workers who have repeatedly voiced their outrage and opposition to various social conditions can hardly be described as "apathetic." Apathy should not be confused with antipathy and alienation. Nor is it clear that these dissident groups are "less informed." What impresses the investigators who actually take the trouble to talk to low-income people is the extent to which they have a rather precise notion of what afflicts them. Certainly they have a better sense of the difficulties that beset their lives than the many middle-class officials who frequently do not even recognize the reality or legitimacy of their complaints.[36]

Voting as an Irrational Response

Civic leaders, educators and opinion-makers usually characterize nonvoters as "slackers" and seldom as people who might be justifiably cynical about the electoral system. Conversely, they portray voters as conscientious citizens performing their civic responsibilities. Certainly many voters seem to agree, especially those who report that they vote primarily because of a "sense of citizenship duty"; often they believe their vote makes no difference and have little regard for the outcome of the election. Thus in the 1956 presidential campaign, 58 percent of those who described themselves as "not much interested" in the campaign voted anyway. Fifty-two percent of those who "didn't care at all" about who won the election voted. Only 13 percent of those with a "low sense of citizenship duty" voted, while 85 percent who had a "high" sense voted. The crucial variable in predicting turnout was "sense of citizenship duty" and not interest in substantive issues.[37] For many citizens, then, the vote seems to be more an exercise of civic virtue than civic power. This raises the interesting question of who really is the "deadwood" of democracy: the "apathetic" or the "civic minded," those who see no reason to vote or those who vote with no reason?

There are, of course, other inducements to voting besides a sense of civic obligation. The tendency to vote for the lesser, or

---

[36]See the citations in the previous footnote.
[37]Angus Campbell et al., *The American Voter* (New York: Wiley and Sons, 1960), pp. 103–106.

lesser known, of two evils has already been noted. Once it is presumed that there are significant differences between the parties, the location of undesirable traits in one party suggests the relative absence of these traits in the other and sometimes becomes enough reason for partisan choice. Thus, the suspicion that Democrats might favor Blacks and hippies leads some middle-class Whites to assume that the Republican party is devoted to their interests, a conclusion that may have no basis in the actual performance of Republican officeholders. Similarly, the identification of Republicans as "the party of big business" suggests to some working-class voters that, in contrast, the Democrats are *not* for business but for the "little man," a conclusion that may be equally unfounded. Not unlike the masks worn by players in Greek drama, the party label gives distinct identities to otherwise indistiguishable and often undistinguished political actors, identifying some as villains and others as heroes. By acting as instigators of partisan spirit and partisan anxiety, the parties encourage participation, stabilize electoral loyalties and build reservoirs of trust and mistrust that survive the performances of particular candidates.

Some people vote because it is "the only thing the ordinary person can do."[38] Not to exercise one's franchise is to cosign one-self to *total* political impotence, an uncomfortable condition for those who have been taught that they are self-governing. An awareness that there are men in exalted positions who exercise fateful power over ordinary people makes it all the more imperative for some citizens to feel that they exercise a control over their leaders. The need to *feel* effective can lead to the mistaken notion that one *is* effective. A faith in the efficacy of voting also allows one to avoid the risks of more unconventional actions and attitudes.

Voting not only induces a feeling of efficacy, it often results from such a feeling. Studies show that persons with a high sense of political efficacy are more likely to vote than those with a low sense. High efficacy is related to a citizen's educational and class level: better-educated people of comfortable income who feel most efficacious in general also tend to feel more politically efficacious than lower-income persons.[39] But while many studies

[38]See Lane, *Political Ideology,* p. 166: Gabriel Almond and Sidney Verba, *The Civic Culture* (Boston: Little, Brown, 1963), p. 131.
[39]See Robert R. Alford and Harry M. Scoble, "Sources of Local Political Involvement," *American Political Science Review,* 62, December 1968, pp. 1192–1206.

relate sense of political efficacy to voting, there is almost nothing relating sense of political efficacy to actual efficacy. In fact there may be little relationship between the two.[40]

The argument is sometimes made that if certain deprived groups have been unable to win their demands from the political system, it is because they are numerically weak compared to White middle-class America. In a system that responds to the democratic power of numbers, a minority poor, for instance, cannot hope to have its way. The representative principle works well enough, but the poor are not strong enough nor numerous enough. Therefore, the deficiency is in the limited numbers of persons advocating change and not in the representative system, which in fact operates according to majoritarian principles. What is curious about this argument is that it is never applied to more select minority interests—for instance, oilmen. Now oilmen are far less numerous than the poor, yet the deficiency of their numbers, or of the numbers of other tiny minorities like bankers, industrialists and millionaire investors, does not result in any lack of government responsiveness to their wants. On many—probably most—important matters the government's policy is determined less by the majoritarian principle and more by the economic strength of policy advocates and the strategic positions they occupy in the wider social structure. The fact that government does little for the minority poor, does not mean that government is devoted to the interests of the great bulk of belabored "middle Americans" nor that it operates according to majoritarian principles.

[40]See Alan Wertheimer, "In Defense of Compulsory Voting" (unpublished monograph, University of Vermont, 1972).

JOE McGINNISS

Honoring the Illusion

At least since the 1952 campaign, when Adlai Stevenson charged
that advertising agencies were trying to merchandise presidential
candidates "like boxes of breakfast food," attention has been focused
on the role of the image makers in the political process. That role
has expanded dramatically. Electioneering has developed into a major
growth industry with the direction of campaigns being turned over
to professional management firms using sophisticated research and
marketing techniques. The amount of money spent in pursuit of the
presidency has doubled every four years. In 1972 it was more than
two hundred million dollars (the figure rises past the one-billion-dollar
mark when the cost of all other campaigns for public office is included), a large part of it going to television. As a campaigning tool,
the medium reigns supreme. But what of the message? In the following selection, journalist Joe McGinniss suggests that at the same
time it is performing cosmetic surgery on the candidate's public
image, television also alters the basic issues of an election.

Politics, in a sense, has always been a con game.

The American voter, insisting upon his belief in a higher order,
clings to his religion, which promises another, better life; and
defends passionately the illusion that the men he chooses to lead
him are of finer nature than he.

It has been traditional that the successful politician honor this
illusion. To succeed today, he must embellish it. Particularly if he
wants to be President.

"Potential presidents are measured against an ideal that's a
combination of leading man, God, father, hero, pope, king, with
maybe just a touch of the avenging Furies thrown in," an adviser

"Honoring the Illusion" (Originally Chapter 2). From *The Selling of the President 1968*
by Joe McGinniss. Copyright © 1969, by Joemac, Incorporated. Reprinted by permission
of Simon & Schuster, Inc., Trident Press Division.

to Richard Nixon wrote in a memorandum late in 1967. Then, perhaps aware that Nixon qualified only as father, he discussed improvements that would have to be made—not upon Nixon himself, but upon the image of him which was received by the voter.

. . .

It is not surprising then, that politicians and advertising men should have discovered one another. And, once they recognized that the citizen did not so much vote for a candidate as make a psychological purchase of him, not surprising that they began to work together.

The voter, as reluctant to face political reality as any other kind, was hardly an unwilling victim. "The deeper problems connected with advertising," Daniel Boorstin has written in *The Image,*

> come less from the unscrupulousness of our "deceivers" than from our pleasure in being deceived, less from the desire to seduce than from the desire to be seduced. . . .
>
> In the last half-century we have misled ourselves . . . about men . . . and how much greatness can be found among them. . . . We have become so accustomed to our illusions that we mistake them for reality. We demand them. And we demand that there be always more of them, bigger and better and more vivid.

The Presidency seems the ultimate extension of our error.

Advertising agencies have tried openly to sell Presidents since 1952. When Dwight Eisenhower ran for re-election in 1956, the agency of Batton, Barton, Durstine and Osborn, which had been on a retainer throughout his first four years, accepted his campaign as a regular account. Leonard Hall, national Republican chairman, said: "You sell your candidates and your programs the way a business sells its products."

The only change over the past twelve years has been that, as technical sophistication has increased, so has circumspection. The ad men were removed from the parlor but were given a suite upstairs.

What Boorstin says of advertising: "It has meant a reshaping of our very concept of truth," is particularly true of advertising on TV.

With the coming of television, and the knowledge of how it could be used to seduce voters, the old political values disappeared. Something new, murky, undefined started to rise from the mists. "In all countries," Marshall McLuhan writes, "the party system has folded like the organization chart. Policies and issues are useless for election purposes, since they are too specialized and hot. The shaping of a candidate's integral image has taken the place of discussing conflicting points of view."

Americans have never quite digested television. The mystique which should fade grows stronger. We make celebrities not only of the men who cause events but of the men who read reports of them aloud.

The televised image can become as real to the housewife as her husband, and much more attractive. Hugh Downs is a better breakfast companion, Merv Griffin cozier to snuggle with on the couch.

Television, in fact, has given status to the "celebrity" which few real men attain. And the "celebrity" here is the one described by Boorstin: "Neither good nor bad, great nor petty . . . the human pseudo-event . . . fabricated on purpose to satisfy our exaggerated expectations of human greatness."

This is, perhaps, where the twentieth century and its pursuit of illusion have been leading us. "In the last half-century," Boorstin writes,

> the old heroic human mold has been broken. A new mold has been made, so that marketable human models—modern "heroes"—could be mass-produced, to satisfy the market, and without any hitches. The qualities which now commonly make a man or woman into a "nationally advertised" brand are in fact a new category of human emptiness.

The television celebrity is a vessel. An inoffensive container in which someone else's knowledge, insight, compassion, or wit can be presented. And we respond like the child on Christmas morning who ignores the gift to play with the wrapping paper.

Television seems particularly useful to the politician who can be charming but lacks ideas. Print is for ideas. Newspapermen write not about people but policies; the paragraphs can be slid around like blocks. Everyone is colored gray. Columnists—and commentators in the more polysyllabic magazines—concentrate on ideology. They do not care what a man sounds like; only how he thinks. For the candidate who does not, such exposure can be embarassing. He needs another way to reach the people.

On television it matters less that he does not have ideas. His personality is what the viewers want to share. He need be neither statesman nor crusader; he must only show up on time. Success and failure are easily measured: how often is he invited back? Often enough and he reaches his goal—to advance from "politician" to "celebrity," a status jump bestowed by grateful viewers who feel that finally they have been given the basis for making a choice.

The TV candidate, then, is measured not against his predecessors—not against a standard of performance established by two centuries of democracy—but against Mike Douglas. How well does he handle himself? Does he mumble, does he twitch, does he make me laugh? Do I feel warm inside?

Style becomes substance. The medium is the massage and the masseur gets the votes.

In office, too, the ability to project electronically is essential. We were willing to forgive John Kennedy his Bay of Pigs; we followed without question the perilous course on which he led us when missiles were found in Cuba; we even tolerated his calling of reserves for the sake of a bluff about Berlin.

We forgave, followed, and accepted because we liked the way he looked. And he had a pretty wife. Camelot was fun, even for the peasants, as long as it was televised to their huts.

Then came Lyndon Johnson, heavy and gross, and he was forgiven nothing. He might have survived the sniping of the displaced intellectuals had he only been able to charm. But no one taught him how. Johnson was syrupy. He stuck to the lens. There was no place for him in our culture.

"The success of any TV performer depends on his achieving a low-pressure style of presentation," McLuhan has written. The harder a man tries, the better he must hide it. Television demands gentle wit, irony, understatement: the qualities of Eugene McCarthy. The TV politician cannot make a speech; he must engage in intimate conversation. He must never press. He should suggest, not state; request, not demand. Nonchalance is the key word. Carefully studied nonchalance.

Warmth and sincerity are desirable but must be handled with care. Unfiltered, they can be fatal. Television did great harm to Hubert Humphrey. His excesses—talking too long and too fervently, which were merely annoying in an auditorium—became lethal in a television studio. The performer must talk to one person at a time. He is brought into the living room. He is a guest. It is improper for him to shout. Humphrey vomited on the rug.

It would be extremely unwise for the TV politician to admit such knowledge of his medium. The necessary nonchalance should carry beyond his appearance while *on* the show; it should rule his attitude *toward* it. He should express distaste for television; suspicion that there is something "phony" about it. This guarantees him good press, because newspaper reporters, bitter over their loss of prestige to the television men, are certain to stress anti-television remarks. Thus, the sophisticated candidate, while analyzing his own on-the-air technique as carefully as a golf pro studies his swing, will state frequently that there is no place for "public relations gimmicks" or "those show business guys" in his campaign. Most of the television men working for him will be unbothered by such remarks. They are willing to accept anonymity, even scorn, as long as the pay is good.

Into this milieu came Richard Nixon: grumpy, cold, and aloof. He would claim privately that he lost elections because the American voter was an adolescent whom he tried to treat as an adult. Perhaps. But if he treated the voter as an adult, it was as an adult he did not want for a neighbor.

This might have been excused had he been a man of genuine vision. An explorer of the spirit. Martin Luther King, for instance, got by without being one of the boys. But Richard Nixon did not strike people that way. He had, in Richard Rovere's words, "an advertising man's approach to his work," acting as if he believed "policies [were] products to be sold the public—this one today, that one tomorrow, depending on the discounts and the state of the market."

So his enemies had him on two counts: his personality, and the convictions—or lack of such—which lay behind. They worked him over heavily on both.

Norman Mailer remembered him as "a church usher, of the variety who would twist a boy's ear after removing him from church."

McLuhan watched him debate Kennedy and thought he resembled "the railway lawyer who signs leases that are not in the best interests of the folks in the little town."

But Nixon survived, despite his flaws, because he was tough and smart, and—some said—dirty when he had to be. Also, because there was nothing else he knew. A man to whom politics is all there is in life will almost always beat one to whom it is only an occupation.

He nearly became President in 1960, and that year it would not have been by default. He failed because he was too few of the things a President had to be—and, because he had no press to lie for him and did not know how to use television to lie about himself.

It was just Nixon and John Kennedy and they sat down together in a television studio and a little red light began to glow and Richard Nixon was finished. Television would be blamed but for all the wrong reasons.

They would say it was makeup and lighting, but Nixon's problem went deeper than that. His problem was himself. Not what he said but the man he was. The camera portrayed him clearly. America took its Richard Nixon straight and did not like the taste.

The content of the programs made little difference. Except for startling lapses, content seldom does. What mattered was the image the viewers received, though few observers at the time caught the point.

McLuhan read Theodore White's *The Making of The President* book and was appalled at the section on the debates.

> White offers statistics on the number of sets in American homes and the number of hours of daily use of these sets, but not one clue as to the nature of the TV image or its effects on candidates or viewers. White considers the "content" of the debates and the deportment of the debaters, but it never occurs to him to ask why TV would inevitably be a disaster for a sharp intense image like Nixon's and a boon for the blurry, shaggy texture of Kennedy.

In McLuhan's opinion: "Without TV, Nixon had it made."

What the camera showed was Richard Nixon's hunger. He lost, and bitter, confused, he blamed it on his beard.

He made another, lesser thrust in 1962, and that failed, too. He showed the world a little piece of his heart the morning after and then he moved East to brood. They did not want him, the hell with them. He was going to Wall Street and get rich.

He was afraid of television. He knew his soul was hard to find. Beyond that, he considered it a gimmick; its use in politics offended him. It had not been part of the game when he had learned

131

to play, he could see no reason to bring it in now. He half suspected it was an eastern liberal trick: one more way to make him
look silly. It offended his sense of dignity, one of the truest senses
he had.

So his decision to use it to become President in 1968 was not
easy. So much of him argued against it. But in his Wall Street
years, Richard Nixon had traveled to the darkest places inside
himself and come back numbed. He was, as in the Graham Greene
title, a burnt-out case. All feeling was behind him; the machine
inside had proved his hardiest part. He would run for President
again and if he would have to learn television to run well, then
he would learn it.

America still saw him as the 1960 Nixon. If he were to come
at the people again, as candidate, it would have to be as something
new; not this scarred, discarded figure from their past.

He spoke to men who thought him mellowed. They detected
growth, a new stability, a sense of direction that had been lacking.
He would return with fresh perspective, a more unselfish urgency.

His problem was how to let the nation know. He could not
do it through the press. He knew what to expect from them, which
was the same as he had always gotten. He would have to circum-
vent them. Distract them with coffee and doughnuts and smiles
from his staff and tell his story another way.

Television was the only answer, despite its sins against him
in the past. But not just any kind of television. An uncommitted
camera could do irreparable harm. His television would have to
be controlled. He would need experts. They would have to find
the proper settings for him, or if they could not be found, manu-
facture them. These would have to be men of keen judgment
and flawless taste. He was, after all, Richard Nixon, and there
were certain things he could not do. Wearing love beads was one.
He would need men of dignity. Who believed in him and shared
his vision. But more importantly, men who knew television as
a weapon: from broadest concept to most technical detail. This
would be Richard Nixon, the leader, returning from exile. Perhaps
not beloved, but respected. Firm but not harsh; just but compas-
sionate. With flashes of warmth spaced evenly throughout.

Nixon gathered about himself a group of young men attuned
to the political uses of television. They arrived at his side by different routes. One, William Gavin, was a thirty-one-year-old English teacher in a suburban high school outside Philadelphia in
1967, when he wrote Richard Nixon a letter urging him to run

for President and base his campaign on TV. Gavin wrote on stationery borrowed from the University of Pennsylvania because he thought Nixon would pay more attention if the letter seemed to be from a college professor.

Dear Mr. Nixon:

May I offer two suggestions concerning your plans for 1968?

1. Run. You can win. Nothing can happen to you, politically speaking, that is worse than what has happened to you. Ortega y Gassett in his *The Revolt of the Masses* says: "These ideas are the only genuine ideas; the ideas of the shipwrecked. All the rest is rhetoric, posturing, farce. He who does not really feel himself lost, is lost without remission. . . ." You, in effect, are "lost"; that is why you are the only political figure with the vision to see things the way they are and not as Leftist or Rightist kooks would have them be. Run. You will win.

2. A tip for television: instead of those wooden performances beloved by politicians, instead of a glamorboy technique, instead of safety, be bold. Why not have live press conferences as your campaign on television? People will see you daring all, asking and answering questions from reporters, and not simply answering phony "questions" made up by your staff. This would be dynamic; it would be daring. Instead of the medium using you, you would be using the medium. Go on "live" and risk it all. It is the only way to convince people of the truth: that you are beyond rhetoric, that you can face reality, unlike your opponents, who will rely on public relations. Television hurt you because you were not yourself; it didn't hurt the "real" Nixon. The real Nixon can revolutionize the use of television by dynamically going "live" and answering everything, the loaded and unloaded question. Invite your opponents to this kind of a debate.

Good luck, and I know you can win if you see yourself for what you are; a man who had been beaten, humiliated, hated, but who can still see the truth.

A Nixon staff member had lunch with Gavin a couple of times after the letter was received and hired him. Gavin began churning out long, stream-of-consciousness memos which dealt mostly with the importance of image, and ways in which Richard Nixon, through television, could acquire a good one.

"Voters are basically lazy, basically uninterested in making an *effort* to understand what we're talking about . . . ," Gavin wrote.

Reason requires a high degree of discipline, of concentration; impression is easier. Reason pushes the viewer back, it assaults him, it demands that he agree or disagree; impression can envelop him, invite him in, without making an intellectual demand. . . . When we argue with him we demand that he make the effort of replying. We seek to engage his intellect, and for most people this is the most difficult work of all. The emotions are more easily roused, closer to the surface, more malleable.

So, for the New Hampshire primary, Gavin recommended

saturation with a film, in which the candidate can be shown better than he can be shown in person because it can be edited, so only the best moments are shown; then a quick parading of the candidate in the flesh so that the guy they've gotten intimately acquainted with on the screen takes on a living presence—not saying anything, just being seen. . . .

[Nixon] has to come across as a person larger than life, the stuff of legend. People are stirred by the legend, including the living legend, not by the man himself. It's the aura that surrounds the charismatic figure more than it is the figure itself, that draws the followers. Our task is to build that aura. . . .

So let's not be afraid of television gimmicks . . . get the voters to like the guy and the battle's two-thirds won.

William Gavin was brought to the White House as a speech writer in January of 1969.

Harry Treleaven, hired as creative director of advertising in the fall of 1967, immediately went to work on the more serious of Nixon's personality problems. One was his lack of humor.

"Can be corrected to a degree," Treleaven wrote, "but let's not be too obvious about it. Romney's cornball attempts have hurt him. If we're going to be witty, let a pro write the words."

Treleaven also worried about Nixon's lack of warmth, but decided that

he can be helped greatly in this respect by how he is handled. . . . Give him words to say that will show his *emotional* involvement in the issues. . . . Buchanan wrote about RFK talking about the starving children in Recife. *That's* what we have to inject. . . .

He should be presented in some kind of "situation" rather than cold in a studio. The situation should look unstaged even if it's not.

Some of the most effective ideas belonged to Raymond K. Price, a former editorial writer for the *New York Herald Tribune*, who became Nixon's best and most prominent speech writer in the campaign. Price later composed much of the inaugural address.

In 1967, he began with the assumption that, "The natural human use of reason is to support prejudice, not to arrive at opinions." Which led to the conclusion that rational arguments would "only be effective if we can get the people to make the *emotional* leap, or what theologians call [the] 'leap of faith.'"

Price suggested attacking the "personal factors" rather than the "historical factors" which were the basis of the low opinion so many people had of Richard Nixon.

"These tend to be more a gut reaction," Price wrote,

> unarticulated, non-analytical, a product of the particular chemistry between the voter and the *image* of the candidate. *We have to be very clear on this point: that the response is to the image, not to the man.* . . . It's not what's *there* that counts, it's what's project- ed and carrying it one step further, it's not what *he* projects but rather what the voter receives. It's not the man we have to change, but rather the *received impression.* And this impression often de- pends more on the medium and its use than it does on the can- didate himself.

So there would not have to be a "new Nixon." Simply a new approach to television.

"What, then, does this mean in terms of our uses of time and of media?" Price wrote.

"For one thing, it means investing whatever time RN needs in order to work out firmly in his own mind that vision of the nation's future that he wants to be identified with. This is crucial. . . ."

So, at the age of fifty-four, after twenty years in public life, Richard Nixon was still felt *by his own staff* to be in need of time to "work out firmly in his own mind that vision of the nation's future that he wants to be identified with."

"Secondly," Price wrote,

> it suggests that we take the time and the money to experiment, in a controlled manner, with film and television techniques, with particular emphasis on pinpointing those *controlled* uses of the television medium that can *best* convey the *image* we want to get across. . . .
>
> The TV medium itself introduces an element of distortion, in terms of its effect on the candidate and of the often subliminal

ways in which the image is received. And it inevitably is going to convey a partial image—thus ours is the task of finding how to control its use so the part that gets across is the part we want to have gotten across.

So this was how they went into it. Trying, with one hand, to build the illusion that Richard Nixon, in addition to his attributes of mind and heart, considered, in the words of Patrick K. Buchanan, a speech writer, "communicating with the people . . . one of the great joys of seeking the Presidency"; while with the other they shielded him, controlled him, and controlled the atmosphere around him. It was as if they were building not a President but an Astrodome, where the wind would never blow, the temperature never rise or fall, and the ball never bounce erratically on the artificial grass.

They could do this, and succeed, because of the special nature of the man. There was, apparently, something in Richard Nixon's character which sought this shelter. Something which craved regulation, which flourished best in the darkness, behind clichés, behind phalanxes of antiseptic advisers. Some part of him that could breathe freely only inside a hotel suite that cost a hundred dollars a day.

And it worked. As he moved serenely through his primary campaign, there was new cadence to Richard Nixon's speech and motion; new confidence in his heart. And, a new image of him on the television screen.

TV both reflected and contributed to his strength. Because he was winning he looked like a winner on the screen. Because he was suddenly projecting well on the medium he had feared, he went about his other tasks with assurance. The one fed upon the other, building to an astonishing peak in August as the Republican convention began and he emerged from his regal isolation, traveling to Miami not so much to be nominated as coronated. On live, but controlled, TV.

LEO BOGART

On Predicting Elections

President Lyndon Johnson once jokingly told an audience that Patrick Henry had conducted a poll before making his "Give me liberty or give me death" speech and that the results had been 46 percent for liberty, 29 percent for death, and the rest undecided. Actually, LBJ, like other politicians, was extraordinarily sensitive to polls and often kept copies of the latest Gallup and Harris surveys in his pocket. The public these polls measured—increasingly opposed to his administration's war policies—had a significant impact on Johnson's decision not to seek reelection.

It has become increasingly difficult to tell where the measurement of public opinion leaves off and the molding of it begins. Along with television, computers, and the other electoral weaponry in the arsenal of political management firms, polls have come to play a central role in America's political life. Pinpointed polls of key precints allow television networks to declare winners before the last votes are cast on election day, while carefully constructed public opinion surveys are increasingly being used by campaign managers to discover what a candidate *should* say. Of this development, one prominent California pollster recently admitted,

> In the world of 1984, voters . . . will first be polled as to what type of candidate they want, even on physical and personal characteristics. The information will be fed into a computer, and the candidates most closely reflecting the voters' choice will be selected to run for office. . . . In the Presidential race, the government will sample the nation to find 1,000 voters and they will make the final selection.

In the following selection, public opinion expert Leo Bogart discusses polls and candidates.

It's like trying to measure a gaseous body with a rubber band.　　　　PAUL CHERRINGTON

Polling is associated in most people's minds with the prediction of election results.[1] It is at election time that polls become a dominant subject in the popular culture—a favorite butt of newspaper cartoonists and television comedians. Yet for all their acceptance as part of the American scene, and for all the general recognition of their power, polls remain for many people a suspect form of activity—for some an occult and perhaps sinister art, for others a hoax that requires restriction.

The fundamental principle of statistical sampling, the basis of polling, seems to be hard for many people to understand. Indeed, 45 percent of the public (in Minnesota, at least) does not think a survey based on 2000 interviews can be accurate. But since this information itself comes from a survey, and since only a comparative handful of the public refuses to answer pollsters' questions, it is evident that most of the skeptics are still willing to accept polls as part of the current political scene.

Many of the limitations of opinion research do not apply to election surveys. The interviewer soliciting a choice of candidates is indeed provoking a meaningful answer; the respondent must choose, much as he would in the voting booth. Preelection polls are closer to consumer studies than are most kinds of opinion surveys. Voting intentions and brand preferences alike represent opinions that are directly linked to actions. Hence they reflect a different order of phenomena than opinions on matters of state, on which the decisions are understood to be in more powerful hands. A market researcher may ask about brand preference, but he usually also goes on to find out from the record of past purchases whether or not the respondent is a likely prospect for the product. By the same token, since 1948 it has been accepted that it is not enough in political polls to determine which candidate the people favor; their past voting record is also needed to assess the likelihood that they will act on their preferences on Election Day. Voting intentions, like brand preferences, may change, but votes, like purchases, are irrevocable.

---

[1]No attempt has been made to review here the extensive research literature on voting behavior. Among the classic studies are Paul F. Lazarsfeld, Bernard Berelson, and Hazel Gaudet, *The People's Choice*, Duell Sloan and Pearce, New York, 1944; Bernard Berelson, Paul F. Lazarsfeld, and William N. McPhee, *Voting*, University of Chicago Press, Chicago, 1954; Angus Campbell, Gerald Gurin, and Warren E. Miller, *The Voter Decides*, Row, Peterson, Evanston, Ill., 1954; Angus Campbell, Philip E. Converse, Warren E. Miller, and Donald E. Stokes, *The American Voter*, Wiley, New York, 1960.

Formal training as a statistician is not a prerequisite for successful performance as an election pollster. Among those who have taken on the augur's mantle are a roach and rodent exterminator in Portland, Oregon, and a Kansas City miller. The miller, in 1948, allowed his customers to select chicken feed decorated with either a donkey or an elephant. He discontinued his "poll" because the Democratic majority (54 percent) ran contrary to the national expectations based on the results of scientific election surveys.

The failure of the 1948 polls was the occasion for intensive self-appraisal on the part of the public opinion research profession.[2] It brought about two major changes in technique: (1) a shift from the less accurate method of "quota" sampling (which gave wide latitude of choice to the interviewer in deciding whom to question) to "probability" sampling (in which interviewers received explicit instructions in order to yield a representative cross section of the public) and (2) a continuation of polling until almost the very eve of the election, in order to take into account the possibility of a last-minute shift in preference (such as seems to have occured in the case of President Truman).[3]

A week before the election, on October 26, 1948, Truman evoked the ghostly memory of the *Literary Digest:*

> In 1936 the Republicans had a poll that told them they had a sure thing. And they did. They met a sure defeat in 1936. . . . These polls that the Republican candidate is putting out are like sleeping pills designed to lull the voter into sleeping on Election Day. You might call them sleeping polls. . . . An overdose could be fatal—can so affect your mind that your body will be too lazy to go to the polls on Election Day. . . . These Republican polls are no accident.

[2]Fred Mosteller, Herbert Hyman, Philip J. McCarthy, Eli S. Marks, and David B. Truman, *The Pre-Election Polls of 1948: Report to the Committee on Analysis of Pre-Election Polls and Forecasts,* Social Science Research Council, New York, 1949. For a topical critique of polls see also Lindsay Rogers, *The Pollsters,* Knopf, New York, 1949.

[3]In January of 1948, long before the election, Gallup found Truman leading Dewey, 49 to 44 percent. But by April, Truman had dropped to 42 percent while Dewey's share had risen to 52 percent. The gap remained at this level or greater until early October, by which time Dewey had dropped to 50 percent and Truman had risen back up to 45 percent. In the popular vote those proportions were exactly reversed, but the pollsters had stopped their surveys by the middle of October. Dramatic swings in voter sentiment can occur in a short period of time as an election campaign reaches its climax. A series of local polls made by Dorothy Corey before the Los Angeles mayoralty election of 1969 found the incumbent's support in one Councilmanic district going from 35 percent on April 12 to 73 percent on May 27 and in another district from 37 to 56 percent.

They are part of a design to prevent a big vote, to keep you at home on November 2 by convincing you that it makes no difference whether you vote or not.[4]

Truman's charges found an echo on election day, 1968, when *Pravda* alleged that the American polls were made to "influence voters. It is as if they are saying to the voter: 'Why are you suffering from doubts when the election has been predetermined?' "

Although allegations of collusion may be dismissed as propaganda or as campaign oratory, it is unquestionably true that pre-election surveys are no longer used merely as a way of informing the public on the latest state of the race, but as a means of influencing the outcome. This is done in several ways:

1. They provide candidates for office with intelligence about where they are strong and where they are weak.
2. They offer guidelines as to what candidates should and shouldn't say to win voter approval.
3. More questionable use of preelection research is the carefully timed, last-minute release of polls to influence convention delegates with demonstrations that Candidate X couldn't possibly win, whereas Candidate Y might.
4. A less guileful but more important effect of polls as an influence on elections comes about when they create the impression that the outcome is a sure thing three or four months before the election itself. What this does to demoralize party workers and to drive away potential contributors to party funds represents a firm example of self-fulfilling prophecy.

If there is reason for concern over the role of preelection surveys, it should not be about their accuracy as a measurement of opinion at the time they are taken, but about the greater question of whether polls that are taken today are in any sense a reliable predictor of the future.

In Britain, the United States pollsters' debacle of 1948 was repeated in the election of June 1970 which unseated Harold Wilson's Labor government in spite of the predictions of four out

[4]In spite of his public expressions of disdain for polls, Harry Truman, while President, commissioned one from Dun & Bradstreet to measure available coal stocks when he was faced with a strike threat from labor leader John L. Lewis.

of the five national polls. The pollsters blamed the low turnout and a last-minute trend to the Conservatives in the few days after their final surveys. Pollster Mark Abrams' post mortem concluded that the biggest factor was abstention from voting.[5] Another after-the-fact analysis demonstrated that polls with impeccably correct samples could still produce the wrong results in a simulated election.[6]

Whatever the excuses, Wilson noted glumly that the pollsters "have not distinguished themselves." This lack of distinction was particularly galling for him because the timing of the election itself, well before the expiration of the normal five-year parliamentary term, was set by the Labor Party's political analysts on the basis of earlier polls which showed a steady upswing in the Prime Minister's popularity.

Predicting election returns from polls is hazardous because of the difficulty of determining who will cast a ballot on Election Day.[7] (One of the reasons for the failure of the 1936 *Literary Digest* poll was that 6 million more voters cast ballots that year than in 1932.) In the 1960 election, one-fourth of the people who in August told the Opinion Research Corporation that they did not intend to vote reported later that they actually did vote, most of them for Kennedy.[8]

In 1968, 60 percent of the 120,000,000 Americans of voting age (or about 80 percent of the registered voters) voted. (This compares with 62 percent of the eligible voters in 1964 and 64 percent in 1960.) Since 1948, the polling organizations have become more and more sophisticated in their ability to screen out probable nonvoters by asking questions on the respondent's certainty in

---

[5]Mark Abrams, "The Opinion Polls and the 1970 British General Election," *Public Opinion Quarterly*, Vol. 34, No. 3, Fall 1970, pp. 317–324.

[6]Richard Rose, ed., *Polls and the 1970 Election*, University of Strathclyde, Strathclyde, 1970.

[7]For an authoritative description of voter behavior see V. O. Key, Jr., *The Responsible Electorate: Rationality in Presidential Voting, 1936–60*, Belknap Press, Cambridge, 1966.

[8]A 1964 survey by the Census Bureau showed that 76.6 million of the 110.6 million eligible voters *claimed* to have voted, but in fact only 70.6 million voters really did so. Of those who did not register in 1966, 8 percent were aliens, 19 percent did not meet state residency requirements, and 63 percent had other explanations. Among those with four years or less of elementary school, only 31 percent voted, compared with 71 percent of the college graduates. Among the college graduates who were not registered, 42 percent mentioned residency restrictions, reflecting the greater mobility of the better educated and well-to-do.

Except for people in the retirement years, the likelihood of voting increases steadily with age. Half of the unregistered people of voting age are under 30.

his voting intentions and on his past record of voting or not voting. The prediction of turnout is especially difficult in primary elections, where fewer go to the polls. A pollster might make different assumptions about the subsequent voting behavior of the undecided voters he interviews and come up with substantially different projections of the same survey results.[9] Among survey respondents who said they were "undecided" in the elections of 1960, 1962, 1964, and 1966, 46 percent eventually voted, compared with 76 percent who said they had made up their minds and expressed a definite preference in the original interview.[10]

Predicting state-by-state results under the American Electoral College system presents added complications. The inexorable laws of statistics require that a state or local survey use a sample of the same size as a national sample to produce results of comparable accuracy. This makes state-by-state polls fifty times as expensive as national polls, and the margin of error still makes predictions difficult in a close contest. In 1948, Dewey would have won the presidency if there had been a swing of 0.001 percent of

[9]Irving Crespi points out that in the final, preelection Gallup survey in 1952, the candidate preferences broke down 47 percent for Eisenhower, 40 percent for Stevenson, and 13 percent undecided. If the pollster were to assume that the undecided voters would end up voting for Stevenson two to one, the final prediction would have been Eisenhower 51 percent, Stevenson 49 percent. If the undecided were allocated three to one, Eisenhower and Stevenson would each have had 50 percent. Harold Mendelsohn and Irving Crespi, *Polls, Television and the New Politics*, Chandler, San Francisco, 1970, pp. 82–83.

[10]Among those originally undecided, however, the percentage that eventually voted varied substantially, from 63 percent in the 1964 Presidential election to 25 percent in the 1966 Congressional election.

Examining the data on Presidential and Congressional elections between 1950 and 1966, Paul K. Perry finds that in the average survey 16.4 percent of the sample of voting age first declared themselves undecided or with no preference. Each of the undecided respondents was then asked a follow-up question about the candidate he was leaning toward even if he had not made up his mind whom to vote for. After this question was asked, the "undecided" proportion fell almost by a half, to 8.6 percent. Among those individuals considered to be "likely voters," because of their answers to a series of questions on voting participation, the undecided dropped further to 6.7 percent. When the same voters were given a secret ballot which forced a choice on their part, the proportion undecided dropped down to 3.9 percent.

Among those ranked as most likely to vote on the voting participation scale, 56 percent were Republicans; among the group rated least likely to vote, 52 percent were Democrats.

In the follow-up interviews with people polled before the elections between 1952 and 1966, the nonvoters numbered about 15 percent more Democrats (as a percentage of the Democratic-Republican preference) than the voters.

(Paul K. Perry and Irving Crespi, "The Measurement of Candidate Preferences and the Role of Issues in the 1968 Presidential Election," a paper delivered before the American Psychological Association, September 1, 1970.)

the voters in Ohio, 0.002 percent in California, or 0.004 percent in Illinois.[11]

In 1968, for the first time in a national election, the leading polling organizations (acting in response to pressures brought within professional circles in previous years) included, in their releases to subscribing newspapers, the number of interviews conducted in each survey. Such information gave specialists, though not the general public, an indication of the margin of error in the survey results. With a sample of 1000 the chances are 19 to 1 that the survey projections obtained for two evenly matched candidates would be within 3½ percentage points above *or* below the true proportions. With a sample of 1500 this margin of error decreases, but only to 3 percentage points, and with 2000 interviews the margin of error is diminished to 2½ percentage points plus or minus. Most presidential elections are decided well within this range of tolerance.

The syndicated pollsters who release their results for publication generally abstain from private polling on behalf of candidates, since this would represent an obvious conflict of interest.[12] (Private polling is generally a much more profitable proposition.) Louis Harris won national attention in 1960 as John F. Kennedy's private pollster and election night companion. (A few years earlier he had managed Franklin D. Roosevelt, Jr.'s, unsuccessful campaign for the New York gubernatorial nomination.) He gave up his political counselling in order to set up his publicly syndicated poll. Samuel Lubell, who had published newspaper columns in many elections as an independent political analyst, worked privately for Governor Nelson A. Rockefeller in the 1970 New York election. Opinion Research Corporation worked privately for Richard Nixon in the 1968 campaign, at the same time that it also (through a different group of research analysts in the same building) ran public surveys on the same subject for the Columbia Broadcasting System. Don Muchmore, a California pollster, worked for both

---

[11] Archibald M. Crossley and Helen M. Crossley, "Polling in 1968," *Public Opinion Quarterly*, Vol. 33, No. 1, Spring 1969, pp. 1–16.

[12] Of 45 senators and governors replying to a poll on the "Contemporary Use of Private Political Polling," 41 used polls in planning their election campaigns. The greatest use of polls reported by congressmen was among freshmen Republicans. Of 46 questioned, 37 reported such use. (It seems probable that the convinced users of polls replied in disproportionate numbers to this poll on their practices.) Robert King and Martin Schnitzer, *Public Opinion Quarterly*, Vol. 32, No. 3, Fall 1968, pp. 431–436.

Ronald Reagan and his opponent Governor Pat Brown, in the same election and has cited this as evidence of his objectivity.

Pollster Oliver Quayle reports that one week before Election Day a midwestern Senator for whom he was doing surveys asked him to do one last "quickie" poll. When Quayle protested that it was a waste of his money, the Senator said, "Do it anyway. I just want to know." But most preelection polling is sponsored with more immediate political aims in mind.

In 1966 Robert P. Griffin, the Republican candidate for the Senate in Michigan, sought to raise funds around the United States using, in support of his appeal, a public opinion poll published in the *Detroit News* which showed him moving slightly ahead of his opponent, G. Mennen Williams. According to the accompanying letter, the poll indicated "that he can win, but only if he is financially able to wage an even stronger campaign in these final hours." Griffin *did* win. The use of such surveys for fund-raising purposes is particularly helpful when the race is contested by a narrow margin. When the polls show a wide gap between the candidates, obviously they are no help to either side, since the apparent winner obviously does not need help and the apparent loser is beyond help.

In the California senatorial primary of 1968, polls showing a drop in the popularity of Senator Thomas H. Kuchel helped his opponent, Max Rafferty, get financial support from conservative backers who originally assumed that he had little chance to beat the incumbent.[13]

In the same year, Paul O'Dwyer, the Democratic contender for the Senate in New York, accused his incumbent Republican rival, Jacob Javits, of trying to create a bandwagon effect to influence the *Daily News* poll, which was starting that day. This was being done, said O'Dwyer, by the release of yet another poll made by the Republican organization, which showed Javits ahead. O'Dwyer commented, "I am in a much better position to judge political trends than any poll taken by amateurs from an undisclosed 1500 people." Javits' victory was as monumental as the polls indicated. However, O'Dwyer had some reason to be skep-

[13]Kuchel, in turn, used a Don Muchmore state poll which showed that the Democratic favorite for the senate nomination, Alan Cranston, would defeat Rafferty but that Kuchel would defeat Cranston. In spite of this poll, Kuchel lost the Republican nomination to Rafferty, who lost the election.

tical. When he ran again in the 1970 Senate primary a poll "leaked" by one of his opponents and duly reported in the *New York Post* of June 2, 1970, later turned out never to have been done at all.

Perhaps the most dangerous misuse of private preelection polls has been not for fund-raising or to create a bandwagon effect among voters, but to manipulate a candidate's public stance on public issues. It has now become quite common for candidates cynically to adapt their campaign utterances to what their private polls show to be publicly acceptable.

A firm of Los Angeles opinion analysts, Decision Making Information, Inc., provides computerized advice to candidates on the acceptability of alternative policy positions to voters, classified into 21 different demographic groups. It also proffers media recommendations based on the known reading and viewing propensities of these different kinds of people. The firm's head, Richard B. Wirthlin, admits, "We haven't refined this enough yet to tell a candidate he should put his television spot in 'Bonanza' rather than 'The Newlywed Game' but with enough polling, there's no reason why we can't."[14] D.M.I.'s polls have guided clients like Governor Ronald Reagan in determining whether or not to intervene in a teacher's strike. In the words of William E. Roberts of D.M.I.'s parent company, Spencer-Roberts, "A well regulated survey can give a candidate a line on what the public wants, and that's a wonderful thing."

During the 1966 Senate campaign in Massachusetts, polls by Opinion Research Corporation indicated that Republican candidate Edward Brooke's silence on the race issue was hurting him. Brooke repositioned himself as a moderate opposed to extremists of both races and he won."[15]

In the same year, political promoter Joseph Napolitan told Democratic Representative Henry Helstoski of New Jersey that 70 percent of his constituents opposed his stand against the bombing of North Vietnam. Helstoski dropped the point from his campaign speeches and managed to win narrowly.

Napolitan used surveys similarly to guide his planning for Hubert Humphrey in the 1968 presidential campaign. In the words of a disaffected advertising agency man, "The polls supposedly

---

[14]*The New York Times*, October 30, 1970.
[15]*Wall Street Journal*, March 8, 1968.

said that the majority of the country thinks the Negro has had too many handouts. So Napolitan advised Humphrey to stop talking about the Marshall Plan for the cities and switch to law and order stuff. We were told, 'Do not show a black man in any commercial.' "[16] Essentially Napolitan was using research as it is traditionally used in testing advertising copy for consumer products: to emphasize strengths and eliminate weaknesses.

In his management of Milton Shapp's (first and unsuccessful) 1966 campaign for the Governorship of Pennsylvania, Napolitan used advertising which cited the findings of his polls. In Catholic areas Shapp spoke out for legalized bingo. In Protestant areas he did not take the opposite view, but merely remained silent on the subject. According to his manager, "He hasn't changed his position. He's for it, but he just doesn't mention it where there is strong opposition to it."[17]

Richard M. Nixon commented on the practice in the course of the 1968 campaign: "I don't think that any political man who has any sense of responsibility at all can change his position every time he takes a poll." But he used many of them himself, for a variety of purposes.

The Nixon-for-President Committee sent out a fund-raising appeal in an envelope stamped "Opinion Survey" on the cover. The enclosure began with a letter which spoke of Nixon and then said, "Do you share his views? If so, here is how you can help. First, you can give us your opinions on the problems facing America. For this purpose a questionnaire is enclosed. Please study it carefully, fill it in, and return it to us. Second, you can make a contribution to Mr. Nixon's campaign." The questionnaire itself, which included a curious assortment of multiple choices on six major issues, concluded with the appeal, "Do you want to see a man in the White House who values your opinion? Then be sure to return this survey promptly. . . . (Please send your personal check made payable to Nixon Finance Committee.)" The accompanying letter was signed by Maurice H. Stans, whom Nixon subsequently appointed to head the Commerce Department.

---

[16] Thomas J. Fleming, "Selling the Product Named Hubert Humphrey," *The New York Times Magazine*, October 13, 1968.
[17] *The New York Times*, November 7, 1966.

The Nixon organization ran a private poll in seven key states "to determine which of seven potential vice presidential candidates would be most popular with the voters."[18] In New Hampshire Nixon's surveys showed that he would get two-thirds of the vote. He said publicly that he would be happy with 35 percent. Actually he got 79 percent and acted "surprised."

At another point in the campaign, after the assassination of Robert Kennedy, Nixon's supporters released a poll showing him running ahead of the field in New Jersey. The poll had actually been taken before Senator Kennedy's death, which radically changed the competitive picture.

The 1968 national election campaign represented a high point in the use of polls by political candidates for their private counsel and in their maneuverings to win the support of convention delegates. More surveys were made in 1968 (by some 200 different polling organizations) than in any other previous campaign, at a cost of some 4 million dollars. The findings were front-page news in newspapers across the country between spring and Election Day.

Early in the year, pollster Archibald Crossley was hired by an anonymous client to conduct a survey of political preferences in New York, Pennsylvania, California, and (at the client's insistence) Stratford County, New Hampshire, which Crossley observes "is not typical of New Hampshire. There were very few interviews there. It is a Democratic County, running 4 to 7 points more Democratic than the State." Crossley agreed to make the survey on the condition that the results not be released without his approval. The study showed President Johnson trailing Nixon by a single percentage point but ahead of other Republicans. The results were leaked by Drew Pearson who said they "proved that Johnson was ahead of Republicans in New York and Pennsylvania and leading them in an unnamed 'bellwether county' in New Hampshire." Crossley commented angrily, "It was supposed to be a confidential relationship, and I have kept my part of the confidence." The client later turned out to be Johnson's close friend and political supporter, Arthur B. Krim, a movie mogul.

---

[18]*The New York Times,* July 28, 1968.

JANE J. MANSBRIDGE

Town Meeting Democracy

Citizens who are white and middle class, recent research has shown, tend to vote more regularly and participate in other public affairs with greater frequency than poorer citizens who are members of some ethnic minority. This difference is not a matter of motivation or intelligence, as has occasionally been suggested, but exists simply because certain groups feel more of a stake in the "system" than others and have greater confidence in their ability to make it reflect their wishes and respond to their needs.

Some social critics have argued that representative government accentuates citizens' feelings of powerlessness. The only way an individual can exercise public responsibility is to cast ballots for candidates whom they nonetheless suspect will forget about them after the election. These critics have looked back nostalgically to a distant, rural past when everyone in the community spoke out at town hall meetings on the great issues of the day. But in her study of a contemporary example of such direct democracy in a small Vermont town, political scientist Jane Mansbridge shows that inequities exist even in this open forum. She suggests that direct democracy "may promote egalitarian values . . . but it does not keep 'cliques' from having disproportionate influence in the decisions of the polity."

Selby, Vermont, is a small town with only 350 people of voting age, a local store, some active farms, a recent influx of summer people and an accompanying land boom. Last year, under state pressure, it began to think about zoning.

At the annual town meeting a familiar drama unfolded. First, the slick lawyer from the state-funded planning commission made an elaborate presentation, supporting his case for zoning with expensive colored maps and quotes from a thick statistical brochure. Then a heavy-set old farmer leaned forward in his chair,

From *Working Papers for a New Society*, Vol. 1, No. 2 (Summer 1973). Reprinted by permission of Jane Mansbridge.

cleared his throat, and began: "That takes away part of the *right* of the man who owns the property! It takes away his rights!"

Farmer Clayton Bedell and the lawyer spent the next ten minutes in a dialogue in which Bedell generated most of the emotions and the lawyer most of the words. Bedell argued that "there's no sense in fighting communism if your neighbor or your selectman can come in and tell you what to do with your property. What are we fighting communism for?" The lawyer responded coolly, "That's a very good and very pertinent question," and swept on to describe again, in terms understandable to a six-year-old, the advantages neighboring towns had realized from the work of the planning commission. "Langford *has* such dreaded things as zoning. *They* know that there are going to be gasoline stations, and *they* want to prepare themselves." He suggested that right must be balanced against right, and that in town meeting everyone could have his say.

Red-faced, Bedell finally exploded, "If I got any say, it'd be the first time I ever had a say!"

The appeal of a direct democracy, where the whole community comes together to make decisions face to face instead of delegating them to elected officials or settling them by referenda, has always been precisely that it "lets everyone have a say." Rousseau, Tocqueville, Emerson, and the early SDS hoped or assumed as much. But for Bedell and many others like him who have actually experienced direct democracy, these hopes have not often been realized.

In theory, direct democracy should accomplish two goals. It should make policy less susceptible to contol by a ruling elite, and it should also enhance the self-respect and personal growth of the citizens.[1] Critics of representative democracy point out that representation usually creates a set of leaders who differ from the rest of the community in social class, in personality, and in their own interests. Even if the community chooses its representatives randomly, as in ancient Greece, the representatives may take on roles and interests that differ from those of their fellow townspeople. Since direct democracy eliminates intermediaries,

---

[1] Robert Wolff, in *In Defense of Anarchism* (New York: Harper & Row, 1970) gives a third argument: that direct, consensual democracy is the only form of decision making that fulfills the Kantian moral imperative to obey only those laws one gives to oneself.

its advocates claim that it will produce results that reflect the general will more closely than will representative democracy.

Advocates of direct democracy also argue that if the community confines its political activity to choosing representatives, it becomes dependent on those it chooses. Most citizens will feel—and be—relatively powerless. They will have no opportunity to develop their understanding and self-respect as they would if they themselves habitually exercised public responsibility.

But does it work? At least in the impure direct democracy of Selby, a class gap persists between those who attend town meetings to make decisions and those who do not. Feelings of alienation and low self-esteem continue. And face-to-face decision making creates new psychological obstacles to participation. Some people, convinced of their own inabilities, fear public ridicule; others are threatened by open conflict; and still others feel excluded by the intimate consensus of an integrated community to which they do not fully belong. One result is that only about 25 percent of the townspeople come to a typical town meeting, whereas 70 to 90 percent vote in state and national elections.

Feelings and Emotions

In the meeting last year, Clayton Bedell, who is one of Selby's poorer farmers and who had been to only one other town meeting in the last ten years, tried to "have his say." He cited state regulations and called forth general principles. But finally he lost his temper, and called the leader of the pro-zoning forces a "conman." The man he accused, a lawyer, stood up, walked over, looked sternly down at the farmer, and threatened, "You keep your mouth shut, Clayton, or you and I'll be in court."

By the end of the afternoon, Bedell's loud insistence that the town pay for the culverts along his road brought groans. And when the road commissioner took him to task for letting manure fall off his spreader onto the road, a number of people laughed aloud.

Months after the meeting, as I talked with people in the town, I gathered the general opinion of Clayton Bedell:

Clayton Bedell is just an ignorant farmer, that's all he is.

We had an occasion this last spring, and it got to a, well, it got to a personal conflict, and the person that got up and made a perfect fool of himself and insulted this taxpayer, it should have been stopped right there and it wasn't.

When people get out of place—I say "people," but I really mean one man—when they're disagreeable, and insult everyone, or actually insult just one man, I don't like it. Of course, he's definitely from the lower strata of society, if you have to say "higher" or "lower," you know.

Some people make a lot of noise, but they aren't the people who ought to control things and they don't.

Some of the poorer and less educated people in town are intimidated by the response to someone like Clayton Bedell. Edith Hurley, living in a dilapidated apartment but managing never to go on welfare, sides with her more affluent neighbors in laughing at Bedell. Yet she quietly draws a lesson for herself. She has not gone to town meeting in the last ten years.

> I don't care to—well, to tell my part, you know, right agin a whole mess of people . . . I don't know, I don't like to get up in town meeting and say, well, this and that . . . well, everybody's looking, or doing something, and they'll say [whisper] "She's a fool!"
>
> There's one man in particular, [Bedell] that's up on this road here, boy oh boy, he's into hot water all the time!
>
> [He talks up in town meeting?] Oh! Gracious to Betsy; I guess he did. [Do people pay attention to him?] Hah, hah, no they don't boy, we just, ah . . .

One of the town's most visible welfare recipients, who lives with her four children in a trailer off one of the town's dirt backhill roads, sympathizes with Bedell but draws the same practical conclusion from what she has heard of the incident. She has never gone to town meeting. Asked why she thought so few people do go, she answers:

> I don't know. If you go there, and you speak up, they make fun of you for speaking up and so on, and I guess people just don't want to go and be made fun of. Why, I don't say anything so they don't just laugh it off anyway.
>
> I mean we have some friends [Bedell] that went last year and the guy stood up and he said some things about a few issues . . . and they just laughed at him. So what good did it do him to open his mouth? I mean, he'd have been better off if he had stayed home.

151

Like Edith Hurley, she too has a vivid picture of what would happen if she spoke:

> They all sit there and they listen while you're talking, but the minute you leave the room or something, they laugh behind your back and poke fun at it because you did open your mouth.

You wouldn't think, offhand, that the Selby town meeting was a frightening place. The town itself is small, a fifth of the people have lived there all their lives, and more than a quarter feel they know almost everyone in town. At the meeting the townspeople dress in work clothes, scrape the mud off their heavy boots, and joke familiarly in deep New England country accents. No one fusses over parliamentary procedure, or worries when the town clerk can't find her arithmetic. Selectmen and school directors— the town's most important officers—are of the same social class as most other residents. One of the selectmen lives in a trailer and runs his own one-man grocery store, while another is the repairman at a nearby state park. As for the school directors, says one newcomer in disgust, "They've got a housewife, a carpenter, and a laborer for running the biggest budget in town."

Yet even in this small direct democracy, where access to decision making is theoretically open, a significant minority (23 percent) feel that "people like me don't have any say about what the town does." Blue-collar workers, people with less than a high school education, and people whose standard of living is fairly low are more likely to feel powerless than others in the town. (About 36 percent of these three groups feel they have no say in the town, compared to only 14 percent or so of their richer and more educated neighbors.)[2]

Many of the poorer townspeople explicitly attribute their unwillingness to go to town meeting, or to speak up if they do go,

---

[2]The results reported here are based on a sample of 69 people who agreed to an unstructured interview of one-half to one-and-one half hours, 55 of whom also returned a structured questionnaire including items devised, tested, and asked nationwide by the Survey Research Center. In addition, a few calculations use a sample of 190 people, who had both registered to vote and were on the town tax list as owning a residence or a trailer. I have taken as a measure of low standard of living an assessment of the value of residence at $3,999 or below.

The population of Selby seems to feel no more efficacious in regard to the national government than others in the United States. Forty percent of the sample that answered my structured questionnaire agreed that "people like me don't have any say about what the government does," compared to 42 percent nationwide in 1968, and 35 percent nationwide in 1970.

Names of towns and individuals are fictitious.

to lack of "education." One farmer, who lives in a decaying house three miles out of town, has only an elementary education. He thinks that the few who speak in town meeting "do just what they want to. They've got more education. . . . I did speak once and pretty near got throwed out. I get to swearing." If he did get up at town meeting and say something, he said, "Why, they'd all laugh at me."

Another older resident who never completed elementary school echoes these sentiments. He explains that he never talks politics with his friends:

> No, I leave that right out. I know what I think, but I can't put it across to people. I've got no education. I can't get it across. Sometimes I'm just speechless. Or I get mad. I'd say too much. If I had education, it'd be a difference.

He feels angry at the way his lack of education has cut him off from influence at the town meetings.

> If you get up and say your piece, they'll call you out of order whether you are or not.
> It is all cut and dried before town meeting. They'll pass right over you if you get up to nominate. It's organized their way before the meeting. No, I never speak. I've seen so many called out of order.

Many, especially the women, view their lack of influence as an appropriate result of their lack of education. One woman, who has never gone to town meeting, says people like her don't usually go.

> A lot of people are not educated enough to understand it, like which I am. I mean, I'm too shy to get mixed into a lot of stuff like this, and I haven't got the education to decide on this stuff like my husband has, and I think that is a lot of it.

Even a wealthy farmer can feel that his lack of education makes him look foolish at the meeting. Old Mr. Thresher has not gone to town meeting for five years. He explains bitterly, gesturing at an old one-room schoolhouse:

> I didn't even have high school. This little box was my main form of education.
> I don't care how smart a fellow may be. We have so many today moving in here—they may be lawyers, professional men, or

153

anything. They can out-talk a native so much that he feels he might as well stay home.

He says that in the old days, folks didn't go to town meetings because:

> A lot couldn't read and write. Today there's none of that, but you will find class distinction has a great deal to do with it. There's no use going.

Later, he adds, "If I should go down there today, nine out of ten of 'em would laugh in my face!"

Seeing yourself in the bottom quarter of a community—whether in education, occupation, or standard of living—may raise self-doubts that are accentuated by public assembly democracy. Face-to-face interaction reinforces the feelings of belonging and commitment of those who already feel integral members of the community, but for those who feel in some way outside the circle, it increases the difficulty of breaking in. Each attempt at participation exposes one to ridicule and threatens rather than increases self-respect.

For these people it takes courage to stand up and argue a potentially unpopular position. When a part from his old harvester flew off, blinding him in one eye, one young owner of a poor and rocky farm concluded in despair that he was "not even a good farmer." Yet he has to master these feelings of failure in order to go to, or talk at, town meeting:

> There's few people who really are brave enough to get up and say what they think in town meeting in this day and age. They'd sit back and say, "Well, it don't make any difference whether I go or not, they're going to get what they want." They're afraid to get up and say what they want.
>
> 'Cause it does take a little bit of courage. 'Specially if you get up and you make a boo-boo. I mean you make a mistake and say something, then people would never get up and say anything again. They feel themselves inferior.
>
> Now, I guess when you basically put down a person, now myself, I feel inferior, in ways, to other people. I mean, at times I'll tell anybody no, it doesn't bother me, when it does, and I won't let anybody let it known that it bothers me. And in the end I'm damn

glad I didn't. Well you got—oh, let's see, forty percent of the people on this road that don't show up for town meeting—a lot of them feel it that way.

Even in a representative democracy, many nonvoters avoid politics because it suggests too much conflict.[3] Face-to-face confrontation increases the level of emotional tension dramatically.[4] This young farmer's anxiety brings him back from town meeting every year with a splitting headache. Another claims he stopped going to the meetings completely because he was afraid for his heart. And a man in the next town tells how his hands shake for hours after the meeting.

In the direct democracy of a small town meeting, even those who do not enter the fray are upset by the emotional consequences of active participation. Mrs. Bettis, a young woman in a neat, new trailer along the state highway, has never been to town meeting. But she says, "Well, to me, all's it is is more or less a fight . . . a big argument." Roy George, in a trailer half a mile down the road, agrees. "Myself, I just get sick of, uh, get sick of it, I say . . . [to] sit and listen to 'em argue and wrangle for four or five hours." Mrs. Joslyn, wife of a farmer who works in the winter for $23.00 a day, says that she goes to town meeting sometimes, "but after they get to arguing about so much and it doesn't amount to anything, I get sick of it." Mrs. Hurley, poor though not on welfare, has never gone to the meeting, but doesn't like that "you get in a lot of hubbub . . . people get quarreling." Mrs. Raynor thinks it's "this bickering back and forth." Mr. Hebert calls the meeting a "nasty argument," Mr. Tenney calls it "a big fight." Mrs. Gross says it's "petty quarrels," and Mrs. Drown says she doesn't like "the way people knowingly go aginst one another." Even Mrs. Allen, who likes a little drama, agrees that many are put off by it. They won't go to the meeting, and when you ask them why, "they'll say, 'too damn many arguments!' " Mrs. Partlow sums up the general feeling when she asserts definitely, "I just don't like disagreeable situations."

Almost a quarter of the people I talked with spontaneously gave some indication that the personal, face-to-face character of the town meeting disturbed them.

[3]Morris Rosenberg, "Some Determinants of Political Apathy," *Public Opinion Quarterly*, 18 (1954–55), p. 349.
[4]Harold J. Leavitt, *Managerial Psychology* (Chicago: University of Chicago Press, 1964), pp. 141–150.

Fear of open conflict makes direct democracies paper over their controversies. If a nasty fight over the office of selectman has hit the town, nothing is said at the meeting. Instead, the election of a new man goes through without discussion and some citizen produces a well-applauded speech of praise for the beaten incumbent. The whole procedure has the unintended effect of making the uninitiated feel excluded and manipulated.

In a direct democracy the fear of conflict, combined with a genuine desire for unity, means that most decisions are made by consensus, in a voice vote that intimidates those who might have objected.[5] The very informality and mutual understanding of a consensual community dramatically excludes the dissenter.

The Advantages of "Certain Groups"

Most governmental polities make decisions that materially benefit one group over another. Groups that participate actively are likely to end up winners, and the nonparticipants to end up losers. Usually, those of higher social or economic status participate more actively and receive more of the benefits.[6] Direct democracy in a town like Selby may slightly reduce this tendency, but it does not eliminate it.

In Selby, blue-collar workers make up a third of the population of the town, but only half of them have gone to a town meeting in the last ten years, compared to three-quarters of those with better jobs. Blue-collar workers are less likely than others to talk at the meeting once they get there. They are less likely to hold a town office, or to go to see a town officer if they have a problem. The same goes for people who haven't finished high school, or who live in trailers or houses valued under $4,000.[7]

---

[5]Most small direct democracies, from early New England towns to present-day village councils in India and Japan, tend to make their decisions by consensus. See references in Mansbridge, "The Limits of Friendship," *NOMOS XVI*, Winter 1975–76.

[6]See Lester W. Milbrath, *Political Participation* (Chicago: Rand McNally, 1965), pp. 110–128, for an overview of the research on class and political participation. Sidney Verba and Norman H. Nie, *Participation in America* (New York: Harper & Row, 1972), pp. 97–101, 125–137, and *passim*, provide a more complex analysis of the class-participation interaction.

[7]The non-blue-collar group includes both independent farmers and white-collar workers. Due to the small size of the sample, only two of the twelve differences (three measures of class by four measures of participation) are statistically significant. All, however, are in the expected direction. In the instance of the greatest gap, only 33 percent of those in residences valued under $3,999 reported having gone to see a town officer, compared to 74 percent of those in more expensive residences. In the instance of the smallest gap, 16 percent of those who had not finished high school held town office, as compared to 19 percent of the high school graduates.

In Selby and in other small New England towns, only about a quarter of the eligible voters show up for town meeting each year.[8] In comparable rural towns in New York State, which are run by elected representatives, have a strong competitive party system, and hold elections every two years, three-quarters of the eligible population votes.[9] Even over a ten-year period, a town meeting brings out fewer people than this. Thirty percent of the people I interviewed in Selby had not been to a town meeting in the last ten years.

Participation in town meeting is, of course, more meaningful than merely casting a ballot. Each person at the meeting hears arguments on both sides of an issue, sees and makes judgments on the character of the protagonists, reflects, and often makes his or her decisions during, not before, the meeting. In a small meeting of 80 or 90 people, like the one in Selby, nearly half the participants say something at some time during the day.[10]

[8]An unpublished study by Frank M. Bryan (St. Michael's College, Winooski, Vermont) in 1970 found an average of about 25 percent attendance, with a high of 45 percent in a town of 751 people and a low of 9 percent in a town of 1,061. These figures include visitors and other nonresidents among the attenders, and are calculated on base of registered voters rather than the eligible population. Consequently, they slightly overestimate the percentage of eligible residents attending the meeting.

Historically, attendance at town meetings has fluctuated, depending on the importance of the questions before the town. In Selby, the first recorded vote in town meeting (1854) gives an attendance of about 46 percent of the eligible (male) voters. (These percentages are calculated on the traditional assumption that one-fifth of the population was eligible to vote. As this estimate often had to be increased to cover the actual gubernatorial and presidential votes, the percentages reported here are probably higher than the actual percentage voting.) In 1857, the attendance was 29 percent; in 1858, 38 percent.

Turnout has declined as the towns have lost importance both politically and in the lives of the townspeople. But, attandance rarely crept over 50 percent, even in the heyday of local power.

The picture of relatively low turnout in Selby's past town meetings is supported by historical research elsewhere. Robert Gross (Columbia University Ph.D., in preparation) reports turnouts in Concord, Mass., averaging 42 percent of the adult males for the period 1826–1840, when the town was split by a bitter political controversy (51 percent if figured on a base of registered voters). Recorded voting in the meetings of nine other Massachusetts towns in this period indicates an average approximate turnout of a little under 50 percent of the adult males, with a high of 65 percent and a low of 26 percent.

[9]The towns of Broome and Conesville, New York, comparable to Selby in physical size, population, percentage of land in farms, average size of farm, and average value of land per acre, had in 1969 a turnout for town elections of 83 and 93 percent of the eligible voters. Other small towns, not as exactly comparable in physical characteristics, had almost as high turnouts. In New York State, town elections are not only partisan, but are combined with the election of county officers (sheriff, county clerk, county treasurer, and county coroners), and occasionally of an associate judge of the state Court of Appeals.

[10]In other towns in Vermont, the percentage of participants speaking at the meeting averages about 37 percent, and 40 percent for towns like Selby, with a population of 600 or less (Bryan, *op. cit.*).

Seventy-three percent of those who have gone to a meeting in the last ten years have spoken at least once.

Yet the fact remains that this participation involves only part of the population. The nonparticipants differ from the participants not only by class, but by personality, and by how well they are connected with the rest of the town socially and geographically.

Festinger's study of an MIT housing project showed that the simple accident of living at the bottom of a stairwell, or at some other point of physical and social communication, increased a student's chances of becoming involved in the internal politics of the project.[11] And so it is in Selby. Living in the central village makes one more likely to learn the date of town meeting, understand local issues, feel that local decisions have a great effect on one's life, go to town meeting, talk at town meeting, go to see town officers, become a town officer, and feel that one has a say in the town.[12]

The diner, the store, the town clerk's office, the gas pump—these spots in the village all serve as focal points for the dissemination of local political information and excitement. One villager drops by the diner before and after work, as well as on Saturdays and Sundays, to get "all the local news and gossip," and says he discusses politics there "all the time." Other villagers say of a local political question that they "discussed it down at the store." Villagers don't make appointments to see town officials; they just "run into them down at the store."

In Selby, physical proximity has produced a village culture of gossip and relatively frequent social contact. The backroaders recognize this culture and dislike it, saying, "Down there they buzz, buzz all the time. I wouldn't live down there for anything because every little thing makes a lot of—what I call gossip." But they also acknowledge that the culture of gossip increases the villagers' political influence. The backroaders say that by town meeting day "the people in the village, they get together and hash it all out. They have their minds all made up." Or, "A certain

---

[11]Leon Festinger, Stanley Schachter, and Kurt Bach, *Social Pressures in Informal Groups* (Stanford: Stanford University Press, 1950), p. 112.

[12]Again, due to sample size, of 11 comparisons only 2 are statistically significant. The greatest gap between villagers and nonvillagers is in political efficacy, with 27 percent of nonvillagers and none of the villagers reporting that they "don't have any say" in the town. In the instance of the smallest gap, 18 percent of the nonvillagers held town office, as compared with 23 percent of the villagers.

few in this town want to run it, and that's the way. And no one in the back roads has anything to say."

Living in the village is only one form of social connectedness that bequeaths a political advantage. If you see people outside your family every day, have lived longer in the community, or recognize a lot of people in town, you are also more likely to participate actively in town politics. The same is true if you say you are a good talker, like competition, and prefer to give orders rather than take them.[13]

These different advantages—wealth, personality, and social and geographical connection—make some people, even in an open democratic community, much more likely to exercise influence. Those without such advantages are left feeling cheated. Consequently, in this small town three-fifths of the community is in some way disgruntled. More than a third actively volunteer that the town is run by a "clique," a "small group," or that "everything is cut and dried a day or two before town meeting,"[14]

An enterprising person who is middle class, not particularly insecure, and used both to taking responsibility and to exerting influence, can fairly easily become part of the not very homogeneous group of active citizens. In the last three years, at least two young middle-class men have moved in and done so. But for the rest the "open" town meeting does little or nothing to dispel the impression of a closed system.

In the absence of political parties, clear factional issues, and representatives who campaign on those issues, influence in a direct democracy must follow the lines of informal social communication.[15] Those who do not participate actively in town affairs are represented (or misrepresented) by those who do participate.

---

[13]Pearson correlations with town meeting attendance: see others every day, .250; length of time in town, .302; recognize others, .304; good talker, .316; prefer to give orders, .245; like competition, .443.

[14]Along with the 22 percent of those who answered the question who actively agreed that "people like me have no say in this town," there were 21 respondents who did not answer that question and 16 who disagreed with it, who elsewhere in the interview or on the questionnaire said they felt powerless in the town. Six used the phrase "cut and dried" to describe the maneuvering before town meeting and the suppression of overt conflict at the meeting itself.

[15]See V. O. Key, *Southern Politics* (New York: Knopf, 1950), p. 37; J. David Greenstone, "Political Norms and Group Process in Private Government: The Case of a Local Union," *Midwest Journal of Political Science* 9 (1965), p. 350; and Paul E. Peterson, "Forms of Representation: Participation of the Poor in the Community Action Program," *American Political Science Review* 64 (1970), p. 502.

No one holds these de facto representatives accountable to the larger group who did not attend the meeting. The nonparticipant loses his rights by his "decision" not to attend. Even those who never go to town meeting and feel quite powerless in the town agree in principle that "you have no right to gripe if you don't go to town meeting."

Yet the activists *are* different from the nonparticipants, and these differences often bias decisions. There are more nonvillagers than villagers in Selby, but the villagers are more active. Thus, on at least one issue the nonvillagers say they "went down and tried our best . . . but those in the village, they outvoted us three to one." When there is a conflict of interest between the groups, as there was over the whole community paying for the installation of a village sewage system, the villagers have an advantage: they live in a climate of more intense political involvement and participate more.

Class differences create the same advantage. If the poorer residents were to try to exercise influence, they might succeed in having the town pay for the culverts along the road, the garbage collection, or the school hot lunch program, instead of having these costs placed on each individual. The poorer residents, however, are the least likely to try to exercise influence.

Losing material benefit may not be as important as losing a sense of full membership in the community. Feeling excluded from consideration in the public but intimate atmosphere of a small direct democracy affects a person's self-respect. Bitterness about control by a "clique" seems intensified by the difficulty of figuring out who has influence, and why. You can't vote the rascals out if they don't hold elective office; indeed, you can't take any form of reprisal if you don't know who the rascals are. As an outsider, if you go to town meeting, you feel manipulated by "those in the know"; if you don't go, you seem to have forfeited your right to gripe.

Ingenuity and Will

Democracies inevitably produce great differences in influence between those who participate actively and those who do not. Instituting direct rather than representative democracy does not change this situation appreciably. It may promote egalitarian values (and thus promote greater equality in the long run) by diminishing the power of formal leaders, opening up the process of decision making for public discussion, and dramatizing the symbolic equality of members of the town. Direct democracy does not, however, keep "cliques" from having disproportionate influence in the decisions of the polity. Nor does it prevent strong and bitter feelings of exclusion among those who lack such influence.

The Power of an Ideal.   Fiddling with institutions cannot, even if one wished to do so, eliminate social stratification and its attendant inequalities of political power. Nor are those people active in a polity generally likely to look out for the interests of the less active. However, an ideal like that of political equality has the power to influence people even against their narrowly conceived self-interest. Idealistic, egalitarian activists, confronted with situations where power is clearly unequally distributed and with methods to distribute it more equally, will often do what they can to divest themselves of power and confer it on others.[16] Idealistic, egalitarian nonparticipants, confronted with an explanation of their own passivity that faults institutions rather than themselves, may move to try to change those institutions.[17] For either to take action, they need concrete ideas on how the institutions can be changed.

Direct democracies that want to spread participation more evenly must do so consciously, by multiplying the number of ways an individual can have an influence. Distributing responsibilities, encouraging small associations, paying for attendance, devising social attractions, and becoming more conscious and less accepting of inequalities of participation: all would have some effect on the distribution and extent of that participation.

Distributing Responsibilities.   Mill once pointed out that holding a public office, even a small one, had a greater educative effect on the individual than the simple act of voting. The more widely

---

[16]See, for example, the Vietnam Summer group, described in Kenneth Keniston, *The Young Radicals* (New York: Harcourt Brace Jovanovich, 1968), pp. 160–173.
[17]This must remain speculative. Those who at any point are not involved in political activity will not be likely in the future to become self-starting. However, in both the black and the women's movements, reducing self-blame has removed a tremendous obstacle to the taking of political initiative.

public responsibilities were distributed, the more people and the more different kinds of people would have an opportunity to have some effect on the system and to grow in their own understanding and self-respect.

In Selby, those people who describe themselves as "outgoing" are more likely to attend town meeting, talk at the meeting, and go to see a town officer. But all nine of the small town offices in my sample have somehow been allotted to people who do not describe themselves this way.[18] Being a fence viewer, a surveyor of wood and lumber, a lister, a trustee of the public funds, or a trustee of the library provides an opportunity to feel part of the town, take responsibility for some of its functioning, and exert influence in an informal way more suited to a quiet personality.

A democratic community can make an effort to allocate major and minor responsibilities as widely as possible. Yugoslavian enterprises rotate membership on the workers' council with the goal of having each member serve at least once in an official capacity.[19]

---

[18]Five of these nine answered the questionnaire, and chose the self-description "keep to myself" or "it depends" rather than "outgoing." Four asked not to answer the questionnaire or did not return it. Three of these clearly indicated by their actions that they would not consider themselves "outgoing." The unclear case would probably have marked "it depends."

[19]Yet in spite of attempts at rotation, Yugoslavian workers' councils seem to be largely composed of skilled rather than semiskilled workers. In 1960 highly skilled and skilled workers made up only 48 percent of the labor force, but held 73 percent of the seats on workers' councils and 80 percent of the seats on management boards. The semiskilled, who made up 25 percent of the labor force, had only 18 percent of the seats on workers' councils, and 13 percent of those on management boards. The unskilled, who made up 27 percent of the labor force, held only 9 percent of the seats on workers' councils, and 6 percent of those on governing boards (Paul Blumberg, *Industrial Democracy* [New York: Schocken Books, 1968], p. 218).

In 1965, in the two enterprises studied by Kolaja, no unskilled workers had seats on the managing board (Jiri Kolaja, *Workers' Councils: The Yugoslav Experience* [London: Tavistock Publications, 1965], p. 14).

In 1967, in one shipyard in Split, only 5 percent of the seats on the workers' council were held by semiskilled and unskilled workers combined. The workers at the shipyard explained this low representation as due to generally low educational levels and the desire for the best men to hold office (Carole Pateman, *Participation and Democratic Theory* [Cambridge: Cambridge University Press, 1970], p. 99).

In Yugoslavia, only one generation removed from a peasant economy, a large percentage of the labor force is still illiterate. Pateman argues that as educational levels rise and workers become familiar with workers' control, the semiskilled and unskilled workers will increase their representation on the workers' councils (Pateman, *op. cit.*, p. 99). However, the trend seems to be in the opposite direction. By 1968, while the proportion of skilled and highly skilled workers on workers' councils remained constant, the percentage of persons with university or other higher education increased to 8 percent, largely at the expense of the unskilled workers.

The demand to have more semiskilled and unskilled workers on the councils is evidently not great. In 1968, only 29 percent of the workers in an automobile works in Serbia felt that unskilled and semiskilled workers should have more representation

A radical workplace like Project Place in Boston rotates membership on the steering committee. A food co-op rotates the planning function.

There may well be a loss in efficiency with such widespread distribution of responsibility, since everyone is not equally competent. Yet many responsibilities do not take unusual competence. When a newcomer complains that a housewife, carpenter, and laborer manage the biggest budget in town, or when a state bureaucrat complains that "the trouble with our road system is that they hire the town drunk to work on the roads," they are often responding to a symbolic incongruity, not to a real mismatching of person and task. Efficiency may also be increased in the long run as more members of a community come to have, through the rotation of office, a view of the entire polity and a stake in it. In an academic department, few professors are naturally competent administrators, but rotation of the departmental chairmanship encourages more of them to see their own interests in the good of the whole.

Small Groups. Radical direct democracies, particularly in the women's movement, have been experimenting with decentralized forms of decision making, using small groups of 5 to 12 people, or federations of small groups. In a community of 300, such groups can form minor social systems to which important information flows through the other contacts of its members. Within a small group, differences in verbal fluency, in education, and in self-confidence can be more readily accommodated. Members of the same social class brought together in a small group become more aware of their interests and more able to fight for them. A small group with inner agreement can legitimate the deviations of its members from a community-wide consensus. Thus the group helps mitigate the effects in a direct democracy of informal social networks, class disabilities, and the closed consensual system.

---

on the council. Even among the unskilled and semiskilled themselves, less than half wanted to see greater representation on the council of their own group. The same year a survey of 92 industrial organizations showed that workers of all classes thought unskilled workers ought to have less influence on decision making in the enterprise than skilled workers, and that both groups ought to have less influence than the middle and top management (Gerry Hunnius, "Workers' Self-Management in Yugoslavia," in Gerry Hunnius, David Garson, and John Case [eds.], *Workers' Control* [New York: Random House, 1973], pp. 297, 300). Forthcoming work by Sidney Verba, Norman H. Nie, and Jae-On Kim also indicates a high correlation between socio-economic advantage and participation in workers' self-management in Yugoslavia.

The small group has often been used to increase citizen participation (in authoritarian as well as egalitarian contexts). The group initiates personal interactions that are more important for most participants than the substantive decisions governing the large institutions that affect their lives. Then, directly or indirectly, the life of the group is tied in with participation in the larger polity.

Active membership, even in a group completely unrelated to politics like a sports association, increases one's subsequent political participation.[20] The relative democracy and high participation in the International Typographical Union stems in part from the large proportion of members who belong to formal and informal groups, most of them quite unpolitical, within the union.[21] If a group takes on a small communal responsibility (e.g., in a neighborhood, holding a bake sale or baseball game for charity; in a workplace, organizing a cleanup campaign or protest to the managerial board; in a voluntary association, making a public statement as a caucus), it brings its members even further into conscious political participation in the community.[22]

Unfortunately, people who are not inclined to participate in large-scale politics are also not inclined to join organizations of any kind, including small groups. Lower- or working-class people, for instance, are less likely than the middle class to join formal voluntary organizations.[23] This is true even when they move to the suburbs, where such organizations normally proliferate.[24] Church groups, coffee klatches, ethnic societies, sports clubs, and gangs do have their share of lower and working-class men and women. But these associations, which usually involve only one sex, are built up slowly through ties of kin and friendship. Groups that form ephemerally, composed of people previously unknown to one another, to deal with specific, perhaps passing issues, have less attraction to someone from a lower- or working-class culture. In the women's liberation movement, "consciousness-raising"

---

[20]Herbert Maccoby, "Differential Political Activity of Participants in a Voluntary Association," *American Sociological Review*, 23 (1958), p. 524; Verba and Nie, *op. cit.*, p. 185.

[21]Seymour M. Lipset, Martin Trow, and James Coleman, *Union Democracy* (New York: Doubleday, 1962), pp. 79, 105, 107, 108.

[22]Verba and Nie, *op. cit.*, pp. 186–194.

[23]Charles R. Wright and Herbert H. Hyman, "Voluntary Association Memberships of American Adults," *American Sociological Review*, 23 (1958), p. 291. See also Lee Rainwater, "Neighborhood Action and Lower-Class Life Styles," in John B. Turner (ed.), *Neighborhood Organization for Community Action* (New York: National Association of Social Workers, 1968), pp. 31–34.

[24]Bennet M. Berger, *Working Class Suburb* (Berkeley: University of California Press 1960), pp. 59–64.

groups have appealed primarily to middle-class women. Working-class women prefer to make intimate friends through social contacts, or to work on projects that are explicitly action-oriented and do not demand commitment to a group of unknown individuals. The same is true for the shy, the loners, and those who have no previous acquaintances who might join a group with them.

As a consequence, any nonselective encouragement of voluntary associations in a polity will reach primarily the middle class, the outgoing, and those already fairly well-connected to the community.[25] Selective organizing efforts aimed particularly at working and lower-class populations,[26] and the encouragement of groups based on prior informal associations (e.g., kinship systems, sharing of a laundromat or a corridor, the regulars at a bar) would be more likely to develop participation among those who now participate least.

Remuneration. An ingenious community might also find ways of paying people both for their explicit political participation (attendance at meetings) and for taking some responsibility in the work of the community. Food co-ops usually give the week's surplus food to the bloc that has had to take the brunt of the work that week. The Athenian city-state paid its citizens to attend meetings. A system of small tax rebates for participating in some community work, a free meal between two sessions of a meeting, or a dance at its end, would have the same function.

Becoming Participation-Conscious. People who are active in, or initiate, a democratic community often assume that the membership will be like themselves—enthusiastic, informed, articulate, and relatively outgoing. The more naive expect direct, face-to-face assemblies to produce decisions that reflect the desires of the entire membership. The more cynical realize that there may be a difference in interest between those who attend and those who do not, and feel that the nonparticipants have lost their right to a voice by their own decision. Early members of SDS used to say exultantly and with some moral self-satisfaction that "freedom

---

[25]Verba and Nie, *op. cit.,* pp. 200–205.
[26]William Hampton and Stephen Hatch, in *Towards Participation in Local Services: Fabian Tract 419* (London: The Fabian Society, 1973), pp. 3, 49, suggest that participatory forms may work to the disadvantage of the working class unless community development officers can increase working-class participation or represent informally those who do not participate.

165

is an endless meeting." They forgot that the rewards and disincentives for attending that meeting were quite differently distributed among their peers.[27]

Activists may rightly fear the consequences of spreading participation too rapidly or too widely. Nonparticipants tend to be less militant[28] and may be less concerned with the collectivity.[29] They are less likely to understand the issues and to be able to make a reasoned decision.[30] While participation contributes to their political education, nonparticipants often begin by being uneducated.[31]

Along with these general fears, activists usually resent encroachments on their power by those of different class, background, personality, or belief. They may also imbue the participative status quo with moral coloring, feeling that those who do not participate under the existing scheme (e.g., public meetings or biennial registration) do not deserve a voice.

If, however, a community wants to make it more likely that political decisions balance the needs of all its members relatively equally, and if it does not want to exclude any of its members from the psychological benefits of participation, it cannot accept the participative status quo. And if participation is to be spread more evenly, the active need to feel more respect for the nonparticipants, and the nonparticipants more respect for themselves. Such respect would be easier if it were more explicit that the shy, the newcomers, those who live and work on the outskirts of the community, the less educated, and the less articulate actual-

---

[27]See Michael Walzer, "A Day in the Life of a Socialist Citizen," *Obligations* (Cambridge: Harvard University Press, 1970), pp. 229–238.

[28]Herbert McCloskey, Paul J. Hoffmann, and Rosemary O'Hara, "Issue Conflict and Consensus Among Party Leaders and Followers," *American Political Science Review*, 44 (June 1960), pp. 406–427.

[29]Samuel A. Stouffer, in *Communism, Conformity and Civil Liberties* (New York: Wiley, 1966), pp. 26–57, indicates that community leaders are more tolerant and more conscious of traditional civil liberties than are ordinary citizens. McCloskey enlarges this notion to suggest that those active in politics are more committed to "the rules of the game." Herbert McCloskey, "Consensus and Ideology in American Politics," *American Political Science Review*, 58 (1964), p. 365.

[30]Discovery in the 1940s of the low education and information levels among the nonparticipating electorate led to a spate of articles in the 1950s suggesting that the voluntary political withdrawal of these people protected the democratic process. See, for example, W. H. Morris Jones, "In Defense of Political Apathy," *Political Studies*, February 1954, pp. 25–37.

[31]This is Kaufman's "paradox of participatory democracy." Arnold Kaufman, "Participatory Democracy: Ten Years Later," *La Table Ronde*, No. 251–252 (1968), pp. 216–228, reprinted in William E. Connolly, *The Bias of Pluralism* (New York: The Atherton Press, 1971), p. 206.

ly find it difficult to participate. These problems are not reduced by the structure of direct democracy which, at least in Selby, requires day-long attendance at a meeting, gives greater weight to informal channels of influence, makes conflict more frightening, and sets up consensual norms that are hard to break.

The point of this essay is not to suggest that there is no substitute for representative government. Those who base their institutions on direct democracy correctly respond to their own needs for active participation, both to influence policy and to feel full members of the community. Even a general assembly of all the members of a community can allow every member to make at least visual contact with the others, can give those who participate actively a feeling of being heard by the whole polity, and can evoke an emotional unity that sustains its members in their prior and subsequent isolation. It may also be the most effective way of giving legitimacy to final decisions.

However, no one trying to set up a democratic community should rely solely on the direct assembly of all the people. Only a small and nonrepresentative percentage of the citizenry will be able to attend the assembly consistently; informal channels of influence will come to dominate decision making; and a large number of those excluded from the informal processes will feel manipulated, angry, or apathetic, cursed with self-blame. Such direct democracies must be supplemented by other institutions, whether a host of minor offices, some elected representatives, decentralization to small groups, or all of these combined.

Almost every radical institution of more than 20 to 30 people that has tried to make its decisions as an egalitarian direct democracy has learned this lesson. Most have developed structures based on the federation of small groups that coordinate their decisions through rotating representation on a steering committee.

Mass meetings have come to serve as theater: dramatizing issues, evoking emotions of community, and giving those who want it a public forum for the expression of their views and the exercise of their forensic talents. These are useful, perhaps crucial functions. Mass meetings also subtly exclude some people from the process of making decisions. An egalitarian democracy will want to exercise both ingenuity and will to provide such members another way of being represented.

ROBERT COLES

The Politics of Middle Class Children

In their study of children and the origins of political belief, *Children in the Political System,* David Easton and Jack Dennis say, "The small child sees a vision of holiness when he chances to glance toward government—a sanctity and righteousness. . . . The government protects us, helps us, is good, and cares for us when we are in need, answer most children." Researchers into children's political attitudes have also noted the early appearance of an unquestioning respect for the presidency and other forms of governmental authority. The dominant ideology conveyed through experiences in school and other socializing institutions is indeed strong. But Robert Coles, who has studied the attitudes of young people extensively, points out in the following essay that young people are also affected by subtle but nonetheless strongly felt lessons of class and race. In this, as much as in the authoritarianism and orthodoxy of their early beliefs, they hold a mirror up to the true nature of this country's political culture.

A black child of eight, a girl who lives in southern Alabama, just above Mobile, told me in 1968 that she knew one thing for sure about who was going to be president: he'd be a white man; and as for his policies, "no matter what he said to be polite, he'd never really stand up for us." Already she knew herself to be a member of "us," as against "them."

A few miles away, a white child of nine, a boy, the son of a lawyer and plantation owner, had a rather different perspective on the presidency: "The man who's elected will be a good man; even if he's not too good before he goes to Washington, he'll probably turn out good. This is the best nation there is, so the leader has to be the best, too."

A child with keen ears who picks up exactly his father's mixture of patriotism and not easily acknowledged skepticism? Yes, but also a child who himself—by the tone of his voice and his earnestness—has come to believe in his nation's destiny, and in the office of the presidency. How about the governor? "He's better known than most governors," the boy boasts. Then he offers his source: "My daddy says that we have a better governor than they do in Louisiana or in Georgia. (He has cousins in both states.) And he says that our governor makes everyone stop and listen to him, so he's real good. He knows how to win; he won't let us be beaten by the Yankees."

Is this more sectional bombast, absorbed rather too well by a boy who now, a teenager, hasn't had the slightest inclination to develop the "cynicism" a number of students of the process of "political socialization" have repeatedly mentioned as prevalent? Or is it, more likely, the response of a child who knows what his parents really consider important, really believe in—and fear? "I took my boy over to my daddy's house," the child's father recalls, "and we watched Governor Wallace standing up to those people in Washington; he told the President of the United States that he was wrong."

The boy was then four, and no doubt even were he to see a child psychoanalyst for several years he would not at nine, never mind at fifteen, recall the specific event his father and grandfather have very clearly in mind. But time and again he has heard members of his family stress how precarious they feel in relation to Yankee (federal) power, and therefore how loyal to a governor who gives the illusion of a successful defense of cherished social and political prerogatives.

Up North, in a suburb outside Boston, it is quite another story. At nine a girl speaks of America and its leaders like this: "I haven't been to Europe yet, but my parents came back last year and they were happy to be home." Then, after indicating how happy she was to have them home, she comments on the rest of the world, as opposed to her country:

> It's better to be born here. Maybe you can live good in other places, but this is the best country. We have a good government. Everyone is good in it—if he's the president, he's ahead of everyone else,

and if he's a governor, that means he's also one of the people who decide what the country is going to do. There might be a war, and somebody has to send the troops by plane across the ocean. If there is a lot of trouble someplace, then the government takes care of it. I'm going to Washington next year to see all the buildings. My brother went two years ago. He really liked the trip. He came back and said he wouldn't mind being in the government; it would be cool to go on the underground railroad the senators have. He said he visited someone's office, and he was given a pencil and a postcard, and he wrote a letter to say thank you, and he got a letter back. His whole class went, and they were taken all over. They went to see some battlefields, too.

She doesn't know which battlefields, however; nor does she know which war was fought on those fields. She is one of those whom southern children of her age have already learned to identify as "Yankees," even know to fear or envy. There are no equivalents for her, however—no name she is wont to hurl at southerners or, for that matter, anyone else. True, she learned long ago, at about four or five, that black children, whom she sees on television but has never gone to school with, are "funny," and the single Japanese child she had as a classmate in kindergarten was "strange, because of her eyes"; but such children never come up in her remarks, and when they are brought up in the course of conversation with a visitor, she is quick to change the subject or go firmly silent. Nor is there any great amount of prejudice in her, at least of a kind which she has directly on her mind. Her drawings reveal her to be concerned with flowers, which she likes to help her mother arrange, with horses, which she loves to ride, and with stars, which she is proud to know rather a lot about.

The last interest prompts from her a bit of apologetic explanation: "My brother started being interested in the stars; my daddy gave him a telescope and a book. Then he lost interest. Then I started using the telescope, and my daddy said I shouldn't, because maybe my brother would mind, but he doesn't." And, in fact, her parents do have rather firm ideas about what boys ought to be interested in, what girls ought to find appealing. Men run for political office, she knows. Sometimes women do, but only rarely; anyway, she won't be one of them. In 1971 she thought the President was "a very good man; he has to be—otherwise he wouldn't be president." The same held for the governor and the town officials who make sure that all goes well in her neighborhood.

When the Watergate scandal began to capture more and more of her parents' attention, she listened and wondered and tried to accommodate her longstanding faith with her new knowledge: "The President made a mistake. It's too bad. You shouldn't do wrong; if you're president, it's bad for everyone when you go against the law. But the country is good. The President must feel real bad, for the mistake he made." After which she talked about *her* mistakes: she broke a valuable piece of china; she isn't doing as well in school as either her parents or her teachers feel she ought to be doing; and not least, she forgets to make her bed a lot of the time, and her mother or the maid has to remind her of that responsibility.

Then she briefly returned to President Nixon, this time with a comment not unlike those "intuitive" ones made by Australian children (from New South Wales) in Professor Robert Connell's book *The Child's Construction of Politics*. "A friend of mine said she didn't believe a word the President says, because he himself doesn't believe what he says, so why should we." What did the girl herself believe? "Well, I believe my parents, but I believe my friend, too. Do you think the President's wife believes him? If he doesn't believe himself, what about her?" So much for the ambiguities of childhood, not to mention such legal and psychiatric matters as guilt, knowing deception, the nature of self-serving illusions, and political guile.

As one listens to her and others like her—advantaged children, they might be called—one wonders, again, where are to be found the symbols of political power, of pomp and circumstance, that are meant to impress, inspire, and intimidate. . . . Of course, there is nothing very dramatic to catch hold of; unlike black children, or Appalachian children, or even the children of well-to-do southern white families, the girl I have just quoted has no vivid politically tinged memories of her own, nor any conveyed by her parents to take possession of psychologically—no governor's defiance, no sit-ins or demonstrations, no sheriff's car and a sheriff's voice, no mass funeral after a mine disaster, no experience with a welfare worker, no strike with the police there to "mediate," no sudden lay-off (not yet, at least), followed by accusations and recriminations—and drastically curbed spending.

Such unforgettable events in the lives of children very definitely help to shape their attitudes toward their nation and its political authority. The black children I have come to know in different parts of this country, even those from relatively well-off homes, say critical things about America and its leaders at an earlier age than white children do—and connect their general observations to specific experiences, vivid moments, really, in their lives. A black child of eight, in rural Mississippi or in a northern ghetto, an Indian or Chicano or Appalachian child, can sound like a disillusioned old radical: down with the system, because it's a thoroughly unjust one, for all that one hears in school—including, especially, those words quoted from the Declaration of Independence or the Constitution: that "all men are created equal," that they are "endowed by their Creator with certain unalienable rights."

The pledge of allegiance to the flag can be an occasion for boredom, at the very least, among some elementary school children; the phrase "with liberty and justice for all" simply rings hollow, or is perceived as an ironic boast meant to be uttered by others elsewhere. Here is what a *white* schoolteacher in Barbour County, Alabama, has observed over the years:

> I'm no great fan of the colored: I don't have anything against them, either. I do my work, teaching the colored, and I like the children I teach, because they don't put on airs with you, the way some of our own children do—if their daddy is big and important. The uppity niggers—well, they leave this state. We won't put up with them. The good colored people, they're fine. I grew up with them. I know their children, and I try to teach them as best I can. I understand how they feel; I believe I do. I have a very bright boy, James; he told me that he didn't want to draw a picture of the American flag. I asked him why not. He said that he just wasn't interested. It's hard for them—they don't feel completely part of this country.
>
> I had a girl once, she was quite fresh; she told me that she didn't believe a word of that salute to the flag, and she didn't believe a word of what I read to them about our history. I sent her to the principal. I was ready to have her expelled, for good. The principal said she was going to be a civil rights type one day, but by then I'd simmered down. "To tell the truth," I said, "I don't believe most of the colored children think any different than her." The principal gave me a look and said, "Yes, I can see what you

mean." A lot of times I skip the salute to the flag; the children start laughing, and they forget the words, and they become restless. It's not a good way to start the day. I'd have to threaten them, if I wanted them to behave while saluting. So, we go right into our arithmetic lessons.

In contrast, among middle-class white children of our northern suburbs, who have no Confederate flag with which to divide their loyalties, the morning salute can be occasion for real emotional expression: This I believe! It is all too easy for some of us to be amused at or, more strongly, to scorn such a development in the lives of children: the roots of smug nationalism if not outright chauvinism. But for thousands of such children, as for their parents, the flag has a great deal of meaning, and the political authority of the federal, state, and local governments is not to be impugned in any way. Among many working-class families policemen, firemen, clerks in the post office or city hall are likely to be friends, relatives, neighbors. Among upper-middle-class families, one can observe a strong sense of loyalty to a system which clearly, to them, has been friendly indeed. And the children learn to express what their parents feel and often enough say, loud and clear.

"My uncle is a sergeant in the army," the nine-year-old son of a Boston factory worker told me. He went on to remind me that another uncle belongs to the Boston police department. The child has watched parades, been taken to an army base, visited an old warship, climbed the steps of a historic shrine. He has seen the flag in school and in church. He has heard his country prayed for, extolled, defended against all sorts of critics. He said when he was eight, and in the third grade, that he would one day be a policeman. Other friends of his, without relatives on the force, echo the ambition. Last summer, when he was nearer to ten, he spoke of motorcycles and baseball and hockey; and when he went to the games he sang the national anthem in a strong and sure voice. Our government? It is "the best you can have." Our president? He's "good."

I pushed a little: was President Nixon in any trouble? Yes, he was, and he might have made some mistakes. Beyond that the child would not easily go. His parents had for the first time voted Republican in 1972, and were disappointed with, disgusted by, the President's behavior over Watergate. But they have been reluctant to be too critical of the President in front of their children: "I don't want to make the kids feel that there's anything wrong with the *country*," the father says. There's *plenty* wrong with the President, he admits, and with the way the country is being run—and, he adds, with big business, so greedy all the time, as well as with the universities and those who go to them or teach at them; but America, he believes, is the greatest nation that ever has been—something, one has to remember, every president's speechwriters, Democratic or Republican, liberal or conservative, manage to work into just about every televised address.[1]

Only indirectly, through drawings or the use of comic exaggeration or metaphorical flights of fancy, does the boy dare show what he has been making of Watergate, news of which has, of course, come to him primarily through television. Asked to draw a picture of President Nixon, the boy laughs, says he doesn't know how to do so (he had had no such trouble a year earlier), and finally manages to sketch an exceedingly small man, literally half the size of a former portrait by the same artist. Then, as he prepares to hand over the completed project, he has some second thoughts. He adds a blue sky. Then he blackens the sky. He puts earth under the man, but not, as is his usual custom, grass. Then he proceeds to make two big round black circles, with what seem to be peices of string attached to them. What are they? He is not sure: "Well, either they could be bombs, and someone could

---

[1]There is nothing like a political crisis, however, to cause even such a child, among others, to have grave doubts about what is happening in the world around him. The recent and continuing racial tension in Boston has prompted apprehension and confusion in this white boy, who lives in South Boston, only three miles from its tragically unsettled high school. The boy lashes out at important city officials, at newspapers and television stations—repeating what he has heard, but also, once in a while, coming up with idiosyncratic and illuminating flashes of social analysis, not to mention empathic generosity:

> The people who called us bad names, like racists, don't have to send their children anywhere except where they want to; their children, a lot of them, go to private schools, even in the suburbs. It's nice and easy to give a sermon from a distance. If I was one of the black kids, I wouldn't give up. I'd keep coming here. I'd keep trying to show I can go anywhere. It's no joke being black. But it's no joke being here, with everyone telling us to behave, and do one thing and do another thing. If you've got money and influence, you can tell everyone off, and no one tells you off.

As for the black children of Roxbury who are being bused, they do indeed feel and put into words what that white child attributes to them. One black youth put it stoically, tersely:

> It's no picnic going to school in South Boston; the schools there are lousy. You take a bus ride and end up in a no good place. But we can't give in. We're fighting to get into America, and you have to get into every part of it, even the no good parts, or else they'll always be trying to keep you out, keep you out.

light the fuse, and they could explode and he'd get hurt, and people would be sad; or they could be balls and chains—you know, if you're going to jail."

Way across the tracks, out in part of "rich suburbia," as I hear factory workers sometimes refer to certain towns well to the north and west of Boston, there is among adults a slightly different kind of love of country—less outspoken, perhaps, less defensive, but not casual and certainly appreciative. In those towns, too, children respond quite directly and sensitively to the various messages they have learned from their parents—and to a number of low-key "spectacles": flags out on July Fourth; the deference of civil employees; pictures of father in uniform during one or another war; and perhaps most of all, conversations heard at the table. "My father hears bad news on television, and he says 'thank God we're Americans,' " says a girl of eleven. She goes on to register her mother's gentle, thoughtful qualification: "It's lucky we live where we do."

Her mother's sister, older and attracted to the cultural life only a city offers, has to live a more nervous life: "My aunt has huge locks on her doors. My mother leaves the keys right in the car." Nevertheless, the United States of America, for the girl's aunt as well as her parents, is nowhere near collapse: "Everything is going to be all right with the country. This is the best place to live in the whole world. That's what my aunt says." The girl pauses. Now is the time to ask her what *she* has to say. But she needs no prodding; immediately she goes on:

> No place is perfect. We're in trouble now. The President and his friends, they've been caught doing bad things. It's too bad. My older brother argues with daddy; he told daddy that it's wrong to let the President get away with all he's done, while everyone else has to go to jail; and he told daddy there's a lot of trouble in the country, and no one is doing anything to stop the trouble. The President, I think he's running as fast as he can from the police. I guess I would if I knew I'd done wrong. But I'd never be able to get to Egypt or Russia, so he's lucky, that President.

It is simply not altogether true, as most studies of "political socialization" conclude, that she and other children like her *only* tend to "idealize" the president, or give a totally "romanticized" kind of loyalty to the country, on the basis of what they hear, or choose to hear, from their parents or teachers. Many parents do select carefully what they say in front of their children; and children are indeed encouraged by their teachers, and the books they read, to see presidents and governors and supreme court justices and senators as figures much larger than life. Yet in no time—at least these days—children can lay such influences aside, much to the astonishment of even parents who *don't* try to shield their children from "bad news" or "the evils of this world," two ways of putting it one hears again and again.

Black children laugh at books given them to read in school, snicker while the teacher recites historical pieties which exclude mention of so very much, and often enough challenge their own parents when they understandably try to soften or delay the realization of what it has been like and will continue to be like for black people in America. White children, too, as James Agee noticed in the 1930s, pick up the hypocrisies and banalities about them and connect what they see or hear to a larger vision—a notion of those who have a lot and those who have very little at all.

"The President checks in with the people who own the coal company," a miner's shy son, aged eleven, remarked last spring in Harlan, Kentucky, where the Duke Power Company was fighting hard to prevent the United Mine Workers from becoming a spokesman of the workers. The child may well be incorrect; but one suspects that a log of the calls made by the President would show him in contact with people very much like those who are on the board of the Duke Power Company, as opposed to people like the boy's parents.

By the same token when a child whose father happens to be on the board of a utility company, or a lawyer who represents such clients, appears to overlook whatever critical remarks his or her parents have made about the United States and instead emphasizes without exception the nation's virtues, including those of its leaders, by no means is a process of psychological distortion necessarily at work. The child may well have taken the measure of what has been heard (and overheard) and come to a conclusion: this is what they really believe, and just as important, the reason they believe what they say has to do with a whole way of life—the one we are all living. So, it is best to keep certain thoughts (in older people, called "views") to myself, lest there be trouble.

Too complicated and subtle an analysis for a child under ten, or even under fifteen? We who in this century have learned to give children credit for the most astonishing refinements of perception or feeling with respect to the nuances of family life or the ups and downs of neighborhood play for some reason are less inclined to picture those same children as canny social observers or political analysts. No one teaches young children sociology or psychology; yet they are constantly noticing who gets along with whom, and why. If in school, or even when approached by a visitor with a questionnaire (or more casually, but no less noticeably, an all too interested face and manner), those same children tighten up and say little or nothing, or come up with remarks that are platitudes, pure and simple, they may well have come up with one of their sophisticated psychological judgments— reserving for another time the expression of any controversial political asides that may have come to mind.

As for some of those children who are a little different, who get called "rebellious" or "aggressive," and sent off to guidance counselors or psychiatrists, they can occasionally help us know the thoughts of many other, more "normal" children—because someone under stress can under certain circumstances be unusually forthcoming. "My poor father is scared," says the son of a rather well-to-do businessman, the owner of large tracts of Florida land, on which work, every year, hundreds of migrant farm workers, who, believe me, are also scared.

What frightens the boy's father? His twelve-year-old namesake, who is described by his teachers as "a behavior problem"—he is, one gathers, fresh and surly at certain times—tries hard to provide an answer, almost as if whatever he comes up with will help him, too:

> I don't know, but there will be times he's sweating, and he's swearing, and he's saying he gave money to all those politicians, and they'd better do right by the growers, or they'll regret it. Then he says he's tired of living here, and maybe he should go back to Michigan where his grand-daddy was born. The other day the sheriff came by and said he didn't know if he could keep those television people out indefinitely. So, daddy got on the phone to

our senator, and we're waiting. But it may cost us a lot, and we may lose. Daddy says we will either get machines to replace the migrants, or we'll go broke, what with the trouble they're beginning to cause. But I don't think he really means it. He's always threatening us with trouble ahead, my mother says, but you have to pour salt on what he says.

That same boy scoffs at what he hears his teachers say about American history; one day he blurted out in class that his father had "coolies" working for him. Another time he said we'd had to kill a lot of Indians, because they had the land, and we wanted it, and they wouldn't "bow to us, the way we wanted." His teacher felt that she had witnessed yet another psychiatric outburst, but a number of his classmates did not. One of them, not especially a friend of his, remarked several days later, "He only said what everyone knows. I told my mother what he said, and she said it wasn't so bad, and why did they get so upset? But she told me that sometimes it's best to keep quiet, and not say a lot of things you think."

It so happens that the child's mother, speaking in front of her three sons, and without any evidence of shame or embarrassment, willingly picks up where she left off a day earlier with one of her boys:

> Yes, I feel we had to conquer Indians, or there wouldn't be the America we all know and love today. I tell my children that you ought to keep your eye on the positive, accentuate it, you know, and push aside anything negative about this country. Or else we'll sink into more trouble; and it's been good to us, very good, America has.

Her husband is also a grower. Her sons do indeed "idealize" America's political system—but when a classmate begins to stir things up a little with a few blunt comments, there is not great surprise, simply the nod of recognition and agreement. And very important, a boy demonstrates evidence of moral development, a capacity for ethical reflection, even though both at home and at school he has been given scant encouragement to regard either migrants or Indians with compassion. Both Piaget and Lawrence Kohlberg have indicated that cognitive and moral development in children have thier own rhythm, tempo, and subtlety. Children ingeniously use every scrap of emotional life available to them as they develop "psychosexually," and they do likewise as they try to figure out how (and for whom) the world works. A friend's remarks, a classmate's comments, a statement heard on television can give a child surprising moral perspective and distance on himself and his heritage—though, of course, he is not necessarily thereby "liberated" from the (often countervailing) day-to-day realities of, say, class and race.[2]

[2]Kohlberg's work is especially helpful. Children come across, in his studies, as lively and thoughtful, as inclined to question and make critical moral judgments of various kinds, within limits set by their developing mental life.

Needless to say, as Jeb Stuart Magruder has indicated in his public remarks and his recent book (*An American Life*, Atheneum, 1974), the acquisition of moral values is very much connected to the child's moral education, obtained not only within the family (as psychiatrists often emphasize) but in the schools and, not least, informally in neighborhood play. See Kohlberg's "Moral and Religious Education and the Public Schools: A Developmental View" in Theodore Sizer, ed., *Religion and Public Education* (Houghton Mifflin, 1967).

PUBLIC POLICIES, PRIVATE INTERESTS

MORTON MINTZ and JERRY S. COHEN

The Regulatory Agencies

Marked by the vigorous exposés of the muckrakers and the "popu-
lism" of such politicians as Robert La Follette, the early years of
the twentieth century witnessed considerable popular antagonism
toward the depredations of the robber barons and the dominating
role big business had come to play in American life. Responding
to a public outcry that crested during the New Deal, the government
began to regulate major industries through independent commissions. The "Big Six" were the Interstate Commerce Commission
(established in 1887); the Federal Trade Commission (1914); the
Federal Power Commission (1930); the Federal Communications
Commission (1934); the Securities and Exchange Commission
(1934); and the Civil Aeronautics Board (1938). (The Federal Reserve
and other agencies would also be given regulatory functions, as
would units of executive departments, such as HEW's Food and Drug
Administration.)

These agencies were given significant autonomy, including quasi-
judicial functions such as issuing licenses. In creating them, Congress had been especially worried about interference from the executive. Yet from the beginning, when businessmen first took their place
as commissioners, the threat was not interference by the White
House but subversion of these commissions from within by exactly
those interests they had been designed to control. This problem is
considered by journalists Morton Mintz and Jerry Cohen in the following excerpt from their best-selling book, *America, Inc.*

> *The public provides public utilities, through rates,*
> *with such experts as the public utilities may require*
> *to protect the utilities' rights, but the public,*
> *through taxes, does not provide adequate funds for*
> *its own protection.*
>
> Florida Public Service Commission,
> quoted in *Washington Post*, April 13, 1969

Excerpts from *America, Inc.* By Morton Mintz & Jerry S. Cohen. Copyright © 1971
by Jerry S. Cohen & Morton Mintz. Reprinted with the permission of The Dial Press.

After John F. Kennedy was elected President in 1960 he asked an old friend of the family, the late James M. Landis, to write what would become the *Report on Regulatory Agencies to the President-Elect*. A former dean of the Harvard Law School, Landis was extraordinarily qualified, having been chairman of the Securities and Exchange Commission in the 1930s and chairman of the Civil Aeronautics Board in 1947. His report dealt concisely with a fundamental problem, the relationships an agency has with the industries it regulates and with the public.

Direct contacts by industry representatives "of necessity . . . are frequent and generally productive of intelligent ideas," Landis said. At the same time, "Contacts with the public are rare and generally unproductive of anything except complaint." The following key sentence contained a warning which is as valid today as it was in 1960:

> Irrespective of the absence of social contacts and the acceptance of undue hospitality, it is the daily machine-gun-like impact on both agency and its staff of industry representation that makes for industry orientation on the part of many honest and capable agency members as well as agency staffs.

Public participation in the regulatory process is minimal. The citizen comes to be regarded as an intruder, if he should attempt to participate at all. Over and over again, regulatory agencies have been discovered using secrecy as a device to make it impossible for representatives of the public to defend their interests, or even to know that their interests need to be defended. At the Interstate Commerce Commission, for example, secrecy played a role in the merger trend in transportation. Staff experts made a report warning the ICC to assert new authority to meet the growing trend among railroads to reorganize as conglomerate corporations. On July 6, 1970, Murray Seeger wrote in the *Los Angeles Times*:

> The report was made in March, 1969, just as the Penn Central Railroad was preparing to transform itself into a holding company. Fifteen months later, when the railroad was bankrupt, the study was still marked "administratively confidential" and was "under study" by the ICC.
>
> Since the ICC did not exert wider authority when it was urged to do so, the new breed of transportation conglomerates are not effectively monitored by government, in the view of many Washington experts. . . .

"More specifically" [the suppressed staff report said], "the conglomerate holding company provides a convenient means for the transfer to other industries of assets now devoted to transportation."

In the view of several congressional investigators, the warnings contained in last year's ICC study have come to reality in the 1970 bankruptcy of the nation's largest railroad.

In the Federal Communications Commission, Nicholas Johnson has said, citizen participation in the decision-making process "is virtually non-existent," with the "necessary but unhappy result . . . that the FCC is a 'captive' of the very industry it is purportedly attempting to regulate." Replying to a questionnaire from a sub-committee of the Senate Committee on the Judiciary, Johnson recalled the case of a Jackson, Mississippi, television station, WLBT. Renewal of its license was opposed by the United Church of Christ, on the ground that WLBT had systematically promoted segregationist views, refused to present opposing views, and excluded Negroes. A favorite technique at WLBT was to flash a "Sorry, Cable Trouble" sign on the screen whenever a network program was presenting somebody or something the station management didn't like. What made the case noteworthy, however, was the refusal of the FCC over a period of years to recognize that the United Church had "standing" to appear and present its arguments. "Petitioners were told, in effect, that they were not even entitled to be heard so far as the FCC was concerned," Johnson said. The issue of "standing" finally was resolved by the United States Court of Appeals for the District of Columbia. In a decision that slapped down the Commission, Judge Warren E. Burger, now Chief Justice of the United States, said:

The broadcast industry does not seem to have grasped the simple fact that a broadcast license is a public trust subject to termination for breach of duty. . . .

We cannot believe that the Congressional mandate of public participation which the Commission says it seeks to fulfill was meant to be limited to writing letters to the Commission, to inspection of records, to the Commission's grace in considering listener claims, or to mere non-participating appearance at hearings.[1]

---

[1] *Office of Communication of United Church of Christ* v. *F.C.C.*, 359 F. 2d 994, 1003.

The passive approach to public participation is so ingrained in regulatory bodies that almost never do they go out into the community to seek the views of affected citizens—say, the blacks who comprised 47 per cent of the population in WLBT's viewer area.

Nicholas Johnson gave several additional examples in testimony in July 1970 before Senator Edward M. Kennedy (D–Mass.). One case involved the issue whether, in bald terms, the FCC as a matter of course will renew existing broadcast licenses each three years in perpetuity. Senator John O. Pastore sponsored legislation to grant just such a bounty to the broadcasters. . . . When his bill failed the FCC rushed into the breach. Johnson testified:

> In January 1970 the Commission, working with White House approval, adopted a "policy statement" which inhibits community groups and other private citizens from competing for broadcast licenses. Under the new policy a potential competitor must show that the existing licensee has not "substantially" served his community in the previous three years. Since the Commission has no standards whatsoever as to what constitutes substantial service, competitors have nothing to go on in determining what licenses to challenge. The Commission, with its traditional preference for the powerful and the status quo, will not say what these standards are. Since the policy statement, not one competing application has been filed for a television station license—which would tend to indicate that the policy statement has served its intended purpose. This statement was adopted without any opportunity for public comment. In fact, the Commission *rejected* such comments before the policy was adopted.[2]

Johnson emphasized that rather than being unique, the FCC "is but a microcosm of what passes for governmental representation of the public generally." Here is a microcosm of what passes for public representation at the Interstate Commerce Commission:

On February 26, 1970, the Southern Railway System filed an application to abolish discounts on all round-trip tickets and to establish a minimum one-dollar fare. The effect on commuters

---

[2]Testimony before the Subcommittee on Administrative Practice and Procedure of the Committee on the Judiciary, United States Senate, on S. 3434 and S. 2544, July 21, 1970.

between Washington, D.C., and suburban Alexandria, Virginia, would have been almost to double the price of a round-trip ticket, which then was fifty-five cents. Neither the ICC nor the railway took any step to notify the commuters, and the fare changes were ordered into effect on April 1. On March 30, however, a friendly ticket agent tipped off one of the commuters. A protest to the ICC followed. The next day, the Commission reversed itself, postponed the increases for seven months, and promised an investigation and a public hearing.[3]

The Civil Aeronautics Board has shown similar disdain for air travelers, even those who happen to be congressmen. Under the law either the CAB or an air carrier may set fares. However rates are set, an airline must incorporate them in a tariff filed with the Board. A carrier that charges rates other than the filed ones violates the law. The Board may change the rates on its own initiative or on receipt of a complaint—but only after serving notice and holding a hearing. Over the years, however, *ex parte*, informal meetings between the CAB and officials of airlines seeking fare increases have undermined the ritual prescribed in law.

Several times, Representative John E. Moss (D–Calif.), a determined fighter for public and consumer causes, protested to the Board about the *ex parte* meetings and, as well, about the Board's lack of standards for testing the reasonableness of fares. His protests went unheeded, and the *ex parte* meetings continued into the summer of 1969. At that time United Airlines filed new fare increases. In early August several carriers followed United's lead. While the proposed increases were pending, CAB members and officials of the airlines scheduled an *ex parte* meeting for August 14.

Moss learned of the meeting. He requested but was denied permission to attend; it goes without saying that an ordinary airline passenger would not have been admitted, either.

Following the closed August 14 meeting with the airlines, the Board issued an order calling for oral argument on whether it should exercise its power to investigate and suspend the new rates before they could become effective. Nowhere in the order did the Board suggest that it might propose a fare formula of its own.

Moss, by now joined by thirty-one other congressmen, not only renewed the complaints about the *ex parte* meetings, but also

[3]*Washington Post*, March 31, 1970, p. A1.

urged the Board to suspend the new rates, to undertake a general investigation aimed at defining with greater precision the standards of reasonableness for fares, and, finally, to use the more precise standards to set fares.

The CAB went ahead and heard oral arguments. Moss and his associates refused to participate, on the ground that the Board had made up its mind in advance and that the proceeding was *pro forma*. Eight days later, on September 12, 1969, the Board ruled. It declared the increases proposed by the airlines possibly unjust or unreasonable and suspended them. But it gave the airlines, which had pleaded their cause in secret, no cause to weep, and the public, which had been excluded from the *ex parte* meetings, no cause to cheer. After all, the Board asserted, the carriers had demonstrated a need for "some additional revenue." And so it held that a 6 per cent fare increase, which, to be sure, was a lesser one than the airlines had formally filed, was necessary. It will be remembered that the Board had not publicly hinted at the possibility that it would outline a fare formula of its own. Yet the CAB not only set out such a formula, but also took the regulatory steps required to make the formula effective almost immediately. The cooperation of the airlines was essential; having met in secret with the CAB, it is not surprising that their cooperation was forthcoming.

Representative Moss and his colleagues then appealed to the Court of Appeals in Washington. A three-judge panel gave them an unprecedented victory. "This appeal," Judge J. Skelly Wright said for the court on July 9, 1970, "presents the recurring question which has plagued public regulation of industry: whether the regulatory agency is unduly oriented toward the interests of the industry it is designed to regulate, rather than the public interest it is designed to protect." Answering the recurring question by sending the case back to the CAB for further proceedings, the court said:

> We hold that the procedure used by the Board is contrary to the statutory rate-making plan in that it fences the public out of the rate-making process.... While we recognize that ... the Board has an obligation to afford the carriers sufficient revenues, that obligation cannot become a *carte blanche* allowing the Board to deal only with the carriers and disregard the other factors, such as the traveling public's interest in the lowest possible fares and

high standards of service . . . we emphatically reject any intimation by the Board that its responsibilities to the carriers are more important than its responsibilities to the public.

Although our focus . . . is on the independent regulatory agencies, it is well to point out that regulatory operations of all kinds have suffered from the lack of public participation. The Federal Trade Commission provided a memorable example in 1963 when it proposed to make the Flammable Fabrics Act applicable to blankets used principally to wrap or clothe infants. "A public hearing was held but there was no government agency or individual who could appear to represent and defend the consumer interest," Commissioner Philip Elman has said. "Incredibly, despite evidence that the fabric used in baby blankets was dangerously flammable and could not legally be used in making clothing for children and adults, and despite the obvious and conceded fact that receiving blankets are worn by infants as clothing, serving essentially the same purpose as a bathrobe or dressing gown, the Commission ruled that baby blankets were not articles of clothing and thus not protected by the Flammable Fabrics Act."[4] Later the law was amended to include baby blankets.

Issues of arcane complexity but substantial importance are commonplace in the regulatory agencies and in units of the Executive with regulatory powers. Whether an antibiotics producer is permitted in the prescribing instructions for physicians to recommend use in particular infections may determine whether a particular product will be a moneymaker or a money-loser—and, if that use is ill advised, whether it will create needless hazards by displacing safer alternative therapy. Whether flammable or fume-producing fabrics and carpeting are permitted in airliners is a matter of money for the airlines—and possibly a matter of asphyxiation for passengers in a plane in which fire occurs. Whether standards are set, and *what* standards are set, for dust levels in the coal mines and for radiation in the uranium mines, determines whether men live or die. Whether the Federal Trade Commission, in measuring tar and nicotine in various cigarette brands, used

---

[4]*Responses to Questionnaire on Citizen Involvement and Responsive Agency Decision-Making,* committee print submitted by the Subcommittee on Administrative Practice and Procedure to the Committee on the Judiciary, United States Senate, Ninety-first Congress, First Session, September 9, 1969, p. 134.

a butt length favored by the tobacco industry or a length favored by public health groups involved a difference of seven millimeters, or 0.27559 inch. However, the butt length favored by the industry tended to make one brand pretty much like another; the length favored by the health groups disclosed large differences.[5]

How "peanut butter" is defined determines whether what is sold under that name is derived mainly from peanuts or is substantially flavored vegetable oil. Whether a bake mix for "blueberry" muffins can contain chemical pellets instead of blueberries; whether a General Foods drink concentrate called "Orange Plus" could contain less orange than orange juice; whether a Carnation Company "eggnog" could contain no eggs—such questions also are regulatory matters.

Rarely has the public been represented in agency proceedings. Never are major industries without representation, usually by platoons and battalions of Washington lawyers—products of the very best law schools.

In 1892, Richard S. Olney, a railroad attorney who became Attorney General under President Grover Cleveland, told the president of the Burlington Railroad that the Interstate Commerce Commission "can be of great use to the railroads. it satisfies the popular clamor for a government supervision of railroads, at the same time that supervision is almost entirely minimal. The part of wisdom is not to destroy the Commission, but to utilize it."[6]

That is really what it is all about.

Founded in 1887 to regulate railroads, the ICC is the oldest regulatory agency and, in terms of volume of cases (8,000 in 1969), the busiest. "Time and time again, the ICC has proved to be protector of the railroads rather than the public interest," Representative Richard L. Ottinger (D–N.Y.) told a House subcommittee. "Time and time again, the railroads have used the Commission as a mere extension of their corporate structures. The ICC's usual attitude is one of torpor; on occasion, it awakens long enough to authorize the discontinuance of a few more passenger trains."[7] A group of law students who, under Ralph Nader's guidance,

---

[5]*Washington Post,* July 2, 1967, p. A1.
[6]Cited by Representative Richard L. Ottinger (D–N.Y.) in testimony before the Subcommittee on Transportation and Aeronautics of the Committee on Interstate and Foreign Commerce, House of Representatives, November 17, 1969.
[7]*Ibid.*

investigated the ICC called it an "elephants' graveyard of political hacks" designed and run to protect transportation industries from consumers. In a report of more than one thousand typewritten pages, the students documented charges of incompetence, subservience to the highway, rail, and water transport industries, suppression of price competition in favor of collusion, and price-fixing and nonenforcement of safety requirements. Robert C. Fellmeth, a Harvard law student who directed the investigators, summed up by saying that the ICC has become so infested by "institutional corruption" as to be "an extension of the [transportation] industry."[8]

Once again a balancing act must be undertaken. No implication is intended that all regulatory agencies have the dismal record of the ICC. It will be recalled ... that in May 1968 Merrill Lynch, Pierce, Fenner & Smith set up its own Effective Government Association and by September 1 had raised reported contributions of $44,775. At the time Merrill Lynch began its enterprise in open political fundraising the firm was under investigation by the Securities and Exchange Commission, which was the most effective of the regulatory agencies until the advent of the Nixon Administration, when a process of disintegration set in. In August 1968 the SEC filed charges of securities fraud against fourteen Merrill Lynch officers and employees. In October William J. La Fleur, treasurer of the Effective Government Association and assistant general counsel of Merrill Lynch, insisted to Walter Pincus of the *Washington Post* that the SEC case had played no part in the decision to set up the association.

Subsequent events provided no basis to doubt this assertion. Merrill Lynch consented to an SEC finding that it had used advance "inside" information from the Douglas Aircraft Company for the advantage of preferred institutional clients, in the process defrauding the investing public of an estimated $4.5 million. On November 26, 1968, the SEC imposed the most severe penalties in its history for misuse of "inside" information. The Commission ordered suspension of one vice president for sixty days, and of another vice president and five salesmen for twenty-one days. The SEC also censured three vice presidents. In an action that is formally said to imply neither guilt nor innocence, the SEC

[8]*Washington Post*, March 17, 1970, p. A1.

191

dropped charges against an executive vice president, a senior vice president, and two plain vice presidents.[9]

Even a strong regulatory law, or strong sections of such a law, can be readily frustrated. Rules to implement the legislation must be drafted, adopted, and interpreted. Each step in the process affords affected industries opportunities to undercut the law and to fight delaying actions in administrative and court proceedings that sometimes seem interminable.

Those who would undertake mergers involving broadcast media are required by law to bear the burden of showing that the public interest would be served, but the law did not deter the Federal Communications Commission from approving, over opposition on antitrust grounds by the Justice Department, the acquisition by the International Telephone and Telegraph Company of the American Broadcasting Companies.

The Interstate Commerce Commission presided over the deterioration of passenger service, which pleased the railroads but was not what the law required or the public wanted. In the eleven years ending in 1969 the number of intercity passenger trains declined more than two-thirds, from 1,448 to 480, and fourteen railroads abandoned all intercity service. Finally the Commission requested authority over standards of passenger service, but, in a signal to the railroads not to worry, Commissioner Kenneth H. Tuggle said, "We do not intend to use that jurisdiction in requiring heavy investment in new passenger equipment."[10]

Now and then an internal critic comes along to tug at the Tuggleses—a Philip Elman in the Federal Trade Commission, but he left in 1970; a Nicholas Johnson in the Federal Communications Commission, but his term is up in 1972. The FCC "has performed as the ally of the broadcasters in every light skirmish with the public," Johnson said in a brutally candid article in the *New Republic*. He continued:

> The FCC once decided that a radio station with more than 30 minutes of commercials per hour was serving the public interest.

[9]*Washington Post*, November 27, 1968, p. A1.
[10]Ottinger testimony, *op. cit.*

It approved the renewal of a station that quite candidly reported it proposed to program no news, and no public affairs. . . . It examined the record of a station guilty of bilking advertisers out of $6000 in fraudulent transactions—while on a one-year probationary status for similar offenses earlier—and found that the station had, nonetheless, "minimally met the public interest standard." And recently the Commission showed its reluctance to enforce even its technical and business standards, when it refused to consider license revocation for a licensee who had been charged with not paying his employees, stealing news, ordering his engineer to make fraudulent entries in the station's logbook, operating with an improperly licensed engineer and 87 other technical violations over a three-year period.

But the broadcasting industry, the Commissioner noted, has to his knowledge never "complained that the kind of intellectually corrupt decisions just mentioned are as much of a disservice to the industry as to the public—as I believe to be the case. The industry has for decades deluded itself into believing, as National Association of Broadcasters Chairman Willard Walbridge put it on "Face the Nation," that "the public says that the programming is fine . . . that they like broadcasting pretty much the way it is."[11]

Many men assume regulatory responsibilities with the intention of someday leaving government to go to work for the industry or specific companies they have been regulating. Congressman Richard Ottinger discussed some examples involving the Interstate Commerce Commission before a House subcommittee. One case involved William H. Tucker, a former chairman. "Mr. Tucker left the ICC, served nine months in the 'purgatory' of his law firm, Maguire and Tucker (which virtually shares offices with the Penn Central Railroad), then became vice president for New England operations of Penn Central," Ottinger said.[12]

In 1969 Bernard F. Schmid, the ICC's managing director and top administrative official, abruptly quit to join the same law firm. The report by the team of investigators led by Ralph Nader charged that Schmid had a "close" relationship with a regulated

---

[11]"We Need the Pastore Bill [by Louis L. Jaffe]; No We Don't [by Nicholas Johnson]," *New Republic*, December 6, 1969, p. 17.
[12]Ottinger testimony, *op cit.*

firm in New York City, U.S. Freight Company, which has several freight forwarders as subsidiaries. The investigators said they were told by past and present ICC staff members that Schmid "frequently called U.S. Freight officials . . . to inform them of the activities of rival freight forwarders in the ICC." Schmid said the charges were "untrue."

While chairman of the Federal Communications Commission, Rosel H. Hyde provided a decisive vote in each of three decisions that staved off a challenge to the renewal of the television license of KSL, which is a cornerstone of the news media empire of the Mormon Church. This performance was consistent with Hyde's votes in similar cases. In March 1970, soon after retiring, Hyde joined Wilkinson, Cragun and Barker, the law firm which represented KSL in the FCC proceedings. On April 6 the National Association of Broadcasters presented Hyde with its Distinguished Service Award.

"The record number of FCC Commissioners and other staff who have left the agency over the years to go to work for the very industries they were supposed to be regulating is not a fact to inspire confidence in the agency's performance," Nicholas Johnson said in his July 1970 testimony before Senator Kennedy. "It is what another witness here today, Ralph Nader, has characterized as the 'deferred bribe.' But as blood curdling as the realities may be of those who are performing at an agency with one eye on their next job, it is even more frightening to find that those who *do* want to stay and serve are driven off one way or another."

While a congressman, Melvin R. Laird, the Secretary of Defense, expressed concern over the possibility that some government regulators would "so position themselves as to (1) obtain lucrative positions with the regulated enterprises and (2) open themselves and their agencies to perhaps valid accusations of conflict of interest."[13] In the case of the Food and Drug Administration, a study made at Laird's request showed that of 813 scientific, medical and technical employees who left in the four years ended December 31, 1963, 83 appeared from available records to have taken positions with FDA-regulated companies. The true

---

[13]Cited by Morton Mintz in *By Prescription Only* (Boston: Beacon and Houghton Mifflin, 1967), p. 176.

figure, however, may have been higher, because data were not available on 98 persons who had left before retirement or on others who may have taken industry employment after retirement. The big exodus from the FDA to industry came after Commissioner Goddard's appointment in 1966. The most important involved Dr. Joseph F. Sadusk, Jr., who had been the agency's top doctor for two years. He was pro-industry from the start. Many of his actions and statements involving, among other things, a long-acting sulfonamide called Midicel and an antiobiotic called Chloromycetin, were considered perilous to children but advantageous to Parke, Davis & Company, the supplier. After a year at Johns Hopkins Medical School Dr. Sadusk joined Parke, Davis as a vice president.

The total annual budget of the federal government is about $200 billion. All of the expenses associated with operating the Congress, the federal judicial system, and all of the major regulatory agencies—all of these expenses together come to approximately $500 million, or one-half of one per cent of the total. The 1970 budget of the independent regulatory agencies was $150 million—less, Ralph Nader has noted, "than women spent on wigs last year." Yet he is among those who say that some agencies get too much money, either because they have outlived their usefulness or because they fritter away much of the money they do get.

Caution must be taken, however, against overreaching implications. The National Highway Safety Bureau, a unit of the Department of Transportation, offers itself as an example. It is so starved for funds that only one professional person is assigned to work with state and local officials on matters of school-bus safety. The Bureau has money for the design *but not the production* of prototype safety cars, which promise great dividends in terms of new safety features. Further, the Bureau has grossly insufficient sums to test vehicles and components, including tires, to be certain that the certifications of safety provided by manufacturers can be relied upon. The inadequate funding of the Bureau, of which more examples could be provided, should be laid alongside its mission: nothing less than to do something truly important about a highway traffic toll that, in 1969 alone, left 56,400 persons dead and 2 million with disabling injuries. On a daily basis the toll amounted to 155 deaths and 5,479 injuries, 365 days a year. The Bureau's

195

budget for fiscal 1970 of $30.2 million could be contrasted with the profits after taxes of General Motors in 1969, $1.7 billion.

Economic concentration aggravates the already formidable difficulties of effective regulation. The point is possibly best illustrated by public utilities. As monopolies they represent concentration in its most extreme form. Efforts to regulate them in the public interest have been gross failures.

The biggest monopoly of them all, of course, is the American Telephone and Telegraph Company. It is a corporation with more assets than any other in the world, more employees than the federal government excluding only those in the Defense and Post Office departments, and more bank deposits than any other firm in the United States. It is, Joseph Goulden said in *Monopoly*, published in 1968, "a corporate state, a Super Government, if you will, whose presence in the United States is felt more keenly on a daily basis than even that of the Federal Government."[14] In addition, Goulden said, "AT&T isn't always a nice company. Indeed, its rapacious attitude toward potential competitors, its frequent contempt for government at all levels, the press and other institutions of a free society, are as disgusting, as brutal, as anything found in the robber baron era of American capitalism."[15] Is it really possible to regulate AT&T? Let us look first at some memorable examples, from Goulden's book, of the impact of AT&T's financial policies on our phone bills.

One example concerned Bell's manufacturing subsidiary, the giant Western Electric Company, and the inability of regulators to determine whether the prices paid by AT&T to Western Electric are fair. Goulden wrote:

> The California PUC [Public Utilities Commission] found a route around this problem in 1964 by deciding that Western Electric's rate of return on its equipment sales should be no more than that allowed the Pacific Telephone & Telegraph Company [which is 89.6 percent owned by AT&T] on its California operations. Had Western Electric been held to this limit during the forty-five-year period 1916–61, chosen by the PUC for study, its earnings from sales to PT&T would have been reduced by $340,746,000 (the difference between its composite earnings of 9.1 percent and the com-

[14]New York: Putnam, 1968, p. 9.
[15]*Ibid.*, p. 11.

posite 6.1 percent authorized by the PUC). Not only did this $340,000,000 come from phone subscribers' pockets, but they also had to pay PT&T an annual return on it averaging 6.1 percent.[16]

Despite such policies, the Federal Communications Commission, whose jurisdiction includes interstate phone charges, did not consider them within the structure of a formal rate case until October 1965—more than three decades after the FCC was established. Until that time rates were negotiated without formal hearings. Thus in October 1953 the FCC authorized interstate rates intended to yield—by AT&T's calculations—6.5 per cent on rate base. Actually, Bell promptly began earning much more than that. The FCC's Common Carrier Bureau repeatedly pointed this out to the Commission, then headed by Rosel H. Hyde, but he would not permit the staff even to undertake informal negotiations to see if AT&T would voluntarily lower long-distance rates. Had Bell been held to 6.5 per cent in the years 1955 through 1957 alone, the staff estimated, the savings to phone users would have been about $159 million. Goulden reported:

> When the House Antitrust Subcommittee headed by Representative Emanuel Celler made growling sounds about the excess profits in the spring of 1958, the FCC busied itself finally with a negotiated reduction of $45,300,000 a year. There was scant effect on Bell. Long-distance returns were 7.9 percent in 1959; 7.8 percent the next year; 7.7 percent in 1961. Again, the FCC declined its staff's recommendation that a serious study be made of AT&T's return. (By this time, according to Celler's computations, AT&T's returns for 1955–61 were $985,000,000 above the authorized 6.5 percent return—*nearly a billion dollars in excess telephone payments by the U.S. public.*) [Emphasis in the original.]
>
> The FCC finally agreed with its critics in 1961 that the difference between AT&T earnings and the permissible limit made an unsightly gap, so it moved to narrow it—by increasing its definition of an "acceptable" return from 6.5 percent to 7.5 percent.[17]

Finally, on October 27, 1965, the FCC authorized an in-depth staff study of AT&T's charges and earnings for its various interstate services. On July 5, 1967, the Commission handed down a

---

[16]*Ibid.*, pp. 320–21.
[17]*Ibid.*, pp. 327–38.

decision in the first phase of the case. It deemed a "fair" return to be in the range of 7 to 7½ per cent, while doing nothing about the excess profits earned, say, in the preceding nineteen months when, during almost half of that period, the rate was at least 8½ per cent. Lest this be dismissed as a bit of nitpicking on our part, remember that we are dealing with a situation in which an increase of only one-tenth of one per cent costs telephone subscribers $60 million a year, or roughly $1.30 per subscriber annually. To drop AT&T's earnings thereafter into the desired percentage range, the FCC ordered interstate rates reduced so as to decrease annual revenues by $120 million. Of course, a great many subscribers found themselves paying more for *intrastate* long-distance calls, and so the actual public benefits were open to question. In addition, the FCC decided to ponder rather than rule on whether to require Bell to adopt accelerated depreciation. While it pondered, the public was forced to pay "about $500,000,000 a year extra in phone bills," Goulden said.[18]

For years, the General Services Administration had a unit called the Transportation and Public Utility Service (TPUS). It acted as counsel to the federal government as a customer of phone companies. Its budget was $300,000 a year. Intervening in rate cases, it won rate reductions of $16 million a year—$160 million over the ten-year life of the major contracts involved—on a defense communications system called SAGE. The success of the twelve-member TPUS team, which was headed by Frederick W. Denniston, doomed it. AT&T launched a massive, coordinated lobbying campaign to eliminate TPUS. The effort was led by Edward B. Crosland, who, Joseph Goulden said in *Monopoly*, "bore the title of AT&T vice president for regulatory matters and the unofficial rank of chief lobbyist." In 1962, during the Kennedy Administration, a battered GSA agreed to take itself out of rate cases, save in instances where "the government is being penalized by rates or services." The story of how Crosland accomplished this, told in detail by Goulden, is a classic in the annals of how corporations govern the government and regulate the regulators—even to the point of regulating them almost out of existence.[19]

[18] *Ibid.*, p. 341.
[19] *Ibid.*, pp. 208–19.

Up to now we have presented an array of examples illustrating how economic power translates into economic power in regulatory agencies at the federal government level. At the same time, we cannot ignore the states. They, too, have regulatory responsibilities, and how these responsibilities are carried out is of great moment to their citizens. By and large, however, state regulation in the public interest has failed dismally.

Gladwin Hill of the *New York Times* provided a powerful example of failure in a story on December 7, 1970, about how representatives of the principal sources of air and water pollution—corporations of one kind or another—sit on and even dominate most of the state boards primarily responsible for cleaning up the air and water. "The roster of big corporations with employees on such boards reads like an abbreviated bluebook of American industry," Hill wrote.

> One Colorado state hearing on stream pollution by a brewery was presided over by the pollution control director of the brewery. For years a board member dealing with pollution of Los Angeles harbor has been an executive of an oil company that was a major harbor polluter. The Governor of Indiana recently had to dismiss a state pollution board member because both he and his company were indicted as water polluters.

But the clearest and most relevant record of inadequate state regulation with great economic impact on the citizenry is in the fields of insurance and public utilities. Here we will illustrate with the utilities, which as monopolies represent concentration in an ultimate form.

A few states, including Texas, avoid hypocrisy by not even attempting to regulate utilities. As for the states that do regulate them, thorough documentation of failure has been provided by Senator Lee Metcalf (D–Mont.) in the extensive hearings that he conducted on his proposed Utility Consumers' Counsel Act, and in *Overcharge*, the book that he wrote together with Victor Reinemer, his executive secretary.[20]

As of 1969, for example, state public utility commissioners were in general agreement on the after-tax rates of return that are

---

[20]New York: McKay, 1967.

reasonable for regulated monopolies—6 per cent on rate base, which is the value assigned to properties, and 9 percent on common stock. In 1967 alone, according to Federal Power Commission figures released by Metcalf, the private power companies' earnings exceeded reasonable rates of return by $1.4 billion. Just one utility, Commonwealth Edison Company of Chicago, had an 8.8 per cent return on rate base and a 14.8 per cent return on common stock. The "overcharge" was $96.9 million—almost double the $50 million spent in the same year by all of the regulatory commissions of the states and the District of Columbia.[21]

Accurate accounting lies at the heart of effective regulation. But in opening hearings on his bill by the Senate Subcommittee on Intergovernmental Relations, Metcalf disclosed that the regulatory commissions of twenty states had only one or two accountants. More than half of the agencies had one or two lawyers—or none at all. The figures on rate analysts were similar.

Arizona's regulatory agency is the Corporation Commission. One of its members, who are elected, is Dick Herbert. Testifying in 1969 before Senator Metcalf, he said that attorneys for the Arizona Public Service Company, which provides electricity or gas or both in twelve of the state's fourteen counties, had prepared the Commission's opinion and order in its last "important rate case." Herbert, who dissented in the case, which was decided in September 1967, said that the company lawyers, going still further, put into the opinion and the order statements of fact and law which had never surfaced in the hearings—even in the company's own testimony and exhibits. A *Washington Post* account added:

> Herbert told Metcalf he recognized that the winning side in a court proceeding commonly prepares an order for the judge to sign.
>
> But, he said, the losing counsel has a chance to review the order. In a rate case in which the Commission is the "judge," however, the consumer would have to be represented to make the situation comparable. In the Arizona case there was, Herbert said, "nobody representing the consumer."
>
> The Commissioner charged that Arizona Public Service filed the opinion, a 35-page document, with "the cases and the language and the parts of the hearing that were most favorable to them,"

---

[21] *Washington Post*, April 13, 1969.

so as to appear to be "one great big benevolent charitable concern." Then, he said, the company used the opinion "as a medium
to disperse company propaganda."

He said that the $380,000 spent by Arizona Public Service to
prepare its case was almost triple the $130,000 spent by the state.[22]

Joseph Goulden's *Monopoly* is a prime source of information
about AT&T's relationships with the states. Norman L. Parks made
another important contribution in a two-part article in the *Nation*
entitled "Who Will Bell the Colossus?"[23] Obviously only a few
points can be touched on here, even if we limit ourselves to those
bearing on state regulation. Discussing regulation by the states
over the years, Parks said it has been mostly "tame." He said
that the bound volumes of *Public Utility Reports* include

> numerous findings, ostensibly written by the commissions, but
> actually the work of Bell officials. These decisions show careful
> preparation; they analyze all of the state operations of the com-
> pany and make elaborate and judicial-sounding findings that point
> by point sustain the claims of the company with respect to revenue,
> expense, depreciation, cost of money and rate of return.
>
> Once issued, such decisions are promptly and successfully
> pressed upon other commissions as precedents. Less compliant
> commissions could find themselves inundated with briefs, exhibits
> and supporting data. At one state hearing the commission was
> confronted with data weighing in excess of 8 tons! ...
>
> Speaking of his eleven years of experience as a Tennessee com-
> missioner, during which time he became known as one of the most
> able and fearless rate experts in the nation, [Leon] Jourolmon
> declared: "I do not believe it is possible to regulate a company
> with as much economic strength as the telephone monopoly. I
> do not think any commission ever has been set up with sufficient
> resources ... to enable it to cope with all the different parts of
> the telephone system on a state-wide basis ... on the Tennessee
> commission I never once saw a rate case in which the results were
> fair to the consuming public."

A few summary points about federal as well as state regulation
by now should be clear. A genetic variation of Newtonian law
operates here: each time a regulatory operation becomes effective

[22]*Ibid.*
[23]October 23, 30, 1967.

in the public interest it generates a larger and opposite counter-reaction. Because concentrated economic power sustains this counterreaction—in the executive mansions, on Capitol Hill, and in the statehouses, as well as in the agencies themselves—it usually prevails sooner or later. Thus, it is imprudent to put too much hope for enduring reform in, say, the appointment of a strong chairman or in reorganizations. Ultimately, these gains founder on the massive economic power of the regulated interests.

CIA COMMISSION ON CIA ACTIVITIES WITHIN THE UNITED STATES

Operation CHAOS

No agency of the United States has caused more controversy than the CIA. Deeply and publicly implicated in such foreign policy disasters as the Bay of Pigs invasion, the war in Indochina, and the "destabilization" of the Allende government in Chile, this "invisible government" has come to be feared and hated by other nations around the world. The clandestine nature of its operations and its impermeability to public scrutiny and control has helped legitimate the assumption of a CIA presence wherever another country is experiencing dissention, intrigue, or political change. However it was not until the revelations associated with the Watergate investigation that CIA involvement in illegal domestic spying and intelligence-gathering became an issue. Amidst concerns that its covert operations could menace civil liberties at home in the same way they affected the fate of foreign governments, a presidential commission (the so-called Rockefeller Commission) was appointed in 1974 to review the agency's activities in the United States. The following selection discusses CIA surveillance of antiwar and other "dissident" groups active during the 1960s and early 1970s.

R esponding to Presidential requests to determine the extent of foreign influence on domestic dissidence, the CIA, upon the instruction of the Director of Central Intelligence, established within the Counterintelligence Staff a Special Operations Group in August 1967, to collect, coordinate, evaluate and report on foreign contacts with American dissidents.

"Operation CHAOS" (Originally "Special Operations Group—'Operation CHAOS' "), by the CIA Commission on CIA Activities Within the United States (Rockefeller Commission). From *CIA Commission Report to the President* (Washington, D.C.: Government Printing Office, 1975), pp. 130–48.

The Group's activities, which later came to be known as Operation CHAOS, led the CIA to collect information on dissident Americans from its overseas stations and from the FBI.

Although the stated purpose of the Operation was to determine whether there were any foreign contacts with American dissident groups, it resulted in the accumulation of considerable material on domestic dissidents and their activities.

During six years, the Operation compiled some 13,000 different files, including files on 7,200 American citizens. The documents in these files and related materials included the names of more than 300,000 persons and organizations, which were entered into a computerized index.

This information was kept closely guarded within the CIA to prevent its use by anyone other than the personnel of the Special Operations Group. Utilizing this information, personnel of the Group prepared 3,500 memoranda for internal use; 3,000 memoranda for dissemination to the FBI; and 37 memoranda for distribution to high officials.

The Operation ultimately had a staff of 52, who were isolated from any substantial review even by the Counterintelligence staff of which they were technically a part.

Beginning in late 1969, Operation CHAOS used a number of agents to collect intelligence abroad on any foreign connections with American dissident groups. In order to have sufficient "cover" for these agents, the Operation recruited persons from domestic dissident groups or recruited others and instructed them to associate with such groups in this country.

Most of these recruits were not directed to collect information domestically on American dissidents. On a number of occasions, however, such information was reported by the recruits while they were developing dissident credentials in the United States, and the information was retained in the files of the Operation. On three occasions, agents of the Operation were specifically used to collect domestic intelligence.

Part of the reason for these transgressions was inherent in the nature of the task assigned to the Group: to determine the extent of any foreign influence on domestic dissident activities. That task necessarily partook of both domestic and foreign aspects. The question could not be answered adequately without gathering information on the identities and relationships of the American citizens involved in the activities. Accordingly, any effort by the

CIA in this area was bound, from the outset, to raise problems as to whether the Agency was looking into internal security matters and therefore exceeding its legislative authority.

The Presidential demands upon the CIA appear to have caused the Agency to forego, to some extent, the caution with which it might otherwise have approached the subject.

Two Presidents and their staffs made continuing and insistent requests of the CIA for detailed evaluation of possible foreign involvement in the domestic dissident scene. The Agency's repeated conclusion in its reports—that it could find no significant foreign connection with domestic disorder—led to further White House demands that the CIA account for any gaps in the Agency's investigation and that it remedy any lack of resources for gathering information.

The cumulative effect of these repeated demands was the addition of more and more resources, including agents, to Operation CHAOS—as the Agency attempted to support and to confirm the validity of its conclusion. These White House demands also seem to have encouraged top CIA management to stretch and, on some occasions, to exceed the legislative restrictions.

The excessive secrecy surrounding Operation CHAOS, its isolation within the CIA, and its removal from the normal chain of command prevented any effective supervision and review of its activities by officers not directly involved in the project.

A.
Origins of Operation CHAOS—
August 1967

In the wake of racial violence and civil disturbances, President Johnson on July 2, 1967, formed the National Commission on Civil Disorders (the Kerner Commission) and directed it to investigate and make recommendations with respect to the origins of the disorders. At the same time, the President instructed all other departments and agencies of government to assist the Kerner Commission by supplying information to it.

On August 15, 1967, Thomas Karamessines, Deputy Director for Plans, issued a directive to the Chief of the Counterintelligence Staff instructing him to establish an operation for overseas coverage of subversive student activities and related matters. This memorandum relayed instructions from Director Richard Helms, who, according to Helms' testimony, acted in response to continuing, substantial pressure from the President to determine the extent of any foreign connections with domestic dissident events. Helms' testimony is corroborated by a contemporaneous FBI memorandum which states:

> The White House recently informed Richard Helms, Director, CIA, that the Agency should exert every possible effort to collect information concerning U.S. racial agitators who might travel abroad . . . because of the pressure placed upon Helms, a new desk has been created at the agency for the explicit purpose of collecting information coming into the Agency and having any significant bearing on possible racial disturbances in the U.S.

The question of foreign involvement in domestic dissidence combined matters over which the FBI had jurisdiction (domestic disorder) and matters which were the concern of the CIA (possible foreign connection). The FBI, unlike the CIA, generally did not produce finished, evaluated intelligence. Apparently for these reasons, the President looked to the Director of Central Intelligence to produce a coordinated evaluation of intelligence bearing upon the question of dissidence.

When the Kerner Commission's Executive Director wrote to Helms on August 29, 1967, requesting CIA information on civil disorders, Helms offered to supply only information on foreign connections with domestic disorder. Ultimately, the CIA furnished 26 reports to the Kerner Commission, some of which related largely to domestic dissident activities.

B.
Evolution of Operation CHAOS—
The November 1967 Study

The officer selected to head what became the Special Operations Group was a person already involved in a counterintelligence effort in connection with an article in *Ramparts* magazine on CIA associations with American youth overseas. In connection with his research and analysis, the officer had organized the beginnings of a computer system for storage and retrieval of information on persons involved in the "New Left."

By October 1967, this officer had begun to establish his operation concerning foreign connections with the domestic dissident scene. In a memorandum for the record on October 31, 1967, he indicated that the CIA was to prepare a study on the "International Connections of the United States Peace Movement."

The CIA immediately set about collecting all the available government information on dissident groups. All field stations of the CIA clandestine service were polled for any information they had on the subject of the study. Every branch of the intelligence community was called upon to submit whatever information it had on the peace movement to the Special Operations Group for cataloging and storage. Most of the information was supplied by the FBI.

All information collected by the Special Operations Group was forwarded to the CIA Office of Current Intelligence, which completed the study by mid-November. Director Helms personally delivered the study to President Johnson on November 15, 1967, with a covering note stating that "this is the study on the United States Peace Movement you requested."

The study showed that there was little evidence of foreign involvement and no evidence of any significant foreign financial support of the peace activities within the United States. As a result of the information gathered for the study, however, the Special Operations Group gained an extensive amount of data for its later operations.

On November 20, 1967, a new study was launched by the CIA at the request of the Director of Central Intelligence. This study was titled "Demonstration Techniques." The scope of the study was world-wide, and it concentrated on antiwar demonstrations in the United States and abroad. The procedure used on the earlier study was also employed to gather information for this new project.

The CIA sent an updated version of the Peace Movement Study to the President on December 22, 1967, and on January 5, 1968, Director Helms delivered to the White House a paper entitled "Student Dissent and Its Techniques in the United States." Helms' covering letter to the President described the January 5 study as "part of our continuing examination of this general matter."

Again, the information bank of the Special Operations Group was increased by the intelligence gathered for these studies.

C.
Evolution of Operation CHAOS—
Domestic Unrest in 1968

Continuing antiwar demonstrations in 1968 led to growing White House demands for greater coverage of such groups' activities abroad. As disorders occurred in Europe in the summer of 1968, the CIA, with concurrence from the FBI, sought to engage European liaison services in monitoring United States citizens overseas in order to produce evidence of foreign guidance, control or financial support.

In mid-1968, the CIA moved to consolidate its efforts concerning foreign connections with domestic dissidence and to restrict further the dissemination of the information used by the Special Operations Group. The Group was given a cryptonym, "CHAOS." The CIA sent cables to all its field stations in July 1968, directing that all information concerning dissident groups be sent through a single restricted channel on an "Eyes Only" basis to the Chief of Operation CHAOS. No other dissemination of the information was to occur.

Some time in 1968, Director Helms, in response to the President's continued concern about student revolutionary movements around the world, commissioned the preparation of a new analytic paper which was eventually entitled "Restless Youth." Like its predecessor, "Restless Youth" concluded that the motivations underlying student radicalism arose from social and political alienation at home and not from conspiratorial activity masterminded from abroad.

"Restless Youth" was produced in two versions. The first version contained a section on domestic involvements, again raising a question as to the propriety of the CIA's having prepared it. This version was delivered initially only to President Johnson and to Walt W. Rostow, the President's Special Assistant for National Security Affairs. Helms' covering memorandum dated September 4, 1968, stated, "You will, of course, be aware of the peculiar sensitivity which attaches to the fact that CIA has prepared a report on student activities both here and abroad."

Another copy of the first version of "Restless Youth" was delivered on February 18, 1969, after the change in Administrations, to Henry A. Kissinger, then Assistant to President Nixon for National Security Affairs. Director Helms' covering memorandum of February 18 specifically pointed out the impropriety of the CIA's involvement in the study. It stated:

In an effort to round-out our discussion of this subject, we have included a section on American students. This is an area not within the charter of this Agency, so I need not emphasize how extremely sensitive this makes the paper. Should anyone learn of its existence it would prove most embarrassing for all concerned.

A second version of "Restless Youth" with the section on domestic activities deleted was later given a somewhat wider distribution in the intelligence community.

The CHAOS group did not participate in the initial drafting of the "Restless Youth" paper, although it did review the paper at some point before any of its versions were disseminated. Intelligence derived from the paper was, of course, available to the group.

D.
The June 1969
White House Demands

On June 20, 1969, Tom Charles Huston, Staff Assistant to President Nixon wrote to the CIA that the President had directed preparation of a report on foreign communist support of revolutionary protest movements in this country.

Huston suggested that previous reports indicated inadequacy of intelligence collection capabilities within the protest movement area. (Helms testified that this accurately reflected the President's attitude.) According to Huston's letter, the President wanted to know:

- What resources were presently targeted toward monitoring foreign communist support of revolutionary youth activities in this country;

- How effective the resources were;
- What gaps existed because of inadequate resources or low priority of attention; and,
- What steps could be taken to provide maximum possible coverage of the activities.

Huston said that he was particularly interested in the CIA's ability to collect information of this type. A ten-day deadline was set for the CIA's reply.

The Agency responded on June 30, 1969, with a report entitled, "Foreign Communist Support to Revolutionary Protest Movements in the United States." The report concluded that while the communists encouraged such movements through propaganda and exploitation of international conferences, there was very little evidence of communist funding and training of such movements and no evidence of communist direction and control.

The CIA's covering memorandum, which accompanied the June 30 report, pointed out that since the summer of 1967, the Agency had attempted to determine through its sources abroad what significant communist assistance or control was given to domestic revolutionary protests. It stated that close cooperation also existed with the FBI and that "new sources were being sought through independent means." The memorandum also said that the "Katzenbach guidelines" of 1967 had inhibited access to persons who might have information on efforts by communist intelligence services to exploit revolutionary groups in the United States.[1]

E.
CHAOS in Full-Scale Operation—
Mid-1969

By mid-1969, Operation CHAOS took on the organizational form which would continue for the following three years. Its staff had

---

[1] In 1967 President Johnson appointed a committee including Nicholas Katzenbach, John Gardner, and Richard Helms to investigate charges that the CIA was funding the National Student Association. The charges were substantiated, and the Katzenbach Committee's recommendation that the government refrain from covert financial support of private educational organizations was adopted as government policy.

increased to 36. (Eventually it totaled 52.) In June 1969, a Deputy Chief was assigned to the Operation to assist in administrative matters and to assume some of the responsibilities of handling the tightly-held communications. There was a further delegation of responsibility with the appointment of three branch chiefs in the operation.

The increase in size and activity of the Operation was accompanied by further isolation and protective measures. The group had already been physically located in a vaulted basement area, and tighter security measures were adopted in connection with communications of the Operation. These measures were extreme, even by normally strict CIA standards. An exclusive channel for communication with the FBI was also established which severely restricted dissemination both to and from the Bureau of CHAOS-related matters.

On September 6, 1969, Director Helms distributed an internal memorandum to the head of each of the directorates within CIA, instructing that support was to be given to the activities of Operation CHAOS. Both the distribution of the memorandum and the nature of the directives contained in it were most unusual. These served to underscore the importance of its substance.

Helms confirmed in the September 6 memorandum that the CHAOS group had the principal operational responsibilities for conducting the Agency's activities in the "radical milieu." Helms expected that each division of the Agency would cooperate "both in exploiting existing sources and in developing new ones, and that [the Special Operations Group] will have the necessary access to such sources and operational assets."

Helms further stated in the memorandum that he believed the CIA had "the proper approach in discharging this sensitive responsibility while strictly observing the statutory and *de facto* proscription on Agency domestic involvements."

The September 6 memorandum, prepared after discussions with the Chief of the Operation, among others, served at least three important functions: First, it confirmed, beyond question, the importance which Operation CHAOS had attained in terms of Agency objectives. Second, it replied to dissent which had been voiced within the CIA concerning the Operation. Third, it ensured that CHAOS would receive whatever support it needed, including personnel.

F.
Agent Operations Relating
to Operation CHAOS

. . .

During the first two years of its existence, Operation CHAOS gathered the bulk of its information from reports issued by other governmental agencies or received from CIA field stations abroad.

By October 1969, this approach had changed almost completely. Operation CHAOS' new case officer was begining to contact, recruit, and run agents directly for the operation. This reversal of approach appears to be attributable primarily to three factors:

- First, and most important, an increasing amount of White House pressure (for example, the June 20, 1969, letter from Tom Charles Huston, Staff Assistant to the President) was brought to bear on the CIA to provide more extensive and detailed reporting on the role of foreign connections with American dissident activities;
- Second, Operation CHAOS had been relatively unsuccessful in obtaining meaningful information through agents associated with other agencies;
- Third, the tempo of dissident activities had increased substantially in the United States.

The extent of CHAOS agent operations was limited to fewer than 30 agents. Although records of the Operation indicate that reporting was received from over 100 other agent sources, those sources appear to have been directed abroad either by other governmental agencies or by other components of the CIA. The information which these sources reported to Operation CHAOS was simply a by-product of other missions.

Operation CHAOS personnel contacted a total of approximately 40 potential agents from October 1969 to July 1972, after which no new agent recruitments were made. (The case officer left the Operation on July 12, 1972.) Approximately one-half of these individuals were referred to the Operation by the FBI, and the remainder were developed through various CIA components.

All contact, briefing and debriefing reports prepared by the case officer concerning all potential and actual agents, from whatever source, became part of the records of the Operation. These reports, often highly detailed, were carefully reviewed by CHAOS personnel; all names, organizations and significant events were then indexed in the Operation's computer. Upon occasion, the information would be passed to the FBI.

The individuals referred to Operation CHAOS by the FBI were past or present FBI informants who either were interested in a foreign assignment or had planned a trip abroad. Eighteen of the referrals were recruited. Only one was used on more than one assignment. In each instance the Operation's case officer briefed the individual on the CHAOS "requirements" before his trip and debriefed him upon his return. After debriefing, the agents once again became the responsibility of the FBI.

In one instance, the FBI turned an individual over to Operation CHAOS for its continued use abroad. Before going overseas, that agent was met by the Operation's case officer on a number of occasions in the United States and did report for several months upon certain domestic contacts.

Seventeen agents were referred to Operation CHAOS by other CIA components. Ten were dropped by the Operation for various reasons after an initial assessment. Four were used for brief trips abroad, with reporting procedures which essentially paralleled those used for the FBI referrals.

The remaining three individuals had an entree into antiwar, radical left, or black militant groups before they were recruited by the Operation. They were used over an extended period abroad, and they were met and debriefed on numerous occasions in the United States.

One of the three agents travelled a substantial distance in late 1969 to participate in and report on major demonstrations then occurring in one area of the country. The CHAOS case officer met and questioned the agent at length concerning individuals and organizations involved in the demonstrations. Detailed contact reports were prepared after each debriefing session. The contact reports, in turn, provided the basis for 47 separate disseminations to the FBI, the bulk of which related solely to domestic matters and were disseminated under titles such as: "Plans for Future Anti-War Activities on the West Coast."

The second of these agents regularly provided detailed information on the activities and views of high-level leadership in another of the dissident groups within the United States. Although a substantial amount of this agent's reporting concerned the relationship of the dissident group with individuals and organizations abroad, information was also obtained and disseminated on the organization's purely domestic activities.

The third agent was formally recruited in April 1971, having been initially contacted by Operation CHAOS in October 1970. During the intervening months the CIA had asked the agent questions posed by the FBI concerning domestic dissident matters and furnished the responses to the Bureau.

Two days after the official recruitment, the agent was asked to travel to Washington, D.C. to work on an interim basis; the mission was to "get as close as possible" and perhaps become an assistant to certain prominent radical leaders who were coordinators of the imminent "May Day" demonstrations. The agent was to infiltrate any secret groups operating behind the scenes and report on their plans. The agent was also asked to report any information on planned violence toward government officials or buildings or foreign embassies.

This third agent travelled to Washington as requested, and was met two or three times a week by the CHAOS case officer. After each of these meetings, the case officer, in accordance with the standard procedure, prepared contact reports including all information obtained from the agent. These reports, many of which were typed late at night or over weekends, were passed immediately to the Chief of Operation CHAOS. And when the information obtained from the agent was significant, it was immediately passed by the Chief to an FBI representative, generally orally.

The Operation's use of these three agents was contrary to guidelines established after Director Helms rejected the initial proposal for Project 1 in March 1968. Helms testified that he was not aware of the domestic use of these agents.

The Commission found no evidence that any of the agents or CIA officers involved with any of the dissident operations employed or directed the domestic use of any personal or electronic surveillance, wiretaps or unauthorized entries against any dissident group or individual. Any reporting by CHAOS agents in the United States was based upon information gained as a result of their personal observations and acquaintances.

G.
Collection, Indexing, and Filing
of Information by Operation CHAOS

The volume of information passing through the CHAOS group by mid-1969 was great. As Director Helms pointed out in his September 6, 1969, memorandum to the Directorates, the Operation's main problem was a backlog of undigested raw information which required analysis and indexing.

Not only was the agency receiving FBI reports on antiwar activities, but with the rise of international conferences against the war, and student and radical travel abroad, information flowed in from the Agency's overseas stations as well.

The Operation had gathered all the information it could from the Agency's central registry. According to the Chief of the Operation, that information for the most part consisted of raw data gathered on individuals by the FBI which had not been analyzed by the Agency because the information contained nothing of foreign intelligence value.

CHAOS also availed itself of the information gained through the CIA's New York mail intercept. The Operation supplied a watch list of United States citizens to be monitored by the staff of the mail intercept. The number of mail items intercepted and sent to CHAOS during its operation were sufficient in number to have filled two drawers in a filing cabinet. All of these items were letters or similar material between the United States and the Soviet Union.

In addition, Operation CHAOS received materials from an international communications activity of another agency of the government. The Operation furnished a watch list of names to the other agency and received a total of approximately 1100 pages of materials overall. The program to furnish the Operation with these materials was not terminated until CHAOS went out of existence. All such materials were returned to the originating agency by the CIA in November 1974 because a review of the materials had apparently raised a question as to the legality of their being held by CIA. The materials concerned for the most part antiwar activities, travel to international peace conferences and movements of members of various dissident groups. The communications passed between the United States and foreign countries. None was purely domestic.

During one period, Operation CHAOS also appears to have received copies of booking slips for calls made between points in the United States and abroad. The slips did not record the substance of the calls, but rather showed the identities of the caller and the receiver, and the date and time of the call. The slips also indicated whether the call went through.

Most of the officers assigned to the Operation were analysts who read the materials received by it and extracted names and other information for indexing in the computer system used by the Operation and for inclusion in the Operation's many files. It appears that, because of the great volume of materials received by Operation CHAOS and the time pressures on the Operation, little judgment could be, or was, exercised in this process. The absence of such judgment led, in turn, to the inclusion of a substantial amount of data in the records of the Operation having little, if anything, bearing upon its foreign intelligence objective.

The names of all persons mentioned in intelligence source reports received by Operation CHAOS were computer-indexed. The computer printout on a person or organization or subject would contain references to all documents, files or communications traffic where the name appeared. Eventually, approximately 300,000 names of American citizens and organizations were thus stored in the CHAOS computer system.

The computerized information was streamed or categorized on a "need to know" basis, progressing from the least sensitive to the most sensitive. A special computer "password" was required in order to gain access to each stream. (This multistream characteristic of the computer index caused it to be dubbed the "Hydra" system.) The computer system was used much like a library card index to locate intelligence reports stored in the CHAOS library of files.

The files, like the computer index, were also divided into different levels of security. A "201," or personality, file would be opened on an individual when enough information had been collected to warrant a file or when the individual was of interest to another government agency that looked to the CIA for information. The regular 201 file generally contained information such as place of birth, family, occupation and organizational affiliation. In addition, a "sensitive" file might also be maintained on that same person. The sensitive file generally encompassed matters which were potentially embarrassing to the Agency or matters obtained from sources or by methods which the Agency sought to protect. Operation CHAOS also maintained nearly 1000 "subject" files on numerous organizations.[2]

Random samplings of the Operation's files show that in great part, the files consisted of undigested FBI reports or overt materials such as new clippings on the particular subject.

An extreme example of the extent to which collection could go once a file was opened is contained in the Grove Press, Inc., file. The file apparently was open because the company had published a book by Kim Philby, the British intelligence officer who turned out to be a Soviet agent. The name Grove Press was thus listed as having intelligence interest, and the CHAOS analysts collected all available information on the company. Grove Press, in its business endeavors, had also produced the sex-oriented motion picture, "I Am Curious Yellow" and so the Operation's analysts dutifully clipped and filmed cinema critics' commentaries upon the film.

From among the 300,000 names in the CHAOS computer index, a total of approximately 7,200 separate personality files were developed on citizens of the United States.

In addition, information of on-going intelligence value was digested in summary memoranda for the internal use of the Operation. Nearly 3,500 such memoranda were developed during the history of CHAOS.

Over 3,000 memoranda on digested information were disseminated, where appropriate, to the FBI. A total of 37 highly sensitive memoranda originated by Operation CHAOS were sent over the

[2]The organizations, to name a few, included:
Students for a Democratic Society (SDS);
Young Communist Workers Liberation League (YCWLL);
National Mobilization Committee to End the War in Vietnam;
Women's Strike for Peace;
Freedomways Magazine and Freedomways Associated, Inc.;
American Indian Movement (AIM);
Student Non-Violent Coordinating Committee (SNCC);
Draft Resistance Groups (U.S.);
Cross World Books and Periodicals, Inc.;
U.S. Committee to Aid the National Liberation Front of South Vietnam;
Grove Press, Inc.;
Nation of Islam;
Youth International Party (YIP);
Women's Liberation Movement;
Black Panther Party (BPP);
Venceremos Brigade;
Clergy and Laymen Concerned About Vietnam.

signature of the Director of Central Intelligence to the White House, to the Secretary of State, to the Director of the FBI or to the Secret Service.

H.
Preparation of Reports
for Interagency Groups

Commencing in mid-1970, Operation CHAOS produced reports for . . . interagency groups. . . . One such report was prepared by the Operation in June 1970. Unlike the June 1969 study, which was limited to CIA sources, the 1970 study took into account all available intelligence sources. In the 1970 analysis, entitled, "Definition of Existing Internal Security Threat—Foreign," the Agency concluded that there was no evidence, based on available information and sources, that foreign governments and intelligence services controlled domestic dissident movements or were then capable of directing the groups. The June 1970 Report was expanded and republished in January 1971. It reached the same conclusions.

I.
Relationship of Operation CHAOS
to Other CIA Components

Substantial measures were taken from the inception of Operation CHAOS to ensure that it was highly compartmented. Knowledge of its activities was restricted to those individuals who had a definite "need to know" of it.

The two or three week formal training period for the operation's agents was subject to heavy insulation. According to a memorandum in July 1971, such training was to be carried out with "extreme caution" and the number of people who knew of the training was to be kept to "an absolute minimum." The Office of Training was instructed to return all communications relating to training of CHAOS agents to the Operation.

The Operation was isolated or compartmented even within the Counterintelligence Staff which, itself, was already a highly compartmented component of the CIA. The Operation was physically removed from the Counterintelligence Staff. Knowledge within the Counterintelligence Staff of proposed CHAOS operations was restricted to the Chief of the Staff and his immediate assistants.

The Counterintelligence Chief was technically responsible in the chain of command for Operation CHAOS, and requests for budgeting and agent recruitment had to be approved through his office. But the available evidence indicates that the Chief of Counterintelligence had little connection with the actual operations of CHAOS. According to a CIA memorandum in May 1969, Director Helms specifically instructed the Chief of the Operation to refrain from disclosing part of his activities to the Counterintelligence Chief.

The Counterintelligence and the CHAOS Chiefs both agree that, because of the compartmentation and secrecy of CHAOS, the actual supervisory responsibility for the Operation was vested in the Director of Central Intelligence. This was particularly so beginning in mid-1969. In fact, the Chief of CHAOS, later in history of his Operation, sought unsuccessfully to have his office attached directly to that of the Director.

Director Helms testified that he could recall no specific directions he gave to the CHAOS Group Chief to report directly to him. To the contrary, Helms said, he expected the Chief to report to the Chief of Counterintelligence, who in turn would report to the Deputy Director for Plans and then to the Director.

The sensitivity of the Operation was deemed so great that, during one field survey in November 1972 even the staff of the CIA's Inspector General was precluded from reviewing CHAOS files or discussing its specific operations. (This incident, however, led to a review of the Operation by the CIA Executive Director—Comptroller in December 1972.)

On another occasion, an inspection team from the Office of Management and Budget was intentionally not informed of the Operation's activity during an OMB survey of CIA field operations.

There is no indication that the CIA's General Counsel was ever consulted about the propriety of Operation CHAOS activities.

It further appears that, unlike most programs within the CIA clandestine service, Operation CHAOS was not subjected to an annual review and approval procedure. Nor does there appear to have been any formal review of the Operation's annual budget. Such review as occurred seems to have been limited to requests for authority to assess or recruit an American citizen as an agent.

The result of the compartmentation, secrecy and isolation which did occur seems clear now. The Operation was not effectively supervised and reviewed by anyone in the CIA who was not operationally involved in it.

Witnesses testified consistently that the extreme secrecy and security measures of Operation CHAOS derived from two considerations: First, the Operation sought to protect the privacy of the American citizens whose names appeared in its files by restricting access to those names as severely as possible. Second, CHAOS personnel were concerned that the operation would be misunderstood by others within the CIA if they learned only bits of information concerning it without being briefed on the entire project.

It is safe to say that the CIA's top leadership wished to avoid even the appearance of participation in internal security matters and were cognizant that the Operation, at least in part, was close to being a proscribed activity and would generate adverse public reaction if revealed.

Despite the substantial efforts to maintain the secrecy of Operation CHAOS, over six hundred persons within the CIA were formally briefed on the Operation. A considerable number of CIA officers had to know of the Operation in order to handle its cable traffic abroad.

Enough information concerning CHAOS was known within the CIA so that a middle level management group of 14 officers (organized to discuss and develop possible solutions to various CIA problems) was in a position to write two memoranda in 1971 raising questions as to the propriety of the project. Although only one of the authors had been briefed on CHAOS activities, several others in the group apparently had enough knowledge of it to concur in the preparation of the memoranda.

Opposition to, or at least skepticism about, the CHAOS activities was also expressed by senior officers in the field and at headquarters. Some area division chiefs were unwilling to share the authority for collection of intelligence from their areas with the Operation and were reluctant to turn over the information for exclusive handling and processing by the Operation. When CHAOS undertook the placement of agents in the field, some operations people resented this intrusion by a staff organization into their jurisdiction.

In addition, some of the negativism toward CHAOS was expressed on philosophic grounds. One witness, for example, described the attitude of his division toward the Operation as "total negativeness." A May 1971 memorandum confirms that this division wanted "nothing to do" with CHAOS. This was principally because the division personnel thought that the domestic activities of the Operation were more properly the function of the FBI. As a result, this division supplied the Operation with only a single lead to a potential agent, and its personnel has little to do with the on-going CHAOS activities.

Apparently the feelings against Operation CHAOS were strong enough that Director Helms' September 6, 1969 memorandum was required to support the Operation. That memorandum, sent to all deputy directors in the CIA, assured them that the Operation was within the statutory authority of the agency, and directed their support.

Director Helms' attitude toward the views of some CIA officers toward Operation CHAOS was further summarized in a memorandum for the record on December 5, 1972, which stated: "CHAOS is a legitimate counterintelligence function of the agency and cannot be stopped simply because some members of the organization do not like this activity."

J.
Winding Down Operation CHAOS

By 1972, with the ending of the American involvement in the Vietnam War and the subsequent lower level of protest activities at home, the activities of Operation CHAOS began to lag. The communications traffic decreased, and official apprehension about foreign influence also abated. By mid-1972, the Special Operations Group began to shift its attention to other foreign intelligence matters.

At the end of August 1973, William E. Colby, the new CIA Director, in memoranda dealing with various "questionable" activities by the Agency, ordered all its directorates to take specific action to ensure that CIA activities remained within the Agency's legislative authority. In one such memorandum, the Director stated that Operation CHAOS was to be "restricted to the collection abroad of information on foreign activities related to domestic matters. Further, the CIA will focus clearly on the foreign organizations and individuals involved and only incidentally on their American contacts."

The Colby memorandum also specified that the CIA was not to be directly engaged in surveillance or other action against an American abroad and could act only as a communications channel between the FBI and foreign services, thus altering the policy in this regard set in 1968 and reaffirmed in 1969 by Director Helms.

By August 1973, when the foregoing Colby memorandum was written, the paper trail left by Operation CHAOS included somewhere in the area of 13,000 files on subjects and individuals (including approximately 7,200 personality or "201" files);[3] over 11,000 memoranda, reports and letters from the FBI; over 3,000 disseminations to the FBI; and almost 3,500 memoranda for internal use by the Operation. In addition, the CHAOS group had generated, or caused the generation of, over 12,000 cables of various types, as well as a handful of memoranda to high-level government officials.

On top of this veritable mountain of material was a computer system containing an index of over 300,000 names and organizations which, with few exceptions, were of United States citizens and organizations apparently unconnected with espionage.

---

[3]A CIA statistical evaluation of the files indicates that nearly 65 percent of them were opened to handle FBI information or FBI requests.

LEWIS W. WOLFSON

Whose First Amendment?

During the early 1970s considerable attention focused on the operation and attitudes of the American press. In the wake of Watergate,
newspapers came to be seen as crusading institutions and journalists
as daring muckrakers involved in cloak-and-dagger work. The sudden
glamour has in many instances obscured the fact that newspapers
and television networks not only disseminate information but often
decide what *is* news. *The New York Times* may have pointed with
pride to its fight with the Nixon Administration over the Pentagon
Papers, but a few years later it acted in behalf of "national security"
to suppress the story of the CIA's salvage operation on a Russian
submarine just as it had suppressed its story on the Bay of Pigs
invasion in the prior decade.

Moreover, at the same time that there has been a renaissance
of investigative reporting consciously aligning itself with the public
interest, there has also been a continuing trend toward chain ownership of newspapers and the creation of huge media baronies. While
60 percent of all American cities had competing newspapers fifty
years ago, less than 4 percent do today. Media conglomerates now
own 58 percent of all daily newspapers, 77 percent of all television
stations, 27 percent of all AM radio stations, and 29 percent of all
FM stations. Control of opinion, in other words, constantly slips into
fewer and fewer hands, raising legitimate questions about the long-
term consequences on First Amendment freedoms and the marketplace of ideas. In the following selection Lewis Wolfson discusses
both the power of the press and the public reaction to it.

The American press is in a self-congratulatory mood these days,
after it exposed Watergate and other government ills while resisting the Nixon Administration's repeated attempts to chip away
at its First Amendment rights. But, in their sweetest moments
of victory, newspapers find too few friends to celebrate with.

Instead, they are being assailed and even taken into court by politicians, frustated advocates of various causes, and even by average readers who mistrust the power of the press and question whether newspapers in actual fact do speak for the people, as they claim they do.

The press's recent vindication of its First Amendment freedom has been worth crowing about. Journalists' persistence in good part helped to oust the President and Vice President who had furiously attacked their independence. The Supreme Court upheld the right of newspapers to publish the Pentagon Papers. And most recently the court, in another landmark decision, has ruled that no one—especially not the Government—can tell a newspaper what it must print.

Last summer the Supreme Court unanimously overturned a Florida Supreme Court ruling which had upheld a state right-of-reply law that guaranteed candidates free space to answer editorial attacks during a political campaign. The U.S. Supreme Court's decision turned back the challenge of Pat L. Tornillo Jr. who, as a candidate for the Florida state legislature in 1972, had petitioned the *Miami Herald* for space to respond to editorial attacks on him.

Noted communications lawyer Floyd Abrams called the decision in *Miami Herald* v. *Tornillo* "one of the great reaffirmations of the First Amendment in this century." The press editorialized glowingly about the outcome. But some newspapers also conceded that *Tornillo* was no reaffirmation of the press's credibility with the public. Thoughtful journalists recognize that the case was no isolated episode, but rather the most serious manifestation to date of reader unhappiness with newspapers. For surveys show that the Nixon Administration's attacks fell on fertile ground. Many people feel that the press speaks less and less for their hopes and needs, and they would just as soon have government do something to curb the press's independent power, no matter what the First Amendment says.

The First Amendment says that "Congress shall make no law . . . abridging the freedom of speech, or of the press. . . ." Through the years, the courts invariably have seen the press as the principal guarantor of free expression and the guardian against government attempts to abridge it. But the public interest lawyers who fought for *Tornillo* favor a new interpretation of the First Amendment which would provide legally guaranteed space for people to speak out in their local newspaper, regardless of how the newspaper itself felt about it.

This would mean that government, in effect, could tell its own watchdog what to print. Few press or legal experts expected that the Supreme Court would accept this argument. Indeed, Chief Justice Warren Burger, in his opinion in the *Tornillo* case, said the purpose of the First Amendment is to keep government out of the editor's chair. But, even as it upheld the press's independence, the Court also seemed to be warning newspapers to look to their public sins. Burger recounted at length the access advocates' arguments that newspaper readers are frustated because, as newspaper chains and media conglomerates grow, their own voice seems to diminish, and they feel powerless to call the monopoly press to account for its abuses of power or judgment.

The problem of access and newspapers' accountability to the public is not a new one. At least two Presidential commissions and countless independent study groups have warned the press in recent years about the possible consequences of the public's mistrust. As far back as 1947, the Hutchins Commission on Freedom of the Press was saying that the press "must know that its faults and errors have ceased to be private vagaries and have become public dangers." Foreshadowing the *Tornillo* threat, the Hutchins Commission concluded that journalists "should put forth every effort to make the press accountable, for if it does not become so of its own motion, the power of government will be used to force it to be so."

Now the press is more than ever under siege. Despite their victory in court, newspapers must contemplate fresh assaults on their credibility and fairness: from politicians irked about the press's power, from antitrust officials eyeing the growth of media monopolies, and from a growing cadre of groups and individuals who feel their message is being shut out. Faced with these pressures, editors have experimented in recent years with ways to make the newspapers more accountable. But, critics warn, with the specter of more court decisions, government actions, and escalating reader unrest, the press will have to move more decisively to earn readers' trust and support—or risk new erosion of its First Amendment freedom.

Public interest lawyers contend that America's newspaper owners, especially chain "press lords" who often have a supermarket mentality about buying and selling newspapers, should not be able to dominate so fully the public's chief channels of communication. The First Amendment, they say, belongs to the people, not to an increasingly monopolistic press; the Constitution did not provide "a grant of press immunity" for whatever newspapers want to do, but "a mandate for press responsibility" to guarantee a voice for many points of view.

Justice Oliver Wendell Holmes set the basis for court interpretation of press freedom when he envisioned a marketplace of ideas that would flourish under the First Amendment's safeguard for the press. The access advocates maintain that there are millions of people today who cannot get a ticket into the marketplace unless the big daily newspaper—and in more and more cases the only newspaper—in their hometown will give them a say. A Tom Paine with a ditto machine in Brooklyn or a Malcolm X on a street corner in Harlem doesn't stand a chance against a majestic utterance from the editorial page of *The New York Times.*

But if monopoly ownership of the means of mass communication implies a new brand of censorship, does that justify bringing in government to decide what is a "fair" award of news or advertising space in order to ensure a flourishing marketplace?

It is a difficult question for liberals. Even the American Civil Liberties Union found itself split in conflict over two not necessarily compatible libertarian values—freedom of the press and assured public access to the marketplace. Members of its Communications Media Committee favored a form of guaranteed public entree, at least to newspaper advertising space. But ACLU legal director Melvin Wulf campaigned against this view; he circulated a fiery memo that said such an interpretation of the First Amendment would be "an invitation to constitutional disaster." As Ben Bagdikian, respected journalist and press critic, puts it, the "disease"—lack of access to big newspapers—is a serious one, but the proposed cure of calling on government to judge is "more dangerous than the disease."

The Supreme Court agreed. Justice Burger, in *Tornillo*, wrote that whatever the merits to the arguments of advocates of a right of reply or any other kind of mandatory press access, "such an enforceable right of access necessarily calls for some mechanism, either governmental or consensual. If it is governmental coercion, this at once brings about a confrontation with the express provisions of the First Amendment and the judicial gloss on that amendment developed over the years." The Court concluded that "a responsible press is an undoubtedly desirable goal, but press responsibility is not mandated by the Constitution and like many other virtues it cannot be legislated."

But, if the press had beaten back the public interest lawyers in this case, it had not stilled other voices which question its power. Spiro Agnew may be gone, but his ghost still haunts American journalism. He unleashed the resentment that many people in public life feel about what they see as press license, and the anger is unlikely to be capped back in the bottle by a few favorable court decisions.

Many frustrated politicians subscribe to the Agnew doctrine that much news coverage is biased and that this is attributable to the concentration of control over newspapers, the news magazines, and broadcast outlets. Though they may be conservatives themselves, they agree with the liberal access lawyers that government should not let this broad power go unchecked. Senator John McClellan, Arkansas Democrat, early in 1974 called on the Senate to study "the right of access by the public to the mass media." He said a "fairness doctrine" for newspapers "would not infringe but would enlarge the use of First Amendment rights by extending their enjoyment beyond those who happen to own newspapers."

Journalists counter that people in government have a generous forum in the press for their statements and for coverage of their political activities—too unquestioning, say some news people. They believe that the press and television overreacted to Agnew's attacks, toning down some of their most incisive analysis of government, and resorting to strained gestures such as the liberal *New York Times's* hiring of Nixon adviser William Safire as its "conservative" columnist.

Scarred by the Agnew-Watergate-Vietnam experiences, journalists have become more skeptical about the words of people in authority. The press no longer can be counted on to reprint politicians' speeches and self-serving statements without question. Columbia University law professor Benno Schmidt, who is director of a study of media access for the National News Council, predicts that reporters' greater independence means new tensions ahead for the press and politicians, even if the worst animosities of the Nixon years abate. Schmidt believes that officials will view the journalist more than ever as "an adversary who cannot be trusted [to protect] government secrets" or to cooperate "informally" in aiding government law enforcement efforts by volunteering information or keeping certain news under wraps, as the press once willingly did.

While the press has been able to rebuff its adversaries, it cannot always expect the courts to see its First Amendment freedom as an unalloyed right. Some judges already have warned newspapers to that effect. In upholding the right-of-reply in the *Tornillo* case, the Florida Supreme Court argued vigorously that government has an obligation to do what it could to offset media monopoly power. It said, "The First Amendment did not create a privileged class which, through a monopoly of instruments of the newspaper industry, would be able to deny people the freedom of expression which the First Amendment guaranteed." Some lower Federal courts have made similar arguments that government should encourage public access in broadcasting cases.

Monopoly control is, in fact, the next battleground for newspapers. Press critic Bagdikian, who is conducting a two-year study of American newspapers, feels that "the growth of [newspaper] chains is so alarming that the press is inviting government interference." Bagdikian says that government could move into this area without infringing on press First Amendment rights simply by changing tax benefits which now encourage chains to buy up newspapers.

The cost of chain ownership to the public, Bagdikian feels, is "perpetual mediocrity" in much of daily journalism. Some papers are improved under the new ownership, he concedes. But he thinks there is a limit to how much of the profits will be reinvested in any one paper in the chain or in its community. Bagdikian points out that a chain's business in the end is to make money for the corporation, while America's most respected newspapers have been built by investment in news quality. He calls it the Howard Johnsonizing of newspapers: your local chain newspaper is "not going to be a poisonous greasy spoon, but it's never going to be distinguished either. You'll always get a good standard hot dog."

The Justice Department already has been fighting media concentration on another front. It has long sought to have the Federal Communications Commission end newspapers' ownership of television stations in the same community by not renewing their licenses. Some publishers argue that cross-ownership means that broadcasting profits have kept alive big dailies which otherwise would have gone under. This is similar to the argument used in their lobbying for the Newspaper Preservation Act, which allows "failing" newspapers to survive by making antitrust-immune operating agreements with healthier papers. While ownership may have a point, the free press banner looks a bit tattered every time publishers swoop down on Washington like oil executives or milk producers, trying to escape antitrust scrutiny or to extract special postal subsidies from the same officials whom the press denounces editorially for bowing to powerful interests.

The paradoxes do not go unnoticed by the public. The "free" press stands impeached in the minds of many Americans. Surveys show that, to many, the local paper is just one more big, impersonal institution that is not sensitive to them, though it claims to be the public's voice. Blacks in the South or in northern ghettos do not believe that their big city papers speak for them. Environmentalists often feel that newspapers have a conservative bias that makes them defer to community business interests which are the worst polluters. Conservative crusaders accuse the big city press—especially *The New York Times* and *The Washington Post*—of giving a "liberal lining" slant to reporting of government and choking out contrary views.

Some newspapers have moved voluntarily to provide free space for divergent views. A number have increased the size of their letters-to-the-editor columns. *The Times*'s decision to open the page opposite its editorial page to other voices has been followed by papers which have "sound-off" columns for people who want to rebut the newspaper's viewpoint or to raise new issues. But many journalists and press critics do not believe that giving readers access to a newspaper's columns is a magic formula for soothing their distress. They believe there is a question of both access *and* accountability, and contend that newspapers must make themselves more answerable to the community in a variety of ways if they are to dispel public mistrust and preserve their freedom.

In fact, before we look further to guaranteed access as the people's salvation, we might better ask what people generally want and need to know from newspapers, and whether they are getting it. The more important question for the press seems to be: Should newspapers bob along, as many of them do, trying to mirror life by reporting a crazy quilt of the latest happenings while they are being used by politicians, the business establishment, and all sorts of groups clamoring for attention? Or can a newspaper assert itself as public educator and an instrument for orderly debate of our problems?

No one should be able to mistake a newspaper, which has a clear-cut public trust, for the Mobil Oils and IBMs many institutions—universities, churches, even Congressional committees—in becoming more accountable by democratizing their internal processes. Many conventional businesses put public members on their board, hold open meetings, and are "concerned with customer relations in more than just a superficial way," as Bagdikian notes. Newspapers, on the other hand, resist, in part because of the legitimate concern about their First Amendment freedom, but also because of what Bagdikian calls "their traditional feeling that it's nobody's damned business how they put out a paper."

How newspapers operate must become everybody's business if they are to win sufficient public endorsement to withstand future attempts by politicians or lawyers to whittle away at their First Amendment freedom. *Tornillo* is only the latest episode. Newspapers have been in court almost continuously in recent years to keep government from the door, as they have deflected official attempts to stop publication of the Pentagon Papers, endeavored to protect jounalists' confidential sources, and opposed gag orders by judges who attempt to throw journalists out of their courtroom.

Some critics feel that if reader discontent persists, the *Tornillo* case may be followed by other attempts to organize to keep the press honest. *Washington Post* investigative reporter Morton Mintz says that if newspapers do not open up, then people might well form their own League of Newspaper Readers to compel the press to explain itself. Says Bagdikian, "There are different ways of waking up newspapers, and most of them can be awakened if you organize and shake hard enough." A few communities have established citizen press councils which review press practices with editors. But most newspapers are skittish about exposing themselves to such questioning. Some think that the key to reform lies in the schools, where students could be taught more about the press and the First Amendment and perhaps publish their own journalism review appraising the newspapers in their community.

The decision in the *Tornillo* case thus has not ended the public's groping for more access and accountability. The press guardians cannot simply go back to humming the old tunes, "Free Press" and "Private Enterprise," while they grow bigger and fatter. The First Amendment belongs to the people; but the press must mind it when the people cannot be there.

The people do not need direct access to the press as much as they need to trust newspapers' judgment. Readers may still resent the messenger that brings the bad news, especially when there is so much of it. But newspapers do not need to be loved; they just need to be needed. They can show that their First Amendment freedom is everybody's freedom by spurring debate on their pages by all voices, and by leveling with people about their own shortcomings. Then, when the press goes after the next ill-conceived war or Watergate rampage, we will all gladly get out bumper stickers that say, *Support Your Local Journalist.*

RICHARD PARKER

The Myth of the Middle Class

After the Second World War social scientists began celebrating America as an affluent society. In this widely accepted utopian vision, politics was said to have vanished in an "end of ideology" just as the social distinctions that had so vexed the nation in the prewar depression years had disappeared in an "end of class." Members of what John Kenneth Galbraith called the "new class"—an upwardly mobile managerial elite operating (and benefiting from) the volatile postwar economy—generalized their own experience into a persuasive theory of a wholly egalitarian America in which everyone, either actively or potentially, was middle class.

The reality, during the postwar years when these theories were taking hold and afterwards, was far different. Poverty was as enduring a feature of the United States as concentrated wealth. As late as 1969 income studies showed that the poorest 20 percent of the population received 5 percent of the nation's income, figures virtually unchanged from similar studies a decade earlier despite the billions spent on the War on Poverty. At the other end of the spectrum, as a 1969 study by economist James D. Smith revealed, the top 1.5 percent of the population received 24 percent of the income and owned over 75 percent of the privately held stock. In between was indeed a "middle class." But as journalist Richard Parker suggests in the following selection, the lessons to be learned from its existence were quite different from what had once been thought.

If you were living in America during the 1950s, there was a theme you heard endlessly repeated: America is the Affluent Society. Television showed it, professors lectured on it, advertising blared it, the government collected statistics to prove it. America—the Affluent Society.

America had the world's highest per capita income. America had more cars, more televisions, more telephones than the rest of the world combined. Americans ate better, dressed better, received better educations and better medical care than any other people in the world. They lived in better homes in nicer communities, enjoyed more leisure, travelled more widely than anyone else. And as if this were not enough, life was going to become better still: automation would gradually take over more and more work, and gains in technology and management would remove the vestiges of burdensome responsibilities, leaving us all free to realize our creative potential as human beings.

Furthermore the Affluent Society was unique in man's history because unlike previous societies, the affluence was shared by all. Whereas past societies had divided into the rich and the poor, America was a country in which the vast majority shared the wealth. In ancient and feudal worlds, only a tiny handful had enjoyed such well-being; in modern America the cornucopia flowed for all. Here even the poorest family had a car and a television, and the vast majority had much, much more. Poverty was an "afterthought" in America; for 70% to 90% of the country, the problem was no longer how to acquire more goods, but what to do with the overabundance of goods they already had. In short, modern America was no longer a nation, like others, divided between rich and poor, but a nation of one homogeneously prosperous middle class.

The promise that this uniform middle class affluence held out was stupendous. In place of the conflict which had characterized human societies from their birth, the Affluent Society would be conflict-free. Because the economic deprivation which had caused so many wars and rebellions was gone, decisions would be reached by rational discussion and efficient planning. Debates would no longer be over the quantity of life, but over the quality of life, and on such questions the society could reach peaceful answers. America, as one writer expressed it, would be the first nation in man's history to put an end to ideology. Barring some international holocaust or some horrible accident of nature, America's future would represent the culmination of all men's dreams for a peaceful and prosperous life.

Today, in the early 1970s, it is hard to find anyone who holds such a completely sanguine vision of America. The sixties reintroduced conflict on a massive scale: war, assassination, riot, and rebellion filled the pages of newspapers. The deaths of a president, a presidential candidate, and a major civil rights leader, plus the deaths of nearly 50,000 Americans in battle are landmarks of the last decade. Widespread poverty and even malnutrition has like-wise been rediscovered, dealing a heavy blow to the image of a homogeneous affluence. Important cities are said to be in a state of crisis, and there is dark talk of impending massive ecologi-cal disasters. The tone of today's social commentators is one of gnawing doubt rather than unlimited hope.

But surprisingly this new tone of doubt does not represent a rejection or even a serious modification of the earlier hopeful vision of a homogeneously affluent America; instead it represents an amendment or deferment of that vision. The Vietnam War is viewed as an accidental involvement, unconnected to the struc-ture of America. The crisis of the cities is seen as the result of rising expectations and the relative starvation of the public sector of the economy. The ecology crisis is thought to be a direct out-growth of America's very affluence—that is, a crisis related to overabundant production and the rapacious consumption of natu-ral resources. Even poverty, which would seem to contradict the notion of affluence most directly, is incorporated into the afflu-ence consciousness by its popular acceptance as a crisis of racial minorities—of black, brown, and red Americans. Only racial dis-crimination excludes them from the general prosperity.

In other words, the basic image of the Affluent Society in the 1970s is still intact. A recent best seller, Charles Reich's *The Green-ing of America*, even goes so far as to reject issues of economics as passé, and to lump 80% of Americans into the category "Con-sciousness I," thereby suggesting the uniformity of both their con-sciousness and their material condition. Another best seller, Alvin Toffler's *Future Shock*, reasserts earlier postwar images of Ameri-ca by resting social analysis on issues of technology and science, and by arguing that the future requires maintaining and managing an already abundant society. (The fact that Toffler is more am-bivalent about the future than many earlier writers does not lead him to challenge their basic attitudes.) In academic journals and textbooks one finds much the same thing: on the one hand, an attempt to reevaluate the goals and character of America, but on the other, an almost matter-of-fact acceptance of its middle-class well-being.

The tenacity of this vision is all the more remarkable because some very authoritative critics have rejected it. Paul Samuelson, Nobel laureate in economics, has warned against thinking that America's wealth is broadly shared by the majority. Displaying his special sense for graphic illustration, he observed of the present income structure: "If we made an income pyramid out of a child's blocks, with each layer portraying $1,000 of income, the peak would be far higher than the Eiffel Tower, but almost all of us would be within a yard of the ground."

Samuelson realized that his description ran counter to popular belief, and sought to buttress his position by further elaboration:

> In the absence of statistical knowledge, it is understandable that one should form an impression of the American standard of living from the full-page magazine advertisements portraying a jolly American family in an air-conditioned mansion, with a Buick, a station wagon, a motor launch, and all the other good things that go to make up comfortable living. Actually, of course, this sort of life is still beyond the grasp of 90 percent of the American public.[1]

Yet in America to be middle class is to have "arrived" for the great majority. Few have the possibility of reaching beyond that point, and in a country specifically founded on the desirability of being middle class, few feel it necessary. However this description is appropriated by all sorts of very different people: those who earn $50,000 a year and those who earn $5,000 a year; by college teachers and corporate executives, and by day laborers and file clerks. The distance between these is obvious, but is daily obscured by the meaninglessness of the term itself. Being middle class can mean comfort bordering on opulence; but it can also mean outright poverty, or deprivation that is only one step removed from poverty.

I

Today, the lower boundary of the American middle class is an income slightly below $4,000 a year, the federal government's definition of poverty for an urban family of four. The upper boundary is more difficult to locate because those who, on the basis of income, are rich compared to most Americans, rarely differentiate themseves. *Fortune* magazine illustrated the difficulty in defining the rich by observing that "a man earning, say, $40,000 a year

---

[1]Paul A. Samuelson, *Economics: An Introductory Analysis*, 7th ed. (New York, 1967), p. 112.

may be hard to distinguish from a man earning $10,000 or $15,000 a year. He is rarely conspicuous in his consumption or ostentatious in his possessions."[2] *Fortune* notwithstanding, a distinction still exists; whether immediately apparent in his spending patterns, life style, goals, or sense of security, the middle class man earning $40,000 is unalterably distinct from his middle class confrere earning $4,000.

Social scientists, having generally conceded the myth by accepting both men as middle class, have however gone on to differentiate between "upper" and "lower" middle classes. This avoids the awkwardness of using a single term to describe two very divergent kinds of lives. But what exactly is a *lower* as opposed to an *upper* middle class, and how do these two very crudely defined groups relate to the rich and the poor who constitute the remainder of our society?

For the sake of argument let us presume the following: that the poor constitute the bottom fifth, and the rich, the upper tenth of the population. Since the government (using its own standards) estimates that poverty afflicts less than 13% of the population, and since the upper tenth includes all those with incomes over $18,000, we can safely assume that we are using a conservative estimate of the size of the middle class. If anything, the remaining seventy percent of the population should show more affluence than if we had chosen a broader model.[3]

Accepting the simple division between the upper and the lower middle class, let us assign the seventy percent by a simple halving. In 1968 ... the upper middle class received 46% of the nation's total money income. In the same year, the lower middle class received 22% or, in other words, less than half the amount received by the upper group.

The situation becomes even more striking if we incorporate the data for rich and poor. According to the Census Bureau, the richest tenth of the country in 1968 received 27% of the money income, while the poorest *fifth* got only 5%. *Stated slightly differently this means that the richest 10% of Americans in 1968 received*

---

[2]Jeremy Main, "Good Living Begins at $25,000 a Year," *Fortune*, May 1968.

[3]Income in 1969 of Families and Persons in the United States," U.S. Census Bureau, *Current Population Reports* (Series P–60, no. 75) and *Statistical Abstract of the United States, 1971* (Washington, D.C., 1972), p. 317, Table 504 and p. 332, Table 513.

more money income than the entire bottom half of the population.
Clearly, economic equality is not a prominent characteristic of
contemporary American society.

But inequality of income is only one part of the problem in
the myth of the middle class in America. For example, liquid
assets—checking and savings accounts, shares in saving-and-loan
banks, credit unions, and government savings bonds—are strong
measures of a family's cushion against disaster and its ability to
plan major investment for the future (such as college education
for the children). But in 1969, one fifth of the population owned
no liquid assets whatsoever, and nearly half of the population
had less than $500. Less than a third had more than $2,000. If
a father was suddenly put out of work, if a family member suffered injuries requiring long-term care, or if a child won admission
to a prestigious college or university, the carefully gathered savings of a lifetime could be quickly wiped out.[4]

Wealth also reflects the imbalance shown in unequal distribution of income. To an economist, the wealth of a family is the
sum of its assets—its home, its car, its savings and investments—
minus its debts on those assets. Among the rich and the upper
middle class, the amount of wealth was understandably large:
among those earning ten to fifteen thousand dollars a year in
1962, two-thirds were worth more than $10,000, and the mean
was a comfortable $28,000. Among the lower middle class, how-
ever, wealth was less generously distributed. The mean was half
that of the ten-to-fifteen thousand group, and over half the group
were worth less than $6,000. If we recall that wealth includes the
value of ownership in the family house and car, $6,000 is paltry
indeed.[5]

For those who survived the Depression, figures like these may
not seem shocking. But few people judge their present prosperity
by the standards of thirty years ago. What these figures mean
is that for the poor, life is marginal, and for the lower middle
class, danger is never far away. Income is annual, and is spent
heavily for the day-to-day maintenance of life; liquid assets and

[4]*Statistical Abstract of the United States, 1970* (Washington, D.C., 1970), p. 321, Table
485.
[5]Federal Reserve Board, *Survey of Financial Characteristics of Consumers* (Washington,
D.C., 1966), Tables A2, p. 98 and A8, p. 110.

debt purchasing are the chief means for the accumulation of comforts, such as additional appliances, a car, or a college education. And debt purchasing, whatever its popularity, can impose not only exorbitant costs in the form of inflated interest charges, but a heavier psychological burden in the loss of a sense of freedom.

II

In the fifties, a great deal of attention was paid to the transition from the primacy of blue-collar work to white-collar work. Sociologists and popular magazines considered it the harbinger of a great social revolution, the movement to the "postindustrial" society. Theorists saw the growth of the service industries as an early sign of the leisure society that was supposed to be just over the horizon. As automation increased, the number of blue-collar jobs would continue to decline, and the service sector would continue to grow.

The thesis was correct as far as it went, but it overlooked two important facts: even if both automation and services continue to expand, there is no way to imagine the disappearance of blue-collar workers in this century; more ominously, income for service workers as a whole is lower than income for blue-collar workers, and by a sizeable amount. In many cases, transition from an industrial to a postindustrial economy many mean not an advance for the lower middle class worker, but simply a lateral movement symbolized by a change in the color of his uniform. As a case in point, the hourly wage in the retail trades actually declined as a percentage of the wages in manufacturing between 1940 and the late 1960s.

Today there are approximately thirty-five million blue-collar workers in America. As a group they have made significant gains since the beginning of this century, gains that have won widespread applause from social reformers and political theorists. But how substantial and enduring are these gains? Industrial sociologist Arthur Shostak, in his recent study *Blue-Collar Life*, has suspicions about the working man's economic status: "On a first reading the record encourages admiration for the progress apparently made by blue-collarites. . . . On a second and more careful reading, however, admiration for these gains gives way to concern for their durability."[6] Shostak concludes that blue-collar prosperity is precariously supported by heavy installment debt and rapidly declining purchasing power. (The take-home pay of a factory worker was smaller in 1970 than in 1965, because of inflation.) The husband's job is uncertain because of technological displacement and stiffer educational requirements. The wife's role is also unstable, because she frequently has had to enter the labor force in order to provide for the family, and finds the dual life of worker and wife-mother difficult to manage. Even the children, who are supposed to have benefitted from increased educational opportunity, have not been as successful as imagined. "Blue-collar children may spend more years in school," Shostak dourly observes, "but high-quality educational content and not time alone influences postschool achievement."

For the blue-collar worker over forty, there is also the nagging memory of the Depression. Many workers feel equally pressured by unending alterations in their own work. Shostak says that "a vast majority of all manual workers are reveling in their persistent fantasies about escaping the factory, and in their hope that their sons will not follow them into blue-collar work." For those who dwell in the larger cities and in adjoining suburbs, there is the further tension of "encroaching" blacks or other nonwhites. Many times the single debt-free possession of any consequence is the worker's home, and in it he has invested not only his labor but a major portion of his psychic status. To feel constantly pressured from "below," to be constantly reminded of the world from which many came and to which one might so easily return, can be a traumatizing experience for those living on the edge as so many blue-collarites do.

This continuous tension shows itself in many ways. The blue-collarites have a high separation and divorce rate. Their children have high dropout rates and high arrest records. They labor under the weight of "an alarming incidence of little-treated physical and mental illness."

Shostak's study is doubly disturbing not only because it excludes both women and nonwhites—who in general do worse than white male workers economically—but also because, as Shostak himself admits, "these observations . . . refer only to the unique

[6]Arthur Shostak, *Blue Collar Life* (New York, 1969), p. 274.

situation of the minority of better-off, modernistic, suburban-dwelling blue-collarites. The vast majority of Caucasian male blue-collarites and their dependents are still less well-off on all counts." And in case anyone has misunderstood Shostak's message, he concludes:

> With respect to most blue-collarites, one comes finally to admire not so much accomplishment as endurance and to envy not so much achievement as persistence. Pathos and "affluence" to the contrary, blue-collarites today in America are *not* especially well-off. Many know this and vaguely sense that somehow things ought to "feel" better. How to make things better eludes almost all of them.[7]

III

But if the lower middle class is to be characterized by endurance, the upper middle class is definitely not. The upper middle class may at one time have merely endured; today it has conquered.

For those families earning between $10,000 and $25,000, life displays many of the accoutrements of affluence that many believe to be the property of all. Just as the lower middle class is dominated by the blue-collar and service worker, so the upper middle class is dominated by professionals and managers. One-quarter of the U.S. labor force is made up of professional and technical workers, managers, officials, and proprietors. At first glance this is not at all remarkable: the professionals and managers have dominated the upper segment of the income scale for decades. Nor is it remarkable, because of all the discussion about it, that the professionals and managers have been steadily increasing in number. This increase has in fact been the subject not so much of discussion as of constant praise. It has provided the foundation for feverish speculation about postindustrial life, and as depicted in *The Organization Man* and other such books, has been used as a paradigm of that future life.

But the speculation has been too naive and too optimistic. It overlooks the fact that all men cannot be managers or professionals, and that the upper middle class, instead of merging into

---

[7] *Ibid.*, p. 275.

a hazy continuum with the lower middle class, has accentuated its differences and raised its admission standards. It would probably be more accurate to say that the professionals and managers display a closer indentification with the rich than with the old middle class, and 'that they see each other as self-conscious members of Galbraith's New Class.

For several years immediately after World War II, optimism was generated by statistics showing a merging of workers' and professionals' incomes. In general, lower groups of workers seemed to be making much faster gains than income groups above them. In some circles, this tendency was even seen as a harbinger of declining income inequality on a vast scale. But what such optimism failed to take into account were the unusual circumstances under which such gains had been made. Wartime conditions, the scarcity of labor, and fat government contracts all accelerated the lower wage levels; once the war was over, however, normal relations began to reassert themselves, and the tendency of lower-paid workers to make more rapid gains than managers and professionals reversed itself by the mid-fifties. Thus, for example, between 1950 and 1960 the median wages for service workers and laborers rose 39%, while for professionals and managers the median rose 68%.[8]

We can see the consequence of these statistics in a different way if we consider the expected earnings of a high school versus a college graduate. In 1968, the median annual income of high school graduates was slightly over $8,000; college graduates, on the other hand, had a median income of nearly $13,000.[9] Projected over a lifetime, this means that the family of a high school graduate will enjoy $230,000 less income than the family of a college graduate. When measured in terms of housing, clothing, education, medical care, or any other index, this is an enormous sum.

The knowledge that his income will continue to rise substantially and evenly allows the upper-middle-class professional or manager to do things which, in lower-middle-class households, would cause financial havoc. For instance, indebtedness has become a crucial way of obtaining the necessities of modern civilization—a house, a car, most major appliances, even health care involves a willingness and ability to sustain long-term indebtedness. For

---

[8]*Statistical Abstract 1970*, p. 111, Table 161.
[9]*Survey of Financial Characteristics of Consumers*, p. 106, Table A6.

families earning between $10,000 and $15,000 in 1962, fully 55% had debts totalling more than $5,000. By contrast, among those families earning between $3,000 and $5,000 (remember that in 1962 the dividing line between poor and lower middle class was $3,000), two-thirds did not even have liquid assets over $500, and hence could not even afford to contemplate indebtedness on the scale of the upper middle class.[10]

There is a further point to be made about the income of the upper middle class. An income that is, say, X dollars above the national median is very different from an income which is X dollars below it. Living decently requires basic expenditures which consume a large and relatively constant amount of income, varying with the size of a family, the age of its members, its locale, etc. Thus for an urban family of four (considered average by the government), the Bureau of Labor Statistics computes an income of $10,700 as necessary for a "moderate," intermediate standard of living.[11] This sum allows for food, clothing, housing, furnishings, transportation, medical care, household operation, reading, recreation, tobacco, education, gifts and contributions, and miscellaneous expenses. The BLS (a division of the Department of Labor) determined the amounts in each category by examining studies of consumer expenditures that are made every ten years. Examination of the amounts used in the "moderate" budget shows that they are less than extravagant. Clothes are replaced over a period of two to four years and furniture over a longer period. Transportation is by used car unless the city has a well-developed transportation system. The recreation allowance allows a movie every two or three weeks. The education allowance covers only the day-to-day expenses, such as books and paper—it does not include saving for higher education.

This "moderate" budget represents what is felt to be reasonable comfort in America today. It is obviously much higher than the government's definition of poverty, but still short of the two-car-in-every-garage, swimming-pool-in-every-backyard image of affluence that often passes for the norm. One can build upon it with additional income to provide for discretionary tastes, but to subtract from it immediately forces cutbacks in what is surely a mod-

---

[10]Bureau of Labor Statistics, "Three Budgets for an Urban Family of Four Persons: Final Spring 1970 Cost Estimates," (Washington, D.C., 1971).
[11]*Ibid.*

est life. The family would not starve, find itself in tatters, or be forced into a rat-infested tenement, were its income cut back by one or two thousand dollars. But it would find itself deprived of simple comforts, it would begin to detect imbalances in its meals—perhaps a marked absence of meat, or an overabundance of potatoes—it might find itself living in a "deteriorating" neighborhood where crime is a constant problem.

Yet one half of American families live *below* the Bureau of Labor Statistics' definition of a "moderate" life.

IV

We have seen the wide disparity between the lower and upper middle classes; . . . there are even greater disparities between rich and poor. Why is it, then, that Americans think of their country as an Affluent Society? How can we speak of America as egalitarian and democratic, when such antitheses contradict equality and endanger democracy?

From numerous interviews, and from cursory observation, it is clear that a majority of Americans publicly identify themselves as middle class (as compared to England, for example, where a majority still identifies itself as working class). Given the fact of this general self-identification, how are we to say that Americans are not middle class without the most patent contradiction?

Part of the answer to these questions lies in the way Americans talk about "the middle class." The American middle class is synonymous with the word majority. To Americans, to be middle class is to stand literally in the middle, to be average, to be the typical man in the street, the Good Joe. The idea of a minority middle class is about as ludicrous to an American as its antithesis was to a European.

Modern social science has reinforced the American notion by incorporating the American concept as part of its analysis. By *assuming* the existence of a broad middle class, and treating it as homogeneous, social scientists have frequently aggregated social economic data in a way that ignores the differences between upper and lower segments of that supposedly unitary class. By stressing the ideal of the middle class's homogeneity over the fact of its diversity, they have assured that the ideal would appear as fact.

But none of this is new; American usage is buried deep in the history of America and in the character of the men and women who founded it. America was born in an age of Rationalist idealism, when the new ideal of equality was sharply contradicted by the reality of European society and, to a lesser extent, by the reality of colonial life as well. It was the hope of many of the Founding Fathers that in America, at least, the ideal would eventually defeat the reality. But instead the idealism of the Founding Fathers launched the country on a wave of anticipation that economic and political institutions were ill equipped to fulfill. Even today it is hard to see how the economic and political systems of America can possibly achieve the ideals which in our rhetoric too often pass for the norm.

It is not hard to see how the myth of the middle class has persisted over time. For lower-middle-class blue-collar and white-collar workers, it removes the sting that a more rigid class structure brings, and gives the workingman the feeling of fraternity in a larger world of equals. For upper-middle-class professionals, managers, and skilled workers, the myth sanctifies above-average wages and privileges on the ground that these are actually available to everyone.

Finally the myth has been enshrined because, over the past two decades, it has helped an elite of the upper middle class to achieve a substantial hegemony over the rest of the community, a hegemony that rarely is challenged successfully because of the New Class's claim to act in the interest of the whole. It is doubtful whether America has ever been the fully participatory democracy claimed by its rhetoric; since World War II, however, this elite of managers and professionals has been able to operate with a freedom that has been only weakly opposed, and then for the wrong reasons.

Their hegemony might not be so bad, were it not for the simple fact that they have misperceived America and perpetuated myths which sustain the inequalities of American life. By naively assuming (or deliberately pretending) that their affluence, advantages, and comforts are universal, instead of unique, and that the middle class includes nearly everyone, they have continued the myth without considering the consequences, neither the injustice which they perpetuate, nor the justice which they promise, but cannot fulfill.

FRANCES FOX PIVEN

The Urban Crisis:
Who Got What and Why

Throughout the summer of 1975 there was talk about the deepening
financial crisis of New York City and even speculation that the largest
and most dynamic of America's metropolises was so saddled with
debt that it would inevitably be forced into receivership or bankruptcy.
As New York teetered on the brink of insolvency, other American
cities, large and small, watched with alarm and wondered about their
own future. The urban crisis, its origins and implications, is the subject
of the following essay by Frances Fox Piven, a leading critic of United
States welfare policies.

For quite a while, complaints about the urban fiscal crisis have
been droning on, becoming as familiar as complaints about big
government, or big bureaucracy, or high taxes—and almost as
boring as well. Now suddenly the crisis seems indeed to be upon
us: school closings are threatened, library services are curtailed,
subway trains go unrepaired, welfare grants are cut, all because
big city costs have escalated to the point where local governments
can no longer foot the bill. Yet for all the talk, and all the complaints, there has been no convincing explanation of just how
it happened that, quite suddenly in the 1960s, the whole municipal
housekeeping system seemed to become virtually unmanageable.
This is especially odd because, not long ago, the study of city
politics and city services was a favorite among American political
scientists, and one subject they had gone far to illuminate. Now,
with everything knocked askew, they seem to have very little to
say that could stand as political analysis.

To be sure, there is a widely accepted explanation. The big cities are said to be in trouble because of the "needs" of blacks for services—a view given authority by the professionals who man the service agencies and echoed by the politicians who depend upon these agencies. Service "needs," the argument goes, have been increasing at a much faster rate than local revenues. The alleged reason is demographic: The large number of impoverished black Southern migrants to the cities presumably requires far greater investments in services, including more elaborate educational programs, more frequent garbage collection, more intensive policing, if the city is to be maintained at accustomed levels of civil decency and order. Thus, city agencies have been forced to expand and elaborate their activities. However, the necessary expansion is presumably constricted for lack of local revenues, particularly since the better off taxpaying residents and businesses have been leaving the city (hastened on their way by the black migration).[1] To this standard explanation of the crisis, there is also a standard remedy: namely, to increase municipal revenues, whether by enlarging federal and state aid to the cities or by

---

[1]This view of the urban problem was given official status by the "Riot Commission." According to the commission:

> [The] fourfold dilemma of the American city [is:] Fewer tax dollars come in, as large numbers of middle-income tax payers move out of central cities and property values and business decline; More tax dollars are required, to provide essential public services and facilities, and to meet the needs of expanding lower-income groups; Each tax dollar buys less, because of increasing costs. Citizen dissatisfaction with municipal services grows as needs, expectations and standards of living increase throughout the community [*Report of the National Advisory Commission on Civil Disorders* (New York: Bantam, 1968), p. 389].

Similarly, Alan K. Campbell and Donna E. Shalala write: "Most of the substantive problems flow, at least in part, from . . . the fact that the central cities have been left with segments of the population most in need of expensive services, and the redistribution of economic activities has reduced the relative ability of these areas to support such services" ["Problems Unsolved, Solutions Untried: The Urban Crisis," in *The States and the Urban Crisis* (Englewood Cliffs, N.J.: Prentice-Hall, 1970), p. 7]. The conventional wisdom is again echoed by the U.S. Advisory Commission on Intergovernmental Relations:

> The large central cities are in the throes of a deepening fiscal crisis. On the one hand, they are confronted with the need to satisfy rapidly growing expenditure requirements triggered by the rising number of "high cost" citizens. On the other hand, their tax resources are growing at a decreasing rate (and in some cases actually declining), a reflection of the *exodus of middle and high income families and business firms from the central city to suburbia* [italics in original] [*Fiscal Balance in the American Federal System: Metropolitan Fiscal Disparities* (Washington, D.C.: Government Printing Office, 1967), Vol. II, p. 5].

Politicians share this view. "In the last 10 years, 200,000 middle-class whites have moved out of St. Louis," said Mayor A. J. Cervantes, "and 100,000 blacks, many of them poor, have moved in. It costs us *eight times as much* to provide city services to the poor as to the middle-class" [italics in original] [*The New York Times*, May 22, 1970].

redrawing jurisdictional boundaries to recapture suburban taxpayers.[2]

It is true, of course, that black children who receive little in the way of skills or motivation at home may require more effort from the schools; that densely packed slums require more garbage collection; that disorganized neighborhoods require more policing. For instance, the New York City Fire Department reports a 300 percent increase in fires the last twenty years. But fires and similar calamities that threaten a wide public are one thing; welfare, education, and health services, which account for by far the largest portion of big city budgets, quite another. And while by any objective measure the new residents of the city have greater needs for such services, there are several reasons to doubt that the urban crisis is the simple result of rising needs and declining revenues.

For one thing, the trend in service budgets suggests otherwise. Blacks began to pour into the cities in very large numbers after World War II, but costs did not rise precipitously until the mid-1960s.[3] *In other words, the needs of the black poor were not recognized for two decades.* For another, any scrutiny of agency budgets shows that, except for public welfare, *the expansion of services to the poor, as such, does not account for a very large proportion of increased expenditures.* It was other groups, *mainly organized provider groups,* who reaped the lion's share of the swollen budgets. The notion that services are being strained to respond to the needs of the new urban poor, in short, takes little account either of when the strains occurred or of the groups who actually benefited from increased expenditures.

These two facts should lead us to look beyond the "rising needs—declining revenues" theory for an explanation of urban

---

[2]As a matter of fact, city revenues have not declined at all, but have risen astronomically, although not as astronomically as costs. Presumably if the city had been able to hold or attract better off residents and businesses, revenues would have risen even faster, and the fiscal aspect of the urban crisis would not have developed.

[3]It should be made clear at the outset that the costs of government generally rose steadily in the years after World War II. This is the subject of James O'Connor's analysis in "The Fiscal Crisis of the State," *Socialist Revolution,* 1, 1 (January/February 1970), 12–54; 1, 2 (March/April 1970), 34–94. But while all government budgets expanded, state and local costs rose much faster, and costs in the central cities rose the most rapidly of all, especially after 1965. Thus, according to the Citizen's Budget Commission, New York City's budget increased almost eight times as fast in the five fiscal years between 1964 and 1969 as during the postwar years 1949 to 1954. From an average annual increase of 5.5 percent in 1954, budget costs jumped to 9.1 percent in 1964 and to 14.2 percent in 1969 (*The New York Times,* January 11, 1960). It is with this exceptional rise that this article is concerned.

troubles. And once we do, perhaps some political common sense can emerge. School administrators and sanitation commissioners may describe their agencies as ruled by professional standards and as shaped by disinterested commitments to the public good, and thus define rising costs as a direct and proper response to the needs of people. But schools and sanitation departments are, after all, agencies of local government, substructures of the local political apparatus, and are managed in response to local political forces. The mere fact that people are poor or that the poor need special services has never led government to respond. Service agencies are political agencies, administered to deal with political problems, not service problems.

Now this view is not especially novel. If there is any aspect of the American political system that was persuasively analyzed in the past, it was the political uses of municipal services in promoting allegiance and muting conflict. Public jobs, contracts, and services were dispensed by city bosses to maintain loyal cadres and loyal followers among the heterogeneous groups of the city. Somehow political analysts have forgotten this in their accounts of the contemporary urban crisis, testimony perhaps to the extent to which the doublethink of professional bureaucrats has befogged the common sense of us all. That is, we are confused by changes in the style of urban service politics, failing to see that although the style has changed, the function has not. In the era of the big city machine, municipal authorities managed to maintain a degree of consensus and allegiance among diverse groups by distributing public goods in the form of private favors. Today public goods are distributed through the service bureaucracies. With that change, the process of dispensing public goods has become more formalized, the struggles between groups more public, and the language of city politics more professional. As I will try to explain a little later, these changes were in some ways crucial in the development of what we call the urban crisis. My main point for now, however, is that while we may refer to the schools or the sanitation department as if they are politically neutral, these agencies yield up a whole variety of benefits, and it is by distributing, redistributing, and adapting these payoffs of the city agencies that urban political leaders manage to keep peace and build allegiances among the diverse groups in the city. In other words, the jobs, contracts, perquisites, as well as the actual services of the municipal housekeeping agencies, are just as much the grist of urban politics as they ever were.

All of which is to say that when there is a severe disturbance in the administration and financing of municipal services, the underlying cause is likely to be a fundamental disturbance in political relations. To account for the service "crisis," we should look at the changing relationship between political forces—at rising group conflict and weakening allegiances—and the way in which these disturbances set off an avalanche of new demands. To cope with these strains, political leaders expanded and proliferated the benefits of the city agencies. What I shall argue, in sum, is that the urban cirsis is not a crisis of rising needs, but a crisis of rising demands.

Any number of circumstances may disturb existing political relationships, with the result that political leaders are less capable of restraining the demands of various groups. Severe economic dislocations may activate groups that previously asked little of government, as in the 1930s. Or groups may rise in the economic structure, acquiring political force and pressing new demands as a result. Or large scale migrations may alter the balance between groups. Any of these situations may generate sharp antagonism among groups, and, as some new groups acquire a measure of influence, they may undermine established political relationships. In the period of uncertainty that ensues, discontent is likely to spread, political alignments may shift, and allegiances to a political leadership may become insecure. In the context of this general unrest, political leaders, unsure of their footing, are far more likely to respond to the specific demands of specific groups for enlarged benefits or new "rights." Periods of political instability, in other words, nurture new claims and claimants. This is what happened in the cities in the 1960s, and it happened at a time when the urban political system was uniquely ill-equipped to curb the spiral of rising demands that resulted.

The Political Disturbances
That Led to Rising Demands

If the service needs of the black poor do not account for the troubles in the cities, the political impact of the black migration probably does. Massive shifts of population are almost always disturbing to a political system, for new relations have to be formed between a political leadership and constituent groups. The migration of large numbers of blacks from the rural South to a few core cities during and after World War II, leading many middle-class white constituents to leave for the suburbs, posed just this challenge to the existing political organization of the cities. But for a long time, local governments resisted responding to the newcomers with the services, symbols, and benefits that might have won the allegiance of these newcomers, just as the allegiance of other groups had previously been won.

The task of political integration was made difficult by at least four circumstances. One was the very magnitude of the influx. Between 1940 and 1960, nearly 4 million blacks left the land and, for the most part, settled in big Northern cities. Consequently, by 1960, at least one in five residents of our fifty largest cities was a black, and in the biggest cities the proportions were much greater. It is no exaggeration to say that the cities were innundated by sheer numbers.

Second, these large numbers were mainly lower-class blacks, whose presence aroused ferocious race and class hatreds, especially among the white ethnics who lived in neighborhoods bordering the ghettos and who felt their homes and schools endangered. As ghetto numbers enlarged, race and class polarities worsened, and political leaders, still firmly tied to the traditional inhabitants of the cities, were in no position to give concessions to the black poor.

Not only was race pitted against race, class against class, but the changing style of urban politics made concessions to conflicting groups a very treacherous matter. Just because the jobs, services, and contracts that fueled the urban political organization were no longer dispensed covertly, in the form of private favors, but rather as matters of public policy, each concession was destined to become a subject of open political conflict. As a result, mayors found it very difficult to finesse their traditional constituents: New public housing for blacks, for example, could not be concealed, and every project threatened to arouse a storm of controversy. Despite their growing numbers and their obvious needs, therefore, blacks got very little in the way of municipal benefits throughout the 1940s and 1950s. Chicago, where the machine style was still entrenched, gave a little more; the Cook County AFDC rolls, for example, rose by 80 percent in the 1950s, and blacks were given some political jobs. But in most cities, the local service agencies resisted the newcomers. In New York City and Los Angeles, for example, the AFDC rolls remained virtually unchanged in the 1950s. In many places public housing was brought to a halt; urban renewal generally became the instrument of black removal; and half the major Southern cities (which also received large numbers of black migrants from rural areas) actually managed to reduce their welfare rolls, often by as much as half.[4]

Finally, when blacks entered the cities, they were confronted by a relatively new development in city politics: namely, the existence of large associations of public employees, whether teachers, policemen, sanitation men, or the like. The provider groups not only had a very large stake in the design and operation of public programs—for there is hardly any aspect of public policy that does not impinge on matters of working conditions, job security, or fringe benefits—but they had become numerous enough, organized enough, and independent enough to wield substantial influence in matters affecting their interests.

The development of large, well-organized, and independent provider groups has been going on for many years, probably beginning with the emergence of the civil service merit system at the turn of the century (a development usually credited to the efforts of reformers who sought to improve the quality of municipal services, to eliminate graft, and to dislodge machine leaders).[5] But although the civil service originated in the struggle between party leaders and reformers, it launched municipal employees as an independent force. As city services expanded, the enlarging numbers of public employees began to form associations. Often these originated as benevolent societies, such as New York City's Patrolmen's Benevolent Association, which formed in the 1890s. Protected by the merit system, these associations gradually gained some influence in their own right, and they exerted that influence at both the municipal and the state level to shape legislation and to monitor personnel policies so as to protect and advance their occupational interests.

The result was that, over time, many groups of public employees managed to win substantial control over numerous matters affecting their jobs and their agencies: entrance requirements, tenure guarantees, working conditions, job prerogatives, promotion criteria, retirement benefits. Except where wages were concerned, other groups in the cities rarely became sufficiently

---

[4]For a discussion of the uses of welfare in resisting black migrants, see Frances Fox Piven and Richard A. Cloward, *Regulating the Poor: The Functions of Public Welfare* (New York: Pantheon, 1971), Chapters 7 and 8.

[5]At least some of the employees in all cities with more than 500,000 inhabitants are now under civil service; in about half of these cities, virtually all employees have such protections.

aroused to block efforts by public employees to advance their interests. But all of this also meant that when blacks arrived in the cities, local political leaders did not control the jobs—and in cases where job prerogatives had been precisely specified by regulation, did not even control the services—that might have been given as concessions to the black newcomers.

Under the best of circumstances, of course, the task of integrating a new and uprooted rural population into local political structures would have taken time and would have been difficult. But for all of the reasons given, local government was showing little taste for the task. As a result, a large population that had been set loose from Southern feudal institutions was not absorbed into the regulating political institutions (or economic institutions, for they were also resisted there) of the city. Eventually that dislocated population became volatile, both in the streets and at the polls. And by 1960, that volatility was beginning to disrupt national political alignments, forcing the federal government to take an unprecedented role in urban politics.

By 1960 the swelling urban black population had a key role in national politics, especially presidential politics. With migration North, blacks became at least nominal participants in the electoral system, and their participation was concentrated in the states with the largest number of electoral votes. By 1960, 90 percent of all Northern blacks were living in the ten most populous states: California, New York, Pennsylvania, Ohio, Illinois, New Jersey, Michigan, Massachusetts, Indiana, and Missouri. It was the heavy Democratic vote in the big cities of these states, and especially the black democratic vote in these cities, that gave Kennedy his slim margin. That narrow victory helped mark the importance of troubles in the cities, especially the troubles with blacks in the cities.

Urban blacks, who had been loyal Democrats for almost three decades, had begun to defect even as their numbers grew, signaling the failure of the municipal political machinery. In 1952, 79 percent voted Democratic; by 1956, the black vote slipped to 61 percent. Kennedy worked to win back some of these votes (69 percent in 1960) by taking a strong stand on civil rights in the campaign.[6] But once in office, his administration backed off from supporting civil rights legislation, for that was sure to jeopardize

---

[6]See Piven and Cloward, *op. cit.*, Chapters 9 and 10, on the impact of the black migration on the Democratic administrations of the 1960s.

Southern support. Other ways to reach and reward the urban black voter were needed.

Accordingly, administration analysts began to explore strategies to cement the allegiance of the urban black vote to the national party. What emerged, not all at once, but gropingly, was a series of federal service programs directed to the ghetto. The first appropriations were small, as with the Juvenile Delinquency and Youth Offenses Control Act of 1961, but each program enlarged upon the other, up until the Model Cities legislation of 1966. Some of the new programs—in manpower development, in education, in health—were relatively straightforward. All they did was give new funds to local agencies to be used to provide jobs or services for the poor. Thus, funds appropriated under Title 1 of the Elementary and Secondary Education Act of 1965 were earmarked for educational facilities for poor children; the medicaid program enacted in 1965 reimbursed health agencies and physicians for treating the poor; and manpower agencies were funded specifically to provide jobs or job training for the poor.

Other of the new federal programs were neither so simple nor so straightforward, and these were the ones that became the hallmark of the Great Society. The federal memoranda describing them were studded with terms like "inner city," "institutional change," and "maximum feasible participation." But if this language was often confusing, the programs themselves ought not to have been. The "inner city," after all, was a euphemism for the ghetto, and activities funded under such titles as delinquency prevention, mental health, antipoverty, or model cities turned out, in the streets of the cities, to look very much alike. What they looked like was nothing less than the old political machine.

Federal funds were used to create new storefront-style agencies in the ghettos, staffed with professionals who helped local people find jobs, obtain welfare, or deal with school officials. Neighborhood leaders were also hired, named community workers, neighborhood aides, or whatever, but in fact close kin to the old ward heelers, for they drew larger numbers of people into the new programs, spreading the federal spoils.

But federal spoils were not enough, for there were not many of them. What the new ghetto agencies had to offer was small and impermanent compared to ongoing municipal programs in education, housing, or health. If blacks were to be wrapped into the political organization of the cities, the traditional agencies of local government, which controlled the bulk of federal, state, and local appropriations, had to be reoriented. Municipal agencies had to be made to respond to blacks.

Various tactics to produce such reform were tried, at first under the guise of experiments in "institutional change." This meant that the Washington officials who administered the juvenile delinquency program (under Robert Kennedy's direction) required as a condition of granting funds that local governments submit "comprehensive plans" for their own reform (that is, for giving blacks something). But the mere existence of such paper plans did not turn out to be very compelling to the local bureaucrats who implemented programs. Therefore, as turbulence spread in the Northern ghettos, the federal officials began to try another way to promote institutional change—"maximum feasible participation of residents of the areas and members of the groups served." Under that slogan, the Great Society programs gave money to ghetto organizations, which then used the money to harass city agencies. Community workers were hired to badger housing inspectors and to pry loose welfare payments. Lawyers on the federal payroll took municipal agencies to court on behalf of ghetto clients. Later the new programs helped organize the ghetto poor to picket the welfare department or to boycott the school system.

In these various ways, then, the federal government intervened in local politics, and forced local government to do what it had earlier failed to do. Federal dollars and federal authority were used to resuscitate the functions of the political machine, on the one hand *by spurring local service agencies to respond to the black newcomers*, and on the other *by spurring blacks to make demands upon city services*.

As it turned out, blacks made their largest tangible gains from this process through the public welfare system. Total national welfare costs rose from about $4 billion in 1960 to nearly $15 billion in 1970. Big cities that received the largest numbers of black and Spanish-speaking migrants and that were most shaken by the political reverberations of that migration also experienced the largest welfare budget rises. In New York, Los Angeles, and Baltimore, for example, the AFDC rolls quadrupled, and costs rose even faster. In some cities, moreover, welfare costs were absorbing an ever-larger share of the local budget, a bigger piece of the public pie. In New York City, for example, welfare costs absorbed about 12 percent of the city's budget in the 1950s; but by 1970 the share going to welfare had grown to about 25 percent (of a much larger budget), mainly because the proportion of the city's population on Aid to Families of Dependent Children increased from 2.6 percent in 1960 to 11.0 percent in 1970.[7] In other words, the blacks who triggered the disturbances received their biggest payoffs from welfare,[8] mainly because other groups were not competing within the welfare system for a share of relief benefits.[9]

But if blacks got welfare, that was just about all they got. Less obvious than the emergence of black demands—but much more important in accounting for increasing service costs—was the reaction of organized whites to these political developments, particularly the groups who had direct material stakes in the running of the local services. If the new upthrust of black claims threatened and jostled many groups in the city, none were so alert or so shrill as those who had traditionally gotten the main benefits of the municipal services. These were the people who depended, directly or indirectly, on the city treasury for their livelihood: They worked in the municipal agencies, in agencies that were publicly funded (e.g., voluntary hospitals), in professional services that were publicly reimbursed (e.g., doctors), or in businesses that depended on city contracts (e.g., contractors and construction workers). Partly they were incited by black claims that seemed to threaten their traditional preserves. Partly they were no longer held in check by stable relationships with political leaders, for these relations had weakened or become uncertain or even turned to enmity: Indeed, in some cases, the leaders themselves had been toppled, shaken loose by the conflict and instability of the times.

---

[7]*Changing Patterns of Prices, Pay, Workers, and Work on the New York Scene,* U.S. Department of Labor, Bureau of Labor Statistics (New York: Middle Atlantic Regional Office, May 1971), Regional Reports No. 20, p. 36.

[8]The dole, needless to say, is a very different sort of concession from the higher salaries, pensions, and on-the-job prerogatives won by other groups. For one thing, the dole means continued poverty and low status. For another, it is easier to take away, for recipients remain relatively weak and unorganized.

[9]That poor minorities made large gains through the welfare "crisis" and other groups did not is important to understanding the furious opposition that soaring welfare budgets arouse. Organized welfare-agency workers were competing for the welfare dollar, of course, but were not nearly so successful as the workers in other services, for they were not in a position to take much advantage of political turmoil. They were not nearly so numerous or well organized as teachers, policemen, or firemen, and they could not use the threat of withholding services to exact concessions nearly so effectively. Unlike school teachers or garbage men, their services were of importance only to the very poor.

In effect, the groups who worked for or profited from city government had become unleashed, at the same time that newcomers were snapping at their heels.

The result was that the provider groups reacted with a rush of new demands. And these groups had considerable muscle to back up their claims. Not only were they unusually numerous and well organized, but they were allied to broader constituencies by their class and ethnic ties and by their union affiliations. Moreover, their demands for increased benefits, whether higher salaries or lower work load or greater autonomy, were always couched in terms of protecting the professional standards of the city services, a posture that helped win them broad public support. As a result, even when the organized providers backed up their demands by closing the schools, or stopping the subways, or letting the garbage pile up, many people were ready to blame the inconveniences on political officials.

Local political leaders, their ties to their constituencies undermined by population shifts and spreading discontent, were in a poor position to resist or temper these escalating demands, especially the demand of groups with the power to halt the services on which a broader constituency depended. Instead, to maintain their position, they tried to expand and elaborate the benefits—the payrolls, the contracts, the perquisites, and the services—of the municipal agencies.

Nor, as had been true in the era of the machine, was it easy to use these concessions to restore stable relationships. Where once political leaders had been able to anticipate or allay the claims of various groups, dealing with them one by one, now each concession was public, precipitating rival claims from other groups, each demand ricocheting against the other in an upward spiral. Not only did public concessions excite rivalry, but political officials lost the ablity to hold groups in check in another way as well; unlike their machine predecessors, they could attach few conditions to the concessions they made. Each job offered, each wage increase conceded, each job prerogative granted, was now ensconced in civil service regulations or union contracts and, thus firmly secured, could not be withdrawn. Political leaders had lost any leverage in their dealings; each concession simply became the launching pad for higher demands. Instead of regular exchange relationships, open conflict and uncertainty became the rule. The result was a virtual run upon the city treasury by a host of organized groups in the city, each competing with the other for a larger share of municipal benefits. Benefits multiplied and budgets soared—and so did the discontent of various groups with the schools, or police, or housing, or welfare, or health. To illustrate, we need to examine the fiscal impact of mounting political claims in greater detail.

Rising Demands and the Fiscal Crisis

Education is a good example, for it is the single largest service run by localities, accounting for 40 percent of the outlays of state and local government in 1968, up from 30 percent in 1948.[10] The huge expenditures involved in running the schools are also potential benefits—jobs for teachers, contracts for maintenance and construction, and educational services for children—all things to be gained by different groups in the local community. Accordingly, the educational system became a leading target of black demands,[11] at first mainly in the form of the struggle for integrated schools. Later, worn down by local resistance to integration and guided by the Great Society programs that provided staff, meeting rooms, mimeograph machines, and lawyers to ghetto groups,[12] the difficult

---

[10]See *State and Local Finances: Significant Features 1967–1970*, U.S. Advisory Commission on Intergovernmental Relations (Washington, D.C.: Government Printing Office, 1969), Figure 6, p. 39.

[11]Conflict and competition over the schools have been further heightened because the proportion of blacks in the schools has increased even more rapidly than the proportion of blacks in the population, owing to the youthfulness of blacks and the flight of whites to private schools. In Washington, blacks constituted 54 percent of the local population in 1965, but 90 percent of the school children; in St. Louis blacks were 27 percent of the population, but 63 percent of the school population; in Chicago, they were 23 percent of the general population, but 53 percent of the school population; in New York City, where blacks and Puerto Ricans make up about 27 percent of the population, 52 percent of the children in the schools were black or Puerto Rican. Of the twenty-eight largest cities in the nation, seventeen had black majorities in the school system by 1965. See *Racial Isolation in the Public Schools*, U.S. Commission on Civil Rights (Washington, D.C.: Government Printing Office, February 20, 1967). Table 11–2.

[12]The federal government was also providing direct funds to improve the education of the "disadvantaged" under Title 1 of the Elementary and Secondary Education Act of 1965. However, although in four years following the passage of the Act, $4.3 billion was appropriated for Title 1, it was widely charged that these funds were misused and diverted from the poor by many local school boards.

257

demands for integration were transformed into demands for "citizen participation," which meant a share of the jobs, contracts, and status positions that the school system yields up.[13]

Blacks made some gains. Boards of education began hiring more black teachers, and some cities instituted schemes for "community control" that ensconced local black leaders in the lower echelons of the school hierarchy.[14] But the organized producer groups, whose salaries account for an estimated 80 percent of rising school costs,[15] made far larger gains. Incited by black claims that seemed to challenge their traditional preserves and emboldened by a weak and conciliatory city government, the groups who depend on school budgets began rapidly to enlarge and entrench their stakes. Most evident in the scramble were teaching and supervisory personnel, who were numerous and well organized and became ever more strident—so much so that the opening of each school year is now signaled by news of teacher strikes in cities throughout the country. And threatened city officials strained to respond by expanding the salaries, jobs, programs, and privileges they had to offer. One result was that average salaries in New York City, Chicago, Los Angeles, Philadelphia, Washington, D.C., and San Francisco topped the $10,000 mark by 1969, *in most instances having doubled* in the decade. Nationally, teachers' salaries have risen about 8 percent each year since 1965.[16] Not only did the teachers win rapid increases in salaries but, often prompted by new black demands, they exploited contract negotiations and intensive lobbying to win new guarantees of job security, increased pensions, and "improvements" in educational policy

---

[13]A series of training guides to such efforts, prepared with federal funds by a local poverty program known as United Bronx Parents, included a kit on "How to Evaluate Your School" and a series of leaflets on such matters as "The Expense Budget—Where Does All the Money Go?" "The Construction Budget—When the Community Controls Construction We Will Have the Schools We Need," as well as an all-purpose handbook on parents rights vis-à-vis the schools. Not surprisingly, Albert Shanker, president of the teachers union in New York City, charged there was "an organized effort to bring about rule in the schools by violence," involving the use of flying squads of disrupters who went from school to school and who, he said, had been trained with government (i.e., poverty program) funds (*The New York Times*, November 16, 1970, p. 2).

[14]See Urban America, Inc., and the Urban Coalition, *One Year Later: An Assessment of the Nation's Response to the Crisis Described by the National Advisory Commission on Civil Disorders* (New York: Praeger, 1969), pp. 34–35. See also, Naomi Levine with Richard Cohen, *Oceanhill-Brownsville: A Case History of Schools in Crisis* (New York: Popular Library, 1969), pp. 127–128.

[15]This estimate was reported by Fred Hechinger, *The New York Times*, August 29, 1971.

[16]Averaging $9,200 in 1970–1971, according to the National Education Association.

that have had the effect of increasing their own ranks—all of which drove up school budgets, especially in the big cities where blacks were concentrated.[17] In Baltimore, where the black population has reached 47 percent, the school budget increased from $57 million in 1961 to $184 million in 1971; in New Orleans from $28.5 million to $73.9 million in 1971; in Boston, school costs rose from $35.4 million in 1961 to $95.7 million in 1971.[18] Total national educational costs, which in 1957 amounted to $12 billion, topped $40 billion by 1968,[19] and the U.S. Office of Education expects costs to continue to rise, by at least 37 percent by 1975. In this process, blacks may have triggered the flood of new demands on the schools, but organized whites turned out to be the main beneficiaries.

What happened in education happened in other services as well. Costs rose precipitously across the board as mayors tried to extend the benefits of the service agencies to quiet the discordant and clamoring groups in the city. One way was to expand the number of jobs, often by creating new agencies, so that there was more to go around. Hence, in New York City, the municipal payroll expanded by over 145,000 jobs in the 1960s, and the rate of increase doubled after Mayor John V. Lindsay took office in 1965.[20] By 1971, 381,000 people were on the municipal payroll. Some 34,000 of these new employees were black and Puerto Rican "paraprofessionals," according to the city's personnel director. Others were Lindsay supporters, put on the payroll as part of his effort to build a new political organization out of the turmoil.[21]

---

[17]State averages reflect the political troubles in big cities. Thus, in an urban state like New York, $1,251 was spent per pupil in 1969–1970 and New Jersey, California, Connecticut, and Massachusetts were not far behind. This represented an increase of about 80 percent in per pupil expenditures since 1965–1966.

[18]Educational costs have also risen sharply outside the central cities, particularly in the adjacent suburban school districts. These rises are a direct reverberation of troubles in the cities. Suburban school boards must remain competitive with the rising salary levels of educational personnel in the central cities, particularly considering the high priority placed on education by the middle-class suburbs. For example, between 1968 and 1969, enrollment in the Westchester, New York, schools increased by 1.5 percent, and the operating budget by 12 percent. In Fairfield, Connecticut, enrollment increased by 5.2 percent, the budget by 13.2 percent. In Suffolk County, New York, enrollment increased by 6.6 percent, the budget by 11.6 percent. In Monmouth, New Jersey, enrollment increased by 4.4 percent, the budget by 19 percent. Moreover, there are also increasing numbers of blacks in some of the older suburbs, with the result that these towns are experiencing political disturbances very similar to those of the big cities.

[19]State and Local Finances, op. cit., p. 39.

[20]Changing Patterns of Prices, Pay, Workers, and Work, op. cit., pp. 7–8.

[21]Some 25,000 of the new jobs were noncompetitive (The New York Times, May 28, 1971). Not surprisingly, the governor suggested that the mayor economize by cutting these, instead of always talking about cutting the number of policemen and firemen.

Most of the rest were new teachers, policemen, and social workers, some hired to compensate for reduced work loads won by existing employees (teachers won reduced class sizes, patrolmen the right to work in pairs), others hired to staff an actual expansion that had taken place in some services to appease claimant groups who were demanding more welfare, safer streets, or better snow removal.[22] As a result, total state and local governmental employment in the city rose from 8.2 percent of the total labor force in 1960 to 14 percent in 1970. A similar trend of expanded public employment took place in other big cities. In Detroit state and local employment rose from 9 percent of the labor force in 1960 to 12.2 percent in 1970; in Philadelphia from 6.9 percent to 9.8 percent; in Los Angeles from 9.8 percent to 12.0 percent; in San Francisco, from 12.2 percent in 1960 to 15.2 percent in 1970.[23]

Another way to try to deal with the clamor was to concede larger and larger salaries and more liberal pensions to existing employees who were pressing new demands, and pressing hard, with transit, or garbage, or police strikes (or sick-outs or slow-downs) that paralyzed whole cities.[24] In Detroit, garbage collectors allowed refuse to accumulate in the streets when the city offered

---

[22]Welfare is the main example of an actual expansion of services, for the number of welfare employees increased largely as a reflection of increasing caseloads. But so were new policemen hired to appease a broad constituency concerned about rising crime, sanitation men to answer demands for cleaner streets, and so forth.

[23]*Changing Patterns of Prices, Pay, Workers, and Work, op. cit.,* p. 9. Moreover, big payrolls were a big city phenomenon. A study showed that, in three states studied in detail, the ratio of public employment per 100 population varied sharply by city size, more so in New Jersey and Ohio, less markedly in Texas. See *Urban and Rural America: Policies for Future Growth*, U.S. Advisory Commission on Intergovernmental Relations (Washington, D.C.: Government Printing Office, April 1968), pp. 47–49.

[24]According to Harold Rubin:
Time lost by state and local government employees due to work stoppages climbed from 7,510 man-days in 1958 to 2,535,000 man-days in 1968, according to the U.S. Bureau of Labor Statistics. Such strikes have not been limited to those performing "nonessential duties." For example, during the first half of 1970 there have been strikes by prison guards (New Jersey), sanitation men (Cincinnati, Ohio; Phoenix, Arizona; Atlanta, Georgia; Seattle, Washington; and Charlotte, North Carolina), teachers (Youngstown, Ohio; Minneapolis, Minnesota; Butte, Montana; Tulsa, Oklahoma; Boston, Massachusetts; Newark and Jersey City, New Jersey; and Los Angeles, California, to list only some of the larger school systems involved), bus drivers (Cleveland, Ohio; Tacoma, Washington; and San Diego, California), hospital employees (State of New Jersey; Detroit, Michigan), policemen (Newport, Kentucky; Livonia, Michigan; and Winthrop, Massachusetts), and firemen (Newark, Ohio, and Racine, Wisconsin) ["Labor Relations in State and Local Governments," in Robert R. Connery and William V. Farr (eds.), *Unionization of Municipal Employees* (New York: Columbia University, The Academy of Political Science, 1971), pp. 20–21].

them only a 6 percent wage increase, after the police won an 11 percent increase.[25] In Cincinnati, municipal laborers and garbage collectors threatened a "massive civil disobedience campaign" when they were offered less than the $945 annual raise won by plicemen and firemen.[26] In Philadelphia garbage collectors engaged in a slowdown when a policeman was appointed to head their department.[27] A San Francisco strike by 7,500 city workers shut down the schools and the transit system and disrupted several other services simultaneously.[28] An unprecedented wildcat strike by New York City's policemen, already the highest paid police force in the world, would have cost the city an estimated $56,936 a year for every policeman (and $56,214 for every fireman), if demands for salaries, pensions, fringe benefits, and reduced work time had been conceded.[29] If these demands were perhaps a bit theatrical, the pay raises for city employees in New York City did average 12 percent each year in 1967, 1968, and 1969. Meanwhile, the U.S. Bureau of Labor statistics reported that the earnings of health professionals in the city rose by 80 percent in the decade, at least double the increase in factory wages. In other cities across the country similar groups were making similar gains; municipal salaries rose by 7–10 percent in both 1968 and 1969, or about twice as fast as the Consumer Price Index.[30]

The cities are unable to raise revenues commensurate with these expenditures; and they are unable to resist the claims that underlie rising expenditures. And that is what the fiscal crisis is all about. Cities exist only by state decree, and depend entirely

---

[25] *The New York Times*, June 13, 1971.
[26] *The New York Times*, January 31, 1970.
[27] *The New York Times*, February 26, 1970.
[28] *The New York Times*, March 17, 1970.
[29] *The New York Times*, March 15, 1971. These estimates were given to the press by the city's Budget Director.
[30] Rising wages and pensions benefits among municipal employees are frequently attributed to unionization, which has indeed spread in the 1960s, rather than to changes in city politics. Membership in the American Federation of State, County, and Municipal Employees increased from 180,000 to 425,000 in one decade; The American Federation of Teachers enlarged its ranks from 60,000 members in 1961 to 175,000 in 1969. But to point to unionization as a cause simply diverts the argument, since the spread and militancy of unionism among city employees in the 1960s must itself be explained. In any case, a Brookings Institution study of nineteen local governments showed no conclusive differences between unionized and nonunionized wages; both had risen substantially. See David Stanley, "The Effect of Unions on Local Governments," Connery and Farr (eds.), *op. cit.*, p. 47.

on the state governments for their taxing powers.[31] Concretely this has meant that the states have taken for themselves the preferred taxes[32] leaving the localities to depend primarily on the property tax (which accounts for 70 percent of revenues raised by local governments),[33] supplemented by a local sales tax in many places, user charges (e.g., sewer and water fees), and, in some places, a local income tax.[34] The big cities have had little choice but to drive up these local taxes to which they are limited, but at serious costs.[35] New York City, for example, taxes property at rates twice the national average, yielding a property tax roll three times as large as any other city. New York City also has an income tax, which is rising rapidly. Newark, plagued by racial conflict, ranks second in the nation in its rate of property tax.[36]

The exploitation of any of these taxes is fraught with dilemmas for localities. By raising either property or sale taxes excessively, they risk driving out the business and industry on which their tax rolls eventually depend, and risk also the political ire of their

---

[31]The New York State Constitution, for example, specifies that:

It shall be the duty of the Legislature, subject to the provisions of this Constitution, to restrict the power of taxation, assessment, borrowing money, contracting indebtedness, and loaning the credit of counties, cities, towns and villages, so as to prevent abuses in taxation and assessments and in contracting of indebtedness by them. Nothing in this article shall be construed to prevent the Legislature from further restricting the powers herein specified [Article VIII, Section 12].

Traditionally the states have granted powers of taxation to the localities only very reluctantly.

[32]Not only do states limit the taxing powers of localities, but they have the authority to mandate local expenditures—e.g., salary increases for police and firemen—with or without adjusting local taxing powers to pay for them. They also have the authority to vote tax exemptions at local expense for favored groups. State legislatures are given to doing exactly that, exacerbating the financial plight of local governments.

[33]This was $27 billion that localities raised in revenues from their own sources in 1967–1968 (*State and Local Finances, op. cit.*, Table 8, p. 31). It should be noted that property taxes are declining relative to other sources of local revenue. At the turn of the century about 80 percent of state and local budgets were financed by the property tax. Today, the states hardly rely on it at all. Nevertheless, local governments still finance about half their budgets with property taxes.

[34]The first city income tax was levied in Philadelphia, in 1939, when the city was on the verge of bankruptcy. The use of the income tax by big cities spread in the 1960s, with Akron and Detroit adopting it in 1962, Kansas City in 1964, Baltimore and New York City in 1966, and Cleveland in 1967. See *City Income Taxes* (New York: Tax Foundation, Inc., 1967), Research Publication No. 12, pp. 7–9. City income taxes must, of course, also be approved by the state, an approval that is not always forthcoming.

[35]By 1964–1965, per capita local taxes in the central cities of the thirty-seven largest metropolitan areas had risen to $200 per capita. In Washington, D.C., taxes were $291 per capita; in New York City $279; and in Newark $273. Overall, central city residents were paying 7 percent of their income in local taxes and in the biggest cities 10 percent (*Fiscal Balance in the American Federal System, op. cit.*, Vol. II, pp. 75–79).

[36]By 1968, official statistics for the nation as a whole showed local property taxes totaling $27.8 billion. The annual rise since then is estimated at between $1 and $3 billion.

constituents. For instance, it was estimated that a 1 percent increase in the New York City sales tax had the effect of driving 6 percent of all clothing and household furnishing sales out beyond the city line, along with thousands of jobs.[37] A New York property tax rate of 4 percent of true value on new improvements is thought by many to have acted as a brake on most new construction, excepting the very high yielding office buildings and luxury apartments. Boston's 6 percent of true value property tax brought private construction to a halt until the law was changed so that new improvements were taxed only half as heavily as existing buildings.[38] Increases in either sales or property tax rates thus entail the serious danger of diminishing revenues by eroding the tax base. To make matters worse, with the beginning of recession in 1969, revenues from sales and income taxes began to fall off, while the interest the cities had to pay for borrowing rose, at a time that local governments were going more and more into hock.[39]

Federalism as a Constraining Influence

If mayors cannot resist the demands of contending groups in the cities, there are signs that the state and federal governments can, and will. The fiscal interrelations that undergird the federal system and leave the cities dependent on state and federal grants for

[37]*Our Nation's Cities* (Washington, D.C.: Government Printing Office, March 1969), p. 24.

[38]*Our Nation's Cities, op. cit.,* pp. 36–37. To understand the full impact of property taxes, one must remember that these are taxes on capital value, and not on income yielded. Thus, a 3 percent of true value tax on improvements can easily tax away 75 percent of the net income that a new building would otherwise earn—a loss, economists generally agree, that tends to be passed on to consumers. See, for example, Dick Netzer, *Economics of the Property Tax* (Washington, D.C.: The Brookings Institute, 1966), pp. 40–62.

[39]Local tax collections increased by 500 percent between World War II and 1967, but costs have risen 10 percent faster, and the bigger the city, the tighter the squeeze. If the process were to continue, and today's growth rate of city spending vs. city revenues to continue, a recent study commissioned by the National League of Cities estimates a gap of $262 billion by 1980 (*Our Nation's Cities, op. cit.,* p. 22). Measured another way, state and local indebtedness combined rose by 400 percent since 1948, while the federal debt rose by only 26 percent (*Fiscal Balance in the American Federal System, op. cit.,* Vol. I, p. 55). In the thirty-six large central cities alone, the cumulative tax gap could reach $25 to $30 billion by 1975 (*Ibid.,* Vol. II, p. 91). A special commission on the Cities in the Seventies, established by the National Urban Coalition, concluded that by 1980 most cities will be "totally bankrupt" (*The New York Times,* September 24, 1971).

an increasing portion of their funds are also a mechanism by which state and federal politics come to intervene in and control city politics. This is happening most clearly and directly through changes in state expenditures for the cities.

With their own taxing powers constricted from the outset, the mayors had little recourse but to turn to the states for enlarged grants-in-aid, trying to pass upward the political pressures they felt, usually summoning the press and the urban pressure groups for help. Since governors and legislators were not entirely immune to pressures from the city constituencies, the urban states increased their aid to the big cities.[40] Metropolises like New York City and Los Angeles now get roughly a quarter of their revenues from the state.

Accordingly, state budgets also escalated, and state taxes rose.[41] All in all, at least twenty-one states imposed new taxes or increased old taxes in 1968, and thirty-seven states in 1969, usually as a result of protracted struggle[42] North Carolina enacted the largest program of new or increased taxes in its history; Illinois and Maine introduced an income tax, bringing to thirty-eight the number of states imposing some form of income tax; South Carolina passed its first major tax increase in a decade. Even Ohio moved to change its tradition of low tax and low service policies

[40]By 1966–1967, per capita intergovernmental aid was substantially higher for the central cities than suburban localities (contrary to popular impression). Per capita aid to Washington, D.C., was $181, compared to $81 in the outlying suburbs $174 to Baltimore, and $101 to the suburbs; $179 to Boston, and $74 to the suburbs; $220 to New York City, and $163 to the suburbs; $144 to Newark, and $53 to the suburbs; $70 to Philadelphia, and $61 to the suburbs; $88 to Chicago, and $55 to the suburbs; $126 to Detroit, and $115 to the suburbs (*State and Local Finances, op. cit.*, Table 29, p. 69).

[41]Arthur Levitt, Controller of the State of New York, recently released figures showing that state spending had increased from $1.3 billion in 1956 to $3.9 billion in 1964, to an approximately $8 billion in 1968. In the four years ending in 1968, state spending rose by an annual average of $875 million, or 18.7 percent. In 1968 the spending increase was $1.4 billion, or 22.1 percent over the previous year (*The New York Times*, April 2, 1969–July 7, 1969). During this same five year period, state revenues from taxes and federal aid increased from $3.7 billion to $7.2 billion. In other words, spending exceeded revenues and by greater margins in each of the successive years. The total deficit for the five year period amounted to $2.5 billion, which, of course, had to be borrowed. A large part of this rise in New York State's budget reflects aid to localities, which increased from $622 million in fiscal 1955 to $1.04 billion in fiscal 1960, to $1.67 billion in 1965, and $3.23 billion in fiscal year 1969. State spending for aid to education has doubled in the last six years, and the state share of welfare and medicaid costs doubled in only four years.

[42]By 1971 the estimated difference between revenues and outlays were in excess of $500 million in New York, California, and Texas. Florida was short $120 million; New Jersey $100 million; Connecticut $200 million (*The New York Times*, January 3, 1971). A handful of rural states, however, were considering tax cuts.

that had forced thirteen school districts in the state to close. Overall, state and local taxes rose from 5 percent of the Gross National Product in 1946 to more than 8 percent of the GNP in 1969. Americans paid an average of $380 in state and local taxes in the fiscal year 1968, $42 more per person than the previous year, and more than double the fiscal year 1967. The rate tended to be highest in urban states: In New York the per person tax burden was $576; in California, $540; in Massachusetts, $453. The low was in Arkansas, with a tax rate of $221.[43]

But raising taxes in Albany or Sacramento to pay for politics in New York City or Los Angeles is no simple matter, for the state capitals are not nearly as vulnerable as city halls to urban pressure groups, but are very vulnerable indeed to the suburbs and small towns that are antagonized by both higher taxes and city troubles. Besides, the mass of urban voters also resent taxes, especially when taxes are used to pay off the organized interests in the service systems, without yielding visibly better services.[44] Accordingly, even while taxes are raised, state grants to the cities are cut anyway. Thus, the New York State legislature reduced grant-in-aid formulas in welfare and medicaid (programs that go mainly to the central cities and mainly to blacks in those cities) in 1969[45] and again in 1971 (1970 was an election year and so

---

[43]Data provided by the Commerce Clearing House, as reported in *The New York Times*, September 27, 1970.

[44]A Gallup poll in 1969 showed that 49 percent would not vote for more money to pay for schools if additional taxes were sought, against 45 percent who would *(The New York Times*, August 17, 1969). Another key fact in understanding the populist character of the tax revolt is that state and local taxes consist mainly in sales and property taxes, and various user charges, all of which tend to be relatively regressive. Even the state income tax, when it is used, is usually imposed as a fixed percentage of income (unlike the graduated federal income tax, which takes more from those who have more, at least in principle). In any case, fully two-thirds of state revenues were raised from sales and gross receipt taxes [*State and Government Finances in 1967*, U.S. Bureau of the Census (Washington, D.C.: Government Printing Office, 1968), Table 1, p. 7]. Consequently the new taxes have had a severe impact on the working and middle classes, who are paying a larger and larger percentage of personal income to state and local government. In New York, state and local taxes now absorb over 13 percent of personal income; in California, over 12 percent; in Illinois and Ohio over 8 percent. As a result of rising state and local taxes (and price inflation), per capita real disposable personal income fell considerably between 1965 and 1969. See Paul M. Schwab, "Two Measures of Purchasing Power Contrasted," *Monthly Labor Review* (April 1971). By contrast, federal taxes declined as a percent of Gross National Product between 1948–1968, during which period state and local taxes rose from about 5 percent to 8 percent of GNP (*State and Local Finances, op. cit.*, Figure 5, p. 29). The "tax revolt" in the states should be no surprise.

[45]Most of the 1969 welfare cuts were restored within a short time, but the 1971 cuts were not.

the governor proposed increased aid to the cities without tax increases). Each time, the cuts were effected in all-night marathon sessions of the legislature, replete with dramatic denouncements by Democratic legislators from the cities and cries of betrayal from the mayors. Despite the cuts, anticipated state spending still rose by $878 million in 1969, the highest for any single year excepting the previous fiscal year in which the rise had been $890 million. By 1970 when the proposed budget had reached $8.45 billion, requiring $1.1 billion in new taxes, the outcry was so terrific that the governor reversed his proposals and led the legislature in a budget-slashing session, with welfare and medicaid programs the main targets.

When Governor Ronald Reagan, a self-proclaimed fiscal conservative, nevertheless submitted a record-breaking $6.37 billion budget for the 1969–1970 fiscal year, he met a storm of political protest that threatened a legislative impasse, leaving California without a budget. The next year Reagan proposed to solve the state's "fiscal crisis" by cutting welfare and medicaid expenditures by $800 million; even so, he submitted another record budget of $6.7 billion. When the long legislative battle that ensued was over, the governor signed an unbalanced budget of $7.3 billion, with substantial cuts in welfare and medicaid nevertheless.

Pennsylvania's former Republican Governor Raymond P. Shafer, in his short two years in office, managed to win the opposition of all but 23 percent of Pennsylvania voters as he and the legislature fought about how to raise $500 million in new revenues. At the beginning of his term in 1967, the governor was forced to raise state sales taxes to 6 percent, despite his campaign pledge of no new taxes, and early in 1969, with the budget $200 million short, he proposed that state's first income tax. When Shafer left office the income tax was enacted by his successor, Democratic Governor Milton Shapp, only to be voided by the Pennsylvania Supreme Court in 1971. A modified income tax law was finally passed, but by that time the state legislature was also making spending reductions, including a 50 percent cut in state education appropriations for ghetto districts.[46]

When Connecticut's 1969 biannual state budget proposal required a $700 million tax increase despite cuts in the welfare budget, the Democratic controlled General Assembly rebelled, forcing a hectic special session of the state legislature to hammer

[46]*The New York Times*, February 16, 1971; June 9, 17, 19, 25, 1971; and July 2, 1971.

out a new budget and tax program. In the tumultuous weeks that followed, a compromise package presumably agreed upon by the Democratic governor and the Democratic majority in both houses was repeatedly thrown into doubt. When the session was over, Connecticut had passed the largest tax program in its history, had borrowed $32.5 million, and Governor John N. Dempsey had announced he would not seek reelection. Two years later Republican Governor Thomas J. Meskill engaged the legislature in battle again over another record budget that the governor proposed to pay for with a 7 percent sales tax—the highest in the country. Not only the legislature, but the insurance industries, the Mayor of Hartford, and 5,000 marchers took part in the protest that ensued, leading to a compromise tax package that replaced the sales tax increase with a new state income tax, together with more borrowing and new welfare cuts as well. A few short months later, after new public protests, the income tax was repealed, the sales tax increase was restored, and more spending cuts were made, mainly in state grants to municipalities and in welfare appropriations.

The New Jersey legislature, at a special session called by Democratic Governor Richard Hughes in 1969 to plead for added revenues for urban areas, rejected a new tax on banks and lending institutions—this despite the urging of the governor, who called the cities of the state "sick" and its largest city, Newark, "sick unto death," and despite the clamor of New Jersey's mayors. The legislature eventually agreed to redirect some existing urban aid funds to pay for increased police and fire salaries—a measure made particularly urgent after Newark's firemen went on strike, forcing the city to make emergency salary arrangements. When Republican Governor William T. Cahill took office later that year he signed a measure raising the New Jersey sales tax to 5 percent, claiming he faced a "major state fiscal crisis" of a $300 million deficit.

Other state governments are locked in similar fiscal and political battles, Michigan began the 1972 fiscal year without authorization to spend money after the legislature had been virtually paralyzed by a six-month struggle over the $2 billion budget, which the governor had proposed to finance with a 38 percent increase in the state income tax. Wisconsin cut welfare and urban aid expenditures over Governor Ody J. Fish's protest and, having enacted a new and broadened sales tax, precipitated a march on the capital by Milwaukee poor. Not long afterward, Governor Fish resigned, imperiling the Wisconsin Republican party. In Rhode

Island, Democratic Governor Frank E. Licht promised no new taxes in his reelection campaign in 1970 and two months later recommended an income tax, amidst loud voter protest. When Texas, having passed the largest tax bill in its history in 1969, faced a deficit of $400 million in 1971, Governor Preston E. Smith vetoed the entire second year of a two-year budget, which totaled $7.1 billion.

In brief, pressures from the big cities were channeled upward to the state capitals, with some response. At least in the big urbanized states, governors and legislatures moved toward bailing out the cities, with the result that state expenditures and state taxes skyrocketed. But the reaction is setting in; the taxpayers' revolt is being felt in state legislatures across the country. And as raucous legislative battles continue, a trend is emerging: The states are turning out to be a restraining influence on city politics, and especially on ghetto politics.

While in the main, grants-in-aid were not actually reduced, they were not increased enough to cover rising city costs either, and the toll is being taken. Some municipalities began to cut payroll and services. By 1971, vacancies were going unfilled in New York City, Baltimore, Denver, and Kansas City. San Diego and Cleveland reduced rubbish collection; Dallas cut capital improvements; Kansas City let its elm trees die.[47] Detroit started closing park toilets. And some city employees were actually being dismissed in Los Angeles, Cleveland, Detroit, Kansas City, Cincinnati, Indianapolis, Pittsburgh, and New York City. "This is the first time since the depression that I have participated in this kind of cutback of education," said Cincinnati's Superintendent of Schools.[48] "You run as far as you can, but when you run out of gas you've got to stop," said Baltimore's Mayor Thomas J. D'Alesandro.

But the biggest cuts imposed by the states were in the programs from which blacks had gained the most as a result of their emergence as a force in the cities. Special state appropriations for health and education in ghetto districts were being cut; nine states cut back their medicaid programs;[49] and most important, at least

---

[47]*The New York Times*, August 30, 1970; November 27, 1970; and May 25, 1971.
[48]Nationally the annual rise in teacher salaries slumped to only 5.5 percent, after rising by about 8 percent each year for several years.
[49]Usually by limiting eligibility, or limiting the types of services covered, or requiring co-payments by patients. See *Health Law Newsletter* (Los Angeles: National Legal Program on Health Problems of the Poor, June 1971), p. 2.

nineteen states reduced welfare benefits by mid-1971, according to a *New York Times* survey. Moreover, new state measures to root out "welfare fraud," or to reinstitute residence restrictions, or to force recipients into work programs threatened far more drastic erosion of black gains in the near future.

There are signs that the federal government has also become a restraining influence on city politics. In the early 1960s, the national Democratic administration had used its grants to the cities to intervene in city politics, encouraging ghetto groups to demand more from city halls and forcing recalcitrant mayors to be more responsive to the enlarging and volatile ghettos, whose allegiance had become critical to the national Democratic party. But a Republican administration was not nearly so oriented to the big cities, least of all to the ghettos of the big cities. Accordingly, the directions of the Great Society programs that the Nixon administration had inherited were shifted; bit by bit the new federal poverty agencies were scattered among the old-line federal bureaucracies, and the local agencies that had been set up in the ghettos were given to understand that confrontation tactics had to be halted. By now the Great Society looks much like traditional grant-in-aid programs; the federal fuel for ghetto agitation has been cut off. And new administration proposals for revenue sharing would give state and local governments firm control of the use of federal grants, unhampered by the "maximum feasible participation" provisions that helped to stir ghetto demands in the 1960s.

There are other signs as well. The wage freeze stopped, at least temporarily, the escalation of municipal salaries, and this despite the outcry of teachers across the country. Finally, and perhaps most portentous for blacks, the administration's proposal for "welfare reform" would give the federal government a much larger role in welfare policy, lifting the struggle for who gets what outside of the arena of city politics where blacks had developed some power and had gotten some welfare.

Nor is it likely, were the Democrats to regain the presidency and thus regain the initiative in federal legislation, that the pattern of federal restraint would be entirely reversed. The conditions that made the ghettos a political force for a brief space of time seem to have changed. For one thing, there is not much action, either in the streets or in the voting booths. The protests and marches and riots have subsided, at least partly because the most aggressive people in the black population were absorbed; it was they who got the jobs and honorary positions yielded to blacks during the turmoil. These concessions, together with the Great Society programs that helped produce them, seem to have done their work, not only in restoring a degree of order to the streets, but in restoring ghetto voters to Democratic columns.

In any case, it was not ghetto insurgency of itself that gave blacks some political force in the 1960s. Rather it was that the insurgents were concentrated in the big cities, and the big cities played a very large role in Democratic politics. That also is changing; the cities are losing ground to the suburbs, even in Democratic calculations, and trouble in the cities is not likely to carry the same weight with Democratic presidents that it once did.

To be sure, a Democratic administration might be readier than a Republican one to refuel local services, to fund a grand new cornucopia of social programs. The pressures are mounting, and they come from several sources. One is the cities themselves, for to say that the cities are no longer as important as they once were is not to say Democratic leaders will want the cities to go under. Moreover, the inflated costs of the city are spreading to the suburbs and beyond, and these communities are also pressing for federal aid. Finally there is the force of the organized producers themselves, who have become very significant indeed in national politics; the education lobby and the health lobby already wield substantial influence in Washington, and they are growing rapidly. But while these pressures suggest that new federal funds will be forthcoming, the rise of the suburbs and the parallel rise of the professional lobbies indicate that it is these groups who are likely to be the main beneficiaries.

The future expansion of the federal role in local services has another, perhaps more profound, significance. It means that the decline of the local political unit in the American political structure, already far advanced, will continue. No matter how much talk we may hear about a "new American revolution," through which the federal government will return revenues and power to the people, enlarged federal grants mean enlarged federal power, for grants are a means of influencing local political developments, not only by benefiting some groups and not others, but through federally imposed conditions that come with the new monies. These conditions, by curbing the discretion of local political leaders, also erode the power of local pressure groups. As localities lose their political autonomy, the forces that remain viable will be those capable of exerting national political influence. Some may view this change as an advance, for in the past local communities have been notoriously oligarchical. But for blacks it is not an advance; it is in the local politics of the big cities that they have gained what influence they have.

The general truths to be drawn from this tale of the cities seem clear enough and familiar enough, for what happened in the 1960s has happened before in history. The lower classes made the trouble, and other groups made the gains. In the United States in the 1960s, it was urban blacks who made the trouble, and it was the organized producer groups in the cities who made the largest gains. Those of the working and middle classes who were not among the organized producers got little enough themselves, and they were made to pay with their tax monies for gains granted to others. Their resentments grew. Now, to appease them, the small gains that blacks did make in the course of the disturbances are being whittled away.

There is, I think, an even more important truth, though one perhaps not so quickly recognized. These were the events of a political struggle, of groups pitted against each other and against officialdom. But every stage of that struggle was shaped and limited by the structures in which these groups were enmeshed. A local service apparatus, which at the outset benefited some and not others, set the stage for group struggle. Service structures that offered only certain kinds of benefits determined the agenda of group struggle. And a fiscal structure that limited the contest mainly to benefits paid for by state and local taxes largely succeeded in keeping the struggle confined within the lower and middle strata of American society. School teachers turned against the ghetto, taxpayers against both, but no one turned against the concentrations of individual and corporate wealth in America. Local government, in short, is important, less for the issues it decides, than for the issues it keeps submerged. Of the issues submerged by the events of the urban crisis, not the least is the more equitable distribution of wealth in America.

MARLENE DIXON

Why Women's Liberation?

Of all the groups struggling for equality during the 1960s the women's liberation movement elicited the most patronizing response. Unlike blacks, chicanos, Asians, and Indians, whose skin color or culture provoked undeniable proof of American racism, women had to work hard to prove that they were indeed oppressed. The following selection was one of the earliest and most perceptive statements to appear on women's liberation. Sociologist Marlene Dixon's arguments are especially interesting given the achievements of the women's movement since this essay was first published in 1969.

The 1960's has been a decade of liberation; women have been swept up by that ferment along with blacks, Latins, American Indians and poor whites—the whole soft underbelly of this society. As each oppressed group in turn discovered the nature of its oppression in American society, so women have discovered that they too thirst for free and fully human lives. The result has been the growth of a new women's movement, whose base encompasses poor black and poor white women on relief, working women exploited in the labor force, middle class women incarcerated in the split level dream house, college girls awakening to the fact that sexiness is not the crowning achievement in life, and movement women who have discovered that in a freedom movement they themselves are not free. In less than four years women have created a variety of organizations, from the nationally-based middle class National Organization of Women (NOW) to local radical and radical feminist groups in every major city in North America. The new movement includes caucuses within nearly every New Left group and within most professional associations in the social sciences. Ranging in politics from reform to revolution, it has produced critiques of almost every segment of American society

"Why Women's Liberation?" by Marlene Dixon. From *Ramparts*, December 1969. Reprinted by permission.

and constructed an ideology that rejects every hallowed cultural assumption about the nature and role of women.

As is typical of a young movement, much of its growth has been underground. The papers and manifestos written and circulated would surely comprise two very large volumes if published, but this literature is almost unknown outside of women's liberation. Nevertheless, where even a year ago organizing was slow and painful, with small cells of six or ten women, high turnover, and an uphill struggle against fear and resistance, in 1969 all that has changed. Groups are growing up everywhere with women eager to hear a hard line, to articulate and express their own rage and bitterness. Moving about the country, I have found an electric atmosphere of excitement and responsiveness. Everywhere there are doubts, stirrings, a desire to listen, to find out what it's all about. The extent to which groups have become politically radical is astounding. A year ago the movement stressed male chauvinism and psychological oppression; now the emphasis is on understanding the economic and social roots of women's oppression, and the analyses range from social democracy to Marxism. But the most striking change of all in the last year has been the loss of fear. Women are no longer afraid that their rebellion will threaten their very identity as women. They are not frightened by their own militancy, but liberated by it. Women's Liberation is an idea whose time has come.

The old women's movement burned itself out in the frantic decade of the 1920's. After a hundred years of struggle, women won a battle, only to lose the campaign: the vote was obtained, but the new millennium did not arrive. Women got the vote and achieved a measure of legal emancipation, but the real social and cultural barriers to full equality for women remained untouched.

For over 30 years the movement remained buried in its own ashes. Women were born and grew to maturity virtually ignorant of their own history of rebellion, aware only of a caricature of blue stockings and suffragettes. Even as increasing numbers of women were being driven into the labor force by the brutal conditions of the 1930's and by the massive drain of men into the military in the 1940's, the old ideal remained: a woman's place was in the home and behind her man. As the war ended and men returned to resume their jobs in factories and offices, women were forced back to the kitchen and nursery with a vengeance. This story has been repeated after each war and the reason is clear: women form a flexible, cheap labor pool which is essential to a capitalist system. When labor is scarce, they are forced onto the labor market. When labor is plentiful, they are forced out. Women and blacks have provided a reserve army of unemployed workers, benefiting capitalists and the stable male white working class alike. Yet the system imposes untold suffering on the victims, blacks and women, through low wages and chronic unemployment.

With the end of the war the average age at marriage declined, the average size of families went up, and the suburban migration began in earnest. The political conservatism of the '50s was echoed in a social conservatism which stressed a Victorian ideal of the woman's life: a full womb and selfless devotion to husband and children.

As the bleak decade played itself out, however, three important social developments emerged which were to make a rebirth of the women's struggle inevitable. First, women came to make up more than a third of the labor force, the number of working women being twice the prewar figure. Yet the marked increase in female employment did nothing to better the position of women, who were more occupationally disadvantaged in the 1960's than they had been 25 years earlier. Rather than moving equally into all sectors of the occupational structure, they were being forced into the low paying service, clerical and semi-skilled categories. In 1940, women had held 45 per cent of all professional and technical positions; in 1967, they held only 37 per cent. The proportion of women in service jobs meanwhile rose from 50 to 55 per cent.

Second, the intoxicating wine of marriage and suburban life was turning sour; a generation of women woke up to find their children grown and a life (roughly 30 more productive years) of housework and bridge parties stretching out before them like a wasteland. For many younger women, the empty drudgery they saw in the suburban life was a sobering contradiction to adolescent dreams of romantic love and the fulfilling role of woman as wife and mother.

Third, a growing civil rights movement was sweeping thousands of young men and women into a moral crusade—a crusade which harsh political experience was to transmute into the New Left. The American Dream was riven and tattered in Mississippi and finally napalmed in Viet-Nam. Young Americans were drawn not to Levittown, but to Berkeley, the Haight-Ashbury and the East

Village. Traditional political ideologies and cultural myths, sexual mores and sex roles with them, began to disintegrate in an explosion of rebellion and protest.

The three major groups which make up the new women's movement—working women, middle class married women and students—bring very different kinds of interests and objectives to women's liberation. Working women are most concerned with the economic issues of guaranteed employment, fair wages, job discrimination and child care. Their most immediate oppression is rooted in industrial capitalism and felt directly through the vicissitudes of an exploitative labor market.

Middle class women, oppressed by the psychological mutilation and injustice of institutionalized segregation, discrimination and imposed inferiority, are most sensitive to the dehumanizing consequences of severely limited lives. Usually well educated and capable, these women are rebelling against being forced to trivialize their lives, to live vicariously through husbands and children.

Students, as unmarried middle class girls, have been most sensitized to the sexual exploitation of women. They have experienced the frustration of one-way relationships in which the girl is forced into a "wife" and companion role with none of the supposed benefits of marriage. Young women have increasingly rebelled not only against passivity and dependency in their relationships but also against the notion that they must function as sexual objects, being defined in purely sexual rather than human terms, and being forced to package and sell themselves as commodities on the sex market.

Each group represents an independent aspect of the total institutionalized oppression of women. Their differences are those of emphasis and immediate interest rather than of fundamental goals. All women suffer from economic exploitation, from psychological deprivation, and from exploitive sexuality. Within women's liberation there is a growing understanding that the common oppression of women provides the basis for uniting across class and race lines to form a powerful and radical movement.

Racism and Male Supremacy

Clearly, for the liberation of women to become a reality it is necessary to destroy the ideology of male supremacy which asserts the biological and social inferiority of women in order to justify massive institutionalized oppression. Yet we all know that many women are as loud in their disavowal of this oppression as are the men who chant the litany of "a woman's place is in the home and behind her man." In fact, women are as trapped in their false consciousness as were the mass of blacks 20 years ago, and for much the same reason.

As blacks were defined and limited socially by their color, so women are defined and limited by their sex. While blacks, it was argued, were preordained by God or nature, or both, to be hewers of wood and drawers of water, so women are destined to bear and rear children, and to sustain their husbands with obedience and compassion. The Sky-God tramples through the heavens and the Earth/Mother-Goddess is always flat on her back with her legs spread, putting out for one and all.

Indeed, the phenomenon of male chauvinism can only be understood when it is perceived as a form of racism, based on stereotypes drawn from a deep belief in the biological inferiority of women. The so-called "black analogy" is no analogy at all; it is the same social process that is at work, a process which both justifies and helps perpetuate the exploitation of one group of human beings by another.

The very stereotypes that express the society's belief in the biological inferiority of women recall the images used to justify the oppression of blacks. The nature of women, like that of slaves, is depicted as dependent, incapable of reasoned thought, childlike in its simplicity and warmth, martyred in the role of mother, and mystical in the role of sexual partner. In its benevolent form, the inferior position of women results in paternalism; in its malevolent form, a domestic tyranny which can be unbelievably brutal.

It has taken over 50 years to discredit the scientific and social "proof" which once gave legitimacy to the myths of black racial inferiority. Today most people can see that the theory of the genetic inferiority of blacks is absurd. Yet few are shocked by the fact that scientists are still busy "proving" the biological inferiority of women.

In recent years, in which blacks have led the struggle for liberation, the emphasis on racism has focused only upon racism against blacks. The fact that "racism" has been practiced against many groups other than blacks has been pushed into the background.

Indeed, a less forceful but more accurate term for the phenomenon would be "social Darwinism." It was the opinion of the social Darwinists that in the natural course of things the "fit" succeed (i.e. oppress) and the "unfit" (i.e. the biologically inferior) sink to the bottom. According to this view, the very fact of a group's oppression proves its inferiority and the inevitable correctness of its low position. In this way each successive immigrant group coming to America was decked out in the garments of "racial" or biological inferiority until the group was sufficiently assimilated, whereupon the Anglo-Saxon venom would turn on a new group filling up the space at the bottom. Now two groups remain, neither of which has been assimilated according to the classic American pattern: the "visibles"—blacks and women. It is equally true for both: "it won't wear off."

Yet the greatest obstacle facing those who would organize women remains women's belief in their own inferiority. Just as all subject populations are controlled by their acceptance of the rightness of their own status, so women remain subject because they believe in the rightness of their own oppression. This dilemma is not a fortuitous one, for the entire society is geared to socialize women to believe in and adopt as immutable necessity their traditional and inferior role. From earliest training to the grave, women are constrained and propagandized. Spend an evening at the movies or watching television, and you will see a grotesque figure called woman presented in a hundred variations upon the themes of "children, church, kitchen" or "the chick sex-pot."

For those who believe in the "rights of mankind," the "dignity of man," consider that to make a woman a person, a human being in her own right, you would have to change her sex: imagine Stokely Carmichael "prone and silent"; imagine Mark Rudd as a Laugh-In girl; picture Rennie Davis as Miss America. Such contradictions as these show how pervasive and deep-rooted is the cultural contempt for women, how difficult it is to imagine a woman as a serious human being, or conversely, how empty and degrading is the image of woman that floods the culture.

Countless studies have shown that black acceptance of white stereotypes leads to mutilated identity, to alienation, to rage and self-hatred. Human beings cannot bear in their own hearts the contradictions of those who hold them in contempt. The ideology of male supremacy and its effect upon women merits as serious study as has been given to the effects of prejudice upon Jews, blacks, and immigrant groups.

It is customary to shame those who would draw the parallel between women and blacks by a great show of concern and chest beating over the suffering of black people. Yet this response itself reveals a refined combination of white middle class guilt and male chauvinism, for it overlooks several essential facts. For example, the most oppressed group within the feminine population is made up of black women, many of whom take a dim view of the black male intellectual's adoption of white male attitudes of sexual superiority (an irony too cruel to require comment). Neither are those who make this pious objection to the racial parallel addressing themselves very adequately to the millions of white working class women living at the poverty level, who are not likely to be moved by this middle class guilt-ridden one-upmanship while having to deal with the boss, the factory, or the welfare worker day after day. They are already dangerously resentful of the gains made by blacks, and much of their "racist backlash" stems from the fact that they have been forgotten in the push for social change. Emphasis on the real mechanisms of oppression—on the commonality of the process—is essential lest groups such as these, which should work in alliance, become divided against one another.

White middle class males already struggling with the acknowledgment of their own racism do not relish an added burden of recognition: that to white guilt must soon be added "male." It is therefore understandable that they should refuse to see the harshness of the lives of most women—to honestly face the facts of massive institutionalized discrimination against women. Witness the performance to date: "Take her down off the platform and give her a good fuck," "Petty Bourgeois Revisionist Running Dogs," or in the classic words of a Berkeley male "leader," "Let them eat cock."

Among whites, women remain the most oppressed—and the most unorganized—group. Although they constitute a potential mass base for the radical movement, in terms of movement priorities they are ignored; indeed they might as well be invisible. Far from being an accident, this omission is a direct outgrowth of the solid male supremist beliefs of white radical and left-liberal men. Even now, faced with both fact and agitation, leftist men find the idea of placing any serious priority upon women so outrageous, such a degrading notion, that they respond with a virulence far out of proportion to the modest requests of movement women. This only shows that women must stop wasting their time worrying about the chauvinism of men in the movement and focus instead on their real priority: organizing women.

Marriage: Genesis of Women's Rebellion

The institution of marriage is the chief vehicle for the perpetuation of the oppression of women; it is through the role of wife that the subjugation of women is maintained. In a very real way the role of wife has been the genesis of women's rebellion throughout history.

Looking at marriage from a detached point of view one may well ask why anyone gets married, much less women. One answer lies in the economics of women's position, for women are so occupationally limited that drudgery in the home is considered to be infinitely superior to drudgery in the factory. Secondly, women themselves have no independent social status. Indeed, there is no clearer index of the social worth of a woman in this society than the fact that she has none in her own right. A woman is first defined by the man to whom she is attached, but more particularly by the man she marries, and secondly by the children she bears and rears—hence the anxiety over sexual attractiveness, the frantic scramble for boyfriends and husbands. Having obtained and married a man the race is then on to have children, in order that their attractiveness and accomplishments may add more social worth. In a woman, not having children is seen as an incapacity somewhat akin to impotence in a man.

Beneath all of the pressures of the sexual marketplace and the marital status game, however, there is a far more sinister organization of economic exploitation and psychological mutilation. The housewife role, usually defined in terms of the biological duty of a woman to reproduce and her "innate" suitability for a nurturant and companionship role, is actually crucial to industrial capitalism in an advanced state of technological development. In fact, the housewife (some 44 million women of all classes, ethnic groups and races) provides, unpaid, absolutely essential services and labor. In turn, her assumption of all household duties makes it possible for the man to spend the majority of his time at the workplace.

It is important to understand the social and economic exploitation of the married woman, since the real productivity of her labor is denied by the commonly held assumption that she is dependent on her husband, exchanging her keep for emotional and nurturant services. Margaret Benston, a radical women's liberation leader, points out:

> In sheer quantity, household labor, including child care, constitutes a huge amount of socially necessary production. Nevertheless, in a society based on commodity production, it is not usually considered even as "real work" since it is outside of trade and the marketplace. This assignment of household work as the function of a special category "women" means that this group *does* stand in a different relationship to production. . . . The material basis for the inferior status of women is to be found in just this definition of women. In a society in which money determines value, women are a group who work outside the money economy. Their work is not worth money, is therefore valueless, is therefore not even real work. And women themselves, who do this valueless work, can hardly be expected to be worth as much as men, who work for money.

Women are essential to the economy not only as free labor, but also as consumers. The American system of capitalism depends for its survival on the consumption of vast amounts of socially wasteful goods, and a prime target for the unloading of this waste is the housewife. She is the purchasing agent for the family, but beyond that she is eager to buy because her own identity depends on her accomplishments as a consumer and her ability to satisfy the wants of her husband and children. This is not, of course, to say that she has any power in the economy. Although she spends the wealth, she does not own or control it—it simply passes through her hands.

In addition to their role as housewives and consumers, increasing numbers of women are taking outside employment. These women leave the home to join an exploited labor force, only to return at night to assume the double burden of housework on top of wage work—that is, they are forced to work at two full-time jobs. No man is required or expected to take on such a burden.

The result: two workers from one household in the labor force with no cutback in essential female functions—three for the price of two, quite a bargain.

Frederick Engels, now widely read in women's liberation, argues that, regardless of her status in the larger society, within the context of the family the woman's relationship to the man is one of proletariat to bourgeoisie. One consequence of this class division in the family is to weaken the capacity of men and women oppressed by the society to struggle together against it.

In all classes and groups, the institution of marriage functions to a greater or lesser degree to oppress women; the unity of women of different classes hinges upon our understanding of that common oppression. The 19th century women's movement refused to deal with marriage and sexuality, and chose instead to fight for the vote and elevate the feminine mystique to a political ideology. That decision retarded the movement for decades. But 1969 is not 1889. For one thing, there now exist alternatives to marriage. The most original and creative politics of the women's movement has come from a direct confrontation with the issue of marriage and sexuality. The cultural revolution—experimentation with life-styles, communal living, collective child-rearing—have all come from the rebellion against dehumanized sexual relationships, against the notion of women as sexual commodities, against the constriction and spiritual strangulation inherent in the role of wife.

Lessons have been learned from the failures of the earlier movement as well. The feminine mystique is no longer mistaken for politics, nor gaining the vote for winning human rights. Women are now all together at the bottom of the work world, and the basis exists for a common focus of struggle for all women in American society. It remains for the movement to understand this, to avoid the mistakes of the past, to respond creatively to the possibilities of the present.

Women's oppression, although rooted in the institution of marriage, does not stop at the kitchen or the bedroom door. Indeed, the economic exploitation of women in the workplace is the most commonly recognized aspect of the oppression of women.

Most women who enter the labor force do not work for "pin money" or "self-fulfillment." Sixty-two per cent of all women working in 1967 were doing so out of economic need (i.e., were either alone or with husbands earning less than $5000 a year). In 1963, 36 per cent of American families had an income of less than $5000 a year. Women from these families work because they must; they contribute 35 to 40 per cent of the family's total income when working full-time, and 15 to 20 per cent when working part-time.

Despite their need, however, women have always represented the most exploited sector of the industrial labor force. Child and female labor were introduced during the early stages of industrial capitalism, at a time when most men were gainfully employed in crafts. As industrialization developed and craft jobs were elim-inated, men entered the industrial labor force, driving women and children into the lowest categories of work and pay. Indeed, the position of women and children industrial workers was so pitiful, and their wages so small, that the craft unions refused to organize them. Even when women organized themselves and engaged in militant strikes and labor agitation—from the shoemak-ers of Lynn, Massachusetts, to the International Ladies' Garment Workers and their great strike of 1909—male unionists continued to ignore their needs. As a result of this male supremacy in the unions, women remain essentially unorganized, despite the fact that they are becoming an even larger part of the labor force.

The trend is clearly toward increasing numbers of women en-tering the work force: women represented 55 per cent of the growth of the total labor force in 1962, and the number of working women rose from 16.9 million to 24 million in 1962. There is every indication that the number of women in the labor force will con-tinue to grow as rapidly in the future.

Job discrimination against women exists in all sectors of work, even in occupations which are predominantly made up of women. This discrimination is reinforced in the field of education, where women are being short-changed at a time when the job market demands higher educational levels. In 1962, for example, while women constituted 53 per cent of the graduating high school class, only 42 per cent of the entering college class were women. Only one in three people who received a B.A. or M.A. in that year was a woman, and only one in ten who received a Ph.D. was a woman. These figures represent a decline in educational achievement for women since the 1930's, when women received two out of five of the B.A. and M.A. degrees given, and one out of seven of the Ph.Ds. While there has been a dramatic increase in the number

CHART A
Comparative Statistics for Men and Women in the Labor Force, 1960

Occupation	Percentage of Working Women in Each Occupational Category	Income of Year Round Full Time Workers		Numbers of Workers in Millions	
		Women	Men	Women	Men
Professional	13%	$4358	$7115	3	5
Managers, Officials and Proprietors	5	3514	7241	1	5
Clerical	31	3586	5247	7	3
Operatives	15	2970	4977	4	9
Sales	7	2389	5842	2	3
Service	15	2340	4089	3	3
Private Household	10	1156	—	2	—

Sources: U.S. Department of Commerce, Bureau of the Census: "Current Population Reports," P-60, No. 37, and U.S. Department of Labor, Bureau of Labor Statistics and U.S. Department of Commerce, Bureau of the Census.

of people, including women, who go to college, women have not kept pace with men in terms of educational achievement. Furthermore, women have lost ground in professional employment. In 1960 only 22 per cent of the faculty and other professional staff at colleges and universities were women—down from 28 per cent in 1949, 27 per cent in 1930, 26 per cent in 1920. 1960 does beat 1919 with only 20 per cent—"you've come a long way, baby"—right back to where you started! In other professional categories: 10 per cent of all scientists are women, 7 per cent of all physicians, 3 per cent of all lawyers, and 1 per cent of all engineers.

Even when women do obtain an education, in many cases it does them little good. Women, whatever their educational level, are concentrated in the lower paying occupations. The figures in Chart A tell a story that most women know and few men will admit: most women are forced to work at clerical jobs, for which they are paid, on the average, $1600 less per year than men doing the same work. Working class women in the service and operative (semi-skilled) categories, making up 30 per cent of working women, are paid $1900 less per year on the average than are men. Of all working women, only 13 per cent are professionals (including low-pay and low-status work such as teaching, nursing and

CHART B
Median Annual Wages for Men and Women by Race, 1960

Workers	Median Annual Wage
Males, White	$5137
Males, Non-White	$3075
Females, White	$2537
Females, Non-White	$1276

Source: U.S. Department of Commerce, Bureau of the Census. Also see: President's Commission on the Status of Women, 1963.

social work), and they earn $2600 less per year than do professional men. Household workers, the lowest category of all, are predominantly women (over 2 million) and predominantly black and third world, earning for their labor barely over $1000 per year.

Not only are women forced onto the lowest rungs of the occupational ladder, they are in the lowest levels as well. The most constant and bitter injustice experienced by all women is the income differential. While women might passively accept low status jobs, limited opportunities for advancement, and discrimination in the factory, office and university, they choke finally on the daily fact that the male worker next to them earns more, and usually does less. In 1965 the median wage or salary income of year-round full-time women workers was only 60 per cent that of men, a 4 per cent loss since 1955. Twenty-nine per cent of working women earned less than $3000 a year as compared with 11 per cent of the men; 43 per cent of the women earned from $3000 to $5000 a year as compared with 19 per cent of the men; and 9 per cent of the women earned $7000 or more as compared with 43 per cent of the men.

What most people do not know is that in certain respects, women suffer more than do non-white men, and that black and third world women suffer most of all.

Women, regardless of race, are more disadvantaged than are men, including non-white men. White women earn $2600 less than white men and $1500 less than non-white men. The brunt of the inequality is carried by 2.5 million non-white women, 94 per cent of whom are black. They earn $3800 less than white men, $1900 less than non-white men, and $1200 less than white women.

There is no more bitter paradox in the racism of this country than that of the white man, articulating the male supremacy of the white male middle class, should provide the rationale for the oppression of black women by black men. Black women constitute the largest minority in the United States, and they are the most disadvantaged group in the labor force. The further oppression of black women will not liberate black men, for black women were never the oppressors of their men—that is a myth of the liberal white man. The oppression of black men comes from institutionalized racism and economic exploitation: from the world of the white man. Consider the following facts and figures.

The percentage of black working women has always been proportionately greater than that of white women. In 1900, 41 per cent of black women were employed, as compared to 17 per cent for white women. In 1963, the proportion of black women employed was still a fourth greater than that of whites. In 1960, 44 per cent of black married women with children under six years were in the labor force, in contrast to 29 per cent for white women. While job competition requires ever higher levels of education, the bulk of illiterate women are black. On the whole, black women—who often have the greatest need for employment—are the most discriminated against in terms of opportunity. Forced by an oppressive and racist society to carry unbelievably heavy economic and social burdens, black women stand at the bottom of that society, doubly marked by the caste signs of color and sex.

The rise of new agitation for the occupational equality of women also coincided with the re-entry of the "lost generation" —the housewives of the 1950's—into the job market. Women from middle class backgrounds, faced with an "empty nest" (children grown or in school) and a widowed or divorced rate of one-fourth to one-third of all marriages, returned to the workplace in large numbers. But once there they discovered that women, middle class or otherwise, are the last hired, the lowest paid, the least often promoted, and the first fired. Furthermore, women are more likely to suffer job discrimination on the basis of age, so the widowed and divorced suffer particularly, even though their economic need to work is often urgent. Age discrimination also means that the option of work after child-rearing is limited. Even highly qualified older women find themselves forced into low-paid, unskilled or semi-skilled work—if they are lucky enough to find a job in the first place.

The realities of the work world for most middle class women—that they become members of the working class, like it or not—are understandably distant to many young men and women in college who have never had to work, and who tend to think of the industrial "proletariat" as a revolutionary force, to the exclusion of "bourgeois" working women. Their image of the "pampered middle class woman" is factually incorrect and politically naive. It is middle class women forced into working class life who are often the first to become conscious of the contradiction between the "American Dream" and their daily experience.

Faced with discrimination on the job—after being forced into the lower levels of the occupational structure—millions of women are inescapably presented with the fundamental contradictions in their unequal treatment and their massive exploitation. The rapid growth of women's liberation as a movement is related in part to the exploitation of working women in all occupational categories.

Male supremacy, marriage, and the structure of wage labor—each of these aspects of women's oppression has been crucial to the resurgence of the women's struggle. It must be abundantly clear that radical social change must occur before there can be significant improvement in the social position of women. Some form of socialism is a minimum requirement, considering the changes that must come in the institutions of marriage and the family alone. The intrinsic radicalism of the struggle for women's liberation necessarily links women with all other oppressed groups.

The heart of the movement, as in all freedom movements, rests in women's knowledge, whether articulated or still only an illness without a name, that they are not inferior—not chicks, nor bunnies, nor quail, nor cows, nor bitches, nor ass, nor meat. Women hear the litany of their own dehumanization each day. Yet all the same, women know that male supremacy is a lie. They know they are not animals or sexual objects or commodities. They know their lives are mutilated, because they see within themselves a promise of creativity and personal integration. Feeling the contradiction between the essentially creative and self-actualizing human being within her, and the cruel and degrading less-than-human role she is compelled to play, a woman begins to perceive the falseness of what her society has forced her to be. And once she perceives this, she knows that she must fight.

WHY WOMEN'S LIBERATION?

Women must learn the meaning of rage, the violence that liberates the human spirit. The rhetoric of invective is an equally essential stage, for in discovering and venting their rage against the enemy—and the enemy in everyday life is men—women also experience the justice of their own violence. They learn the first lessons in their own latent strength. Women must learn to know themselves as revolutionaries. They must become hard and strong in their determination, while retaining their humanity and tenderness.

There is a rage that impels women into a total commitment to women's liberation. That ferocity stems from a denial of mutilation; it is a cry for life, a cry for the liberation of the spirit. Roxanne Dunbar, surely one of the most impressive women in the movement, conveys the feelings of many:

> We are damaged—we women, we oppressed, we disinherited. There are very few who are not damaged, and they rule. . . . The oppressed trust those who rule more than they trust themselves, because self-contempt emerges from powerlessness. Anyway, few oppressed people believe that life could be much different. . . . We are damaged and we have the right to hate and have contempt and to kill and to scream. But for what? . . . Do we want the oppressor to admit he is wrong, to withdraw his misuse of us? He is only too happy to admit guilt—then do nothing but try to absorb and exorcize the new thought. . . . That does not make up for what I have lost, what I never had, and what all those others who are worse off than I never had. . . . Nothing will compensate for the irreparable harm it has done to my sisters. . . . How could we possibly settle for anything remotely less, even take a crumb in the meantime less, than total annihilation of a system which systematically destroys half its people.

JESSICA MITFORD

What Counts as Crime?

It often appears that America has become convulsed by anarchy and crime. Newspapers play up official crime statistics. And while politicians have moderated their inflammatory appeals to "law and order" somewhat in the last few years, officials still frequently use terms like "epidemic" in referring to the country's lawlessness. Budgets for police departments have risen over 100 percent in ten years, yet because of growing paperwork and effort spent on victimless crimes, police services have actually declined during the same period, and Pinkerton's and other detective firms have experienced phenomenal growth as citizens and businesses spend billions each year on guard services and security equipment. In this next selection Jessica Mitford considers some of the subtleties often hidden behind what threatens to become a national obsession with crime.

Press statement prepared by J. Edgar Hoover:

For release Monday P.M., June 22, 1970—According to figures made available through the FBI's Uniform Crime Reports and released by Attorney General John N. Mitchell, serious crime in the U.S. continued its upward trend, recording a 13 percent rise nationally for the first three months of 1970 when compared to the same period in 1969.

Press statement released by the Attorney General:

For release Monday P.M., June 22, 1970—Attorney General John N. Mitchell announced today the FBI's Uniform Crime Reports show that the rate of increase in violent crimes in the first three months of 1970 slowed 7 percent in the major cities of the nation—and 3 percent in the nation as a whole.

From KIND AND USUAL PUNISHMENT, by Jessica Mitford. Copyright © 1973 by Jessica Mitford. Reprinted by permission of Alfred A. Knopf, Inc.

WHAT COUNTS AS CRIME?

This falling-out between the purveyors of mathematics for the millions came to light when reporters discovered that for the first time in four decades the attorney general had done a bit of creative copy-editing of the late J. Edgar Hoover's annual crime statistics press release. Traditionally, preparation of the release has been the prerogative of the FBI director, who year after year dangles before an accommodating press his "new all-time high" in the rate of crime increase, thus assuring suitably lurid crime-wave headlines. Well and good for the FBI's purposes (for the higher the crime rate, the easier to pry ever-larger appropriations out of Congress), this did not suit an Administration elected largely on a pledge to "make our cities safe from crime"; hence the attorney general's judicious use of the juggler's craft.

While to the statistician the two releases are not necessarily contradictory (for, as the practitioner of that uncanny discipline will explain, a 13 percent *rise* in crime is not imcompatible with a 7 percent slowing of the *rate of increase*), the newspapers were understandably muddled. Next day some papers reported crime was rising, others said it was tapering off, and still others, with one foot firmly planted in each camp, quoted Hoover as saying the risk of being a crime victim was rising and Mitchell as saying crime rates were slowing down. Be that as it may, this tug of war between the mastodons of crime-busting is mainly instructive for what it tells us about clever ways with figures. The public opinion polls show most people have long since come to accept the FBI's annual "all-time high" as an article of faith—for example, in a survey conducted by the Joint Commission on Correctional Manpower, 89 percent of those polled said they believe crime rates have increased in recent years.

The Uniform Crime Reports, single most influential and most widely quoted source of crime and information, basis for nightmarish popular fears and sweeping legislation crackdowns, are regarded by many criminologists as highly suspect—not only are they subject to cynical manipulation for political purposes but they give a grossly distorted picture of the crime scene.

What, then, lies behind the familiar headline "Major Crimes Up From 4.4 Million In 1968 To 5.6 Million In 1971"?

Crime rates (and crime waves) are based on "Index Crimes," also known as "major crimes" and "serious crimes," that come to the attention of police; most are reported by citizens, some are discovered in the course of police work. The figures are forwarded by local police departments to FBI headquarters and there compiled into what *The New York Times* calls "virtually impenetrable" tables of statistics, the Uniform Crime Reports. These in turn are summarized and presented in vastly simplified form, with suitable interpretation, to the media.

Like Deadly Sins, the Index Crimes are seven in number, listed as follows by the FBI: willful homicide, forcible rape, aggressive assault, robbery, burglary, car theft, larceny over $50. To list them in this order is, it develops, somewhat like listing national population figures beginning with Luxembourg and ending with China, since the eye-catching first two (murder and rape) account for only about 1 percent of the total and the first four (crimes against the person as distinct from property crimes) for about 13 percent. About half of all reported "serious crimes" in the Index consist of larceny and car theft, which includes joy-riding, mere misdemeanors under the laws of many states.

Venturing further into the thicket of figures, it is surprising to learn that the rate of most crimes against persons—presumably everybody's least favorite and most feared of the Index Crimes—has actually declined over the years. According to the President's Crime Commission Report, the rate of Index Crime No. 1— murder—when adjusted to rising population figures, has decreased by about 30 percent from its high in 1933 and the robbery rate by about 15 percent in the same period. In *The Honest Politician's Guide to Crime Control* Norval Morris and Gordon Hawkins say, "Looking further back to the 1870's and the late 1890's it seems clear that rates of murder, non-negligent homicide, rape, and assault have all appreciably declined with the passage of time."

Furthermore the spectre of the marauding stranger conjured up by the FBI figures is largely mythical, for the great majority of murders (88 percent according to one survey quoted in the President's Crime Commission Report) are committed within the family or among acquaintances. The same is true of other crimes of violence: a District of Columbia study showed that two thirds of rape victims were attacked by boyfriends, members of the family, or other acquaintances, and that only 25 percent of aggravated assault victims were unacquainted with their assailant—which prompts the fanciful speculation that one might be safer out alone in the dark city streets than waiting cozily at home for a convivial troop of relatives and neighbors to drop in.

Moving on down the Index to the property crimes—burglary, car theft, larceny over $50—we discover that the alleged soaring rise in the rate of these is not all it seems, either. For one thing the number of police departments that participate in the reporting program is constantly rising: in 1957, 7,000 departments participated; by 1964, 8,000. For another, much depends on the local police chief; thus there was an 83 percent increase in "major crimes known to the police" in Chicago between 1960 and 1961 when a zealous new chief revised reporting procedures. In a study of the 1963 Uniform Crime Reports, Professor Albert D. Biderman of the Bureau of Social Science Research made these observations.

> More than half of the rise in the Index in recent years—the basis for the alarm expressed about the "mounting crime rate"—comes from increases in the reports people make to the police about things being stolen from them. . . . To be reflected in the Index, a reported theft has to involve the stealing of an automobile or of something worth $50 or more.

Thus in a period of inflation, when things cost more, thefts that would formerly not have made the Index—because the items involved were worth less than $50—now show up to swell the surging crime wave. Affluence, too, is an important factor in reported thefts: not only are there more valuables around to steal (stolen bikes alone accounted for about 20 percent of all reported larcenies) but due to the spectacular rise in comprehensive homeowners' insurance policies, people are far more likely to report thefts than heretofore. While this may add up to more work for police, says Mr. Biderman, it is hardly a useful indicator for measuring how much lawbreaking is occurring. Musing over the problems of the criminal in these times of soaring inflation, Professor Leslie T. Wilkins of the School of Criminal Justice in Albany, points out that, "If the cost of living legally goes up, presumably the cost of illegal living also rises. If persons who live by illegal means increase their productivity proportional to the increase in the cost of living, does this really mean that 'crime' has increased?"

Thus the foregoing authorities—Morris and Hawkins, Albert D. Biderman, and Leslie T. Wilkins—seem inclined to the view that crime may have remained relatively stable over the past several decades, and in some categories may even have decreased. If this is so, why the almost universally held belief that crime has increased dramatically, reaching horrendous proportions? One probable answer is that in the days of which Morris and Hawkins speak, and up until fairly recently, such crimes as purse-snatching, burglary, robbery, and assault were largely confined to slums and ghettos, where they attracted the attention of nobody outside those areas. The police as a matter of policy seldom interfered in the crimes of poor against poor, black against black; nor did the newspapers bother to report such incidents.

I recall a conversation of some twenty years ago with a black newspaperwoman who lived in Harlem. On a sultry summer night she had dozed off for a few seconds while reading in bed. When she opened her eyes, her small bedside radio had vanished—a cat burglar had scaled seven stories to snatch this almost worthless item through her open window. She mildly derided my shock and amazement over this frightening episode, and assured me such incidents and worse were common, everyday experiences of the ghetto-dweller. Today, they are becoming commonplace on Park Avenue, on the Loop, in Pacific Heights. The middle and upper classes, once insulated from street crime and theft, are now targets of these crimes, which have become a national obsession reflected in myriad dinner party conversations, in the polls, the press, the get-tough platforms of politicians.

In addition to its précis of the Uniform Crime Reports, the FBI releases other crime news when and as the spirit moves it. If certain categories of violent incidents show a decrease, they may mysteriously vanish altogether from the annual report. For example, in recent years the bureau has furnished figures for racial disturbances in American cities, disorders in secondary schools, numbers of police officers killed or injured by members of the Black Panther Party. All were missing from the 1972 release. Asked by reporters to supply the figures, the bureau reluctantly complied (incidents in all three categories were sharply down from the previous year), and a spokesman explained to the press: "One year doesn't compare to another. I don't think you are supposed to take last year's report and compare it with this one. You can't include everything. One of the problems is to keep this in workable length."

In sum, FBI crime-reporting is shrewdly tailored to focus attention on crimes of those perceived by the Establishment as the dangerous classes: poor people, ghetto-dwellers, political dissidents. These are the crimes that make headlines, sell newspapers, frighten and upset people—and create a solid platform for the politician pledged to vote more money for the FBI.

Absent from the Uniform Crime Reports are crimes committed by the rich and powerful against the rest of the population:

murder, assault, and theft via violation of health and safety codes by slum landlords, mine owners, construction companies, robbery by the food industry through deceptive packaging, and organized crime that depends on corruption of public officials, to name a few. That these crimes cause infinitely more death, injury, and impoverishment than those listed in the Index is documented in official government reports and in the annals of criminology. Some random examples of such crimes at high levels, culled from recent newspaper accounts: "The Blacksville No. 1 coal mine, which has been sealed, making it the tomb of nine miners given up for dead, was cited for 485 safety violations since it opened four years ago . . ." "The Sunshine Mining Co. in Kellogg, Idaho, where 91 silver miners perished in a fire, had been cited for 14 fire and safety violations over the past 21 months . . ." "Lockheed Shipbuilding and Construction Co. was accused by the Department of Labor of willful negligence in the San Fernando Tunnel explosion that killed 17 men on June 24. . . ." It is a safe bet that nobody will go to prison for these deaths.

The annual figure on "aggravated assault" given in the Uniform Crime Reports runs around 200,000. In *New Horizons in Criminology*, Barnes and Teeters say that from 8 to 15 percent of all food consumed in this country is contaminated and that each year more than 3 million people are made "seriously ill" as a result of eating tainted or doctored food. Is this not a form of "aggravated assault" committed by the food industry?

According to the President's Crime Commission Report, corporate and business crime, which goes largely unreported and unprosecuted, is absolutely vast in scope, its depredations far exceeding those of the ordinary thief. As George Bernard Shaw put it,

> We may take it, then, that the thief who is in prison is not necessarily more dishonest than his fellows at large. . . . He snatches a loaf from the baker's counter and is promptly run into gaol. Another man snatches bread from the tables of hundreds of widows and orphans and simple credulous souls who do not know the ways of company promoters; and, as likely as not, he is run into Parliament.

The commission estimates that price-fixing by 29 electrical equipment companies alone probably cost utilities, and therefore the public, more money than all the burglaries put together in a year.

As to white-collar crime in general, the commission says it is "committed in the course of their work by persons of high status and social repute," who are thus differentiated from "low status or disreputable persons" and who are "rarely dealt with through the full force of criminal sanctions." I was afforded a glimpse into why this is so by a friend who owns a chain of restaurants. To her extreme annoyance, she discovered one day that her book-keeper had embezzled $50,000 of the company's money. I asked her if she intended to prosecute. "Heavens, no! What good would he be to me behind bars? I want him to pay my money back." She added that she was most anxious that word of the bookkeeper's dereliction should not leak out, as she was actively seeking a job for him among her business acquaintances. "I think I'll try to get him placed in a bank," she said reflectively. "That should provide the necessary scope for his particular talents."

Quite naturally, since FBI statistics are compiled from "crimes known to police," crimes committed *by* police figure nowhere in the computations, and the extent of police crime has hitherto been largely unknowable. The public was asked to make an educated guess about this in an opinion survey conducted for the President's Crime Commission. The question: "Do you think the police around your neighborhood are almost all honest, mostly honest, with a few who are corrupt, or are they almost all corrupt?" Difference of response by race was, the commission found, "more than striking. It was startling." Sixty-three percent of whites and only 30 percent of nonwhites thought police were "almost all honest." One percent of whites and 10 percent of nonwhites thought the police were "almost all corrupt." Polls cited by the Kerner Commission showed that nationwide 35 percent of black men thought there was police brutality in their areas, while 7 percent of white men thought so. (In urban ghettos the percentage of black men who believed there was police brutality was far higher; 79 percent in Watts, 82 percent in Detroit.)

That the blacks had the better grasp of reality in these matters can be inferred by subsequent disclosures from three sources: Professor Albert J. Reiss, Jr., and his team of police observers, the Knapp Commission hearings in New York, and Professor Paul Takagi's study of civilian killings by police.

At the request of the President's Crime Commission Professor Reiss assembled and trained 36 observers whose task it was, seven days a week for seven weeks, to accompany policemen in patrol cars and monitor booking procedures in "high crime" precincts of Boston, Chicago, and Washington, D.C. Their staggering findings[1]: although the policemen were fully aware that their every action was being scrutinized and recorded, one out of every five was "observed in criminal violation of the law." Among the crimes reported: stealing from drunks and "deviants," taking bribes in cash and merchandise in return for not giving traffic tickets or for altering sworn testimony, looting establishments that had been burglarized. The observers also found that 4 out of every 10 policemen routinely violated such departmental regulations as those against drinking or sleeping on the job and falsification of reports.

The observers reported 44 instances of police assault against citizens, 37 of them unprovoked; 13 assaults took place in the station house when at least 4 other policemen were present. "The lock-up was the scene of some of the most severe applications of force," writes Professor Reiss. "Two of the three cases requiring hospitalization came about when an offender was 'worked over' in the lock-up."

Some of the scenes described by the observers:

A white traffic violation suspect had been handcuffed and brought to the station—". . . the policemen began to beat the man. They jumped him, knocked him down and beat his head against the concrete floor. He required emergency treatment at a nearby hospital."

"One man brought into the lock-up for threatening a policeman with a pistol was so severely beaten by this policeman that he required hospitalization. During the beating, some fellow policemen propped the man up while others shouted encouragement."

Two black teen-agers, arrested at gunpoint on suspicion of refusing to pay their bus fares, were handcuffed and beaten in an interrogation room. "One of the boys hollered, 'You can't beat me like this! I'm only a kid, and my hands are tied.' Later one of the policemen commented to the observer, 'On the street you

---

[1]Apparently the President's Crime Commission feared the consequences of making these astonishing revelations public, for although the commission had ordered and paid for the survey, none of the findings appear in its report, "The Challenge of Crime in a Free Society." To the contrary, the commission says it "believes that the corruption at all levels and the widespread use of physical coercion that prevailed in many police departments during the era of Prohibition is largely a thing of the past." According to John P. MacKenzie of the Washington *Post*, Commission Chairman Nicholas deB. Katzenbach dismissed reports that the study had found evidence of widespread police corruption, physical abuse, and discourtesy as "inaccurate" and "misleading" (*The New York Times*, November 18, 1971). Professor Reiss eventually published his findings in a sociology textbook, *The Sociology of Punishment and Correction.*

can't beat them. But when you get to the station, you can instill some respect in them.' "

Although during their rounds in the patrol cars the observers noted a substantial number of police contacts with middle- and upper-class citizens, some of them offenders, none of these was the victim of excessive force or of verbal abuse; on the contrary, they were treated with considerable politeness and respect. Without exception, says Professor Reiss, the victims of assault, both white and black, were "from the lower class."

Beating heads and breaking bones is, it seems, perfectly safe and sound procedure from a police standpoint. In only one of the 37 instances of brutality witnessed by the observers did the victim file a formal complaint. Nor would the victims have been likely to get any satisfaction from the higher-ups, for the reaction of police administrators with whom Professor Reiss discussed his findings was mainly one of annoyance that their patrolmen should have done these things while they knew they were being watched. As one said, "Any officer who is stupid enough to behave in that way in the presence of outsiders deserves to be fired." Speculating on why his observers were able to see as much police crime as they did, Professor Reiss suggests that people do not easily change their habitual conduct in the presence of others, may easily forget they are being observed and continue to behave as they normally do. He adds, "But should one cling to the notion that most policemen modify their behavior in the presence of outsiders, one is left with the uncomfortable conclusion that our cases represent a minimal picture of actual behavior."

The findings of Professor Reiss should go far to dispel the popular myth, assiduously fostered by law enforcement people everywhere, that police misconduct involves only the "occasional rotten apple in the barrel." David Burnham of *The New York Times*, a leading authority on police work whose series on police corruption triggered the Knapp Commission investigation of the New York police department in 1971, told me he estimates that between 75 percent and 80 percent of police accept some sort of graft and that virtually all of those charged with enforcing gambling laws get payoffs. Among the Knapp Commission's revelations: construction costs in New York are increased by 5 percent because of bribes paid by contractors to police. In Harlem, the average take from addicts and pushers by one crime-prevention squad was $1,500 a month; "heavy scorers" made as much as

$3,000 a month. Police regularly furnished addicts with lists of cigarettes, liquor, and other merchandise they wanted stolen in return for "laying off." In the course of their daily rounds, the police themselves become pushers, doling out daily fixes to their addict informants from their immense stores of confiscated heroin.

The great police funeral, replete with honor guards of law enforcement men massed in tribute to their fallen comrade, is becoming commonplace in large American cities. So are front-page newspaper stories about the alarming increase in police killings, and presidential pledges of tougher measures to safeguard police lives.

What is the converse of this picture? Occasionally killings of civilians by police break into the headlines (as in the Chicago armed raid of Panther headquarters), but the run-of-the-mill "suspect shot while fleeing arrest" gets little newspaper attention and, since his death is almost invariably labeled "justifiable homicide," he does not appear in the statistics of crime victims.

Curious about reported police killings by citizens and unreported killings of citizens by police, Professor Paul Takagi of the University of California and Philip Buell, public health department statistician, did some detective work in the archives of government statistics. Their inquiry disclosed that, contrary to popular belief and official dictum, the *rate* of police killings, while it fluctuates from year to year, has hardly changed since 1963. For, while FBI reports show the numbers of such homicides rose from 55 in 1963 to 86 in 1969, during that period there was an increase of nearly 50 percent in the number of full-time police officers.[2]

Finding out about civilian deaths at the hands of police proved more complicated. Professor Takagi discovered that these are recorded on death certificates as "Justifiable Homicide by Legal Intervention of Police." After disappearing into the maw of the computer, these records eventually surface as "Cause of Death Number 984" in the annually published official volumes of Vital Statistics. From this obscure source he learned that between 1963 and 1968, police killed 1,805 men and 21 women; about half were black. In the same period, 362 policemen were killed by civilians.

---

[2]According to *The New York Times* (August 22, 1971) the rate of police killings by civilians in New York fell from 5.4 policemen killed for every 10,000 in 1930 to 1.9 for every 10,000 in 1970.

The rate of civilian killings by police, says Professor Takagi, is rising throughout the nation: in California it increased two and a half times between 1962 and 1969. The California totals, 1961–69: 59 policemen killed by civilians, 363 civilians (of whom 3 were women) killed by police, for a ratio of 6 to 1.

David Burnham tells me he believes these official figures may grossly understate the actual numbers of civilians killed by police. "The New York Police Department, for example, in 1971 told me that their men killed 50 persons," he said. "The medical examiner for the city reported only 16 such deaths, the state 17. Presumably, when Vital Statistics gets around to publishing the figures, New York will show up as 16½ killings."

Surveys in other areas would indicate that ratios similar to those cited by Takagi and Buell obtain throughout: 54 New Yorkers were killed by city police in 1970, during which year 8 policemen were reported "killed in the line of duty." Californians and New Yorkers can take comfort from the fact that despite these shocking figures they are still safer from police gunfire than residents of Chicago, which leads the nation in police killings of civilians. The Chicago Law Enforcement Study Group found that more persons were killed by police in that city than in any other: in 1969–70, 79 persons, of whom 59 were black, perished at the hands of police. To this disclosure the Chicago Patrolmen's Association responded that one reason for the figures was "aggressive police work, responsible for Chicago's low crime rate."

When is conduct a crime, and when is a crime not a crime? When Somebody Up There—a monarch, a dictator, a pope, a legislator—so decrees. If one were to extend Ramsey Clark's imaginary map of high-crime areas into the adjacent suburbs, one might find manufacturers of unsafe cars which in the next year will have caused thousands to perish in flaming highway wrecks, absentee landlords who charge extortionist rents for rat-infested slum apartments, Madison Avenue copywriters whose job it is to manipulate the gullible into buying shoddy merchandise, doctors getting rich off Medicare who process their elderly patients like so many cattle being driven to the slaughterhouse, manufacturers of napalm and other genocidal weapons—all operating on the safe side of the law, since none of these activities is in violation of any criminal statute. Criminal law is essentially a reflection of the values, and a codification of the self-interest, and a method of control, of the dominant class in any given society. (One might suppose that some conduct, such as murder, is universally considered a horrendous crime and punished as such. Not so. Professor Laura Nader, an anthropologist, tells me that in some primitive communal societies murder is considered a relatively trivial matter, involving as it generally does merely a quarrel between two individuals; whereas polluting the river, which affects the whole community, is on the order of high treason.)

History is replete with examples of acts which at one time or another have been subject to criminal sanctions. In Europe between the fifteenth and eighteenth centuries, when the Church was supreme, some quarter of a million people were executed for the crime of witchcraft. In Henry VIII's reign it was a crime to predict the death of the king. With the rise of the Industrial Revolution, statutes embodying new needs of the emerging capitalist class proliferated; in the United States, the number of statutory crimes under federal law alone rose from 33 in 1790 to almost 600 by the mid-twentieth century. Barnes and Teeters say that at least three quarters of American prisoners could not have been incarcerated fifty years ago, since the acts for which they were convicted were not then criminal violations.

As the legislature conjures crimes into being, so too can it will them away. Thus public insobriety, first made a criminal offense in England by a 1606 law entitled "An Act for Repressing the Odious and Loathsome Sin of Drunkenness," has been illegal in this country since the Puritans first came over. But in 1967 the President's Crime Commission discovered that the business of processing drunks through the criminal justice system was wildly inefficient, had become an intolerable burden on police, courts, and jails. One third of all arrests in the United States, the commission found, were for drunkenness; in the District of Columbia, more than half the arrests were for this offense. In some places drunks occupied over 90 percent of the available space in local lock-ups, regrettable in the commission's view because as a consequence "resources are diverted from serious offenders." Taking account of these pragmatic considerations, the commission put its seal of approval on what medical men have been saying for generations: alcoholism is an illness, should be treated as such, should be removed from the inappropriate ministrations of judiciary and jailers, and placed under the jurisdiction of public health workers. District of Columbia skid-rogues may now stand up and cheer, for shortly after the commission pronounced these self-evident facts Congress ordained that henceforth drunkenness is no longer a crime in the District. State legislatures are beginning to follow suit: in the past five years Maryland, Florida, North Dakota, Connecticut, and Massachusetts have all enacted new legislation eliminating public drunkenness from the criminal statutes.

While they were at it, why did not the commissioners take the further step of proposing repeal of the laws against such victimless crimes as homosexuality, prostitution, adultery, gambling, narcotics, and a host of other forms of behavior now legally proscribed thanks to the baleful influence of latterday Puritans? One answer is suggested by Peter Barton Hutt, a consultant to the commission, in an analysis of the task force report on drunkenness. "I have not conducted any research into their personal habits or private lives, and I would not suggest that I or anyone else do so," he writes.

> Nevertheless, a few generalizations can properly be made. First, it is likely that almost every member of the commission consumes alcoholic beverages. It is virtually certain that they have friends and relatives who have drinking problems and may even be alcoholics.... They live in a society that condones drinking and tolerates even excessive drinking. Current social mores therefore preconditioned them to acceptance of the position that drunkenness should be handled as a public health problem rather than as a criminal problem. In contrast, I think it fair to assume that something less than a majority of the commission members smoke marijuana or have performed an abortion or have engaged in prostitution.

Had the President chosen to appoint nineteen college students instead of these representatives of the Bourbon Generation, Mr. Hutt thinks the commission might have taken a different tack and would have been more inclined to recommend repeal of the marijuana laws than repeal of drunkenness statutes.

Within the general framework of laws established to preserve the system from subversion, protect property, and enforce the Puritan ethic so dear to the hearts of our lawmakers, there is wild disparity in statutory sanctions imposed at various times by various state legislatures and the federal government. Violation of the Smith Act (advocating overthrow of the government by force and violence, the federal statute under which scores of Communists and other radicals were prosecuted at the height of the McCarthy repression) is punishable by five years in prison. Under the Texas "Communist Control Law," the maximum penalty is twenty years. Texas also authorizes imprisonment of up to twenty-five years for offenses labeled "Insult to United States Flag," "Disloyalty in Writing," "Possessing Flag of Enemy," and "Disloyal Language."

For rape, minimum sentences vary from one year in six states to death in four. Often no distinction is made between forcible rape and sexual intercourse with a consenting under-age female. The minimum penalty for armed robbery is one year in ten states, five years in twelve, and death in two.[3]

California has a maximum prison sentence of fifty years for the crime of incest; in Virginia the same offense is considered a misdemeanor with a one-year maximum sentence. At one time California punished indecent exposure as a misdemeanor, with a sentence of up to one year, no matter how often a person was convicted of it. But in 1952, following a wave of public hysteria about sex crimes, the legislature imposed a statutory penalty of one year to life in state prison for a second conviction for this offense. In Nebraska the penalty for possession of up to one pound of marijuana is seven days in jail. In Texas, possession of a single marijuana cigarette carries a sentence of two years to life.

If statutory penalties are the products of the whims and biases of legislators, their application to convicted defendants reflects the quirks and caprice of judges. Prison literature by authors on both sides of the bars abounds with grotesque examples of disparate sentences imposed on defendants charged with the same offense: in *I Chose Prison*, James V. Bennett, former chief of the U.S. Bureau of Prisons, tells of the disposition in the same year by two federal judges of similar crimes of forgery committed by men in almost identical circumstances, both honorably discharged veterans, unemployed, fathers of young children. One, who had no prior police record, got fifteen years imprisonment. The other, who had previously served time for drunken driving and failure to support his family, was given thirty days in jail. In *An Eye for an Eye*, a convict writer relates the outcome of two armed robberies in Wyoming. A thief in the northern part of the state

---

[3]The death penalty for these crimes was nullified by the 1972 U.S. Supreme Court ruling on capital punishment.

who stole $7.50 was given a twelve-year sentence, another in the southern section drew three years for stealing $124.

That sentencing is in the nature of a dice game is shown by figures furnished by the Federal Bureau of Prisons on penalties imposed by federal courts in New York State for the crime of transporting stolen cars. Defendants sentenced to prison from Brooklyn Federal Court in 1970 for this offense received an average sentence of 51 months. Those sentenced in Manhattan Federal Court for the same crime were given an average of 30.7 months; in the Federal District Courts for Northern New York, the average was 20.9 months.

One maxim about the sentencing process urged on judges by the modern penologist is to fit the punishment to the criminal, not the crime. The evidence is overwhelming that judges do just that, for the criminal justice system functions not only to put some lawbreakers behind bars but to keep others out. The white middle-class offender, social equal of the judge, will be let off lightly: "Most judges justify the minimal sentences they give to businessmen-criminals—fines, probation, or exceedingly short jail terms—on the ground that when such a man is convicted, he generally loses his job, his standing in the community, and his family's respect," reports Lesley Oelsner of *The New York Times*. The poorer and darker the convicted defendant, the more onerous will be his punishment. His job, his standing in the community, his family's respect weigh lightly in the scales of justice as manipulated by the judges.

Just how the dice are loaded, and against whom, is documented in Oelsner's detailed survey of current sentencing practices. Noting that "crimes that tend to be committed by the poor get tougher sentences than those committed by the well-to-do," she cites these examples: 71 percent of people convicted of car theft in 1970–71 went to prison for an average term of three years. In the same year the average penalty imposed for violation of elevator safety regulations in Manhattan was an $18 fine. In at least two such cases the elevators went unrepaired after the owners were prosecuted, and subsequently caused fatal accidents.

Defendants who, unable to afford a lawyer, must make do with court-appointed counsel are sentenced nearly twice as severely as those with private counsel, says Oelsner. Nonwhites serve much longer sentences than whites convicted of the same crime. Federal Bureau of Prisons records show that in 1970 the average sentence

302

for whites was 42.9 months, compared to 57.5 months for non-whites. Whites convicted of income tax evasion were committed for an average of 12.8 months and nonwhites for 28.6 months. In drug cases, the average for whites was 61.1 months and for nonwhites, 81.1.

Those who have the temerity to proclaim their innocence of the crime with which they are charged and to demand a trial will, if convicted, serve more than twice as long a sentence as those who "cop a plea" of guilty, says Oelsner. Over 90 percent of all criminal cases are dealt out through the plea-bargaining process; judges say that if every accused or even a majority were granted a trial, the criminal courts would become so hopelessly clogged they would soon grind to a halt.

Until a few years ago this pervasive practice, which consists of an accused agreeing to plead guilty to a lesser crime than the one for which he was charged in return for a promise of lighter sentence, was not officially sanctioned or recognized by the courts, since a guilty plea obtained under promise of leniency was an illegally entered plea. It was one of these "secrets" that everybody involved knew about—judge, prosecutor, defense lawyer—but nobody openly acknowledged. The better to preserve the fiction, a standard question was asked of the defendant under oath by his lawyer: "Has any promise been made to you which has caused you to plead guilty?" To which the defendant, coached in advance, would primly and perjuriously answer, "No."

By 1969 the U.S. Supreme Court had rendered this bit of play-acting unnecessary by putting its seal of approval on plea-bargaining, providing it is done with "full understanding of what the plea connotes and of its consequences," and that the judge assembles an "affirmative record" of the proceedings, meaning that the agreement must be officially recorded and is not, as heretofore, an under-the-table deal between defense lawyer and prosecutor.

As characterized by one public defender, plea-bargaining is "trial by trick and deceit." In a typical plea-bargaining situation the prosecutor will pile on felony charges, regardless of whether he has evidence to support them, in order to pose the threat of long years in the penitentiary should the accused put the state to the expense and trouble of a trial and be found guilty. The defendant who, unable to raise bail, has already spent months in jail under atrocious conditions, will be delighted to plead guilty to one of the many offenses he is charged with, even if he is in fact innocent of *any* crime, in exchange for a promise of probation or a short sentence with credit for time served. (According to Gregory J. Hobbs, Jr., writing in the *California Law Review*, conditions in one California jail condemned by Federal District Judge Alphonso J. Zirpoli as "barbaric" and "cruel and unusual punishment for man or beast" are deliberately kept that way as an extra coercive lever to make those awaiting trial more amenable to plea-bargaining.)

Since trial judges have made such a notorious hash of dispensing justice, some crime watchers reason, the sentencing power should be removed from their erratic ministrations and placed in the hands of an independent body of experts. In *The Honest Politician's Guide to Crime Control*, Norval Morris and Gordon Hawkins go so far as to propose that the length of time served by the convicted lawbreaker should be determined by the prison administration:

> ... within the limits set by prescribed maximum and minimum, the correctional administration should be free to decide how long the prisoners ought to be held beyond the minimum. The correctional administration is in the best position to judge when the release of the prisoner will be safe, and here it can take advantage of any improved methods developed by the behavioral sciences for predicting behavior and identifying dangerous offenders.

JACK NEWFIELD and JEFF GREENFIELD

Them That Has, Keep

Writing about nineteenth-century Paris, Anatole France observed that the law, in its majestic equality, punishes rich and poor alike for stealing purses and sleeping under bridges. Whether or not such a dual system of justice exists in modern America, social critics have charged that a basic hypocrisy is reflected in such areas of public policy as taxation. In the following excerpt from their book *A Populist Manifesto* journalists Jack Newfield and Jeff Greenfield argue that America's "progressive" tax system actually "reinforces . . . the power of wealth."

Anybody has a right to evade taxes if he can get away with it. No citizen has a moral obligation to assist in maintaining the government. If Congress insists on making stupid mistakes and passing foolish tax laws, millionaires should not be condemned if they take advantage of them.

J. P. MORGAN

A man making $6,000 a year spends almost all of it on the things he needs to live: food, shelter, clothing. A man making $200,000 a year has a far wider range of choices: two houses, three cars, European and Caribbean vacations, servants, private schools for his children. A fair tax system understands this fact of economic life; that is why a tax on incomes is graduated—it takes not just more, but a higher percentage of a wealthy man's income, because the rich need a much smaller share of their incomes for necessities. A progressive tax is also a kind of balance. You have your wealth, such a system says to the rich, but you will help pay for the schools that will give the children of the un-rich a chance to compete with your children; you will help finance the hospitals to care for the men and women injured in your plants and by your products; you will help pay for the costs of pollution and disease.

That is what is supposed to happen. It does not. The American tax system is a fraud. It has been so manipulated by the legal and political hired guns of the rich that it *reinforces,* rather than equalizes, the power of wealth in America.

Legalized tax evasion has been written into the legislation, regulation, and court opinions of our tax structure. In April, 1971, two Census Department officials revealed that the *real* tax rate of $50,000-a-year families was the same as for $5,000-a-year families—because the affluent family had so many opportunities to deduct, exempt, and shelter their actual wealth. In 1968, Treasury Secretary Joseph Barr told the Congress that middle-income Americans—those making between $7,000 and $20,000 a year—paid a higher percentage of their incomes to the federal government than the richest 1 per cent of Americans. In fact, he revealed, in 1967, 155 taxpayers who earned $200,000 or more—including 21 millionaires—paid *no tax at all.* (By 1970, there were 301 tax-dodgers in the $200,000–plus bracket.) And those millionaires who did pay tax paid an effective rate of 25 per cent—the rate that is supposed to hit those with one-fiftieth of a millionaire's income.

This legal larceny flows from the special privileges granted to corporate America and its beneficiaries. In a hundred different ways, the tax law says: "All Americans are equal; but the rich are more equal than others." The pattern of unfair tax advantage is total. A $50 business lunch at a plush restaurant is deductible; nobody pays for it except ultimately the ordinary taxpayer, who must make up the business expense deduction. The $1.15 coffee shop lunch of a clerk or secretary, the $.40 hot dog in a company cafeteria, is paid for by the wage-earner. Even the cost of criminal behavior can be deducted from a tax bill—if the criminal is a corporation instead of a street thief. In the early 1960's, twenty-nine of America's biggest electrical companies were convicted of massive price-fixing and forced to pay treble damages to the customers they had bilked. Thanks to the influence of high-priced, well-connected Washington lawyers, the Internal Revenue Service permitted the companies to deduct the cost of the fines—as an *ordinary and necessary business expense![1]*

---

[1]The 1969 Tax Reform Act limited these deductions substantially by permitting companies to deduct only the one-third of the fines that represented actual reimbursement to the cheated parties.

The impact of our rich man's tax system can be seen by looking at the most favored of American industries, the oil industry. Despite the 1969 law trimming the oil depletion allowance to 22 per cent from 27½ per cent, (a cut that made a *real* difference of only 1 per cent according to Senator Fred Harris), the oil industry continues to rack up enormous profits while paying a smaller share of taxes than a badly paid worker. In 1970, the big oil companies earned profits of $8.8 billion—a 10 per cent jump from 1969— and paid an average tax rate of 8.7 per cent. By contrast, a $6,000-a-year worker—earning barely half of what a family needs for a moderate standard of living—paid a federal tax rate of 16 per cent. What this means, in brief, is that one of the most important perceived grievances of working-class Americans—that the "big boys get away with murder"—is absolutely true.

Some of the big companies pay next to nothing—or less than nothing. In 1970, Texaco, with an income of $1.1 billion, paid 6.4 per cent in taxes; Standard Oil of California paid 5 per cent; Gulf paid 1.2 per cent. Standard Oil of Ohio not only paid *nothing* on an income of $66 million, but got a 10.4 per cent *tax credit*, to charge off against any future taxes it might have to pay.

The tax laws also shelter other concentrations of wealth. Mutual savings banks in 1967 paid an effective tax rate of 5 to 6 per cent; savings and loan associations coughed up 15 per cent; and commercial banks paid about half of what the average industry rate is. These bank privileges alone cost more than a billion dollars a year—twice the cost of the appropriation for education vetoed by President Nixon in 1969 as "inflationary." And the tax rate of private utility companies dropped from 14.7 per cent of revenues in 1955 to 11.6 per cent in 1967. What these companies do not pay in taxes goes to stockholders in the form of excess profits —and stockholders are overwhelmingly the richest of Americans.

Tax favoritism is not confined to rich institutions; it extends as well to rich individuals. Right-wing polemicists make much of the high rates of taxation at the federal level—theoretically, those with incomes in the top bracket once paid 91 per cent in taxes, and now pay 65 per cent (in 1973, the top rate will drop to 50 per cent). But the truth is that *almost nobody pays these rates because money earned by the wealthy is taxed less severely than money earned by the average American.*

When a taxpayer buys stock and sells it at a profit (a transaction not a normal part of an $8,000-a-year life style) that profit is *not* taxed at "ordinary income" rates, but at a "capital gains" rate—a tax that exempts half of the profit from taxation and that costs the Treasury $20 billion a year. No such special privilege is given to a worker who earns extra money through overtime, or to a family in which both husband and wife work. That kind of earnings is "ordinary income."

When a rich man dies and leaves his stock to his heirs, there is no tax whatever as long as the stock is not sold. All of the enormous economic advantages of stock ownership—power to influence corporate decisions, collateral for borrowing funds for new ventures, and the like—accrue to the sons and daughters of the rich without any cost; it's a kind of economic representation without taxation. There is no such escape for the wage-earner; every dollar he makes is subject to withholding at the federal and state level.

An individual or financial institution with capital can completely escape the force of the tax law by investing money in state and local bonds, which are tax-free, risk-free, and which—despite the low return on interest—actually are more profitable than high-interest taxable investments. (To a taxpayer in the 50 per cent bracket, a 5 per cent tax-free municipal is the equal of a 10.5 per cent taxable investment.)

"Charity" is another loophole by which the rich dodge taxation. A corporation or family trust can create a foundation, and can channel the largely tax-free proceeds of this institution into whatever fields it chooses.[2] If a millionaire decides that his foundation will support psychic research, or the private school of which he is an alumnus, he can do so and reap the tax benefits. And whether he decides to underwrite medical research, or community-action groups, it is *his* money and *his* choices—all beyond public influence. The wage-earner has no choice. His income taxes go directly to Washington and the state. He has no way to disapprove the spending of his money on projects with which he disagrees. And thus the tax law further enhances the power of the wealthy: the monies of the rich make public policy every day; between elections, the rest of us just send the tax payments to the decision-makers.

The enormous injustices written into the federal tax code were underscored by Stanley Surrey, a former Assistant Secretary of

---

[2]In 1969, a 4 per cent tax on the income from foundation investments was established, and some controls on the unsupervised abuses of foundations were established for the first time; before 1969, all income from foundations was completely tax-exempt.

the Treasury, in a 1971 paper for the Council on Policy Evaluation. These exemptions from the tax code, Surrey said, are really "tax expenditures"—subsidies to the wealthy, which in 1970 totaled $50 billion. Although these exemptions are offered under the guise of aiding social goals, the real consequence is, as Surrey puts it, that "we achieve our social goals by increasing the number of tax millionaires."

These hidden "tax expenditures" mean, for example, that a $200,000-a-year family "gets" a $70 subsidy for every $100 of mortgage payments it makes; while a $10,000 a year couple gets only $19. The incentives for housing rehabilitation mean, in effect, that the richest of taxpayers gets a 19 per cent investment credit, while an average-bracket payer gets only a 5 per cent break. The measure of the outrages legislated into the tax code is that if these kinds of "expenditures" were voted on as subsidies, not a senator or congressman would have the chutzpah to vote for them. But they are just as real as welfare checks for millionaires even though they are buried under mountains of technicalities.

The inequity of taxation at the federal level is, if anything, worse at the state and local levels. Most communities finance their schools from the local property taxes; an inherently unfair method that enables wealthy communities, sealed off from their less affluent neighbors by zoning and construction restriction, to raise funds for their own children and leave the wage-earner and the poor to fight over the remaining scarce resources. States base much of their revenue-raising on the sales tax: a regressive tax, since it makes no distinctions based on ability to pay.[3]

The inequity of the property tax is compounded by the free ride given to giant "public" or "charitable" institutions in the form of exemptions from the property tax. Nearly *one-third* of the $850 billion of real estate in America is tax-exempt, leaving the homeowner and the marginal shopkeeper, as well as the big real estate and financial interests, to pick up the slack. Some of these exemptions are legitimate: hospitals, purely religious or charitable institutions, and the like. But billions of dollars worth of property that is exempt actually enriches the wealthy; private clubs, for example, in the big city, or foundation offices that would normally

---

[3]Two concepts many people fail to grasp are (1) an income tax at the state level may be far more desirable for the average wage-earner than a sales or property tax increase, and (2) a 6 per cent sales tax is *regressive, not equal*, since it makes no distinction on ability to pay; the millionaire and the waitress pay the same tax rate on food, clothing, and recreation.

be assessed at several million dollars. In some cases, the financial return to the elite is direct, and directly at the expense of the nonwealthy.

Say, for example, a bank, financial institution, or millionaire purchases the bonds of the Port Authority of New York—an interstate compact with the responsibility for running both the bridges and tunnels between New York and New Jersey and the three metropolitan airports. The Port Authority can decide—as it has—to enrich itself by going into the real estate business and building two 110-story kleenex boxes called the World Trade Center. Because they are a "public" institution, no public authority can stop the Port Authority—not the mayor, not the governors of New York and New Jersey, not the city council or state legislature or Congress; not even a public referendum. The Port Authority has total power to condemn the property, wiping millions of dollars off the tax rolls, and to construct tax-exempt giants that compete in space rentals with tax-paying real estate businesses. It can lease space for restaurants, shops, all manner of businesses that gain in lower rent from the unfair advantage of tax exemption. The profits from the Port Authority's commercial operations—$12 million a year from JFK Airport restaurants alone—go back to the investors, whose profit is tax-free. Moreover, so narrowly is the Port Authority's financial operation conceived by its directors, that hundreds of millions of dollars in surpluses, which could be used to salvage New York's collapsing mass transit system, are kept in reserve—not for the people of New York City, but for the bondholders. Thus does public authority and private power come together in a massive fusion of wealth that leaves the ordinary, tax-paying New Yorker as its victim. (There is a special added attraction to the Port Authority's situation. The World Trade Center was built during a time when the office boom in New York City suffered a setback because of the recession. Two 110-story *unrented* kleenex boxes would have meant financial difficulty for the Port Authority and its bonds. But Governor Nelson Rockefeller came to the rescue by renting fifty-eight floors of the center for New York State offices. What is one of the biggest financial institutions with holdings in the Port Authority? The Chase Manhattan Bank. And who is the chief executive and biggest stockholder in Chase Manhattan Bank? *David* Rockefeller.)

As with so many other areas of public life, the question of who wins and who loses economic privileges from the tax law is a political question; Congress and the president determine the shape of our revenue system. And, as in so many other areas, those who hold wealth also control great political leverage. Rich people can be liberal, conservative, reactionary, radical; they may oppose the war or favor equal rights for racial and religious minorities; they may want to fight pollution or cure cancer. But there just aren't that many people who are on the long end of the stick who will voluntarily surrender tax privileges that save them thousands of dollars a year. Consequently, those with protected wealth offer massive campaign contributions in return for the "right" vote to block tax reforms. This strength has produced in liberal as well as conservative presidents a pattern of building inequity into the tax structure.

In 1971, for example, with one of the biggest peacetime federal deficits in history, President Nixon authorized a new set of rules governing capital depreciation that will cost the federal treasury—and therefore the American taxpayer—$39 billion by the end of the decade. This is perhaps no surprise, given Nixon's lifelong career of pandering to the economic interests of big business.

But liberals like John Kennedy and Lyndon Johnson did little better. The tax cut of 1964—originated by Kennedy and passed under Lyndon Johnson—was nothing less than a windfall for the rich. Economist Leon Keyserling noted this breakdown of benefits:

The one-third of American taxpayers who earned less than $3,000 got 3.7 per cent of the cut.

The 1.9 per cent earning $20,000 a year got 21.1 per cent of the cut.

And the one-third of 1 per cent of taxpayers making $50,000 got 8.3 per cent of the cut.

This windfall came at a time when corporate profits had grown by more than twice as much as the economic growth rate and by almost four times as much as a worker's weekly earnings.

The damage to our political system spawned by this pattern of privilege cannot be overstated. A $150-a-week employee may not know the details of the capital gains law; but if he knows that he pays more of his income in taxes than the people who own the plant he works in, that is enough to breed cynicism in the most patriotic of citizens. It has been, too, one of the prime reasons for the bitter reaction of working-class whites against programs to promote social justice. When a wage-earner sees "socially conscious" businessmen promoting government programs for the poor, when he hears rich executives tell him to "give a damn," he knows that given the way the tax system is rigged *those advocates will not be paying their fair share of the program.* His son's job security may clash directly with the demand of racial minorities to be admitted to a union; Head Start centers in ghettos may mean more competition for inadequate openings in a state university in another fifteen years; but however much social justice for the poor may cost the not-quite-poor, the top wealth-holders will continue to evade their share of taxes. In this sense, the growing belief among working Americans that the very rich and the very poor are squeezing him from both sides turns out to have a hard economic basis in reality.

Despite the Byzantine complexities of the tax system—which by itself amounts to a full employment program for the nation's tax lawyers—the theory remains strong that the tax code is not an instrument of social policy, that its sole function is to raise revenue. In fact, this is nonsense. Every exemption, deduction, credit, and surcharge amounts to a statement of policy. We encourage private charities; we believe that those who are blind, over sixty-five, or dependent deserve special consideration. Those are, in principle, unobjectionable social policies.

But our tax law as it now stands encourages—intentionally or not—a plethora of policies that directly promote the concentration of economic power. The merger wave of the late 1960's was in part the result of companies looking for tax advantages through take-overs; the absorption of large tracts of land by corporate conglomerates is encouraged by depreciation laws that enable these companies to sell land at enormous profits without taking on a high tax load; the growing use by insurance companies of the "equity kicker"—demanding part ownership in a development enterprise in return for investing capital in it—reflects the tax breaks available under that kind of practice. The result of all of these practices is *concentration;* the use of capital not so much to start new enterprises, but to absorb old ones. And thus, while our antitrust policies encourage diversity, competition, and a halt to concentrated ownership, our tax laws promote exactly the reverse.

SIDNEY LENS

Unmasking the Goliath

In his famous farewell address after eight years in office, President
Eisenhower warned,

> The conjunction of an immense Military Establishment and large arms
> industry is new in the American experience. . . . In the councils of
> government we must guard against the acquisition of unwarranted
> influence whether sought or unsought, by the military-industrial com-
> plex. The potential for the disastrous rise of misplaced power exists
> and will persist.

Today the annual budget of the Department of Defense is well over
one billion dollars, constituting over 60 percent of the annual budget
for all federal agencies. Twenty thousand firms throughout the
country are engaged in production for the military, but the one
hundred largest firms receive nearly three-quarters of the prime contracts. Mammoth firms like Lockheed can count on close to two billion
dollars in contracts each year. Nor is there any great outcry from
the Pentagon when costs exceed estimates. In fact, when former
Deputy Scretary of the Air Force A. Ernest Fitzgerald revealed collusion between the Defense Department and Lockheed to conceal
nearly two billion dollars in overrun on production of the C-5A transport plane, his reward was summary dismissal from his position. In
the following essay journalist Sidney Lens considers some of the
consequences of the military-industrial complex on the country's
domestic and foreign policies.

The one useful result of the Vietnam War may be that it has
finally made the military establishment fair game for criticism.
Until the war proved "unwinnable," the Pentagon wore a halo.
Its words on weapons, strategy, and budgets were sacrosanct.

From *The Military-Industrial Complex* by Sidney Lens. Reprinted by permission of the
author.

When it came to the higher mathematics of procurement, its judgment was accepted like a message from Mount Sinai, and the nation followed it from one weapons system to another, from one enlarged budget to another, with humble awe. From 1946 to 1967, according to the statistics of Senator J. William Fulbright, the federal government spent $904 billion, or 57.29 percent of its budget "for military power," and only $95 billion, or 6.08 percent for "social functions," such as education, health, labor and welfare programs, housing and community development.[1] Convincing the American people that they ought to spend nine times as much on guns as on human welfare was an act of mesmerism by the military establishment without parallel. Both the people and Congress rubber-stamped an arsenal of horror that began with the 20-kiloton Hiroshima atom bomb, equivalent to 20,000 tons of dynamite, and escalated to a stockpile of multi-megaton hydrogen bombs, equivalent to millions of tons each; that began with a modest bomber plane of limited range and escalated to intercontinental bombers, then unmanned missiles, and finally multi-weapon missiles independently targeted; that began with a capacity to kill a few million people and grew in a single generation, with hydrogen bombs, missiles, and chemical and biological weapons, to a capacity to kill all living things on this planet dozens of times over.

Except for a handful of pacifists, radicals, and, periodically, a few members of Congress, no one questioned the utility or sanity of all this. The Department of Defense alone, not to mention the Atomic Energy Commission (AEC), the National Aeronautics and Space Administration (NASA), and tens of thousands of defense contractors, employed 66,000 scientists and engineers as of 1966.[2] In 1961, when the defense budget was only $44 billion, America was spending $247 for every man, woman, and child in the country on the military, as against $19 per head on foreign economic assistance.[3] Since then the former figure has grown by about two thirds; the latter has declined. As a barometer of the nation's sense of values, the aircraft and missile industry spent $5.4 billion for research and development in 1966, most of it supplied by the

---

[1] J. W. Fulbright, "The Great Society Is a Sick Society," *The New York Times Magazine,* Aug. 20, 1967.

[2] *Reviews of Data on Science Resources,* National Science Foundation, No. 14, April 1968.

[3] *New Republic,* Nov. 24, 1962, p. 19.

federal government, while the Department of Health, Education, and Welfare was allotted a fourth as much.[4] Andrew Hamilton estimates that the Pentagon will spend $30 billion in the next 10 years on three weapons—the F-14A supersonic plane, the Safeguard anti-ballistic missile (ABM), and the Advanced Manned Strategic Aircraft (AMSA). This $3 billion a year, if invested in federal domestic programs, would:

- nearly double federal support for primary and secondary education; or
- double federal job and training programs for the unemployed and disadvantaged; or
- triple the present level of food assistance programs to combat hunger; or
- provide nearly 20 times the present level of federal assistance for urban mass transportation.[5]

"There is something intrinsically obscene," writes former ambassador to India, John Kenneth Galbraith, "in the combination of ill-fed people and well-fed armies deploying the most modern equipment."[6] But the populace, until now at least, has been willing to upgrade war and downgrade hunger, because it was convinced the Pentagon "knew what it was doing."

Vietnam, however, has tarnished the image of infallibility. Defense secretaries and generals kept promising that a few more dollars and a few more men would bring victory, but there has been no victory. In 1953, when the United States was underwriting most of France's expenses against the Viet Minh, Secretary Charles E. Wilson assured all and sundry that "French victory is both possible and probable." Admiral Arthur W. Radford echoed these sentiments: "The French are going to win." Six years later when the French had already lost and new guerrilla movements were rising in South Vietnam, Lieutenant General S. T. Williams gave it as his expert assessment that "the guerrilla threat in Vietnam has receded to a point where one single territorial regiment could handle it." By 1962, when the United States had

---

[4]*Reviews of Data on Science Resources, op. cit.*, No. 12, Jan. 1968. Also *Federal Funds for Research, Development, and Other Scientific Activities*, Vol. XVII, National Science Foundation, p. 5.

[5]Andrew Hamilton, "High Flying in the Pentagon," *New Republic*, May 31, 1969, p. 16.

[6]Quoted by Senator Joseph Clark, "Farewell to Arms," *Trade Union Courier*, Jan. 1967.

8,000 "advisors" in Vietnam and the Ngo Dinh Diem regime was deploying many divisions against the guerrillas, Secretary Robert S. McNamara was "tremendously encouraged" by developments on the fighting front and pledged that there was "no plan for introducing combat forces into South Vietnam." McNamara's subsequent prophecies are notable for their misjudgment: "The corner has been definitely turned toward victory" (May 1963); "The major part of the U.S. military task can be completed by the end of 1965" (October 1963); "We have every reason to believe that plans will be successful in 1964" (December 1963); "The U.S. hopes to withdraw most of its troops from South Vietnam before the end of 1965" (February 1964). And in November 1965, after all these trumpets of near-victory, he announced that "we have stopped losing the war."[7] The same synthetic optimism has come from the lips of Generals Wheeler, Taylor, Westmoreland, and others, to the point where all of it finally lost its credibility. The war was not being won; at best it was stalemated. "The frustration of the United States in Vietnam," commented historian Arnold J. Toynbee, was "one of the wonders of the world."[8]

In the face of this unimpressive record the latent critics of the military rose to the offensive. Wisconsin's Senator William Proxmire and his Subcommittee on Economy in Government began revealing late in 1968, in scathing detail, the Pentagon's proclivity to "excessive costs, burgeoning military budgets, and scandalous performances."[9] With the aid of a few people in the Pentagon itself, such as A. E. Fitzgerald, who were ready to talk regardless of personal consequences, Proxmire's subcommittee has uncovered a miasma of waste, inefficiency, and probably corruption, which draws stern attention to the military's clay feet. Half the Senate, including many hawks of yesteryear—Stuart Symington (Dem.-Mo.) for instance—have joined in opposition to the Safeguard ABM and came within a single vote of defeating it. And journalists by the carload are now working up exposés on the "military-industrial complex" which a year or two ago would have received the silent treatment. The term itself—military-industrial complex—has become, for many people, one of opprobrium, and the military has been put to considerable

[7]Chicago's American, July 17, 1967.
[8]N. D. Houghton, ed., Struggle Against History (New York: Simon and Schuster, 1968), p. xxxii.
[9]Congressional Record, Vol. 115, No. 42, p. S2518.

trouble trying to prove there was nothing sinister or conspiratorial about it.

What is still lacking, unfortunately, is a sense of historical perspective. How did the military-industrial complex arise in the first place? What is its role and purpose? Why do we have one now when we didn't have one before? What has it done to our institutions that the old "merchants of death" did not do? How does it affect our future as a nation and as individuals?

These questions are not yet being probed, except by the off-stage peace movement. Yet the story of overruns and misused resources may be a beginning to the search for more fundamental answers. It is a story so incredible it leaves conscientious citizens all but wilted.

The Pentagon, it has become evident, wastes the taxpayer's money like the proverbial sailor on a drunken binge. C. H. Danhoff of the Brookings Institution records in his study "Government Contracting and Technological Change" that "during the 1950s virtually all large military contracts . . . ultimately involved costs in excess of original contractual estimates of from 300 to 700 percent."[10]

By all accounts the situation has not improved since then. C. Merton Tyrrell, a former Air Force consultant, told Proxmire's subcommittee in June 1969 that the Minuteman II, which was expected to cost $3.3 billion will actually cost $7 billion, an overrun of almost $4 billion. The C-5A cargo plane, built by Lockheed, was bid at $3 billion but will run at least $2 billion more. Eight hundred Mark IIs were first figured at $610 million but are now expected to cost at least $2.5 billion. The SRAM missiles, estimated at $301 million in January 1968, by December 1968 were expected to cost upward of $636 million. The Navy DRSV—deep submersible rescue vessel—which was supposed to be built for $36.5 million for 12 vessels is now priced at $480 million for six; and according to Senator Proxmire there is only a single instance in the last 40 years where such a rescue vessel could have been of use.[11] Defense Secretary Melvin Laird conceded on June 20, 1969 that the overrun on nine projects alone was $3.5 billion—twice as much as the nation spends each year on its antipoverty program. Since

---

[10]Quoted in the *Congressional Record, ibid.,* p. S2519.

[11]For these and most of the other data that follow see Senator Proxmire's speech, March 10, 1969, *Congressional Record, ibid.,* pp. S2518 ff., and Report of the Subcommittee on Economy in Government, "The Economics of Military Procurement," May 1969, *Milwaukee Journal,* June 15, 1969.

1946 the figure undoubtedly runs into many tens of billions, though no one has yet been permitted to dig into the files of Pentagonia to discover exactly how many.

Ironically, the 22,000 prime contractors who do business with the Department of Defense (DOD) are all fervid advocates of the free enterprise system and competition—except for themselves. Ninety percent of all weapons procurement is now done without competitive bidding—simply by negotiations between a colonel or general and the specific company. The contractor, therefore, makes a low estimate to begin with, so as not to unduly alarm the Secretary of Defense or congressional skeptics; and then goes on to spend two or three times as much, with little fear that the Pentagon will, or can, cancel his order.

The Pentagon, Proxmire shows, treats its industrial allies with regal generosity. It has made available to defense contractors $13.3 billion of government-owned land, buildings, machinery, and materials, saving them the job of financing their own investments. Lockheed, for instance, is building the C-5A cargo plane on government facilities that had an original acquisition cost of $113.8 million. This is a form of "private socialism," in which the public takes the risk, the companies the profit.

The same generosity is evident in patent policy. The federal government pays for the research and development, but it "permits contractors to obtain exclusive patent rights, free of charge, on inventions produced in the performance of government contracts." The Boeing 707 commercial plane was essentially an "off-shoot" of the KC-135 military jet tanker. Hundreds of spinoff products, first developed with DOD, NASA, or AEC money, are now being marketed commercially by the corporations, for their own profit.[12] Additionally, DOD sometimes winks an eye at the practice of using government money for nondefense research. A glaring example brought to light involved three firms who were paid $22.4 million for work on the Minuteman, but diverted $18 million of these sums for research that was not remotely connected with either missile or any other defense work. The Pentagon spares no effort—or money—to make its industrial suppliers happy. While they are still fabricating the weapons, contractors may receive substantial "progress" payments, which in effect are interest-free loans. On incurred costs of $1.278 billion, as of De-

[12]See Amaury de Riencourt, *The American Empire* (New York: Dial Press, 1968), pp. 292–93.

cember 27, 1968, Lockheed, for instance, was given "progress" payments of $1.207 billion. All it had to raise was $71 million of its own cash for a transaction involving cost and facilities close to a billion and a half dollars. Any nondefense manufacturer in America would give his left eyetooth for terms so favorable.

Yet despite the Government's unbounded benevolence, weapons come off the assembly line "two years later than promised," on the average, and fall far below specifications in the contract. Proxmire reports that "of 13 major aircraft and missile programs with sophisticated electronic systems built for the Air Force and Navy since 1955 at a cost of $40 billion, only four, costing $5 billion, could be relied on to reach a performance level of 75 percent or above of their specifications." Four others, costing $13 billion, "broke down at a performance level which was 75 percent or less than their specifications." Two, for which the taxpayer paid $10 billion, were so poor they had to be scrapped after three years because of "low reliability," and two, costing $2 billion, had to be canceled.[13]

To round out the gaudy picture, at least 68 weapons systems, worth $9 billion, had to be abandoned as unworkable, including the nuclear-powered plane on which $512 million was lost, the B-70 superbomber (a loss of $1.5 billion), the Snark robot bomber ($678 million), the Navaho missile ($680 million), and others.[14] This waste does not include incidents of outright theft such as the disappearance of three million gallons of gasoline in Thailand or innumerable peculations of the same sort in Vietnam.[15]

Editors of the authoritative *Congressional Quarterly,* after interviewing "highly placed sources in the Pentagon," concluded that $10.8 billion could have been cut from the 1969 defense budget without impairing the military posture one iota. A former Pentagon official, Robert S. Benson, puts the figure at $9 billion that could be saved "without reducing our national security or touching those funds earmarked for the war in Vietnam." Proxmire claims further that of the $45.8 billion in "our military supply pipeline," 28 percent, or $12.7 billion, is unneeded excess.

But if waste is monumental it doesn't prevent the inefficient corporations from being lavishly rewarded. A *Washington Post* article of June 17, 1969, reports that "a defense contractor who

---

[13]*Congressional Record,* Jan. 31, 1969, p. S1125.
[14]*Newsweek,* June 9, p. 79.
[15]*Congressional Record,* May 1, 1969, Vol. 115, No. 71, p. S4461.

produced substandard guidance 'brains' for the Minuteman II missile has received an estimated $400 million in additional orders for the same device." Far from being penalized, the contractor was rewarded. As far as profits are concerned, not enough is known about them to be definitive, first because DOD does not make adequate studies on the subject, and second because corporations include civilian and defense work profits in one lump. There are strong indications, however, that the military industrialist does considerably better than his counterpart in the consumer industries. Prof. Murray Weidenbaum made a comparison of large defense firms doing three fourths of their business with the Government and industrial firms of comparable size selling their wares on the commercial market. He found that the former earned 17.5 percent on investment from 1962 to 1965, as against 10.6 percent for the latter.

Admiral Hyman Rickover told the Proxmire subcommittee that propulsion turbine suppliers today insist on profits of 25 percent of costs, where a few years ago they were willing to accept 10 percent. Shipbuilders, he said, have doubled their rate of return in the past two years. According to Colonel A. W. Buesking, "profits based on return on investment in the Minuteman program, from 1958 to 1966, were 43 percent." North American Aviation evidently hit the jackpot, in the opinion of a 1962 tax court, by earning 612 percent and 802 percent profit on its investment in two successive years.

Such tales of greed, waste, and inefficiency would stagger any normal business and any other government agency, but when it comes to "defense" spending the nation has become so accustomed to deferring to the military that tens of billions of dollars seem inconsequential. A proposal by Senator George McGovern and 14 others for an excess profits tax on war production is not likely to garner any support in the defense industry, or in Congress itself for that matter.

There is a hint in the Proxmire hearings that more than human error is involved. In fiscal 1968, says the senator, the 100 companies that did more than two thirds of the prime military work, held on their payrolls "2,072 retired military officers of the rank of colonel or Navy captain or above."[16] Lockheed aircraft (of C-5A

---

[16]*Congressional Record*, March 24, 1969, Vol. 115. No. 50, pp. S3072 ff.

fame) led the pack with 210; Boeing came next with 169; McDonnell Douglas Corporation, 141; General Dynamics, 113; North American Rockwell, 104; General Electric, 89. Retired military officers must be a valuable asset, for in 1959 the 100 largest defense contractors employed only a third as many as today—721 as against 2,072. Many of the same men who negotiated the lush deals with private business when they wore Pentagon hats used their influence and inside knowledge on behalf of defense companies after retirement. Pentagon regulations forbid a retired officer to "represent anyone other than the United States in connection with a matter in which the United States is a party or has an interest and in which he participated personally and substantially for the Government." But as a Pentagon spokesman points out, no one, to his knowledge, has ever been prosecuted for such conflicts of interest. Admiral William Fechteler, a former chief of naval operations, told a House subcommittee some years ago how he got around this difficulty. As a $30,000 a year employee for General Electric, plus $8,500 incentive pay, plus $12,000 retirement pay from the Navy, he would simply introduce company officials to the Secretary of the Navy or key admirals, and politely leave the room while they talked contracts.[17] If this is not corruption it certainly skirts the thin edges.

What can one say, for instance, of the fact that an Assistant Secretary of Defense, Thomas Morris, went directly from his post as chief procurement officer at the Pentagon to a top job with Litton Industries? In his last full year in government, Morris and his subordinates approved a 250 percent jump in Litton's defense orders, from $180 million to $466 million. Now as a Litton executive he will be dealing with former underlings to raise the ante. With Morris "coaching the Litton team," asks Senator Proxmire, "how objective will Morris' former subordinates be in deciding whether or not to give the big profitable jobs to Litton? . . . Morris' vice-presidency of Litton can be viewed both as a payoff for the huge Pentagon business shifted to Litton in 1968 and as assurance of immense future influence for Litton."[18]

Litton has 49 retired high-ranking officers on its payroll. Retired General Carl A. Spaatz is on its board of directors. John H. Rubel, a senior vice-president, is a former assistant Secretary of Defense.

---

[17]John M. Swomley, Jr., *Military Establishment* (Boston: Beacon Press, 1964), p. 107.
[18]*Congressional Record*, May 5, 1969.

With all these men opening doors into the right Pentagon office it is little wonder that Litton jumped from thirty-sixth largest prime defense contractor in 1967 to fourteenth in 1968. On the same basis, to a greater or lesser degree, the 2,072 former active officers try to achieve similar results for their companies and are being similarly rewarded.

These are all alarming facts, strongly hinting that aggrandizement has been more important than patriotism in stoking the fires of preparedness. Whether it is or isn't, however, one may be sure that, despite the efforts of Senator Proxmire and others, the full story of waste and corruption in the Pentagon's expenditure of more than a trillion dollars since World War II has not yet been told.

More will undoubtedly come to light in the near future, for Proxmire is an honest man with a passion for fiscal rectitude. Interestingly, he is no antiwar maverick in the tradition of one of his Wisconsin predecessors, Robert M. La Follette. After the 1964 election "Prox" defended Lyndon Johnson against the charge of implementing the Goldwater policy on Vietnam like a parish priest defending his pope. His anti-communism has sometimes been more fierce than that of the Establishment—for instance, in his opposition to aid for independent Yugoslavia on the ground that it is Communist. He believes in most of the clichés of the Cold War, including the need for "preparedness." He is angry at the military-industrial complex only because it is shortchanging the American people; it isn't giving enough "bang for a buck," as one of his speeches puts it.

Important as is the criticism of overruns and similar issues by men like Proxmire, its value is limited and it is not likely to bring any but superficial changes. For if the American people accept the fundamentalist thesis that the military is our bastion of "defense," a few wasted tens of billions will not alarm them into anti-military heresy. DOD will accept some of Proxmire's accounting proposals, such as "zero-cost" budgeting; expenditures will be trimmed a few billion; contractors will be instructed to make more realistic bids—and there the matter will rest.

There are issues far more urgent than cost overruns, however. The military, Senator Fulbright asserts, "is a direct threat to American democracy." Is that true, or is it an exaggeration? Does the military-industrial complex make the United States stronger, as most people claim, or weaker? Does it assure victory—whatever that means—or hasten defeat? For a quarter of a century Americans have accepted without question certain assumptions—about communism and freedom, about Brezhnev, Mao, and Castro, about the ideals of their leaders and generals, about military theories like "deterrence." It is time to ask now, "Are they valid?" In the light of the Pentagon's obvious inadequacy in Vietnam, has it also been wrong in its basic strategy?

"The American people," said Senators Symington, Stephen Young (Dem.–Ohio), and Daniel K. Inouye (Dem.–Hawaii) in a dissent to the ABM,

> have lived with fears of a Soviet attack . . . ever since World War II and have expended a thousand billion dollars on defense in recognition of this possible danger. These gigantic expenditures have been detrimental to many other plans, programs, and policies which now also appear vitally important to the security and well-being of this nation.

Journalist I. F. Stone speaks of the same issue much more sharply:

> The truth is that we have spent a trillion dollars . . . on a gigantic hoax. The U.S. emerged from World War II, as from World War I, virtually unscathed, enormously enriched and—with the atom bomb—immeasurably more powerful than any nation on earth had ever been. The notion that it was in danger of attack from a devastated Soviet Union with 25 million war dead, a generation behind it in industrial development, was a wicked fantasy. But this myth has been the mainstay of the military and the war machine.[19]

In the September 1969 issue of *Esquire*, Ernest J. Sternglass, professor of radiation physics at the University of Pittsburgh, asserts that if the United States were able to intercept with antiballistic missiles the five hundred 25-megaton SS-9 missiles that Secretary Laird claims the Russians soon may have, it would be disastrous. The vast amounts of "long-lived strontium 90 necessarily released into the world's rapidly circulating atmosphere" would kill off all Russian and American infants in the next generation, "thus ending the existence of the Russian people, together

---

[19]*I. F. Stone's Weekly*, July 29, 1969.

with that of all mankind." Sternglass, DOD will no doubt argue, is wrong. But who knows? And what if he is right?

What is needed clearly is a probe of fundamentals. The highest peacetime military budgets of the past ranged from $600 to $900 million a year under Franklin Roosevelt—a rate of expenditure which prompted the liberal *New Republic* to castigate Roosevelt as a "warmonger." Today's level is $80 billion, excluding space expenditures which are defense-related and some cloak-and-dagger funds for the Central Intelligence Agency and similar groups. Forty-four billion of these sums go to 22,000 prime contractors and 100,000 subcontractors for procurement, creating in their wake a vast constituency interested in prolonging the arms race.

The Pentagon puts its wealth at $202.5 billion—a figure which Richard F. Kaufman severely questions because it has "greatly underestimated" the value of land and other items listed at *acquisition* costs a long time ago rather than real worth today.[20] The Pentagon owns 29 million acres of land—almost the size of New York state—plus another 9.7 million acres under the control of the Army Civil Works division, valued, all-told, at $47.7 billion. It is custodian of $100 billion worth of weaponry and $55.6 billion in supplies and plant equipment. Its true wealth undoubtedly ranges from $300 to $400 billion, or about six to eight times the annual after-tax profits of *all* American corporations.

The question is how an institution of these dimensions expanded so mightily in 25 years. It is not enough to say that it "grew like Topsy" or that it is the result of a "conspiracy," because history shows it blossomed with the support and encouragement of the civilian leaders in Washington. It is inconceivable, moreover, that men as conversant with the mechanism of power as our politicians would have yielded such power to the military goliath if they hadn't felt it carried out their own goals. Nor would they have turned their backs on a century and a half of anti-militarist tradition unless they felt they were thereby serving a drastically redefined—and correct—national purpose.

Ever since George Washington, America has been an anti-militarist state. It has engaged in many wars, to be sure—as of

[20]Richard F. Kaufman, "As Eisenhower Was Saying," *The New York Times Magazine,* June 22, 1969.

1924 six major ones and 104 minor ones—but it has always been opposed to large standing armies and large military establishments. At the end of the War of the Revolution, Washington dissolved the army entirely and sent it home, leaving defense to the ragged and inept state militia. When he later asked for a small regular force—denied, incidentally—he conceded that a large military "hath ever been considered dangerous to the liberties of a country." In June 1784 Congress passed a resolution in the same vein—that "standing armies in time of peace are inconsistent with the principles of republican governments, dangerous to the liberties of a free people, and generally converted into destructive engines for establishing despotism."

As of 1845, just before the Mexican War, the military contingent stood at 9,000 officers and men; as late as 1904 at a relatively small 53,000; and on the eve of World War II, 139,000. Today there are more than three and a half million in 470 major bases, camps, and installations, and 5,000 lesser ones around the nation, as well as 429 major bases and 2,972 minor ones overseas.[21] The military establishment, far from being dismantled as in previous postwar periods, is increasing its wealth and power from year to year. Even the conclusion of the Korean War in the early 1950s led to a reduction in military spending of only a few billion for two or three years, and since then it has almost doubled. It is now seven times what it was in 1948 and 80 times what it was before World War II.

For good or ill—and in this writer's view, for ill—all this represents a qualitative change in the American way of life. It has concentrated too much unchecked power in too few hands. It has corrupted the process of "government by consent of the governed." It has *necessarily* put us in the same bed with dozens of dictators and established us as a policeman rather than a negotiator in our relations with the rest of the world.

One may say that regrettable as these results may have been they were necessary to curb an aggressor, to defend America from Communist Russia or Communist China—in a nuclear age. But the Soviets did not have an atom bomb until the Cold War was already a few years old, and were not expected to have one, in

---

[21] *The New York Times*, April 9, 1969.

the view of Lieutenant General Leslie R. Groves, in charge of the American atomic project, for at least five years under the best circumstances, and probably 20 years.[22] Pointing to a potential aggressor begs the question anyway, for we have always had foreign enemies we claimed threatened our security—England, France, England again (in 1812), Spain, Mexico, Germany, Italy, Japan. Moreover in the early days of the Republic both England and France were far more potent than the United States—even with an ocean in the way. Yet we never before tolerated a permanent military establishment of any consequence, and certainly not of the present size. We never before consented, as Eugene McCarthy puts it, to permitting a "Republic within the Republic."

There must be an explanation for the rise of the military-industrial complex, therefore, that goes beyond the issue of security. Or, to say it in another way, the word security must have a connotation somewhat different from what it has had in the past.

[22]See *The New York Times*, Oct. 10, 1945; and D. F. Fleming, *The Cold War and Its Origins, 1917–1950* (New York: Doubleday, 1961), Vol. I, p. 323.

STUDS TERKEL

Working:
Phil Stallings

However advanced American capitalism is said to be, the fact remains
that most of the nation's workers do their job in a setting that may
be dirty and dangerous and is more often than not filled with cruel
monotony. As the following excerpt from Studs Terkel's *Working*
shows, individuals face a difficult task in keeping the work place
from eroding their humanity and sense of worth.

He *is a spot welder at the Ford assembly plant on the far South
Side of Chicago. He is twenty-seven years old; recently married.
He works the third shift: 3:30 P.M. to midnight.*

"I *start the automobile, the first welds. From there it goes to
another line, where the floor's put on, the roof, the trunk hood,
the doors. Then it's put on a frame. There is hundreds of lines.*

"*The welding gun's got a square handle, with a button on the
top for high voltage and a button on the button for low. The first
is to clamp the metal together. The second is to fuse it.*

"*The gun hangs from a ceiling, over tables that ride on a track.
It travels in a circle, oblong, like an egg. You stand on a cement
platform, maybe six inches from the ground.*"

I stand in one spot, about two- or three-feet area, all night. The
only time a person stops is when the line stops. We do about
thirty-two jobs per car, per unit. Forty-eight units an hour, eight
hours a day. Thirty-two times forty-eight times eight. Figure it
out. That's how many times I push that button.

The noise, oh it's tremendous. You open your mouth and you're liable to get a mouthful of sparks. (Shows his arms.) That's a burn, these are burns. You don't compete against the noise. You go to yell and at the same time you're straining to maneuver the gun to where you have to weld.

You got some guys that are uptight, and they're not sociable. It's too rough. You pretty much stay to yourself. You get involved with yourself. You dream, you think of things you've done. I drift back continuously to when I was a kid and what me and my brothers did. The things you love most are the things you drift back into.

Lots of times I worked from the time I started to the time of the break and I never realized I had even worked. When you dream, you reduce the chances of friction with the foreman or with the next guy.

It don't stop. It just goes and goes and goes. I bet there's men who have lived and died out there, never seen the end of that line. And they never will—because it's endless. It's like a serpent. It's just all body, no tail. It can do things to you . . . (Laughs.)

Repetition is such that if you were to think about the job itself, you'd slowly go out of your mind. You'd let your problems build up, you'd get to a point where you'd be at the fellow next to you—his throat. Every time the foreman came by and looked at you, you'd have something to say. You just strike out at anything you can. So if you involve yourself by yourself, you overcome this.

I don't like the pressure, the intimidation. How would you like to go up to someone and say, "I would like to go to the bathroom?" If the foreman doesn't like you, he'll make you hold it, just ignore you. Should I leave this job to go to the bathroom I risk being fired. The line moves all the time.

I work next to Jim Grayson and he's preoccupied. The guy on my left, he's a Mexican, speaking Spanish, so it's pretty hard to understand him. You just avoid him. Brophy, he's a young fella, he's going to college. He works catty-corner from me. Him and I talk from time to time. If he ain't in the mood, I don't talk. If I ain't in the mood, he knows it.

Oh sure, there's tension here. It's not always obvious, but the whites stay with the whites and the coloreds stay with the coloreds. When you go into Ford, Ford says, "Can you work with other men?" This stops a lot of trouble, 'cause when you're working side by side with a guy, they can't afford to have guys fighting. When two men don't socialize, that means two guys are gonna do more work, know what I mean?

I don't understand how come more guys don't flip. Because you're nothing more than a machine when you hit this type of thing. They give better care to that machine than they will to you. They'll have more respect, give more attention to that machine. And you *know* this. Somehow you get the feeling that the machine is better than you are. (Laughs.)

You really begin to wonder. What price do they put on me? Look at the price they put on the machine. If that machine breaks down, there's somebody out there to fix it right away. If I break down, I'm just pushed over to the other side till another man takes my place. The only thing they have on their mind is to keep that line running.

I'll do the best I can. I believe in an eight-hour pay for an eight-hour day. But I will not try to outreach my limits. If I can't cut it, I just don't do it. I've been there three years and I keep my nose pretty clean. I never cussed anybody or anything like that. But I've had some real brushes with foremen.

What happened was my job was overloaded. I got cut and it got infected. I got blood poisoning. The drill broke. I took it to the foreman's desk. I says, "Change this as soon as you can." We were running specials for XL hoods. I told him I wasn't a repair man. That's how the conflict began. I says, "If you want, take me to the Green House." Which is a superintendent's office—disciplinary station. This is when he says, "Guys like you I'd like to see in the parking lot."

One foreman I know, he's about the youngest out here, he has this idea: I'm it and if you don't like it, you know what you can do. Anything this other foreman says, he usually overrides. Even in some cases, the foremen don't get along. They're pretty hard to live with, even with each other.

Oh yeah, the foreman's got somebody knuckling down on him, putting the screws to him. But a foreman is still free to go to the bathroom, go get a cup of coffee. He doesn't face the penalties. When I first went in there, I kind of envied foremen. Now, I wouldn't have a foreman's job. I wouldn't give 'em the time of the day.

When a man becomes a foreman, he has to forget about even being human, as far as feelings are concerned. You see a guy

329

there bleeding to death. So what, buddy? That line's gotta keep goin'. I can't live like that. To me, if a man gets hurt, first thing you do is get him some attention.

About the blood poisoning. It came from the inside of a hood rubbin' against me. It caused quite a bit of pain. I went down to the medics. They said it was a boil. Got to my doctor that night. He said blood poisoning. Running fever and all this. Now I've smartened up.

They have a department of medics. It's basically first aid. There's no doctor on our shift, just two or three nurses, that's it. They've got a door with a sign on it that says Lab. Another door with a sign on it: Major Surgery. But my own personal opinion, I'm afraid of 'em. I'm afraid if I were to get hurt, I'd get nothin' but back talk. I got hit square in the chest one day with a bar from a rack and it cut me down this side. They didn't take x-rays or nothing. Sent me back on the job. I missed three and a half days two weeks ago. I had bronchitis. They told me I was all right. I didn't have a fever. I went home and my doctor told me I couldn't go back to work for two weeks. I really needed the money, so I had to go back the next day. I woke up still sick, so I took off the rest of the week.

I pulled a muscle on my neck, straining. This gun, when you grab this thing from the ceiling, cable, weight, I mean you're pulling everything. Your neck, your shoulders, and your back. I'm very surprised more accidents don't happen. You have to lean over, at the same time holding down the gun. This whole edge here is sharp. I go through a shirt every two weeks, it just goes right through. My coveralls catch on fire. I've had gloves catch on fire. (Indicates arms.) See them little holes? That's what sparks do. I've got burns across here from last night.

I know I could find better places to work. But where could I get the money I'm making? Let's face it, $4.32 an hour. That's real good money now. Funny thing is, I don't mind working at body construction. To a great degree; I enjoy it. I love using my hands—more than I do my mind. I love to be able to put things together and see something in the long run. I'll be the first to admit I've got the easiest job on the line. But I'm against this thing where I'm being held back. I'll work like a dog until I get what I want. The job I really want is utility.

It's where I can stand and say I can do any job in this department, and nobody has to worry about me. As it is now, out of say, sixty jobs, I can do almost half of 'em. I want to get away from standing in one spot. Utility can do a different job every day. Instead of working right there for eight hours I could work over there for eight, I could work the other place for eight. Every day it would change. I would be around more people. I go out on my lunch break and work on the fork truck for a half-hour—to get the experience. As soon as I got it down pretty good, the foreman in charge says he'll take me. I don't want the other guys to see me. When I hit that fork lift, you just stop your thinking and you concentrate. Something right there in front of you, not in the past, not in the future. This is real healthy.

I don't eat lunch at work. I may grab a candy bar, that's enough. I wouldn't be able to hold it down. The tension your body is put under by the speed of the line . . . When you hit them brakes, you just can't stop. There's a certain momentum that carries you forward. I could hold the food, but it wouldn't set right.

Proud of my work? How can I feel pride in a job where I call a foreman's attention to a mistake, a bad piece of equipment, and he'll ignore it. Pretty soon you get the idea they don't care. You keep doing this and finally you're titled a troublemaker. So you just go about your work. You *have* to have pride. So you throw it off to something else. And that's my stamp collection.

I'd break both legs to get into social work. I see all over so many kids really gettin' a raw deal. I think I'd go into juvenile. I tell kids on the line, "Man, go out there and get that college." Because it's too late for me now.

When you go into Ford, first thing they try to do is break your spirit. I seen them bring a tall guy where they needed a short guy. I seen them bring a short guy where you have to stand on two guys' backs to do something. Last night, they brought a fifty-eight-year-old man to do the job I was on. That man's my father's age. I know damn well my father couldn't do it. To me, this is humanely wrong. A job should be a job, not a death sentence.

The younger worker, when he gets uptight, he talks back. But you take an old fellow, he's got a year, two years, maybe three years to go. If it was me, I wouldn't say a word, I wouldn't care what they did. 'Cause, baby, for another two years I can stick it out. I can't blame this man. I respect him because he had enough will power to stick it out for thirty years.

It's gonna change. There's a trend. We're getting younger and younger men. We got this new Thirty and Out. Thirty years seniority and out. The whole idea is to give a man more time, more time to slow down and live. While he's still in his fifties, he can settle down in a camper and go out and fish. I've sat down and thought about it. I've got twenty-seven years to go. (Laughs.) That's why I don't go around causin' trouble or lookin' for a cause.

The only time I get involved is when it affects me or it affects a man on the line in a condition that could be me. I don't believe in lost causes, but when it all happened ... (He pauses, appears bewildered.)

The foreman was riding the guy. The guy either told him to go away or pushed him, grabbed him ... You can't blame the guy—Jim Grayson. I don't want nobody stickin' their finger in my face. I'd've probably hit him beside the head. The whole thing was: Damn it, it's about time we took a stand. Let's stick up for the guy. We stopped the line. (He pauses, grins.) Ford lost about twenty units. I'd figure about five grand a unit—whattaya got? (Laughs.)

I said, "Let's all go home." When the line's down like that, you can go up to one man and say, "You gonna work?" If he says no, they can fire him. See what I mean? But if nobody was there, who the hell were they gonna walk up to and say, "Are you gonna work?" Man, there woulda been nobody there! If it were up to me, we'd gone home.

Jim Grayson, the guy I work next to, he's colored. Absolutely. That's the first time I've seen unity on that line. Now it's happened once, it'll happen again. Because everybody just sat down. Believe you me. (Laughs.) It stopped at eight and it didn't start till twenty after eight. Everybody and his brother was down there. It was really nice to see, it really was.

DEMOCRATIC VISTAS

RICHARD GOODWIN

The System Must Change

Social scientists frequently describe the United States as a "pluralistic" society. This term does not refer to the fact that America is a polyglot nation comprised of semiassimilated minorities and ethnic groups. "Pluralism" is meant rather to describe the arrangement of social and political power—the way public policies evolve as a result of the competition between a broad spectrum of interest groups, no one of which can ever attain permanent advantage over another and all of which are constantly re-forming as a result of social mobility.

Opposed to this view are those who believe that America is governed by a "power elite," that large economic interests sit atop the "system," and that democracy and freedom are ultimately incompatible with advanced capitalism. Those at the bottom have an interest in fundamental change but no power; those at the top with the power are uninterested in change. Richard Goodwin, author of the following essay, was for years a leading figure in the Kennedy and Johnson administrations.

In 1959, little over a year after graduating from law school, I went to work in the Senate office of John F. Kennedy, from which, the next fall, 49.7% of the American voters unwittingly sent me to the White House as assistant special counsel to the president. A few hours after the Inaugural Parade, while exploring our new quarters in the now notorious West Wing of the White House, my employer called me through the open door of the Oval Office.

"Did you see the Coast Guard Academy in the parade?"

I tried to remember. Were they in blue? Or was that the Navy? But he did not wait for an answer.

"There wasn't one black face. Call Dillon [the new secretary of the treasury, the department with jurisdiction over the Coast Guard]. Have him do something."

I took the stairs to my West Wing office three at a time. It was real. The controls were in our hands, liberal and still tough-minded; we could now proceed to build a better, freer country, starting with the Coast Guard Academy.

On Friday, December 14th, 1963, along with Arthur Schlesinger, I sat in the attorney general's spacious office, whose walls had drawings by his young children Scotch taped to the wood paneling, while we discussed some difficulties which Governor Averill Harriman was having with the State Department.

"I don't want to see Averill Harriman get hurt, or anyone else," said Robert Kennedy.

> Harriman's got his faults. I've got my faults. We've all got faults. The secret is collective action. I haven't thought through how to go about it. But the secret is collective action. There are hundreds of guys around here in positions of influence. We're important to Johnson. I'm the most important because my name happens to be Kennedy. But we're all important. I haven't thought it through yet, but we are.

He stood rigidly next to his desk, beside the special telephone connected to the White House, his hands tensely at his side, head down, working to suppress a show of emotion.

"Sure I've lost a brother. Other people lose wives," his voice trailed off.

> I've lost a brother. But that's not what's important. What's important is what we were trying to do for this country. We got a good start.
>
> We had a committee working on poverty. A juvenile delinquency study. You can't do a lot in three years, but we'd gotten started. We could have done a lot in five more years. There are a lot of people in this town. They didn't come here just to work for John Kennedy, an individual, but for ideas, things we wanted to do.
>
> It's one thing if you've got personal reasons for leaving, like you may want to leave, Arthur. But I don't think people should run off. We're very important to Johnson now. After November 5th we'll all be dead. We won't matter a damn. A lot of people could scramble around now, get themselves positions of power and influence. I could do that. But that's not important. What's

important is what we can get done. Remember, after November 5th we're all done. We won't be wanted or needed.

As we got up to go, I pointed out a column in the afternoon paper in which public-opinion analyst, Samuel Lubel, reported that Southerners violently opposed Kennedy for vice president but that Negroes were for him. Kennedy, still standing, studied the paper and, without raising his head, mused flatly, "Well, Johnson's already got the Negroes . . . but he's already got the Negroes."

Late one evening in the spring of 1968, just a few days before his victory in the Indiana primary, Robert Kennedy sat talking in an Indianapolis restaurant after a 12-hour campaign day of that continual movement which reduces towns and neighborhoods to an almost indistinguishable series of platforms, crowds and outstretched hands. "Even if I get to be president," he said to me, "how can you do everything you want to do with Congress, and the newspapers, and the establishment pressing down on you all the time? How can you accomplish anything important?"

Within four months, my passage from the confident ambitions of 1960 was complete. The events of one day in a Los Angeles hospital and a week in a maddened Chicago catalyzed a steadily growing awareness that we had misconceived the nature of America's afflictions, failed to understand fully the sources of that oppressive power which was now visibly constricting the fair expectations and the freedom of the citizen.

Surely the declining conditions of a colossal society could not be ascribed to misjudgments, flawed character, accident or conspiracy. And if we had not been America's "best and brightest," still we were as good and intelligent as any likely to inhabit the government. If one could expect better only from a government staffed by men of improbable and unprecedented nobility, then perhaps we were asking of politics what it could not give; perhaps, at our best moments, we had been battling imaginary enemies for an illusory prize.

In 1969 I moved to a farm overlooked by the mountains of west central Maine, thus concluding a decade-long engagement with public life. The isolated study and writing of the nearly five years which followed gradually enlarged my understanding of society, and of the relationship between politics and the economic structures which dominate society.

This did not, however, constitute a belated acquiescence in the anti-liberalism which was proclaimed by every infant Lenin of the televised Sixties. For New Left politics, lacking any roots in economic radicalism, can be placed alongside the politics of Richard Nixon as a demonstration that liberalism is the most benign form of public power possible within the present structure of American society. But it is also true that no form of truly liberating politics is possible within that structure. It is the structure itself which must be changed. And that task is beyond the reach of politics.

Politics—the acquisition and use of power—is an institutional process created by the civil society, the nation, to reconcile the competing claims of the varied interests, human and material, which constitute that society. Since politics is the agent of the civil society, those interests which dominate the life of the nation also dominate its politics. Even though government can make reforms, it cannot change, in any important way, the social structure, the distribution of power within society, on which it is based. Of course, economic relationships, the patterns of economic power, can themselves be changed, and, if they are, then the political, always anxious to please, will submit.

This is a relationship which is as inescapable as it is fundamental. Nor are politicians cynics, who secretly believe themselves the agents of private power. Most of them share the assumptions which dominate social thought; that, for example, it is possible for government to serve "all the people"—to guard with equal vigilance the welfare of businessman and farmer, rich and poor, banker and worker. Yet if this means anything at all, it is that no one is to be damaged or reduced in order to benefit another. Thus existing relationships, the distribution of social power and rewards, will be preserved.

Many in public life are American utopians who share the ideological fantasy that there are no mortal and irreconcilable differences of interest and desire; that social conflict is the product of misunderstanding or changeable public attitudes, that our problems and difficulties can be resolved simply by perfecting the techniques of our present social structure.

During the heyday of the Great Society, in 1964 and 1965, when Lyndon Johnson's mastery over Congress made almost anything

seem possible, high officials sat around the White House conference table to draft sweeping new measures to improve the quality
of American life—to remodel cities and restore the physical requirements for community, to clean up the environment, to complete the civil rights revolution by enlarging black economic
opportunity. Yet, despite White House intentions, somehow, the
boldest departures were flattened, altered into conformity with
established patterns of government regulation. It did not occur to
me then, as it has since, that the inability to exercise power is
an almost infallible demonstration that the power doesn't exist.

This helps explain why none of the significant modern movements for social change were begun by that enlightened and moral
political leadership we continually pursue. They began with Martin Luther King in Birmingham, Ralph Nader and irate consumers,
anti-war students and community groups anxious to save their
towns and purify their rivers.

The political structure responded after these groups had acquired power and support within the private society, and this
response began to diminish once these movements collided with
the superior strength of dominant economic relationships. This
is not a demonstration of correctable flaws in the contemporary
political process. It evidences an enduring relationship. Important
social change never begins with politics. Lincoln did not invent
the anti-slavery movement, nor did the government persuade
workers to organize.

This argument is deeply repellent to the American character, a
heretical contradiction of that secular faith which evoked Lord
Bryce's observation that "the federal Constitution is, to their eyes,
an almost sacred thing, an Ark of the Covenant." This belief explains why, even though we see that public authority is being
used to serve the interests of large economic institutions, we believe such behavior to be the consequence of a conspiracy which
might be shattered or corruption which should be punished.

Last month I completed a book-promotion tour of major cities.
In dozens of interviews I discussed the subordination of politics
to the civil society, and then went on to detail some of the oppressive consequences of large-scale industry and finance, after which
the interviewer would ask me, "Do you think Teddy Kennedy would
change that if he were elected president?" Since most of these
interviewers were intelligent, had clearly understood the point I

was making and had frequently nodded agreement, I soon became aware that I was in the presence, not of ideas, but of a "faith that surpasseth all understanding."

Before examining some of the evidence, however, let us dispose of that misleading phrase—the "public interest." The term "public interest" is not a harmlessly convenient label. Like all sloppy and deceptive language it tends to cripple thought, hindering us from asking of every political act: "Who wins and who loses?"

The "public" is neither Hamilton's "great beast" nor the "sovereign people." It is an abstraction, a creation of that mysticism which, in our secular age, is called ideology. There is no "public," only individuals, alone or in groups: you and me, Bob Dylan, Billy Graham and Harold Geneen; each different in ambition, need and possession. It is not the "public" but private individuals who attend schools, walk in parks, drive the highways and vote for presidents.

Thus, there can be no "public interest," only citizens with common private interests. What convention calls the "public interest" consists primarily of those private interests which can be enforced by government, a category which cannot be defined in terms of numbers and which extends from the interest of almost everyone in protection against foreign invasion to the interest of a single individual in casting his ideas against the hostility of the entire population.

A recent law requires that whenever goods are purchased on the installment plan the buyer must be given a clear statement of the total interest to be paid. This means we prefer to protect debtors against the consequence of their ignorance or arithmetical ineptitude, rather than to reward the agile entrepreneur who might benefit from those incapacities. For a long time the "public interest," as expressed in the legal maxim *caveat emptor* (let the buyer beware), was thought to require the opposite judgment. A more subtle analysis of this change in our concept of the "public interest" might reveal a modern awareness that production is maximized when consumers are on the edge of bankruptcy, not over it.

Use of the term "public interest" in order to stimulate or explain particular acts of government is only an expression of preference among competing private interests. This is true of the most benign and irreproachable policies, even those which seem to benefit almost everyone, such as the financing of cancer research. Every allocation of resources is an expression of priority; that which is spent for one purpose is not available for other purposes. It is ordinarily the most affluent who rank cancer among their highest concerns, being exempt from the malnutrition or the ravages of slum living which preoccupy others.

This conclusion does not constitute moral censure. It is the function of politics to enforce private interests. The issue is which interests and to what end. The standards which determine that resolution are not those of morality, the Constitution's "general welfare" or the Declaration's "pursuit of happiness," but of power within the society.

A complete description of the private interests which dominate American society would require a large treatise. But mere identification is no more difficult than finding Wilt Chamberlain among a delegation of visiting Pygmies. There are more than one-and-a-half million American corporations. One hundred of them possess nearly 50% of the country's corporate assets—well over a quarter of a trillion dollars. Add the next hundred and, together, they have more than 60% of the assets.

And these figures modestly understate the economic importance of the super-corps, for the fortunes of many smaller units— car dealers, TV repairmen, suppliers of plumbing—are linked to their behavior. The long-term policies and recent actions of large oil companies, for example, have damaged a multitude of "independent businesses," from record manufacturers dependent upon vinyl, to the small farmer who must use chemical fertilizer. Similarly the policies of steel companies influence the cost and type of new construction. If these companies are inefficient—if their equipment is obsolete—if they are successful in blocking imports by foreign competitors, then the costs of the steel industry's deficiencies must be paid for by every business which uses their product.

The statistics of concentration by themselves would have been startling when we were still a capitalist country; today they only hint at the extent to which economic power has been consolidated.

The ideology of capitalism, although often corrupted and ignored, opposed a unitary control over important economic activities. The source of this principle was not hostility to bigness, but the expectation that corporate warfare—called the free market—would stimulate economic progress and benefit the general public. Competitive success would go to those who offered a better product at a better price; the conditions of struggle would encourage the most productive use of resources: greater efficiency, innovation and enterprise. The anti-trust laws were designed, not to punish size, but to combat the natural tendency of the capitalist to evade the rigors of competitive capitalism.

If we analyze corporations from the standpoint of their actual operation within the society, we cannot regard them as distinct and autonomous simply because they have different names, shareholders and managers, but only to the extent they compete in a free market. It makes little difference if there are one, three or seven automobile companies, if they produce essentially the same product in the same way at the same price. In the world of the megacorporations there is little practical distinction between monopoly and domination by a handful of companies, i.e., oligopoly. Seven oil companies and three automobile companies have the same power over the market—the ability to prevent serious price and product competition—as do IBM and the telephone company. Functionally, they are one.

At one time it was thought that vigorous enforcement of the anti-trust laws could guarantee a competitive marketplace. And we still retain some of this faith. Were a militant attorney general to break up General Motors into three companies, it would be greeted as a major turning point in our economic life. Yet the behavior of the automobile industry would be unchanged, and we would still not be able to buy better or cheaper cars. (A hundred automobile companies would be a different story, but that cannot be accomplished by a lawsuit, only by dismantling the present economic structure.) The anti-trust laws have gone the way of the law of supply and demand, whose present decrepitude was recently disclosed by the president of Chrysler Corporation when he announced, without a hint of irony, that sales had dropped and prices must rise.

To uncover the extent of concentration in today's economy, one would have to examine the actual behavior of corporations, the extent to which they compete, not simply to seduce consumers, but in terms of price, product, increased efficiency, lower cost and technological innovation. Such a functional analysis of the economy would reveal that the hundred corporations, with more than half of the assets, operate as an even smaller number of gigantic bureaucracies. We would find an immense and accelerating concentration spreading into fields, from growing tomatoes to selling hamburgers, previously exempt from such control, and rapidly overflowing national boundaries. Through devices such as the "franchise" and the "chain" the domination of large enterprise is extended over activities once reserved for the small and independent businessman.

These institutions and the economic relationships which sustain them rule the American economy; their increasing ascendency has been the most important phenomenon of post World War II America. The power of its repositories has increased through all the tumults and divisions of politics: during liberal administrations and conservative ones, under strong political leadership and weak, while McCarthyism preoccupied the country, during the glory days of the New Left and in the era of Watergate. These are the interests—the institutions and the way in which they conduct business—which the political structure often serves, sometimes modifies or "reforms," and never attacks.

Unless one, blinded to the changing conditions of American life, should assume this growth in control to be wholly beneficent, in the "public interest," this history alone should dispel the illusion that some new leader, the advent of some ideal government, will reverse the process and dismantle the sources of our afflictions.

Nevertheless, the yellow brick road of politics does not lead to some hapless, almost pitiable, creature secreted within the towers of sovereignty. For government is immense and important, its power increasingly vital to the well-being of private economic relationships. It would require a dispiriting volume to depict the manifold ways, small and large, in which government serves the large economic bureaucracies; but a few fragmentary sketches are adequate to show the unmistakable shape of this relationship.

Most federal money, like most other money, goes to benefit the large institutions of the private economy. In 1971, as an illustration, the federal government spent about $150 billion (omitting the trust funds like Social Security, which are forms of public insurance and which, for the most part, take in more than they pay out). About $90 billion of this went to defense, "international affairs," space and veterans programs. About $20 billion was divided between interest payments to financial institutions on the national debt and the financing of transportation to more goods or expand the horizons of the automobile.

About $5 billion went to agriculture, much of it ultimately assisting the growth of that corporate agriculture which labors heroically to reduce the quality of food while raising the price. Indeed, government-sponsored research has helped America's burgeoning tomato magnates develop a fruit tough enough to travel every corner of the land without bruise or scar, a peerless tomato whose only defect is an almost complete absence of flavor. Over $4 billion was spent to run the government; about $3 billion for water resources and power. We allocated $8 billion to education and manpower training, which has important human benefits, but is also consistent with the need for a supply of skilled workers and educated consumers.

It can be seen that the pattern of federal spending supports the economic objectives of large enterprise—primarily through direct subsidies or purchases, but also by investments in activities necessary to the well-being of enterprise, but which are inherently unprofitable or which cannot be owned by particular industries, e.g., various forms of transportation, power, shipping, etc.

This fact alone does not condemn such expenditures. Some of them serve the general welfare and some would be necessary in any form of economy. But, whatever the merit of particular expenditures, the federal budget is an effective instrument for transferring wealth from the middle class to large private enterprise. This task, a little more difficult in a democratic society than elsewhere, is eased by a network of tax breaks and "incentives," all the more valued for being virtually incomprehensible. "Tax incentive" is simply a polite word for subsidy. The result is the same as if the government had taxed everyone on the same basis and then returned money to those it favored. One man's break is another man's burden.

Stanley Surrey, in charge of tax matters for the Treasury Department under President Johnson, has calculated that loopholes, credits and incentives represent a direct yearly federal payment of $51.5 billion to business and wealthy individuals. By contrast, federal public-assistance payments to the poor are around $10 billion. The method of payment is different—the poor receive checks while the rich and powerful are excused from writing them—but it all comes from the same place, the pockets of the good, gray middle class.

The more blatant inequities of government getting and spending are more visible and easier to debate than are the voluminous assortment of laws, agencies and commissions through which government "regulates" the private economy. Many of these laws were drafted by men filled with zeal for the public welfare, supported by those indignant at the reckless greed of business, enacted over the bitter protests of the affected enterprise. But passion is not power. And, as one would expect, regulation has become an instrument to strengthen, not just the regulated industry, but all the institutions and relationships which dominate the economic structure.

One of the first acts of the New Frontier, in 1961, was to appoint a distinguished scholar and law-school dean, James Landis, to evaluate the regulatory agencies. His long friendship with the Kennedy family guaranteed him White House support and attention, and his final report to the president concluded that the agencies were more anxious to serve the interest of business than that of the public interest and recommended radical changes. The report was carefully read at high levels of government, released to an admiring press, thoughtfully discussed in editorials, and tenderly immured in the government archives.

Our mistake was to think we were dealing with a regulatory system that had failed. In fact, it was performing, and performing well, a very important function—that of protecting businesses from the public and from each other. The beneficiaries of this "regulatory" purpose, and their congressional allies, formed a constituency powerful enough to resist all assaults. Even now, when the same conclusions have become clear to the most casual observer, there is no serious movement for change.

In the era of free-market capitalism, government intrusion could, for the most part, only interfere with the ambitions of large enterprise. But the economic forces which govern today's society need the assistance of government. Industries where concentration is not far enough advanced to eliminate the rigors of the marketplace are shielded by government subsidies and rules designed to ward off the hazards of competition. General Motors sets automobile prices, and a federal agency fixes airline fares, while the Federal Communications Commission guarantees exclusive control over the national airwaves to three networks.

Economic enterprises which are necessary to the well-being of many other businesses—enterprises such as telephone, airlines, banking and financial structures—are protected against economic adversity and, at the same time, prohibited from using their control over vital services to benefit particular industries at the expense of competitors. As once, for example, the railroads gave special rates to favored customers.

The regulatory structure also helps to insulate the economic process from the hazards of public fashion or the vagaries of misguided politicians. Protests against poisoned air, ineffective drugs or unsafe products result in government regulations, boards and speeches which manage to calm the turbulence of the moment while ultimately imposing the minimum burden consistent with public order. A caricature of this function was the establishment, in April 1970, of the National Industrial Pollution Control Council, composed of 63 executives of major polluting companies, without any representatives of consumers, conservation groups or the general public.

This description is not intended to deny that the public also receives benefits from government regulation, nor does it support an unregulated economy. It shows a pattern of behavior in government's relationship to business—behavior which also extends to those policies by which government influences the national economy. It is no longer possible to debate the wisdom of government interference with the private economy; its intervention is inescapable.

Federal spending amounts to about one-fifth of the gross national product, while government financial institutions control the supply and cost of money. These activities, combined with a host of others, such as control over the tax structure of public guarantees of collective bargaining, help determine the distribution of national wealth and income. They decide the extent to which various groups will share the rewards of the fat years and the burdens of the lean. Therefore, to oppose new economic policies on the grounds that they constitute unwarranted interference by government is simply to express support for the existing patterns of interference. It is the demagogic form through which beneficiaries of present policies express their opposition to change.

When prosperity is increasing and the economy booms, the essential bias of economic policy is obscured by the fact that nearly everyone is doing better. Nonetheless, some do much better than others. The two decades of economic growth from 1950 to 1970, when the gross national product almost tripled, greatly accelerated the concentration of corporate wealth. But the distribution of personal income was unchanged. Today, as at the beginning of the boom, the wealthiest receive 45% of all family income, while the bottom fifth are still alloted their five percent share.

Now we are in more difficult times and it is much harder to conceal the preferences contained in economic policy. Around 1967–68 the postwar boom began to falter. Nevertheless, over the last six years the gross national product increased by more than $160 billion (all these figures are in "real" dollars, i.e., the numbers have been changed to reflect the declining purchasing power of the dollar since 1967). Yet the average weekly earnings of the American worker did not increase at all; he made about $103 a week in 1968 and makes $103 now. And in the same period, the total financial assets of all American consumers actually declined. There can be little doubt what happened to the increased national wealth: Some of it went to rich individuals, most of it returned to the corporate structures whence it came.

The last pretenses to fairness are now being dissolved by an inflation which has brought a serious drop in the income, purchasing power and living standard of most Americans. A closer look at the present "recession" reveals that corporate profits in most sectors of the economy have risen at an almost unprecedented rate over the last year. Most banks have increased profits 20–40%, largely because the government has raised interest rates. Naturally some industries, like automobiles, have not done well, but they will be permitted to raise prices and try to catch up.

Some economists, faithful to a primitive Keynesianism, think inflation and recession are unrelated; nevertheless, like Bonnie and Clyde, they always go together. While democrats express outrage and Republicans offer the ancient consolation "this too shall pass," the economic policy of the government is unchanged. But it is not inert. Since the government can never do nothing, the failure to adopt new policies constitutes a decision to continue the old. This decision is a sure sign that economic distress is not universal.

From the standpoint of major enterprise, current economic policies are wise and desirable. The almost unanimous political opposition to economic controls corresponds to the awareness by big business and organized labor that they have the economic power not only to keep ahead of inflation but also to profit from it. It is the rest of us—most of us—who are hurt.

The term "economic policy" itself reveals its function. Its ordinary meaning is restricted to fiscal and monetary policy, whose instruments are taxation, federal spending, interest rates and control over the supply of money. Economic policy is not thought to include modification of the economic structure itself. Yet many of our current difficulties are due to the misuses of national resources by large economic bureaucracies—the inefficiency, stifling of competition, failure to innovate, etc. But these matters are beyond the present power of politics.

The inclination of public authority to support the ruling relationships of private life is not a modern phenomenon, a consequence of technology, the cold war or future shock. It is an attribute of all organized society, comprehended by thoughtful men long before the industrial age.

In the tenth Federalist paper, James Madison explained that society was divided into "factions," and that

> the most common and durable source of faction has been the various and unequal distribution of property. . . . A landed interest, a manufacturing interest, a moneyed interest, with many lesser interests, grow up of necessity in civilized nations, and divide them into different classes, actuated by different sentiments and views. The regulation of these various and interfering interests forms the principal task of modern legislation. . . . And what are the different classes of legislators but advocates and parties to the causes which they determine . . . and . . . the most powerful faction must be expected to prevail.

Unlike many of us, Madison did not believe this danger to the general well-being could be avoided by strong and benign leadership. "It is vain to say that enlightened statesmen will be able to adjust these clashing interests, and render them all subservient to the public good." His remedy was to disperse political power among public institutions and across a large "extent of territory," so that government would represent a multiplicity of divergent interests.

"A rage for paper money, for an abolition of debts, for an equal division of property, or for any other improper or wicked project," Madison explained, incidentally betraying his own allegiances, "will be less apt to pervade the whole body of the Union than a particular member of it. . . ."

We are greatly changed from the America whose circumstances gave persuasive force to Madison's expectation; a country where Southern planters and Northern merchants, manufacturers who wanted protection and shipowners desirous of commerce, Western fur traders and pioneers, impoverished debtors and bankers, were all scattered across a territorial expanse containing disparate economic conditions and lifestyles. Madison could not have foreseen the rise of industrial and financial structures large enough to dominate the economic life of an entire continent. But that change does not invalidate his understanding that government could not suppress private power, "that the causes of faction cannot be removed, and that relief is only to be sought in the means of controlling its *effects.*"

Madison's exposition was a premonition of Marx's more profound analysis. It is a historical misfortune that much of our public dialogue is conducted as if Marx had never made his important discoveries, as if history or social problems or personal values could be understood apart from the ecomonic forces which shape them. In part this rejection reflects the hostility of the pragmatic American temperament to intellectual systems, a hostility which was strengthened when Marxism became an ideological weapon in the struggle for power both within and between nations. The use of Marx's ideas to increase our understanding of history and the social process was to risk being thought an advocate of Soviet world rule, international communism or bloody revolution.

However, Marx himself would be the first to deny that hostility to his ideas could be explained by political circumstances or intellectual attitudes alone. Economic relations sustain their authority by imposing a structure of beliefs, an ideology, which helps to insulate them from direct attack by denying the fact of their domination. It is analogous to the way in which that other 19th-century discovery, the unconscious mind, conceals and strengthens its rule through a mechanism of repression.

Until recently many of Marx's works were not available in English translation. And just a few weeks ago the Harvard Department of Economics rejected the proposal of a faculty committee, headed by Nobel Prize-winner Kenneth Arrow, that some knowledge of Marx's ideas be required of graduate students in economic theory. The chairman of the department explained that Harvard expected its students to master the standard body of economic knowledge and then, if they wished, they could study other "interesting things," like Marx. One can well imagine the Department of Psychology at Moscow University saying that once its students had mastered the techniques of Pavlov, there would be no objection if they wanted to read other interesting people, like Freud.

The most common intellectual evasion is to avoid the consequences of Marx's general principles by demonstrating the flaws in his economic analysis of capitalism and its future. It is like denying the unconscious by asserting that Freud was wrong about women.

Marx wrote a century ago, and whatever the validity of his economic descriptions at that time, they refer to a system of production, to economic relationships which no longer exist. Among the distinguishing features of his "capitalism" was the fact that the owner of capital, the capitalist, bargained with the helpless and isolated worker. That does not describe the relationship between General Motors, which no one owns, and the United Automotive Workers, which has the power to shut down production. The vigorous free-market competition, which was an attribute of 19th-century capitalism, remains only in the most nostalgic memory.

Indeed, Marx was right. The "capitalism" of his day was doomed, although he did not foresee either the manner or the consequences of its demise. In any event, one cannot dispose of Marx's understanding of the relationships between economic activity, history and the social process by disproving his technical economics or pointing to flaws in his power of prophecy.

There are at least two ways to destroy the vitality of ideas; by ignoring them or by sanctifying them as a ruling ideology. The social thought of Marx has become the political constitution of the Soviet state. It is made to appear that an attack on the state is an attack on Marx, an absurdly self-contradictory use of Marx's ideas.

If a Marxist critique were made, however, it would reveal a Soviet society dominated by a massive bureaucratic economy not subject to the general or community will and which is, therefore, by Marx's criteria, oppressive. To paraphrase Marx, the Soviet state is merely the organized power of the bureaucratic class for oppressing the working class.

Because Americans usually see social problems in political terms, even when we are intellectually receptive to Marx, we tend to ignore in practice his discovery that economic relations—the way in which wealth is produced—influence all the circumstances and life of society.

Yet it is clear thet those who control the resources of society (not necessarily those who own them—as for example, we all own the Defense Department—but those who direct their use) decide, consciously or not, what we shall receive in exchange for that large portion of our humanity poured out in labor. They determine the structure of our physical environment—of our homes and cities and land—and establish the nature of work. To decide what is to be produced by the resources and knowledge of the entire society, and in what way, is to have control over that external world which begins to form ideas and values from infancy.

Since politics is the creation of civil society, Marx explained, the interests and classes which dominate that society also rule politics. One can no more expect government to attack the sources of economic power than one can anticipate that rock and roll groups will espouse the dissolution of the record industry.

It is not possible, or necessary, to explore Marx's argument fully. A few quotations will make the point:

- "The material life of individuals . . . their mode of production and their form of intercourse . . . are the real basis of the State. These real conditions are not created by the State power; they are rather the power which creates it."
- "Only political superstition believes at the present time that civil life must be held together by the State, when in reality the state is upheld by civil life."

  Since those who control civil life also control the State—
- ". . . The State is the form in which the individuals of a ruling class assert their common interests, and in which the whole civil society of an epoch is epitomized. . . ."

  Or, in more polemical terms—
- "Political power, properly so called, is merely the organized power of one class for oppressing another."

  And in a caution especially to be heeded by Americans, the most political of people:
- ". . . the more political a country is, the less likely it is to seek the basis of social evils and to grasp the general explanation of them . . . in the structure of society, of which the State is the active, conscious and official expression . . . the clearer and more vigorous political thought is, the less it is able to grasp the nature of social evils."

Of course, political power is not pure illusion, whose every act can be traced to the needs of commanding private interests. The institutions and relationships which dominate society are not the entire society. It is largely the quality of political life which determines whether other interests will also be protected. There are many matters vital to human freedom and well-being—compassion and help for the poor, protection of civil liberties, justice for minorities—whose resolution will not challenge the structure of economic power or the reach of economic bureaucracy. There are a multitude of suffering and oppressed—in the Mississippi Delta or Northern ghettos, incarcerated in prisons or housing projects for the elderly—whose fate will not affect the assets or market control of IBM. These must rely upon that sense of justice which a people express, in part, through their political institutions.

And even though the political structure is the creation of civil society, it is also part of that society, and influences the claims and the behavior of important private interests. There could be, for example, no Ralph Nader or consumer movement in a country like the Soviet Union where political and economic power have been fused.

Moreover, private interests, even the most powerful, have divergent needs and purposes. The skill with which political leadership reconciles such conflicts affects the well-being of society; while failure, as in the 1850s or during the early days of the labor movement, means that force, not politics, will decide the issue.

Despite those reforms which politics does accomplish, we must resist the idea that political authority is superior to the private relationships which govern civil society. To attribute to the government a power to alter the society in any fundamental way is to assume that the City of Washington, like the City of God, hovers somewhere outside or beyond the social process and the forces which rule it. It is thus made transcendent, revealing that we are in the presence of mystic revelation, a belief resistant to the contradictions of experience and logic.

Political faith, which is nowhere stronger than in America, diverts the energies of discontent and the purposes of those anxious for social change into the struggle of parties and candidates, thus reducing the possibilities of serious challenge to private power. Even the most enlightened politics will withdraw its support once movements for social change seriously threaten ruling economic relationships.

The civil rights movement of the Sixties made rapid progress only until it became an economic movement whose goals required large amounts of money, new union policies and changes in the patterns of employment. The collision was fatal, especially as it coincided with a period of relative economic stagnation. More recent forms of protest, such as consumerism or the environment movement, have discovered a willingness to yield only until the sources of dominant social power appear to be threatened. While many of those changes in social behavior which appear to be a successful revolution, sexual or drug, are fully consistent with the ideology of an economic structure which depends upon the readiness of people, i.e., consumers, to gratify their individual desires.

There are times when government seems to be responsible for fundamental social change. In all cases, however, if we examine historical conditions more closely, we will find it is responding to previous shifts in the distribution of social power. Indeed, the greatest virtue of the American political system has been its capacity to ratify and legitimate the outcome of social conflict without prolonged and violent turmoil. The Jacksonian revolution of 1828 was a response to the shift of population and economic activity away from the Eastern domain of the Founding Fathers. For reasons similar to these, the Eastern establishment, the ministers of finance, no longer directs the fortunes of the Republican party. And the Supreme Court's "one man, one vote" decision in 1966 was a belated recognition that we had become an urban society.

Our afflictions require basic changes in the direction of society, and, therefore, new forms of control over our resources and productive capacity; in that pursuit, the ability to respond to changing social power is the most important quality of American politics.

The modern economy depends on the middle class—those of low income as well as the more affluent—on its skills and labor and, more importantly, on its capacity and willingness to consume. The income and savings of the middle class—not the accumulated wealth of owners and managers—are the source of corporate assets and earnings.

This economic reality has not been translated into economic power because the middle class is fragmented, lacking either a common purpose or the understanding of causes and possibilities from which a common purpose might evolve. Yet it is their freedom, the possibilities of their existence, which is being constricted by the process of modern life.

The road to social change, therefore, lies in mobilizing and organizing the discontented majority, not simply to elect a president or reform the nomination process, but to understand and

353

assert their wants and interests against the forces which now rule their lives. It is organized purpose which transforms economic importance into economic power. And that power alone can create the political leadership which history may later enshrine as the bearer of a more liberating time.

SHELDON S. WOLIN

From Jamestown to San Clemente

The Watergate affair raised profound questions not only about the Nixon presidency but also about the American political system. Were the Nixon years an aberration or were they in some deeper sense the logical fulfillment of tendencies present in the national political climate at least since the beginning of the Cold War era? After being sworn into office President Ford attempted to soothe an agitated nation into believing that the "long nightmare" was indeed over: "Our Constitution works, our great Republic is a government of laws and not of men." But in the following essay written shortly after the Ford inaugural, political scientist Sheldon Wolin draws quite different conclusions about Watergate.

[The question a member of the House Judiciary Committee asked—"How in the world did we get from the *Federalist Papers* to the edited transcript?"—] is likely to be forgotten quickly, overborne by the universal relief following Nixon's resignation and by the new myth which is beginning to take hold already. The new myth turns relief into national self-congratulation, old fears and outrage into childish fantasies: it tells us that the near-impeachment of Nixon proves that "the system works" and that, therefore, it is time to return to the real business of government. The courts have upheld the rule of law; Congress has discharged its constitutional duties in exposing the misdeeds of the President; a new president has been installed; and we may even expect that, in 1976, the opposition party will peacefully regain the presidency.

Before we are wholly numbed by the refrain "the system has worked," we may want to raise a few questions: What is the sense in which the system has worked? What system is it that has worked? What system is it that is working when, for the first time, we now have a president who, in no sense, has been elected;

who is the hand-picked appointee of the man who was nearly impeached; and who has now presented us with our second un-elected vice president in less than a year?

The most common answer to the first question is that Nixon was almost impeached by the system prescribed in the law and the Constitution and carried out in various ways by the courts, House and Senate committees, and special prosecutors. The common answer, however, has an uncommon side that is likely to be expressed by professional politicians, lawyers, and political scientists when they try to explain the sense in which the system has worked. The system was successful because it kept the issue of Nixon's removal within the narrowest possible legal bounds. Beginning with the investigations of the Ervin committee, continuing through the House committee's debates on the articles of impeachment, and persisting in the present efforts to protect Nixon from prosecution, there has been an unrelenting pressure to confine the issues to legal categories, the hearings to courtroom norms, and the abuses to the standard of the criminal law. The pressures came not only from the President's lawyers but from congressmen and senators as well. They worked to prevent a broad political debate about our recent past and the continuing crisis in our national life.

The surface signs of the crisis were first evident in 1968 at the turbulent convention of the Democratic party when two things became visible: the emergence of the presidency as an immense apparatus of power and the Vietnam war as the measure of its uncontrollability. The special significance of the convention was that, a few months earlier, Johnson had been forced to resign at the end of his first full term. His acknowledgment that he could not run again signified something new in American politics, something that we have been encouraged to forget. Johnson's resignation was not the result of congressional or party pressures, but of the political climate created mainly by the extralegal and unofficial politics which flourished during the Sixties, the politics of the campuses, ghettos, streets, and suburbs. Although the economic demands of minority groups were an important element in the ferment, the peculiar quality of that politics was that it was significantly political and cultural.

The official system was unaccustomed to noneconomic politics in which bargains and trade-offs were not second nature. And so, with the help of psychiatrists and social scientists, the political renewal that took place was diagnosed either as a "generational" revolt (although that analysis was forgotten when all of the young Nixon men went before the bar) or as confusion on the part of the middle class about the proper relationship between revolution and deprivation. Nonetheless, the political culture of the Sixties persisted, penetrating the movies, the press and television, schools, and everyday life, and preparing the American consciousness for the unthinkable, the indictment of its highest official and symbol of national unity.

Without that preparation, it is doubtful that Nixon would have ever resigned. From the outset Congress did not want either resignation or impeachment; it accepted the latter course not simply because Nixon forced it or because the evidence was overwhelming, but because impeachment afforded a better chance of limiting the scope of the problem. At the same time that Congress was instinctively trying to prevent new political forms and values from entering the official system, it was also defending a political system significantly different from the one prescribed by the Constitution. The system that "worked" is the one familiar to political and social scientists: the system that mutes issues and screens out popular dissidence; a system which is affiliated to the idea of democracy only by rhetoric and whose highest art is to encourage democratic illusions without arousing democratic expectations. This system has a constitution but it is not confined to the Constitution. It stretches beyond the president, Congress, the civilian and military bureaucracies, the major political parties, to include the corporate structures of business, agro-business, and finance, big science and education, trade unions, and the press and television.

It would be foolish to contend that this system has stage-managed the recent spectacle of Watergate; but it is correct to say that it succeeded in establishing limits to the controversy and controlling its effects. It will give us the phony issue of campaign expenditures, knowing full well that no one is going to legislate big money out of politics unless they mean to destroy the existing party system and the network of influence which connects politics to the power centers of society. It will not tolerate, however, reopening the question of the secret bombing of Cambodia because that would inevitably raise the great question of presidential power.

The reason why that question is a sensitive one and why, since the Gulf of Tonkin resolution, Congress has raised it only halfheartedly is that the inflation of presidential power has become a fundamental part of the new constitution.

Several years ago a famous constitutional scholar observed that the end of World War II marked the completion of a constitutional revolution in which our system had evolved from a constitution of restraints to a constitution of powers. Subsequently any "reasonable" exercise of power would be countenanced by the courts so long as procedural niceties were respected. The main beneficiaries of the new system were the president and, through him, the civilian and military bureaucracies. But at the same time that governmental power was being increased, the structures of power outside government were also increasing: big business was joined by big labor, big education by big science. Since each thrived on expansion and growth, it was inevitable thet they should realize their dependence on one another.

They learned, too, that the presidency was the one political institution which possessed the power to galvanize expansion. Congress was too fragmented in its leadership to serve as anything but a tactical device, useful when obstruction was called for. All that was needed to complete the new constitution was for its constituent parts to realize how to convert dissidence into a force for expansion. If, for example, women and minorities could be taught to package their demands in the form of economic opportunities within the system, then the forces of change would be linked to economic expansion and made to promote the power of the new system.

A notable example of how the new system has reshaped the old is in the institution of the opposition party. The traditional justification for a two-party system is that the party out of power will help to control the party in power by exposing misbehavior and proposing alternatives. To be sure, we have all become educated to believe that no substantial differences distinguish the two major parties; but we had not been prepared for the policy of silence which the Democratic party has observed since the summer of 1972. The reason, of course, is obvious: the Democrats hope to inherit the system that produced Watergate.

It might seem that the role of opposition party has been picked up by the press, which discovered Watergate and kept it alive.

This interpretation is plausible if we remember that the mass media belong to the same system of power which has been super-imposed on the traditional constitutional arrangements. Its affiliations are with big business and finance, advertising, big science, and the multiversity. If this is true, then it is possible to explain the tenacity with which the press and the networks pursued Richard Nixon.

From the beginning the Nixon Administration served notice of its intention to "get" the media, or rather, their most powerful representatives. The situation came to a head in the court battle over the Pentagon Papers. It was clear then that the press was fighting for its existence not as defined by the First Amendment but as defined by the new constitution of corporate structures. Nixon could get away almost indefinitely with violations of the old Constitution if he had not egregiously threatened the new system. Anyone who has doubts about the system to which the loyalties of the media are attached need only recall the media's treatment of the movements of the Sixties. That experience, combined with the Eagleton affair, the McGovern campaign, and, now, Nixon's resignation, reveal the new role of the press and television in our new system: they are the power that defines the tolerable limits of deviation within the new system.

It is, then, the new system that has worked to produce Nixon's resignation and to prevent his impeachment. Its success has obscured what should have been the ultimate political significance of Watergate and of Richard Nixon. Watergate was America's first genuine experience of tyranny. The Huston Plan, the role of the FBI and CIA, the attempts to bribe and corrupt the courts, the efforts to make the federal bureaucracy into an instrument of ideology, the studied contempt for Congress, the promotion of repressive legislation—it is a catalogue of abuses fit to be placed alongside the list which the colonists attached to the Declaration of Independence.

But Nixon's tyranny was not George III's. In his inept and visionless way he was the underlaborer of the new system, clearing away the debris of the old system, accomplishing his task in a faceless, private way, indifferent to the value of public things except as pomp or squalid profit, preaching political quietism in the guise of the work ethic. It is fitting that technological society, which dwarfs men by things, should have found so mean an instrument.

EDWARD WEISBAND and THOMAS FRANCK

Growing Up Toward Ethical Autonomy

In the early stages of the antiwar protest, demonstrators were condemned as much for their comportment as for their message about
the dangers of America's presence in Southeast Asia, for their willingness to choose obedience to their own moral imperatives over adherence to the policies of their government. In their book *Resignation
in Protest*, from which the following selection is taken, Edward Weis-
band and Thomas Franck consider the same problem at the level
of government. Reflecting both on the lack of protest in the Nixon
Administration against the abuses culminating in Watergate and also
on the absence of principled public stands by Robert McNamara,
John Gardner, and other of Johnson's cabinet officials who eventually came to oppose the war, the authors conclude that the cultural
emphasis on "teamwork" raises serious issues for the future of
American government. In England a cabinet official with severe reser-
vations about the direction of government would resign in protest
and take a public role of leadership in opposition to these policies.
The fact that such a choice would lead to political suicide in America,
say the authors, is the ultimate consequence of an authoritarian
political atmosphere that, for all its talk about the individual, often
chooses to see personal ethical decisions as evidence only of
disloyalty.

No constitutional change, by itself, can transform a society's view
of what constitutes appropriate behavior by its public officials.
In positing as a positive good the willingness of some top officials
to be publicly "disloyal" to the President, we cut across the deep
grain of social decorum—what people have come to believe is
"meet, right, and our bounden duty." It is this sense of what is
fitting that must be reconsidered.

The social sense of propriety is one to which we are initiated early in life. Very soon we come to learn that decent, honorable persons do not betray the confidences of their peers, do not "squeal" or "tattle tell." This lays the groundwork for the conformist adult. It prepares us for the demands of our employers and our peer groups, convincing us that loyalty and cohesiveness is the highest value of all. Jean Piaget, the leading authority on child development, in an experiment told 100 Swiss primary school children of various ages the following story:

> Once, long ago and in a place very far away from here, there was a father who had two sons. One was very good and obedient, the other was a good sort, but he often did silly things. One day the father goes off on a journey and says to the first son: "You must watch carefully to see what your brother does, and when I come back you shall tell me." The father goes away and the brother goes and does something silly. When the father comes back he asks the first boy to tell him everything. What ought the boy to do?[1]

Piaget posed this problem in order to discover whether the children believed that they should obey the adult and be loyal to the authority and law, or whether they should respect the principle of solidarity with their peers. He found that, among the younger subjects between the ages of six and seven, the predominant reaction was that the parent should be told everything. If the parent asks you to tattle, the small child believes, then it is right to submit completely to that wish. The adult looms larger in the child's life than the brother. Among older children between the ages of eight and twelve, however, the reaction was quite different. Predominantly, they indicated total solidarity with brothers and friends, their peers, against adult authority. Nothing should be volunteered to the parent or teacher. Some of the older children, when told Piaget's story, even felt that they should lie to protect the brother. They felt it wrong to betray an equal for the benefit of an adult.[2]

From this as well as other story-telling experiments with children, Piaget concluded that the more progressed the child's moral judgment, the less willing he is to engage in tattle-telling. The

---

[1]Jean Piaget, *The Moral Judgment of the Child* (New York: The Free Press, 1965), p. 290.
[2]*Ibid.*, pp. 290–293.

morally immature tattler breaks the solidarity of his peer group in favor of adult authority. Piaget postulates two personality types: *le petit saint,* who tattles and ingratiates himself with authority figures, and *le sport,* who sides with his peers and who is regarded by more mature children as a "moral" person.

Except among very young children, tattle-telling is regarded as a serious offense deserving punishment, particularly in the form of exclusion from the group. In the words of a British children's rhyme:

> I know a little girl, sly and deceitful
> Every little tittle-tat she goes and tells the people.
> If you want to know her name, her name is Heather Lee.
> Please, Heather Lee, keep away from me;
> I don't want to speak to you, nor you to speak to me.[3]

Even more venomous is this bit of children's doggerel:

> Tell tale tit,
> Your tongue shall be slit,
> And all the dogs in town
> Shall have a little bit.

Tom Brown's School Days, published in Britain in 1857, presents an excruciating example of a schoolboy's inability to break peer ranks by "squealing" on an older fellow student who has tortured him so severely as to warrant his hospitalization. Many other boys also witnessed the torture, yet though they disapproved, none reported it to the school authorities. This incident amply illustrates the power of the schoolboy peer group to enforce its rules of loyalty.

Children are not alone in deploring the tattler in their ranks. It is part of the adult world's perception of child-rearing that, at a certain state of maturity, children ought to balance respect for parental authority with loyalty to their neighborhood playmates or school chums. This is part of learning to develop reciprocal, mutually beneficial relations with peers. Parents, even at some cost to their own authority, generally want their children to be

---

[3]Dorothy Barclay, "What Tattling Really Tells," *The New York Times,* August 12, 1962, Section VI, p. 46.

"in" with peer groups that can be useful to them, and tend to deem it important that they "get along" with the right pals, learning to recognize in them the potential allies needed to win the battles of life. Thus, after a certain age, parents often ally themselves with the child's peer group in disapproving of tattling. If a child's tattling persists at, say, the age of twelve, parents tend to be worried rather than pleased, fearing arrested development. In Piaget's words, such a child is in danger of becoming a "narrow-minded moralist" with excessive deference to authority figures and no autonomous moral standards.[4]

The social disapproval of tattling remains a factor in group behavior past adolescence and into adulthood. Throughout literature, the "squealer" or tattler is the subject of an opprobrium which reflects this socialization theme. Judas Iscariot, Benedict Arnold, the war prisoner who sides with his captors are all objects of public loathing which attaches to adult tattlers. In the words of one observer of this phenomenon, "Martin Luther seems to be about the only figure of note to make much headway with public opinion after doing an inside job on a corrupt organization."[5] Ibsen's Dr. Thomas Stockmann, in threatening to expose the medical dangers in the therapeutic baths being developed by his enterprising fellow townspeople, is stoned as "an enemy of the people."

Life imitates literature. At the very least, tattlers are generally regarded with scorn. Persons who have "blown the whistle" by speaking up against an organization for which they had been working are perceived—and eventually report that they perceive themselves—as being on an ego trip. *The New York Times*, before committing itself to spreading the word of one adult tattler who had purloined government documents—Daniel Ellsberg—attacked another—Otto Otepka—by calling the latter's revelations to a Senate subcommittee a "dangerous departure from orderly procedures."[6]

In short, the lot of the tattletale in our society, child or parent, is not a happy one—not, that is, after about the age of eight.

This social conditioning against tattle-telling is deplored by some students of the subject. One authority cautions parents to

[4]Piaget, *op. cit.*, pp. 294–95.
[5]Charles Peters and Taylor Branch, *Blowing the Whistle: Dissent in the Public Interest* (New York: Praeger, 1972), p. 19.
[6]*Ibid.*, p. 230.

distinguish between children who are merely ingratiating themselves with authority or trying to do damage to another child from those who are conveying valid information.[7] A child telling his parents that another child is in the process of setting fire to the garage is different from one revealing that his brother has not brushed his teeth after breakfast.

Among adults, it is far more inappropriate to lump together as tattlers all those who convey confidential information damaging to a peer, because in adult life tattling occurs in a different social context and often serves a different purpose. In an adult, tattling can be useful as a check on unbridled authority. It may be as significant a sign of the adult's ethical emancipation as tattle-telling in children may be indicative of arrested moral growth.

This different value that ought to attach to tattling in childhood and in maturity reflects its quite different function and social value at the early and at later stages in the individual's development. As we have seen, the animosity linked with tattle-telling in childhood serves as an indicator and aspect of the child's moral development, attesting to the growth of individuation and a degree of autonomy in place of authority fixation and favor-currying. By discouraging an infant's tendency to tattle, we encourage him or her to develop reciprocal relations with the peer group rather than continue excessive infantile dependence on the superior authority of the adult. Reciprocal dependence is the halfway house on the steep road from parent-authority dependence to ethical emancipation, mature individuation, and responsible self-determination. The child learns to broaden his universe and his sense of responsibility, coming to care about the effects of his conduct on the opinions and responses of both the parents and his peer group, rather just the parents alone.

But in our society, the opprobrium against speaking out or going public, against telling tales out of school, lingers long after it has ceased to be socially functional. Even when most of us have already shed our dependence on parental authority and ceased playing up to mother, father, and teacher, we still feel constrained not to tattle-tell on fellow workers, neighbors, or superiors when we see them breaking the law or acting antisocially.

---

[7]Lawrence Kohlberg, "The Development of Modes of Moral Thinking and Choice in the Years 10 to 16" (Ph.D. dissertation, University of Chicago, 1958), pp. 339, 346.

Our peer group—the profession, club, team, office, social set, political party, White House staff, the President's "official family," or that vague but real establishment of "men who govern"—continues to demand group solidarity, even though such rigorous solidarity may have lost its positive, emancipating social function. Worse, this adult group solidarity tends to be regarded admiringly by the public at large, persons who are not members of the in-group, and who are too often victimized by the in-group's machinations. We tend mindlessly to admire the "virtues" of group loyalty and solidarity quite regardless of the social outcomes.

There are instances, of course, where it is quite appropriate for childhood values of group unity against parents and teachers to continue into adulthood. For example, in a society where a political dictatorship replaces the parent, fostering a new but still immature dominance-dependence relationship with its citizens, a continuing conspiracy of silence, of tight peer-group solidarity against tattlers, may continue to be functional. But in a democracy, where the ultimate government is the people, a rigorous anti-tattling ethic is socially dysfunctional. It is one thing to betray Jesus to the Romans, but obviously quite another to report a fellow airplane passenger to the San Francisco airport authorities for carrying a concealed weapon. Whether adult tattling is very childish or very mature depends on the specific circumstances. In a democratic society, to disclose a fellow citizen's antisocial conduct may be the highest manifestation of ethical autonomy, whether that citizen is a fellow Rotarian, shopworker, the president of General Motors or of the United States. This assumes, always, that the matter being disclosed is one which is properly within the public-policy concerns of the citizens of a democracy. If so, speaking up is an act of courageous maturity, an emancipation from ingrained adolescent peer-group pressures "not to rat."

The very groups of peers which, early in life, helped us emancipate ourselves from infantile parent dependence fight to hold us in the thrall of peer-group dependence. Some people remain Choate old boys, sons of Eli, or Harvard men all their lives. The social sanctions we have developed against those who "tell tales out of school"—again the term is reflective of the level of adolescent development it reinforces—can prevent the adult from breaking out of dependence on his peer group to achieve a new level of responsible reciprocal relationship with the community as a whole. It may reinforce the adult's tendency, learned in childhood, to think of his responsibilities in terms of the team or clique, without attaining a higher level of responsibility to a larger community consisting of his nation or, even, all humanity.[8] Serpico, the New York cop whose revelations of police corruption triggered the Knapp Commission, was led into a near-fatal ambush and hounded out of the force by his fellows because "He had broken an unwritten code that in effect put policemen above the law, that said a cop could not turn in other cops."[9] As he discovered, the road to ethical autonomy can be lonely and sometimes even dangerous.

A higher consciousness of one's wider responsibility to society—beyond the peer group—is, however, the apex of personal maturity. And it is equally functional to individual self-emancipation and to the collective survival of an interdependent world. Paradoxically, it is only through the extension of our individual sense of responsibility to an all encompassing humanity that we attain true responsibility to ourselves—not in partiality, as son, fraternity member, or White House aide, but as a total, autonomous singular being. "The greatest thing in the world," Montaigne said, "is to know how to belong to ourselves." Each of us comes to belong to himself to the extent that he perceives himself as *one* of *all*. Our reciprocal special relations with "teams" are most mature if they are in the context of an overriding responsibility to our society and to humanity.

Professor Lawrence Kohlberg of Harvard has pointed out the flaw in Piaget's contention that the moral maturity of a person can be measured merely by his recognition of reciprocal relationships with his peer groups. Such reciprocal relations, he says, may play a role in emancipating a child from parent-authority dependence, but this progress is achieved by substituting group-authority dependence. It has been observed that the child learns to establish "I'll scratch your back if you'll scratch mine" relations with members of a gang, club, clique, and prep-school class, then carries this apparently successful way of "getting along" into his or her Ivy League college, fraternity, and sorority, and, even, in later life, the department where he works, or the Presidential

---

[8] Pressures to uniformity in groups is comprehensively analyzed in Dorwin Cartwright and Alvin Zander, eds., *Group Dynamics*, 3rd ed. (New York: Harper & Row, 1968), esp. pp. 139–51.

[9] Peter Maas, *Serpico* (New York: The Viking Press, 1973), p. 23.

Administration in which he serves.[10] Yet, the development of peer-group loyalty is only one step toward the ultimate goal of growing up, of self-emancipation, of becoming an autonomous being capable of making principled decisions on the basis of one's own internalized values without excessive fear of displeasing the authorities, the group, or the law. The final stage of the moral evolution of the individual, according to Kohlberg and others,[11] comes when life decisions and actions are rooted in an autonomous, principled judgment of right and wrong, in full consciousness of responsibility to the larger social community.

This definition does not prejudge the social utility of any particular decision made by an individual, but only the degree of genuine autonomy with which decisions are made and whether they are made by reference to generalized principles of right conduct that are genuinely those of the individual—i.e., which he has freely and deliberately chosen and made his own. In other words, adult tattle-tellers may be the most mature, the most autonomously principled, of adults if by going public they are breaking out of group conformity to inform the entire community of something it ought to know. But most members of society, still living in the early stages of the growing child's moral development, continue to regard the practice with disgust and disdain. Many an official who might have resigned from government in public protest against the Vietnam escalation has reported an unwillingness to be seen as a traitor by his "team" and a tattle-tale by his countrymen.

That no major figures in the Johnson or Nixon Administrations quit and spoke up in protest during the Vietnam war or Watergate

[10]Barclay, *op. cit.*

[11]See, for example, Piaget, *op. cit.*, and the works of Kohlberg, including *op. cit.*, and "Development of Moral Character and Moral Ideology," in M. L. and L. W. Hoffman, *Review of Child Development Research* (New York: Russell Sage Foundation, 1964); "Stage and Sequence: The Cognitive-Developmental Approach to Socialization," in David Goslin, *Handbook of Socialization Theory and Research* (Chicago: Rand McNally, 1969); for other writers that differ in some respects with Piaget and Kohlberg but confirm the validity of their observations as stated above regarding the nature and development of principled autonomous judgment in children, consult Robert Peck and Robert Havighurst, *The Psychology of Character Development* (New York: John Wiley and Sons, 1964); Havighurst and Hilda Taba, *Adolescent Character and Personality* (New York: John Wiley and Sons, 1967): Elizabeth B. Hurlock, *Child Development*, 4th ed. (New York: McGraw-Hill, 1964); William A. Kay, *Moral Development: A Psychological Study of Moral Growth from Childhood to Adolescence* (New York: Schocken Books, 1969).

is a comment, therefore, not solely on the ethical state of the men who occupy high office, but also on the ethical climate of the nation. We positively do not *want* to be told. We reject those who break faith with the system, even if they do it to keep faith with us. We prefer officials to be loyal to the President even if they are thereby disloyal to the constitution and themselves. The men and women at the breaking point in the executive branch know this, and trim accordingly.

Obviously, going public is not invariably the mark of the ethically emancipated adult. A person may rightly be stigmatized for tattle-telling when he reveals confidential information the publication of which is not necessary to the well-being of those to whom it is revealed. An adult, like a child, may "rat" not out of a sense of obligation to society but solely in order to ingratiate himself with those in authority, for personal gain and publicity, or to damage rivals gratuitously. Those involved in the Watergate scandal who bargained for reduced sentences or immunity, in return for giving evidence against colleagues, are fairly stigmatized to the extent that they spoke up only because—and when—it served their personal interests rather than out of conviction that the nation needed to be told. But an official resigning over Vietnam and speaking out against the Kennedy, Johnson, or Nixon policies of escalation could not be suspected of doing so in deference to authority—the full weight of Presidential power would have come down against him or her—nor in the hope of personal gain. Only in the years after 1968 could a public antiwar stand be suspected of being politically opportune, and then only for persons intending to run for elected office from certain primarily urban parts of the country or seeking the favor of certain of the media. Yet officials like Charles Frankel who resigned and, to a limited extent, expressed their negative views of Presidential policies report the pressures from others, and from their own internal social conditioning, to maintain a "decent" silence about what they had seen and heard.

Social psychologists have begun to make some progress in the scientific measurement of our pilgrimage toward ethical autonomy. Kohlberg postulates six measurable levels which help us verify the relation between an individual's ethical maturity and, for example, his willingness to speak out against the team. Some further recent experiments conducted by New York University graduate students under our supervision indicate that, in a group of 96 law students at New York University, there could be found a distinct pattern of direct correlation between their willingness to go public in a dispute with authority and their level of moral development as measured by tests based on Kohlberg's theoretical six stages.[12] There thus appears to be a connection between the individual's stage of moral development and his or her ethical autonomy.

Kohlberg's work suggests that higher levels of moral development are more likely to be found in persons actively and broadly involved in social and interactional roles in the community.[13] Politicians, at least some of those who succeed in being elected to important state or Congressional office, fit this description. They have learned to listen to many points of view and many voices but have also acquired the habit of eventually making their own decisions, for which they are accountable not to a small, tightly knit organization or group but to a variegated public. This could conceivably be one more reason to surround the President with a political rather than a banker-lawyer cabinet.

Ultimately, however, a transformation in the structure of the executive branch depends upon a change in the level of moral maturity and ethical autonomy, not only of the cabinet but of the American public. The lesson of the Vietnam and Watergate eras is not merely that the government must be populated with ethically autonomous persons able to resist their President and, if necessary, to quit and take their case to the public. Of what use is it to go public if the public has been conditioned to despise and mistrust those who violate confidences, to turn a deaf ear to those who place the dictates of their own consciences before loyalty to "the Chief"? What hope is there for a true systemic transformation as long as the public extracts fearsome price from those who try to open crucial policy dialogues to the public? Not that Americans should line the streets to cheer anyone who quits the cabinet and tells everything he knows to *The Washington Post*.

---

[12]Joseph H. Moskowitz and Bertram I. Spector, "Profiles of the Growler and the Insider: Two Styles of Dissent in Government," New York University Center for International Studies, unpub. manuscript, 1974.

[13]Kohlberg, dissertation, pp. 140–142: Richard Kramer, "Changes in Moral Judgment Response Patterns During Late Adolescence and Young Adulthood: Retrogression in a Developmental Sequence" (Ph.D. dissertation, University of Chicago, 1968), p. 44; Kohlberg and Kramer, "Continuities and Discontinuities in Childhood and Adult Moral Development," *Human Development*, vol. 12, 1969, 100–101.

But acts of public protest should be judged on their merits, not by a reflexive social condemnation of tattlers.

Vietnam and Watergate: the names are synonymous with insufficiently fettered Presidential discretion. If America is ever to construct a working system of checks and balances within the executive branch, it will have to revise its judgment of those who exercise their option to "exit" with "voice." It will have to excuse, and even reward, that disloyalty to a President which bespeaks a higher loyalty to the democratic system.

Such a popular acceptance of disloyalty at the top will have to grow out of a much more universal inventory of the costs and benefits of the American emphasis on team play, at all levels of social and political organization. Our society will have to reconsider whether, and to what purpose, it wants to continue to reward nonautonomous and punish autonomous behavior in a wide range of institutional settings.

If we were asked by an official like George Ball whether, in 1966, after resigning, he should have led a public campaign against the Johnson Administration's Vietnam policies, our answer would be something like this: "Yes, for the sake of the republic, for the good of the democratic political system, as well as for the cause of Vietnam disengagement. It would have been very useful to have had you take a lead in the antiwar movement. It would have restored the faith of the young in the system, would have given credibility and weight to the war's opponents, would have created the basis for an informed, civilized public debate of the Vietnam issues. But it would also, in all probability, have ended your political career and led to your being ostracized by the professional and social circles in which you work and relax. It would have brought you to a severe crisis of self-esteem. You have spent your life as a team player, a loyal peer-grouper. You would suddenly have found yourself being categorized as a non-team-player by that small elite on whose amiability your professional and private life is built. The costs to you would have been enormous."

It has not been the point of this book that men like George Ball should pay these costs, although we would be less than candid if we did not admit to a vast admiration for the few, like William Jennings Bryan, who spent themselves heedlessly for the public weal and for their principles, without concern for the costs to their careers.

But it is unrealistic to expect many senior officials at the top of what Disraeli called "the greasy pole" to be unmindful of costs. Only a fanatic would climb to the top of that pole in order to immolate himself, no matter how brightly his light would shine. It would be unhealthy for the executive branch to be heavily populated by men and women of such unshakable ethical autonomy, for they would probably make government both more difficult and more dangerous in their unbending self-assertiveness and reckless rectitude.

It follows that, while we would applaud a higher incidence of strongly self-assertive consciences in the immediate vicinity of the White House, we believe that a better balance within the executive branch can best be attained not by surrounding the President with persons of iron principles, cheerfully willing to sacrifice everything, but by lowering the costs the ordinarily ambitious political aspirant must pay to have, and to manifest, a healthy amount of ethical autonomy.

We believe that, in a different institutional setting, the kinds of men and women who now elect to remain silent could persuade themselves to speak up. . . . And the costs of resigning would certainly be less if the public were to decide to lower them: by respecting the dissident, the man or woman who refuses to subordinate his conscience or his duty to the public, and by weighing thoughtfully what he has to say, rewarding or punishing in accordance with the social importance and political validity of his or her dissent.

"Unhappy the land that needs a hero," Brecht's Galileo says to us. Inevitably, the fate of the republic will, from time to time, depend on the emergence of a hero. And heroes will emerge bidden or not. Yet the system ought not to be built on them, but on normally ambitious, reasonably benevolent, relatively mature persons who do the right thing because they are encouraged—or at least are not drastically discouraged—to live up to their own highest ideals and ethical standards.

DAVE DELLINGER

Countering Society's Inhibition on Love, Trust, and Democracy

The mid-1960s witnessed a radical break with a past that had stretched back without interruption or challenge to the early years of the Second World War. First civil rights workers and then antiwar activists broke through the Cold War consensus and raised serious questions about the nature of American society. Were the country's institutions infected with racism? Was the nation dependent on a permanent war economy? Was it ruled by a corporate elite?

Although a measure of "normalcy" appears to have returned with the final withdrawal from Vietnam and the Nixon resignation, such questions remain unanswered. More than a handful of protestors have been left with doubts about the future. A poll taken by the Hart Associates in July 1975, for instance, revealed that a surprising 33 percent of those responding felt that "American capitalism had peaked," while 41 percent felt that "things must change from what they are at present." With international crises in oil and food supplies and the global change from a bipolar power organization based on the United States–Soviet Union confrontation to a multipolar one involving China and the Third World as well, these tides of change are affecting the world at large.

One of those interested in the shape of future American society is Dave Dellinger, community organizer for thirty years, pacifist, and one of the Chicago Seven defendants tried for the disturbances at the 1968 Democratic Convention. While the following selection is more or less addressed to the remnants of the "movement," it raises issues that have a broader relevance.

Between 1956 and 1973 there were times when the movement engaged in civil-rights and antiwar campaigns seemed little short of miraculous, with its commitment, inventiveness, solidarity, sense of humor, and rejection of both establishment hypocrisy and leftist dogma. But anyone who worked full time as a movement organizer for a few months or more knew that it was riddled with contradictions. This was probably most clear to women and blacks.

It was a movement capable of expressing incredible energy and love one week and of collapsing into indifference or pompous factionalism the next. Too many of us vacillated between euphoria at our imagined self-liberation from a money-grubbing, power-seeking, uptight society and depression at the failure of our new life style to bring unremitting happiness or of our new politics to achieve a speedy reversal of policies that began with slavery and doing to the Indians what the United States was trying to do to the Indochinese. There was far too much emphasis on expanding consciousness through the shortcuts offered by drugs and superficial sexual encounters and not enough on the hard work and self-discipline required in order to attain lasting spiritual growth and mutually satisfying interpersonal relationships. It was a movement whose members frequently were ready to die for a black sharecropper or for Vietnamese peasants but whose males and females rarely knew how to interact as equals. In the late sixties it was a movement which, for all its emphasis on racial equality and its history of civil-rights struggle, was shocked into action when white students were killed at Kent State but could only turn out a few hundred hard-core activists when black students were killed at Orangeburg, Jackson State, and Southern University.

It wasn't as if the press made it easy for the American people to respond equally to events that were of equal importance to anyone believing in the unity of the human family. It made headlines of some of these events and treated others as if they were minor incidents. The families of the black victims were not given equal time with the families of the white students, who were shown in tears on national television and were quoted and photographed for weeks in the press. It would be interesting to know, for example, how many readers can even identify the Orangeburg massacre. On February 8, 1968, South Carolina highway patrolmen fired buckshot into a crowd of demonstrating students, killing three of them. The press reported that an "exchange of gunfire" had occurred, with officials quoted as saying that the students "fired first." Later it was established that *none* of the blacks had been armed. Nine patrolmen were acquitted of all charges in a federal trial, five of them after having received promotions. Cleveland Sellers, a gentle and much-beloved member of the Student Nonviolent Co-ordinating Committee, who had frequently been beaten, jailed, and shot at during the course of his work, was convicted of incitement to riot. Apparently he was selected because of his persistence and effectiveness. Sellers lost his appeal in the federal courts and more than four years after the murder of his comrades had to leave a teaching job at Cornell University to serve five months in a southern jail. In the meantime, white police officers shot and killed two black students at Jackson State College, Mississippi, in May 1970, and two more black students at Southern University, Baton Rouge, Louisiana, in November 1972. In neither instance was any officer convicted of any crime.

We are a movement whose members are still being crippled by the society from which we are trying to free ourselves and others. Contrary to some interpretations, the movement's erraticism and inconsistency tell us more about the sickness of the society against which we are in revolt—and about the corrosive effects of that sickness on all the members of that society—than about any immutable limitations imposed by human nature. This cannot be proven scientifically, at least not to the satisfaction of those who have not experienced the kind of human nature that flowers from time to time in movement endeavors. But as Susan Sontag has pointed out, "Someone who has enjoyed . . . a reprieve, however brief, from the inhibition on love and trust this society enforces is never the same again."[1] Or as Emma Goldman wrote half a century earlier:

> Poor human nature, what horrible crimes have been committed in thy name! . . . The greater the mental charlatan, the more definite his insistence on the wickedness and weakness of human nature. Yet how can one speak of it today, with every soul in a prison, with every heart fettered, wounded and maimed? John Burroughs has stated that experimental study of animals in captivity is absolutely useless. Their character, their habits, their appetites undergo a complete transformation when torn from their soil in field and forest. With human nature caged in a narrow space, whipped daily into submission, how can we speak of its potentialities?

[1]Susan Sontag, *Trip to Hanoi*, Farrar, Straus, and Giroux, p. 90.

> Freedom, expansion, opportunity and, above all, peace and re-
> pose, alone, can teach us the real dominant factors of human nature
> and all its wonderful possibilities.[2]

The reprieves granted by the movement from society's inhibi-
tions on love and trust are brief and erratic, but they give us
a glimpse of human possibilities that make it impossible for most
of us ever again to accept the cynical assumptions of the present
society about human nature. We can no longer believe with Richard Nixon and millions of alienated Americans that "no other
motive, no matter how noble-sounding, can replace the profit
motive." We can no longer believe that the best way to deal with
bank robbers (or as revolutionaries, with robber bankers) is to im-
prison or execute them. We can no longer believe with the idola-
tors of Chairman Mao that in the struggle to do away with violence
and injustice "all power comes out of the barrel of a gun." We
may not have learned yet how to deepen, regularize, and fully
apply the alternative motives and methods of power we have
experienced, but for many of us the faith that this can be done
and the attempt to do so is what the movement is about.

The movement's very failings are tributes to its relevance. The
contrast between our best experiences and our worst teaches us
the urgency of creating an environment that will be more favorable to the development of a new human than the environment
that produced us. We have learned in Mississippi, in jail, and
at the siege of the Pentagon that to be human can be beautiful.
We are working for the day when "human *is* beautiful," because
human nature is nurtured in a society that is dedicated to that
proposition.

By contrast, the professional patriots of both the Center and
the Right seem to hope that the energy and hope of the sixties
will be submerged in the cynicism and despair of the seventies.
From the liberal media to Richard Nixon, they comment with
undisguised glee on every sign of movement confusion or re-
treat—as if the country should be pleased and reassured if those
who have been trying to fulfill the American dream are thwarted,
frustrated, and discouraged. No matter how much the liberals
and the Right-wingers may hate each other or struggle against

---

[2]Emma Goldman, *Anarchism: What It Really Stands For,* reprinted in *Nonviolence in America: A Documentary History;* Staughton Lynd, editor; Bobbs-Merrill.

each other for dominance, they agree in condemning all movement initiatives that try to operate outside the narrow limits of
conventional electoral politics or that cannot in some manner be
controlled from above by those of lesser vision and greater access
to the present instruments of wealth and political power. They
shudder at attempts to reintroduce the revolutionary enthusiasm
and unpredictability of the country's birth and early years.

Ironically, these paper patriots constantly declared their faith
in American democracy, but the operative word is "American,"
not "democracy." Their approach to every crisis—from recurring
assassinations to the war in Vietnam, from the Pentagon Papers
to Watergate—is to handle it in a way that will preserve the people's faith in the existing American system. None of them speaks
of developing a system which is based on faith in the people,
though in theory that was the original goal of the American experiment. I cannot recall a single editorial or political speech by liberal
critics of Watergate seriously suggesting that we try to reorganize
either the government or the society to help restore the people's
faith in themselves. Yet without it there can be no day-to-day
democracy, though there may be periodic elections. In June 1973,
liberal opponents of Richard Nixon were speaking of sparing an
obviously guilty Nixon in order to preserve the people's faith in
the presidency. A few were speaking of impeaching him in order
to accomplish the same objective. The time may come rather
rapidly when they will agree to get rid of him in order to cover
up for the system, much as they sacrificed Lyndon Johnson in
1968, in order to be able to continue the war a little longer without
completely destroying the people's faith in the system. In 1968
the country had turned against the war, and they had to do something dramatic to appease the people. They decided to get rid
of Johnson so that they would not have to get rid of the war.
In 1973 or 1974, a majority of those in Congress and a majority
of those whose money and power influences Congress will save
or destroy Nixon not because they agree or disagree with his
brutal, undemocratic politics, not because they think he is guilty
or innocent of major crimes against Indochinese and Americans,
but because they estimate that that is the best way to head off
popular initiatives to probe the workings of the system and to
make it significantly more democratic. If they think that it will
help tame popular indignation and revolt, they will gladly unite

behind a Gerald Ford, who, as a member of the Warren Commission, is guilty of a far more devastating cover-up than Nixon's cover-up of Watergate, the cover-up of the Kennedy assassination.

The insistence of prejudging and predetermining the range of allowable remedies for a sickness as deep and pervasive as that revealed by Vietnam and Watergate is in itself a violation of democracy: The outcome of a genuinely democratic process must always be unpredictable and beyond the control of any elite of political managers. Insofar as the corporate and governmental trustees of the people's will are able to control events, they allow the public to have only as much information as they think is good for it. Nixon is not alone in both withholding and tampering with information that might disillusion or inflame the public. Every branch of the government does the same, including Congress and the courts. They all regularly "classify," "seal," and conceal information crucial to the public's ability to know what is going on and do something about it.[3]

With corporate control of the mass media, the public is not allowed to participate directly in the major debates, let alone the decision-making. A public debate is thought to be one in which the public is allowed to listen to the spokesmen for rival cliques, all of whom represent or are beholden to some segment of the power elite. The struggle for democracy is reduced to a struggle to force the representative of the "in" faction to debate the challenger from the "out" faction, or to force the President to hold a press conference at which the establishment press can ask questions. Some of the questions may be embarrassing to the incumbent and useful to the public, but they do not come from the people, let alone from people who oppose the system, whether from its Left or its Right. George Wallace and Spiro Agnew were certainly correct when they accused the liberal press of looking down on the people and failing to mirror their interests, even though both men may be dishonorable and their reasons for making the charge may have been self-serving.

---

[3]In the contempt trial that grew out of the conspiracy trial of the Chicago Seven, we chanced upon a tape of conversations between Judge Hoffman and another judge, made when the court reporter turned her machine on too soon. They revealed the judge's determination to convict us long before the government had presented its case, but we were not allowed to use it in our case or publicize it in press conferences on a theory of judicial privilege that paralleled Nixon's claims of presidential privilege.

During the war years, when several thousand underground papers were flourishing, not to mention the college press and college- and listener-sponsored radio stations, to the best of my knowledge none of these was ever allowed to take part in a presidential news conference. Even after all the polls reported that a *majority* of the country opposed continuation of the war in Vietnam, there never was any mechanism whereby the organized antiwar movement, which had led the way in arousing the opposition, could confront the President or Congress in public debate or even at a news conference.

In March 1965, the movement devised its own partial substitute for this lack of genuinely democratic dialogue in the United States. It organized teach-ins at which opponents of the war and its defenders from the State Department or Pentagon could present their conflicting views. The results were disastrous for the prowar apologists, and the government soon refused to let its spokesmen participate. For a while their refusal was dramatized by placing an empty chair, marked "State Department," in a conspicuous place on the platform.

Later, denied debate, sections of the movement fell into the trap of crowding into halls where government spokesmen were scheduled to speak in splendid isolation and trying to prevent them from speaking or at least from being heard. In my view this tactic (which more recently has been repeated in the case of *debates* arranged with William Shockley, who argues that blacks are genetically inferior) is wrong in principle and ultimately counterproductive in its effects. At first it may have communicated legitimate anger and seriousness of concern, but it soon degenerated into hooliganism, or at least the appearance of hooliganism. It promoted the dangerous notion that free speech is an expedient rather than a principle. Even from the point of view of expedience it was a bad tactic, since it is easier for local and national authorities to deny us effective freedom to be heard than it is for us to deny them—a fact tacitly recognized by those who argue that the tactic is justified since under existing power relationships effective free speech is a myth. Worse, it identified the movement in the public mind with the totalitarian practices of Soviet bloc countries. It violated the public's sense of fair play and hardened movement sensibilities. Finally, it reduced the likelihood that searching questions or brief interjections could expose the flabbiness and dishonesty of the government's position in the manner accomplished (admittedly under more favorable circumstances) in the early teach-ins. I do not mean to suggest that before or after the speeches of notorious war criminals, after particularly offensive statements or outside the hall, the protesters could not boo, hiss, chant, or hold aloft signs expressing their condemnations. I do not mean by any means to rule out other forms of dramatic action, such as countergraduations, timed mass walkouts, etc., in which the primary message is opposition to the government or the corporations rather than apparent opposition to free speech and civil liberties.

A great deal is being written today about forcing the President to share some of his power (which is power over *our* lives) with Congress or even with his Cabinet. It is rarely suggested that ways are needed for sharing that power with us, ways of returning power to the people. Outside the movement, there is little if any serious effort to devise methods by which the public airwaves, television channels, and other technological resources can be utilized to transfer decision-making to the people. The networks and President Nixon may be having a bitter personal quarrel, with each trying to destroy the other, but neither one speaks for the people. Neither *is* the people. I don't mean the people as an undifferentiated blob or mass called the public (or in some Left-wing circles, the masses or "the workers"). I mean people in the communities and institutions where they live, work, go to school, make purchases, pay taxes, breathe the air, and re-create; in the communities and relationships they have to leave when they are sent to war or prison.

Today the public is "represented" in far-off Washington by ambitious politicians who, by the most generous analyses, keep one eye on the public and the other on the business and financial interests and sources of governmental power (patronage and contracts) that can make or destroy them in the next election. Between elections the people's political views are expressed through "public opinion" polls conducted by private commercial enterprises (such as Gallup, Harris, Yankelovitch) that decide what questions to ask, how to phrase them, and who to ask. Usually the opinion of the country is authoritatively announced on the basis of a *few hundred* inquiries, sometimes not even face-to-face but on the telephone. The poll takers are under pressure to keep the sampling small because doubling the number of inquiries would double the variable costs and reduce the profits. Once again the profit motive adulterates the product and undermines even this pseudo-democratic procedure. Since we now know that intelligence and aptitude tests have given faulty results for years because of the middle-class biases and verbalisms involved, it is not hard to imagine how faulty the public-opinion polls are, formulated as they are by an educational elite and carried out by middle-class pollsters who seek out (or are most apt to receive an unintimidated response from) their own kind.

An unprecedented development in technology, transportation, and industry in the past hundred years, a population explosion, and a cancerlike drive for power, profits, and national prestige led to a centralization of government and an extension of the territory and numbers of people under its control that was undreamed of by the framers of the Declaration of Independence and the Constitution. From 1790 to 1960, the territory of the United States expanded from 864,000 to 3,628,000 square miles and the population from 3,900,000 to 183,285,000. Yet Washington has powers today that the signers of the Declaration and the framers of the Constitution would never have tolerated—not to mention the powers it asserts over the lives of Asians, Latin Americans, Africans, and Europeans. The centralization of power in Washington was mistakenly encouraged in the thirties by Leftists who assumed that the way to check the power of the banks and corporations was to increase the power of the federal government, forgetting that power corrupts and that the greater the power the greater the ultimate corruption. This was the thirties' parallel to today's illusion that the way to check the power of the presidency is to increase the power of Congress and the separate governmental departments, instead of decentralizing and dispersing power throughout the population. Ironically, the present level of technology now makes possible as well as necessary a revolutionary emphasis on returning power to the people where they live, work, and have their being. The contemporary drives to overcome alienation, powerlessness, and war, expressed most self-consciously through the movement, including the counterculture and groups emphasizing spiritual growth, point in that direction, although in the short run, sections of the movement get deflected into campaigns to get better rulers rather than self-rule.

Today decisions affecting the whole world are made at secret summit meetings between Nixon and Brezhnev, Kissinger and Chou En-lai, men whose authority does not derive in an organic way from the people or functional groups (neighborhoods, factories, etc.) in the countries they presume to represent, though Chou undoubtedly comes the closest. Even less can they legitimately claim to represent the people and institutions in the countries and spheres of influence they seek to divide among themselves, from Czechoslovakia and Cuba to Vietnam, Korea, Pakistan and Sri Lanka, from Zaïre to Saudi Arabia and Venezuela. Because we have been so horrified at the prospect of the catastrophic wars that might result from super-power rivalries, we tend to be grateful for détente and to overlook the long-run implications of tolerating such procedures. It's a mad, mad world, out of touch with the most elementary concepts of democracy or people's decision-making when meetings of two, three, or four super-power tyrants to divide up the world into agreed on "spheres of interest" (read domination and profit) are hailed by their subjects as signs of sanity. Impinging on these meetings and holding separate decision-making meetings of their own are huge transnational corporations, such as ITT, IBM, Exxon, and General Motors, and financial conglomerates whose existence and names are barely known to the people whose lives they interfere with. The beginning of sanity and the possibility of valid worldwide co-operation and solidarity require the return of both corporate and governmental power to local units. From there decision-making can flow outward to embrace countries, regions, and the world, whenever the questions to be decided affect these larger areas.

Today there is nothing in the United States even remotely comparable to the old-fashioned town meetings with which this country began and in which issues were openly debated and decided by the people whose lives were involved (always excepting, of course, black slaves, native Americans, and, in most cases, women). As recently as fifty years ago, when I was growing up in Wakefield, Massachusetts, close to Lexington, Concord, and Boston Harbor, the town meetings were a significant force in the political process. They were not ideal: For one thing, much of their power had already been pre-empted by officials and bureaucrats in Boston and Washington; for another, the mechanisms of class and sexist training, confidence and prestige affected the proceedings, as they still affect all relationships in the United States. But everyone from the town fool to the town radical, from the town laborers to the town multimillionaire had a chance to speak. Town officials had to argue their policies and defend their actions. Sometimes the governor himself had to appear or suffer a serious loss of face. "Meet the Public" in face-to-face encounters had not yet been replaced by "Meet the Press" on the one-way tube.

In the civil-rights and antiwar movements at their best, participants began to rediscover the lost practice of democracy. They began to learn self-reliance, communal solidarity, participatory decision-making, nonelectoral politics, direct action, and local, country-, and worldwide co-operation. They began to experiment with communal interactions and multidimensional coalition programs that gave satisfaction to the minorities in their ranks as well as the majority. They began not only to savor a reprieve from society's inhibition on love and trust but to explore more dynamic methods of asserting their collective will than pulling a lever on a voting machine every two to four years and hoping that the lesser-evil candidate would win and not totally betray her or his campaign promises. No one knows fully what all these alternate methods are or can become, what new sets of checks and balances and initiatives will develop within the practice of a decentralized, more direct democracy. But in a period when the country's indirect, representative democracy clearly excludes 99 per cent of the population from meaningful decision-making, the movement's drive for racial equality, economic justice, and an end to the war led it—almost by accident, as it were—to experiment with corrective measures that can begin to overcome the political powerlessness and apathy of the people.

These attempts to assume and encourage active democratic responsibility for what happens in the country make a lot of people nervous, from Richard Nixon and Gerald Ford to the New York *Times* and Walter Cronkite, from Nelson Rockefeller and Ronald Reagan to Eugene McCarthy, George McGovern, and Teddy Kennedy. One of the reasons some of these men finally wanted to end the war was to kill the antiwar movement. They spoke as if the most exciting development in American politics in more than thirty years—the passionate attempt by a significant proportion of the population to involve itself in decision-making about foreign policy, about the uses to which their work and their lives would be put, about whether their town should shelter a factory manufacturing napalm or fragmentation bombs—was a tragedy. They spoke of the need to put an end to the country's "division and conflict," as if the "experts," representatives, and holders of undemocratic power should not have to face the people whose lives they presently control, as if democracy should be synonymous with tranquility and the existence of a bland national consensus in which political differences are so minor that there is no need for strikes, boycotts, marches, civil disobedience, protest demonstrations, and passionate controversy. No doubt many of these men and other men and women like them were sincerely affronted by the war, shocked by its human toll and by the crude lies and deceptions of the military and the governing administrations. At the same time, their limited conception of democracy, their fear of populist movements, and their own ambitions to play a dominant political role led them to hope that bringing the troops home from Vietnam would cause the people to abandon their democratic initiatives and settle back into passivity. They were desperate to prevent the antiwar movement from maturing into a self-reliant anti-imperialist movement for social justice. They wanted to prove that the system could correct its "mistakes" and curb its "excesses," to convince the American people that they should work through the two discredited parties to make whatever adjustments the system might require. The problem is that the fruits of that system include the CIA; Watergate; ITT; corporate control of the economy (with effective control by less than one half of 1 per cent of the population); the Soviet wheat deal, which led to millions of dollars of private profit and sent the prices of bread and meat skyrocketing; disastrous manipulations of gasoline, fuel oil, and milk; more than five thousand military bases in foreign countries; nuclear warheads; forty million Americans below the poverty level; wire-tapping and other invasions of privacy; prisons; rampant racism and sexism; terrifying rates of mental breakdown, suicide, murder, muggings, drug addiction, alcoholism, and infant mortality; pollution of air, water, soil, and food; and ruthless competition for self-advancement at the expense of love, trust, honesty, and mutual aid.

The spokesmen for conventional politics are trying to convince tired movement veterans and the new generation of youth that a parapolitical movement is automatically doomed to impotence and failure, that democracy must be limited to ward heeling, lobbying, and periodic election of a few leaders who will run the country for the rest of us. James Reston gave typical expression to this defeatist attitude when he wrote shortly after a major escalation of the war that students should

> turn their energies to quiet, legal, political organization. . . . More violence by campus militants [*as if that were the dominant characteristic of the anti-war movement and the only alternative to electoral politics*] who are even less popular than when they helped elect Mr. Nixon in 1968, is only going to divide the country further and perpetuate the very things they fear and hate the most. . . . The universities cannot persuade or bully them with demonstrations, but they have the power of political registration and organization.[4]

Note how Reston conveniently blames Nixon's election on those who opposed him and did something about it. He promotes the "backlash" theory of democracy under which the safest course is to "stay in your place" and not offend anyone by fighting for your rights. Kill and die in Vietnam while waiting for the next election. If you lose the election—or if you win and your candidate fails to live up to his "campaign oratory"—drop bombs on Vietnamese villages as ordered, or risk death on a search-and-destroy mission, since the decision that you should do so was "democratically" arrived at.

Washington *Post* columnist Nicholas von Hoffman has a far better understanding of the impact of parapolitical activity:

> In truth he [Nixon] was forced out because he had nothing left to fight with. The war slid out from under him as it once slid down on top of us. . . . The Army had quit on him a couple of years ago. He claims he pulled half a million troops out as if he had a choice. Had he left them there, by now they would have been in a state of open opium addiction and naked mutiny. Next came the fleet. Sabotage, race riots and desertion. . . . The last to crack was the Air Force. . . . It finally got to them and they started cashing in their pilot's wings.

Without trying at this point to assess the role of demonstrations and protests in helping foster the moral and political climate that encouraged these developments in the armed forces, we should

[4]New York *Times*, April 23, 1972.

at least remember that most of the GIs in question had witnessed, heard about, or in some cases even participated in protests during the years immediately prior to their induction. Whatever encouragement the widespread domestic antiwar activity provided, the main thing to notice is that *it was direct action by the GIs, not their absentee ballots,* that played a major role in forcing an end to the war.

Von Hoffman continues:

> The marchers, the protesters, that rabble, they're the ones who served honorably. It will be a long time before you hear anyone in the White House say that. They will continue to repeat that the movement had no effect on them, that while the peaceniks marched they watched the Washington Redskins, but don't you believe it. They were peeking through the curtains.
>
> Likewise the late-joining, more conventional antiwar sorts will say that it was your Eugene McCarthys and George McGoverns who made the difference. McCarthy lent the movement respectability, is how the thought is usually phrased. Actually, it was the other way around. The only respectability in politics is power; and men like McCarthy got it by hitching on to the peace movement.[5]

. . .

The glory of the movement for civil rights and against the war in Vietnam is that they produced the beginnings of a counterculture in the midst of direct confrontations with the present society. They discovered the essence of a new satisfying life style and entered into the joys of community in the jails, hideaways, offices, houses, picket lines, and occupied buildings where they shared the risks, plans, food, work, and financial and security problems of an ongoing campaign.

[5]Washington *Post,* January 1973.

A	6
B	7
C	8
D	9
E	0
F	1
G	2
H	3
I	4
J	